FROM LENINIST DISCIPLINE
TO SOCIALIST LEGALISM

From Leninist Discipline to Socialist Legalism

Peng Zhen on Law and Political Authority in the PRC

PITMAN B. POTTER

STANFORD UNIVERSITY PRESS
STANFORD, CALIFORNIA
2003

Stanford University Press
Stanford, California

Printed in the United States of America on acid-free, archival-quality paper.

Library of Congress Cataloging-in-Publication Data

Potter, Pitman B.
From Leninist discipline to socialist legalism : Peng Zhen on law and political authority in the PRC / Pitman B. Potter.
p. cm.
Includes bibliographical references and index.
ISBN 0-8047-4500-5 (cloth : alk. paper)
1. Rule of law—China—History. 2. Law reform—China—History. 3. Peng, Zhen. I. Title.
KNQ2025.P68 2003
340'.092—dc21 2002012186

Original Printing 2003

Last figure below indicates year of this printing:
12 11 10 09 08 07 06 05 04 03

Typeset by Alan Noyes in 10/12.5 Palatino

Contents

This book is dedicated to
all my teachers.

Acknowledgments

THIS BOOK ORIGINATED with a paper written at the invitation of Timothy Cheek and Carol Hamrin and published as "Peng Zhen: His Evolving Views Toward Party Organization and Law" in their edited volume, *China's Establishment Intellectuals* (21–50; Armonk, N.Y.: M. E. Sharpe, 1986; portions of this text appear in Chapter 1 and are used with permission). At Tim's urging, and with the kind support of Rod MacFarquhar, I was invited to continue the project as a research associate at the Fairbank Centre for East Asian Research. My thanks go to Professor MacFarquhar, who was extraordinarily generous with his time while he was on sabbatical, and to Nancy Hearst of the Fairbank Library, who was extremely helpful. I received generous financial support from the Social Sciences and Humanities Research Council of Canada, for which I am deeply thankful. I owe a debt as well to the Universities Service Centre at the Chinese University of Hong Kong (CUHK), which invited me to visit the Centre and deliver a talk on December 6, 1994, in which I addressed many of the issues set forth in this book. The paper presented to CUHK was published as "From Leninist Discipline to Socialist Legalism: Peng Zhen on Law and Authority in the PRC" (Hong Kong: Chinese University of Hong Kong, 1995; used with permission; portions contained in Chapter 5). I thank the Centre for its financial support, particularly Professor Kuan Hsin-chi and Jean Hung for their generous assistance and hospitality during my visit. A paper on Peng Zhen's impact on the ideology of law in post-Mao China was presented to the 1996 Annual Meeting of the Association for Asian Studies and appeared in print as "Foundation and Emblem of PRC Elite Legal Culture: Peng Zhen in the Deng Era," *Problems of Post-Communism* 45, no. 3 (May–June 1998): 17–28; revised portions of this text appear in Chapter 5 and are used with permission (copyright M. E. Sharpe Inc.). I thank Jim Feinerman and the panel participants, as well as an anonymous reviewer, for their thoughtful comments on that paper.

Many people took the time to read and comment on various portions of the manuscript during its incarnation, including Sarah Biddulph, Pete Chamberlain, Tim Cheek, David Goodman, Nina Halpern, Kathleen Hartford, Philip Huang, Diana Lary, Paul T. K. Lin, Rod MacFarquhar, Michael Schoenhals, Scott Tanner, and Jim Townsend. David Goodman kindly shared a copy of Peng Zhen's 1938 speech to Jin Cha Ji CPC committee activists (from *Jinzhong shizhi ziliao*, no. 2, 1984). Michael Schoenhals generously provided materials from his extensive collection of Cultural Revolution documents—thanks in particular for providing copies from Yuan Beijing shiwei jiguan Mao Zedong sixiang hongqi bingduan (Mao Zedong thought red flag battalion of the original Beijing Municipal Committee organs), ed., *Da yexing jia, da yinmou jia: Peng Zhen zui 'e shi (1925–1966)* (*Big careerist and conspirator: The most odious history of Peng Zhen [1925–1966]*, Beijing: 1967) and *Qingli jieji duiwu* (*Purify class ranks*; ca. 1969, title page and publisher information missing). Several individuals in China who wish to remain anonymous also commented on various parts of the manuscript.

I thank my students at the University of British Columbia (UBC), Meera Bawa, Paul Cowsill, Kelly Lautt, Tim Xia, and Kelly Zhu, for their tireless assistance on this project. My thanks go as well to Karen Jew, Marietta Lao, and Cathy Lovering at the Institute of Asian Research and to Joanne Chung, Lillian Ong, and Deanna Clark at UBC Law Faculty for their secretarial and administrative assistance. I also thank my colleagues and friends at the Vancouver office of Borden Ladner Gervais LLP for their ongoing support for my work.

I thank Muriel Bell at Stanford University Press for her steadfast support in bringing the book to press. Sumathi Raghavan, Caroline Casey, and Tony Hicks at SUP also provided invaluable assistance for which I am deeply grateful.

Finally, I owe a particular debt of gratitude to my wife Vicki and to my daughters Kathleen and Jessie, without whose support and patience the completion of this book would not have been possible.

Despite the assistance and advice received from the individuals mentioned above, and from others whom I may have neglected to mention, the volume contains many shortcomings, for which I alone am responsible.

Pitman B. Potter
Vancouver, British Columbia
March 2003

Introduction

LEGAL SYSTEM development has been a cornerstone of government policy in China since 1978, as part of the broad program of reform associated with Deng Xiaoping and the post-Mao political leadership. More recently, China's accession to the World Trade Organization has seen further efforts to strengthen China's economic and civil law regimes. Ongoing pressure from foreign governments and international nongovernmental organizations has stimulated limited reforms in the areas of criminal justice and human rights. Despite these changes, however, debate continues over the limits and possibilities of legal reform.[1] Although the resolution of these questions ultimately awaits the judgment of history, important indicators of the parameters of possibility for legal reform in China may be found in official norms about the rule of law. To the extent that the PRC ruling elite supports legal reform and ascribes juridical significance to the terminology of the Chinese legal system, official legal culture remains an important guide to understanding the meaning of Chinese law.[2]

Few members of the PRC elite have been as closely associated with the socialist legal system as Peng Zhen (1902–1997). Peng's responsibilities for political–legal work in the Communist Party of China (CPC) Politburo during the 1950s and again in the early 1980s allowed him to play a significant role in shaping Party policy on law and legal institutions, and his role as chair of the National People's Congress (NPC) Standing Committee offered unparalleled opportunities to affect the content and process of legislation. However, unlike other political figures associated with the PRC legal system such as Dong Biwu, Wang

Hanbin, and Qiao Shi—much less members of the growing cohort of Western-trained legal specialists currently working its way through the system—Peng Zhen devoted much of his career to the furtherance of Party supremacy. Accordingly, Peng's views on the role of law in China remain influential. The 1982 Constitution, of which Peng was the architect, continues as amended to serve as the fundamental articulation of the basic policies of the state and the Party.[3] Peng's oft-repeated phrase "the Party leads the people in enacting the law and leads the people in observing the law" (*dang lingdao renmin zhiding falu, ye lingdao renmin zunshou falu*)[4] has become a familiar slogan used by Jiang Zemin, Li Peng, and other top leaders to explain principles of ruling the country by law (*yifa zhiguo*).[5] Peng's edict on the role of law as an instrument for implementing Party policy[6] has been incorporated as well into the legal education curriculum of the Central Party School.[7] Peng's stature and the continued influence of his views were underscored when his official obituary claimed Peng's purported loyalty for the leadership of Jiang Zemin.[8]

Peng's views on law and political authority evolved significantly over time. Throughout most of his early career, Peng was associated with the more repressive aspects of Communist rule in China and devoted his leadership of the *zheng-fa* system to ensuring popular submission to Party rule. However, during the post-Mao period, Peng called for increased reliance on formal rules and procedures as mechanisms of governance. The transition in Peng Zhen's stated views on law and political authority afford a penetrating glimpse into the legal culture of the PRC elite and permit preliminary conclusions to be drawn as to the future of law and legal institutions in China.

Biographical Sketch

Peng Zhen's views on law and political authority reflected the circumstances of his life and career.[9] Like his contemporaries, Peng lived through periods of tumultuous change in China. He was born before the fall of the Qing Dynasty and lived through periods of warlord strife, Japanese invasion, and civil war. His career in the CPC saw him rise from underground operative to Politburo member, as well as his return from political disgrace to chair the PRC legislature. The scope of Peng's career marks him as a significant political actor in twentieth-century China.

Peng Zhen was born into a poor peasant family in 1902 in the town of Houma in Quwu county, Linfen Prefecture, in Shanxi Province.[10] His education was limited to primary and middle school, although he displayed an early grasp of Marxist theory in a piece written for his high school journal on the labor situation in China.[11] Peng joined the CPC in 1923. During the mid-1920s, he was active in labor organizing work among factory and railway workers in Shijiazhuang.[12] In 1926 he was made secretary of several departments in the Tianjin Party cell, and by 1927, he was heading the Organization Department in the Tianjin CPC Committee. In 1927 he was sent by the CPC's Xunzhi Provincial Committee to Yutian and Tangshan to organize insurrection under what was later deemed a "left opportunist" plan for insurrection in North China.[13] In 1928 he headed the Organization Department of the Xunzhi Provincial CPC Committee. The next year, Peng was arrested and sent to Tianjin's No. 3 Prison, where he served as secretary for a secret Party cell and organized hunger strikes and ongoing political work among the inmates.[14] He was transferred to Beijing No. 2 prison in 1931 and was released in 1935. Although Peng was at the time and throughout his career closely associated with many other underground CPC cadres working in the White Areas who were imprisoned by the Kuomintang, the evidence seems clear that Peng was not among the so-called 61 Cadres who were released from prison after making CPC-mandated confessions (and who were attacked for this during the Cultural Revolution).[15] Upon his release from prison, Peng was appointed deputy secretary of the Tianjin CPC Committee and served as representative of the North China Bureau in East Hebei, then as director of the Organization Department of the North China Bureau.[16]

In 1936 Peng began what was to become a long-standing relationship with Liu Shaoqi when Liu took over the Party's North China Bureau in Tianjin. One source suggests that Liu Shaoqi had troubled relations with the CPC's Hebei Provincial Committee and that Peng Zhen was the only local cadre who consistently sided with Liu.[17] Certainly Peng's experience and his persistent activism would have made him a valuable subordinate. He played an important role as a Party liaison worker during the December 9th Movement of 1935, reporting back to Liu and the North China Bureau and conveying Party ideas to the movement leadership. With the onset of the Sino-Japanese War in 1937, Peng continued working on Party organization in Tianjin and Beiping. In 1938 Peng was appointed party secretary and later chairman of the Government Council of the Jin Cha Ji (Shanxi, Chahar, Hebei) Border Region. Peng went to Yan'an in 1941 to become vice president of the

Central Party School, where he led the work of the Party rectification campaign in 1942.

In 1944 Peng was appointed head of the Party's Urban Work Department. He was also appointed acting director of the Party Organization Department, with the full directorship coming to him the following year. He was appointed to the Politburo at the Seventh National CPC Congress in 1945 and served as an alternative member of the Secretariat. After the Japanese surrender, Peng was appointed secretary of the Northeast Bureau in Manchuria and political commissar for the army commanded by Lin Biao. Peng was removed from these posts in 1946 in the wake of policy conflicts with Lin Biao and Mao Zedong over matters of political and military strategy, primarily the question of whether to emphasize urban (Peng) or rural (Mao, Lin) areas as the focus of attacks on Nationalist power.[18] Although this effectively ended Peng's brief involvement in military matters, his antagonistic relationship with Lin Biao continued in subsequent years and was an important factor in the attacks on Peng during the Cultural Revolution. The Manchurian affair also colored Peng's ties with Deng Xiaoping and Chen Yun, each of whom sided with Mao in the brokered resolution to the policy dispute that saw Peng recalled to the Centre. From 1947 to 1949 Peng's energies were directed toward land reform issues in Jin Cha Ji and other liberated areas of the North China Plain, and he played an increasingly important role in preparations for the capture and ultimately the administration of Beijing.[19]

After the Communist victory, Peng was made secretary of the Beijing Party Committee and held concurrent posts in the Chinese People's Political Consultative Conference and in the Central People's Government Council. His power base in Beijing continued until his purge in 1966. Peng was also appointed vice chairman and Party secretary of the government's Political–Legal Affairs Commission, thus beginning his long career in this area. In 1953 he was appointed a member of the election-law drafting committee under Deng Xiaoping,[20] and in 1954 he served as head of the Central Political–Legal Cadre School. Peng was appointed secretary and vice chair of the First NPC Standing Committee in 1954. Although Peng's star seemed on the rise during the mid- and late 1950s, he was passed over in favor of Deng Xiaoping for the position of General Secretary of the Party at the Eighth CPC Congress in 1956, although he did obtain appointment to the Secretariat and had general responsibility for day-to-day operations.

In the early 1960s, Peng was given responsibility for the Party's cultural policy. In the politically combative atmosphere following the Great Leap Forward, indirect criticism of Mao became prominent in the literary circles under Peng's control. His support for writers such as Deng Tuo (with whom Peng had worked in the Jin Cha Ji Base Area) brought him into increasingly open conflict with Mao, and ultimately his efforts to protect Beijing vice mayor and playwright Wu Han were to play an important role in Peng's downfall. In 1965, as head of the five-man Cultural Revolution Group charged by Mao to direct the criticism of Wu Han and his play, *Hai Rui Dismissed from Office*, Peng attempted to confine criticism of Wu to academic rather than political issues. This led to the final break with Mao, and Peng's dismissal from his posts was finalized at the meeting of the Party Secretariat on May 16, 1966. Peng was formally expelled from the Politburo at the Eleventh Plenum of the Eighth CPC Central Committee in early August 1966. On December 4, 1966, he was "arrested" by Red Guards, and on December 12, he was paraded through the streets of Beijing to a violent struggle session.[21] Aside from heralding a new phase of open conflict in the Cultural Revolution, the persecution of Peng Zhen was particularly ironic because it represented the imposition of extralegal punishment on the Politburo member most closely associated with the Chinese legal system. He was dragged before mass struggle sessions repeatedly during the summer of 1967.[22] Peng was initially confined at one of the Central Case Examination Group prisons in the outskirts of Beijing,[23] but after 1975 he appears to have been exiled to remote Shaanxi Province.[24]

After the decision of the landmark Third Plenum of the Eleventh Central Committee to rehabilitate Cultural Revolution victims, Peng Zhen returned to Beijing in December 1978[25] and reappeared publicly on January 27, 1979, at a tea party celebrating the Spring Festival.[26] It has been suggested that Peng's return was delayed by Deng Xiaoping, even though Chen Yun reportedly had advocated a reversal of verdicts on Peng following the downfall of the Gang of Four in 1976.[27] On February 23 Peng was appointed chairman of the NPC Committee for Legislative Affairs,[28] and in July he was once again elected a vice chairman of the NPC Standing Committee. In September he regained his former position on the Politburo.[29] On June 10, 1981, Peng resigned his post on the Legislative Affairs Committee to take up responsibilities as vice chairman of the Committee for Revising the Constitution.[30] In December 1982 Peng became first secretary of the Party's Central Political–Legal Committee, although he was passed over for appointment to the CPC Politburo Standing Committee. Instead, he was appointed chairman of the Sixth NPC Standing Committee in June 1983.[31] In this position, he played an active role in the drafting of a wide range of legislation, including the General Principles of Civil Law and the Bankruptcy Law. Peng resigned from the Central Committee and the Politburo in October 1987 and was replaced by Wan Li as chair of the NPC Standing Committee the following spring.

Peng continued to be active politically, participating on the informal council of elders that advised Deng Xiaoping on key issues, including the handling of the Tiananmen crisis in 1989. Empowered by his status as an elder statesman, Peng continued to make periodic pronouncements on legal reform throughout the late 1980s and early 1990s. Gradually, however, his advanced age and associated health problems confined him to a wheelchair, and despite occasional televised inspection tours of Beijing in 1995 and 1996, he limited his public appearances. Peng was formally listed as a member of Deng Xiaoping's funeral committee in February 1997, although illness prohibited him from attending. Peng Zhen died April 26, 1997, at the age of ninety-five.

From Leninist Discipline to Socialist Legalism

Peng Zhen played a significant role in the legal reform efforts undertaken in post-Mao China, both as head of the *zheng-fa* system at the Politburo level and as chair of the NPC Standing Committee. Although the Chinese legal system has the potential to beget institutions and processes that are recognizable to lawyers trained in the European and North American traditions of liberal private law, it retains many elements of socialist ideology and of traditional Chinese norms that will continue to set it apart for the foreseeable future. Many of these are attributable to Peng Zhen, whose discourse on law and political authority infused the PRC legal system with complementary elements of modern Chinese socialism and traditional Chinese legalism.

Although the complexities of Peng's career argue for caution in drawing unidimensional conclusions about his ideas on law and political authority, a broad trend is evident, namely a transition from strict reliance on the Leninist revolutionary party's disciplinary edicts of particularist application to a call for a coercive system of formal norms and processes of general application that would be articulated and enforced by the socialist party-state. This transition from Leninist discipline to socialist legalism stands as Peng Zhen's legacy to the PRC legal system. Leninist discipline represents a typology of political organization that places a premium on strict compliance by subordinates with Party policies decided at higher levels; by extension, members of society submit to Party leadership generally.[32] Long associated with the organization and behavior of the CPC underground in North China before liberation, the control and compliance features of Leninist discipline were justified by the requirements of revolutionary class struggle.[33] Under norms of Leninist discipline, power and accountability flow in one direction, as party and state officials responsible only to their superiors have broad authority to direct and sanction subordinates in their organizations and in society at large. Socialist legalism describes a modality of regulation which combines policy goals of socialism with operational norms that echo principles of the pre-Han legalist school of governance.[34] The element of socialism emphasizes the importance of collective ownership of the means of production and the continued role of the Party in promoting collective economic and social welfare. The element of legalism embodies an emphasis on formalism, generality, and punishment in the content and application of rules.

When Peng Zhen began his career as an underground CPC organizer, he was part of an organization whose primary goals were survival and revolution. This required strict adherence to the dictates and norms of the Party organization—the top-down discipline of the Leninist revolutionary party. The Leninist approach to political organization called for clear channels of authority and communication within institutions of political power. Essential to this approach was a process that included collective decision making at the Centre, which could then impose its edicts on lower levels, from which was expected unquestioning obedience. This grew, of course, from the needs of revolution but was expanded significantly in the context of governance as well. The relationship between consensus at the top and disciplined adherence below was grounded in that familiar rubric of "democratic centralism." Although the extent of true collective decision making within the CPC elite varied significantly, the continued insistence on rigid compliance at lower levels remained. These norms of Leninist discipline were dominant through much of Peng Zhen's career, from the December 9th Movement, when the consequences of failing to enforce organizational discipline came into stark relief, through the Jin Cha Ji and Yan'an periods, when Peng worked actively to institutionalize norms of discipline both inside and outside the Party.

After Liberation, however, the revolutionary Party was thrust into the role of governance, where the utility of, and indeed the need for, the kind of rigid compliance with ideological and policy dictates that characterized the revolutionary period came into question. Disagreement arose over the exact nature of the ideological guidance that was to serve as the source of Party policy, as evidenced in part by the move, allegedly initiated by Peng Dehuai and supported by Peng Zhen and others to remove the reference to "Mao Zedong Thought" from the CPC Constitution.[35] During the period of state-building during the 1950s, Peng Zhen's expressed views on governance began to suggest a different approach to discipline. No longer could the Party be concerned merely with discipline for its subjects and political allies. In Peng's view, the Party must also bring greater discipline to its own internal decision making. The 1950s saw significant changes in Peng's expressed views about the conditions of society and the implications these had for Party rule. For the first time, Peng began to articulate views about law that would bind not only the subjects but also the sources of political rule.

Although this thematic direction in Peng's doctrinal position was interrupted by the political crisis of the Cultural Revolution, it took on new vitality during the 1980s. What emerged was a doctrine of socialist legalism—a view that combined adherence to socialist ideologies of state-planning in the economy and narrowly limited parameters for social and cultural discourse on the one hand, with a system reminiscent of pre-Han legalism that embodied formal laws and institutions characterized by coercive norms of general application on the other. By combining tenets of socialism and legalism, Peng modeled a discourse that stands as a powerful paradigm for legal reform in China.

Organization and Methods

This book examines the evolution of Peng Zhen's discourse on law and political authority from an historical and contextual respective. As with most research on political elites in China, reliance on the published record and on interviews must be handled with caution. Every effort has been made to contextualize official records and personal recollections of Peng's career, such that review and analysis of Peng's published writings and speeches is augmented by off-the-record interviews, comparison with the views of others in the political leadership, and discussion of the political and policy environment of the day.

Chapter 1 examines complexities of Peng Zhen's personality, offering important context for the more detailed discussion that follows.

Chapter 2 addresses Peng's work during the pre-Liberation period, with particular attention to his work in the December 9th Movement, the Jin Cha Ji Border Region, and the Yan'an Party School. This period may generally be characterized as one in which the emphasis in Peng's writings and speeches was on building Leninist discipline and organization in pursuit of Party directives. Chapter 3 examines the process by which Peng's focus on the pursuit of revolution and political power was gradually transformed into one that gave greater attention to establishing more formal processes for the Party's own decision making. Chapter 4 reviews the political and policy conflicts that emerged over the Great Leap Forward and depicts how Peng came to articulate more forcefully the need to institutionalize the dynamics of CPC decision making and governance. During the pre–Cultural Revolution period, Peng's published statements revealed a transition from focusing on discipline for the subjects of authority to discipline for the sources of authority. This was, of course, cut short when Peng was purged at the outset of the Cultural Revolution. After his return to elite politics after 1978, Peng resumed activity in the *zheng-fa* system and took a lead role in orchestrating the post-Mao legal reforms. This process is the subject of Chapter 5, which addresses the transition to socialist legalism in Peng's discourse on law and political authority.

Although Peng's formal statements on law and political authority reflected the policy discourses and political environments in which he operated, his organizational stature in the *zheng-fa* apparatus lend his views particular importance. Peng's close personal and political ties with Liu Shaoqi, Nie Rongzhen, and other patrons made it inevitable that Peng's speeches would reflect the policy preferences of his factional sponsors, particularly during the earlier years of his career. As his stature rose, however, Peng's views can be seen to take on greater independence. This can be seen in the post-Mao period as well, when early on, Peng tended to support Deng Xiaoping's line on political and economic reform, although later, as Peng's position became more established, he began increasingly to depart from Deng's orthodoxy. Although Peng was accused by Cultural Revolution Red Guards of using staffers such as Deng Tuo and Wang Hanbin to draft speeches and articles for him,[36] and doubtless he made full use of talented associates such as Yao Zhen and Xu Liqun, interviews with Peng Zhen's staffers in Beijing yielded consistent statements that Peng was intimately involved in preparing his own speeches, often drafting large portions of them himself. Whether Peng Zhen's official expressions on law and political authority primarily reflect his own personal views, views based on his view of political expediency, or the views of factional superiors or subordinates, the fact remains that Peng established a discourse on law and political authority that remains an important and influential component of legal and political culture in China today. It is this discourse, its historical and political context, and its implications for China's legal reform project that are the focus of this book.

CHAPTER 1

The Complexities of Peng Zhen: Four Personae

PENG ZHEN'S LONG association with the *zheng-fa* system in China lent a complex and often contradictory tone to many of his public statements on law and political authority. The same man who during the 1950–1951 campaign against counterrevolutionaries opposed the use of formal regulations that might inhibit attacks on class enemies also held, not three years later, that all should be equal before the law. During the early 1960s Peng Zhen lent support to a vigorous community of intellectuals whose critical views of certain Communist Party of China (CPC) policies would no doubt have been criticized a few short years previously during the Anti-Rightist Campaign, in which Peng was an effective participant. Shortly after his rehabilitation in 1979, Peng asserted the primacy of Party leadership, although not more than five years later, he suggested that the Party should be subject to legal constraints. It would be easy to dismiss such contradictions as mere political expediency—and indeed many of Peng's statements and much of his behavior can be ascribed to his role as a politician in the CPC elite. On the other hand, many of the apparent contradictions in Peng Zhen's expressed views can be ascribed to the complexities of his personality and to the widely differing requirements of his career positions. Peng Zhen's expressed views on law and political authority may usefully be viewed by reference to four distinct yet interrelated personae that reveal individual characteristics of toughness and intelligence, political traits of task orientation and relationship building, Party organizational abilities, and a focus on institutionalization and process associated with law making. These four personae—the individual, the politician, the

CPC organizer, and the lawgiver—explain much about Peng Zhen's evolving views on law and politics.

The Individual

Peng Zhen's life and career reveal a complex array of individual characteristics, including toughness, intelligence, and comradeliness. First and foremost, Peng Zhen was a tough individual. Peng's heritage as the child of a poor peasant family no doubt steeled him for the rigors of revolution and Chinese elite politics. Peng's hometown of Houma is located in the southern Shanxi county of Quwu in Lin Fen Prefecture, an area so desolate that efforts after 1949 to build up towns along the Tatung railway between Taiyuan and Xian went unfulfilled.[1] While in jail in Tianjin and Beijing for his labor and Party organizing activities, Peng organized hunger strikes and other forms of resistance. Each of these came at significant personal cost—to the point where He Long later indicated how impressed he was with the young Peng's ability to withstand twenty days without food.[2] Peng's association with the ascetic Liu Shaoqi and his work in the underground Party cells in the "White" areas of North China required a capacity for self-denial, whereas Peng's work in isolated Jin Cha Ji and in the bloody battles of the Manchurian campaign would have further toughened his capacity to withstand hardship.

Peng was also mentally tough—his work in the Yan'an rectification campaign and in the campaigns of the early 1950s against counterrevolutionaries, and against the urban bourgeoisie (*wu fan*) and corrupt officialdom (*san fan*) made him a dark figure during the period of transition to PRC rule.[3] Peng's image as a tough enforcer of Party policy may have contributed to the impression that he was harsh supporter of the Anti-Rightist Campaign, although the record remains mixed on this score.[4] Although he may have couched his language in encouraging terms, Peng's thinly veiled threats to the Panchen Lama and National People's Congress (NPC) Delegate Ngapoi Ngawang Jigme over implementation of collectivization in Tibet in 1959 revealed the steely determination that underlay Peng's political behavior.[5] During the Cultural Revolution, he was paraded through the streets and suffered considerably during struggle meetings and at the hands of case group interrogators, but he still refused to make a thorough self-criticism—essentially toughing it out in the face of mob demands and the Maoist inquisition.[6] Although these attributes of personal toughness were shared by other Chinese Communist leaders with similar experiences, Peng held them in ample doses.

A second personal attribute was Peng's intelligence. Although largely without formal education—Peng's attendance through middle school was a most unusual opportunity provided by the Party's largesse—Peng's intelligence was spoken of many times by Liu Shaoqi and even Mao.[7] Upon visiting Yan'an, the writer Gunther Stein commented on being unsure whether the peasant or the intellectual element was foremost in Peng's thinking.[8] Peng was said to be extremely well read, and shared with Mao a love for history and the classics.[9] Peng's posting to the Central Party School in 1941 after his return from Jin Cha Ji; his increased responsibility for education policy under the Secretariat in the early 1960s; and his close dealings with intellectuals, first in Jin Cha Ji, and more obviously during the 1960s before the Cultural Revolution, all suggest the extent to which Peng's intelligence was recognized by his colleagues. Indications of Peng's intelligence have been confirmed by members of Peng's NPC staff interviewed in Beijing. Peng is said to have easily grasped the complexities not only of Marxism but also of modern economic theory, philosophy, and world affairs. On many occasions, he is said to have sat through lengthy and detailed policy presentations and was then able to ask incisive and difficult questions that revealed his mastery of latent complexities and contradictions. He is said to have been quite flexible in his thinking—rejecting dogmatic application of existing ideology and policies in favor of careful tailoring to meet practical needs and existing conditions.[10] Peng's powers of memory were also prodigious: Peng is said to have been able, while in his eighties, to commit a four-hour speech to memory and speak from only a few pages of notes. Peng's intelligence also benefited from his mental toughness; reportedly, during the 1950s and early 1960s, he was the first to arrive and the last to leave his NPC offices when the NPC was in session.[11]

Peng's traits of toughness and intelligence were complemented by his affable personality—an important element in building political connections. While in Jin Cha Ji and Yan'an, he organized local opera performances,[12] and there are numerous descriptions of him shmoozing with associates, thoroughly enjoying the performances—indeed, Peng was criticized during the Cultural Revolution for being too fond of classical operas.[13] Peng is described rather glowingly by Deng Tuo as strolling casually with his immediate superior Nie Rongzhen along the Sha River in Jin Cha Ji.[14] He was a noted fishing partner of He Long.[15]

In contrast to Liu Shaoqi's rather ascetic demeanor, Peng was not averse to living the good life, and he was accused of throwing elaborate parties at his compounds in Beijing.[16] Peng's affability extended to his professional life, where he was described as demanding but collegial. His subordinates referred to him as *Peng Laoshi*—the teacher who was solicitous toward his protégés. One former colleague insisted that Peng was genuinely interested in his associates' views, constantly asking them to say what they really thought, not simply what they thought he wanted to hear.

The Politician

From his early days as an underground labor organizer, Peng Zhen revealed a variety of political traits that complemented his personal attributes. A major aspect of Peng's political persona was his ruthless pursuit of political goals set for him by his superiors. As Liu Shaoqi's deputy in the North China Bureau, Peng was charged with investigating problems of leftism in the December 9th Movement. Peng's activities were instrumental in providing information for Liu's report of April 1936 critiquing the movement.[17] During the critical stages of consolidating the Party's control over the movement in early 1936, Peng represented Liu and the North China Bureau in articulating CPC policies at the first meeting of the North China National Salvation Association (*Huabei jiu guo hui*) and maintained constant contact with the student movement.[18] But Peng was critical of the inability of the movement to eliminate leftist errors, and his reporting ultimately formed the basis for reorganizing the Beiping CPC Committee.[19] Peng's work was later incorporated into Liu Shaoqi's "The Lessons to be Drawn from the Beiping Question"—a summary critique of leftist errors that was later published as "On the Beiping Question" in the North China Bureau's journal *Huoxian* (*Fireline*).[20]

Peng's participation in the Yan'an rectification campaign revealed a similar commitment to carrying out political directives from above in the context of intra-Party struggle. While Peng's appointment as deputy director of the Central Party School was in part an effort by Liu Shaoqi to insert his protégé into the rectification movement, possibly to rein in whatever excesses might have emerged from Mao in his capacity as director of the Central Party School, Peng nonetheless seemed committed to carrying out the purge. Peng seemed to enjoy a cooperative relationship with Mao, as indicated in part by a well-publicized photograph of Mao shaking Peng's hand at the Yan'an airport in the company of Zhu De, Chen Yi, Nie Rongzhen, and Li Fuchun.[21] Peng's 1942 speech summarizing the twenty-two articles that were to be the focus of study during the rectification movement characterized the opportunism associated with Wang Ming and the "returned students" as class conflict—thus opening the door for virtually unrestrained attacks on dissidents within the Party: "We represent the proletariat class, but all erroneous opportunistic points of view represent another alien class."[22] Elsewhere in the speech, Peng claimed that Hegelian materialism permitted a degree of absolutism in areas of doctrine and ideology, thus suggesting that Mao's views could not be easily dismissed as but one component of a dialectic process of contending views.[23] Peng's support for Mao's concern that Yan'an was rife with spies and class enemies contributed to the vehemence of this attack.[24] With the drawing down of the campaign in 1944, Peng adopted a more conciliatory stance, although this too seemed dictated by superiors, as Peng's 1944 speech summarizing the rectification effort emphasized the Maoist dicta of "saving the patient" and maintaining the enthusiasm of Party cadres.[25]

Peng's zealotry in carrying out political attacks on Party enemies continued after liberation. His direction of the 1950–1951 campaign against counterrevolutionaries included public condemnation and execution meetings in which Peng is portrayed as an enthusiastic participant:

> "Is it cruelty to execute these criminals?" The answer came back, "It is not cruelty." The mayor [Peng Zhen] commented: "Truly it is not cruelty. It is mercy. We are protecting the lives of the people whom they harm. . . . We are here representing the people. It is our duty to do the will of the people. We suppress the anti-revolutionaries. This act we perform according to the law. Those who have to be killed, we kill. In cases where we could kill or not kill, we do not kill. But when it has to be killing, we kill . . . Now you all want them to be suppressed. Tomorrow the Court will pronounce the judgment and they will be executed."[26]

In his reporting on the campaign, Peng decried the problems of overleniency (characterized as a problem of "rightism"), which were seen as alienating the masses anxious to redress past wrongs.[27] Similarly, during the *wu fan* campaign, Peng urged unremitting harshness for corruption in commerce and industry: "Bribery is serious in nature, and dealt with seriously. If we take care of only a small number of people and do nothing about the majority this would be excessively lenient [*shi zhi guo kuan*]."[28]

Following his rehabilitation in 1979, it appeared Peng had lost none of his skills for political attack. In one of his first speeches after returning to the central political elite, Peng took a leading position supporting Deng Xiaoping's effort to reregister Party members in an effort to eliminate leftist influences in the leadership. Citing the spirit of the Fifth Plenum of the Eleventh Central Committee, and Deng's dicta on practice as the sole criterion for truth and the need to liberate thought, Peng argued for vigorous rectification at leadership departments in the political–legal sector as a necessary step in clarifying major issues of Party line.[29] Clearly Peng was lending his services to support Deng's attacks on Cultural Revolution holdovers in the government. Peng's activist bent was directed as well toward problems of social order and economic crime during the early 1980s, as he approved the use of administrative sanctions (particularly reform and reeducation through labor) in lieu of the criminal sanctions provided under the PRC Criminal Law and the Criminal Procedure Law, which offered more formal, albeit flawed, protections for the criminally accused.[30]

However, Peng Zhen's political skills extended beyond being merely a subservient functionary. He also actively cultivated political allies in an effort to bolster his political position and independence. From his earliest days in Tianjin, Jin Cha Ji, and Yan'an, Peng developed a network of political mentors on whom he would come to rely throughout his career. The most familiar of these was Liu Shaoqi, for whom Peng worked in the North China Bureau in Tianjin after his release from prison in 1935. Liu obviously saw Peng's value during the December 9th Movement and used Peng's work as a basis for his own reporting to the Party Centre. Peng's career was linked closely to Liu's throughout the latter's life, and indeed Peng's fortunes may be said to have depended on Liu's power and ultimately on his inability to manage Mao Zedong. Liu tried repeatedly, without success, to have Peng elevated to the Politburo Standing Committee during the late 1950s and early 1960s, only to be stymied by Mao's support for Deng Xiaoping. Peng's fall at the outset of the Cultural Revolution reflected in part Liu's inability to protect him.

In Jin Cha Ji, Peng cultivated relations with a network of Party workers such as Cheng Zihua, Liu Lantao, and Liu Fuzhi. Indirect links with cadres such as An Ziwen, who played a key role in implementing in Northern Shanxi the moderate economic policies associated with Peng Zhen's Jin Cha Ji program,[31] and fellow Shanxi native Bo Yibo led Cultural Revolution Red Guards to claim the existence of a

"Shanxi Counterrevolutionary Stronghold."[32] Although the charge was spurious—Peng is hardly mentioned in the portions of An Ziwen's biography dealing with Shanxi and it is widely reported that Peng and Bo have never been close (in the words of one Chinese observer, they "bicker constantly")—the impression of Peng assiduously cultivating a political network remains powerful.[33]

Peng Zhen's military connections were somewhat less strong. Although his work in Jin Cha Ji permitted contacts with Nie Rongzhen and other military officials[34] and he was on the distribution list for important military directives,[35] Peng was unable to build the kind of network of military contacts that later would permit Deng Xiaoping to rise to the apex of the CPC hierarchy. Part of the explanation lies in the fact that Peng was considered primarily to be a civilian administrator, rather than a political commissar working directly with military units.[36] Peng's career in the CPC began in the North China underground, and he did not participate in the Long March—a further barrier to close military links. As well, Peng's sole foray into military strategy and tactics was disastrous—his proposal that the civil war in Manchuria emphasize urban centers was rebuked publicly by Mao and even Liu Shaoqi and led to Peng's recall from the Northeast.[37]

As he rose in the hierarchy, Peng maintained ties with his Shanxi roots while cultivating subordinates from previous assignments.[38] He used his position as mayor of Beijing and head of Beijing Party Committee to promote careers of former Jin Cha Ji associates such as Liu Ren (deputy director of the CPC Centre's Jin Cha Ji Sub-Bureau, later Peng's deputy mayor in Beijing before the Cultural Revolution), Deng Tuo (general secretary of Jin Cha Ji Provincial CPC Committee and editor *Jin Cha Ji Daily*, later secretary of the Beijing CPC Committee and editor *People's Daily* before the Cultural Revolution), and Wang Feiran (Jin Cha Ji Administrative Council alternate, later chief judge of the Beijing People's Court before the Cultural Revolution).[39] Peng apparently secured lasting loyalty from those of his associates who survived the punishments of the Cultural Revolution by attempting to take responsibility for their alleged errors.[40] After his rehabilitation, Peng continued to promote careers of former subordinates from Beijing Party Committee such as Wang Hanbin and Zheng Tianxiang. Peng's position as Chair of the NPC Standing Committee also provided an opportunity to cultivate high-level associates such as Wang Renzhong and Chen Peixian, as well as staffers such as Yang Jingyu, Xiang Chunyi, and Qiao Xiaoyang, who served as secretaries (*mishu*)[41] to Peng at the NPC.

Peng's cultivation of a formidable network of political allies extended to the use of family members as well. Peng relied extensively on his wife Zhang Jieqing and her links to other senior officials' spouses, such as Deng Xiaoping's wife Zhou Lin.[42] Zhang Jieqing also served as Peng's *mishu*, suggesting that for all his political networking and contacts, Peng's experience during the Cultural Revolution had convinced him that family was the best protection against betrayal.

Peng Zhen was also a pragmatic bureaucratic infighter. This became particularly evident during the late 1950s and early 1960s when, despite being passed over for the post of Party General Secretary at the Eighth CPC Congress in 1956, Peng began to take on individual political significance as a leader of growing stature. Peng's success in using Beijing municipality as a political power base motivated Mao to comment that under Peng's leadership, the city was controlled so tightly that not even a needle or a drop of water could penetrate.[43] Peng's infighting skills, combined with his control of Beijing, were evident in the circumstances surrounding the Changguanlou meetings in 1961.[44] Presumably with the knowledge of Liu Shaoqi and perhaps Deng Xiaoping as well, Peng directed Deng Tuo to supervise an investigation of mistakes in central economic policy that had caused the economic disaster of the Great Leap Forward. In November 1961 several meetings were held at the Changguanlou (Broad View Tower) in the Beijing Zoo during which central policy documents on the Great Leap Forward were analyzed. A lengthy report was generated and delivered to Peng,[45] who apparently intended to use it and various accompanying materials to challenge the Great Leap policies at an enlarged meeting of the CPC Central Committee.[46] On the basis of these reports, Peng hinted broadly at Mao's policy errors at the "7,000 Cadres Conference" in January 1962 and criticized the tendency to avoid individual responsibility.[47] Ultimately, Mao's self-criticism at the conference blunted the attack and the Changguanlou report was never formally presented, although it probably helped to prompt Mao's withdrawal from the front line of economic policy making.

The Changguanlou report serves as a telling example of Peng's capacity to manipulate what could formally be explained as officially sanctioned activities to serve his own political ends. The Changguanlou report appears to have been an outgrowth of a series of investigations of Great Leap policies being carried out by the CPC Secretariat.[48] Indeed, one staff participant at the meetings indicated that he considered the meetings at the time to be a fully authorized policy review. And even while this effort was under way, Peng apparently expressed support for Mao to lower-level officials.[49] Yet there is little doubt that the results of the meeting were used for purposes that Mao certainly did not support—namely a critique and reversal of the policies of the Great Leap Forward.

In the growing conflicts with Mao, Peng's use of the dictum "All Are Equal Before the Truth" revealed as well his facility for ideological argument.[50] Peng's suggestion that the "truth" required a recognition of the failure of Mao's Great Leap Forward (and by implication supported Peng Dehuai's challenge at the Lushan Plenum), was difficult to refute. Peng's reference to equality before the truth was bolstered by the acceptance already extended to the notion of equality before law in the state constitution. Although there was no direct policy linkage between equality before the law and equality before the truth, the rhetorical analogy remained powerful. For if the law could be seen as applicable equally to citizens, so too could the truth be applicable equally to CPC leaders. The reference to equality before truth now suggested the ultimate equality of individual leaders based on objective conditions—a view that Mao would find hard to counter and remain true to his expressed ideas about inner Party democracy.[51] Peng's dictum posited notions of objective truth that undermined Mao's claims to political supremacy even as it challenged Mao's emphasis on class analysis.[52] Despite being the obvious point of attack, Mao was hard pressed to oppose Peng's statement, in part because this would have meant a direct challenge to existing Party orthodoxy. In his rather weakened political condition at the time, Mao was not prepared to launch such a challenge. Such constraints were fleeting, however, and within a few short years, the dictum was expressly attacked by Cultural Revolution radicals with Mao's blessing.

During the Socialist Education Campaign, Peng's call for reliance on local Party officials to control the conduct of the campaign reflected yet again the politician at work protecting local networks—his own and those of his associates.[53] Although Mao's First Ten Points on the campaign had emphasized the importance of poor and lower middle class peasant organizations as the main force for mobilizing popular participation,[54] Peng's Latter Ten Points put local officials in charge, confining higher-level Party work teams to staff support roles.[55] Although Peng allowed work teams to replace "bad" officials in some instances, he generally admonished against interference in local administration.[56] Peng's view of the work teams, however, was later reversed by Liu Shaoqi's Revised Latter Ten Points, which urged that work teams sent from higher levels should take charge of local Party reform.[57]

Peng's handling of Mao's criticisms of Wu Han also revealed his skills as a political infighter.[58] First he used control of Beijing cultural apparatus to prevent, or at least delay, publication of Yao Wenyuan's critique of *Hui Rui Ba Guan*, and then to mitigate its effects by terming it an academic discussion. Later he held a private meeting with Mao to discuss Wu Han and to delay a final political resolution while seeking to explain privately to Mao the general terms of the February Outline. Finally he tried to portray Mao as having approved the February Outline. These actions all speak of a political infighter maneuvering to control access to information and the interpretation of policy in order to protect his political position and to nullify his opponents. Peng's political tactics may be contrasted with the style of Liu Shaoqi. Consistent with his writings on the principle that cadres should accept criticism and not engage in factional intrigue, Liu seemed willing to confine his challenges to the formal organizational realm—as for example where he chaired the Politburo Standing Committee meeting that approved distribution of Peng Zhen's February Outline.[59] The fact that Peng was ultimately unsuccessful suggests that his skills did not yet match those of the Chairman, who apparently had already made up his mind on Peng's fate and can be seen manipulating Peng into a position where he could be removed fairly easily.[60] In this context, Peng was in company with many of Mao's opponents.

During the post-Mao period, Peng actively used his position as chair of the NPC Standing Committee and the banner of socialist legality as platform to promote his own political position.[61] Peng quickly began to transform the NPC Standing Committee into a politically active body. Estranged from Deng Xiaoping's inner circle, Peng brought many senior officials such as Chen Peixian and Wang Renzhong over to the NPC Standing Committee, where he began to play an increasingly significant role in the policy process. Peng was to take pride in noting the discomfort caused by the NPC Standing Committee transcending its former function as a rubber stamp.[62] By attempting to monopolize the organizational framework for legislation, Peng made the NPC Standing Committee a force to contend with, and one that provided him an institutional platform from which to pursue his political career.

The Party Organizer

Throughout his career, Peng was involved with the building and operation of Party organizations as instruments to ensure compliance by lower levels with central Party policies. Although his attention to organizational structures and procedure tended toward a formalistic emphasis on form over substance and a reluctance to depart from formal decisions, his record as a Party organizer remained an enduring feature of Peng's approach.

Peng's experience during the December 9th Movement and his conclusions about the need for organizational discipline no doubt played a role in his thinking about Party work in the Jin Cha Ji border area, where he took over as Party secretary in 1938. Peng's main role in Jin Cha Ji was to serve as a conduit for disseminating and ensuring enforcement of Party policies in the border region in such areas as economic administration, security work, education, and war mobilization. One of Peng's first assignments was to direct the First Representative Congress of Jin Cha Ji held in August 1938 and to convey the policies of the Party Centre.[63] Peng's Twenty-Point Program aimed at strengthening Party control in three areas: (1) elimination of enemies through the use of tribunals dominated by Party loyalists; (2) Party building through use of "filtered democracy" in election laws and other regulations designed to ensure Party dominance; and (3) institution building through the use of formal regulations on government institutions that permitted Party domination.[64] Ultimately, Jin Cha Ji was held up as a model for other border regions to follow in the area of building Party power—a tribute to Peng Zhen's organizational work.[65]

Peng's work in Yan'an afforded further opportunities to apply his organizational skills. Charged with the Central Party School rectification program, Peng drafted the "plan" for rectification in the Central Party School, whose aim was to break down old organizational loyalties and to ensure that newly recruited cadres, many of whom had recently defected from the nationalists, were brought within the ambit of Party discipline and organization.[66] The plan called for the assignment and arrangement of students in the Party School to be based on educational level and "theoretical ability and the ability to work independently," rather than factors such as age, time of joining the Party, and organizational background. This meant that cadres from the same organization would not necessarily be trained together and permitted the education program to transcend personal and institutional relations in the molding of cadre students into disciplined subjects of Party policy. It also meant that the school—and particularly the Party Secretariat and the Organization Department, which approved and coordinated recruitment—would determine which cadres would be selected for advancement, thus avoiding promotions made on the basis of personal or institutional ties. Peng's work at the Central Party School revealed his capacity for using organizational arrangements to promote Party authority and suggested as well that he was fully aware of the potentially disruptive consequences of parochial organizational and personal loyalties.

After Liberation, Peng's work on the Government Administrative Council's Political–Legal Commission provided additional opportunities to carry out his ideas about Party organization work. Peng's work in political–legal matters included serving on the drafting committee for the Election Law, where his experience with the use of "filtered democracy" to ensure Party control in Jin Cha Ji would play a crucial role. Although he was not a member of the drafting committee for the 1954 Constitution, Peng had ample opportunity for input to the document before it was enacted.[67] In his speech to the First NPC, Peng elaborated on the dictum of the 1954 Constitution that all citizens are equal before the law, indicating that this meant not substantive or procedural equality for all, but rather that once the content of particular rules were set, implementation should be disciplined and in keeping with organizational procedures.[68] Although the content of specific statutes might permit disparate treatment of different types of people (counterrevolutionaries and other bad classes, for example), the statutes themselves were to be enforced equally according to their terms. Thus the permitted scope for interpretation and adjustment of the application of legal rules was to be sharply constrained. Because the revolutionary conditions that justified empowering enforcing officials with discretion to determine when and how the law would be enforced no longer existed, the differential application of legal rules based on the subjective circumstances of the citizenry was no longer necessary. As the fount of policy and its expression through law, the Party might still determine that by their terms, laws should apply differently to different classes and in different situations, but this authority was no longer to be delegated informally to enforcing organs and officials.

In the area of judicial institutions, Peng frequently discussed the need to coordinate relations and division of labor between and among the Public Security Bureau, the People's Procuracies, and the People's Courts.[69] He emphasized coordination and mutual supervision among these institutions and the use of procedural arrangements to ensure that no single organ could become too powerful and that all organs would comply with central Party directives and policies.

After his rehabilitation in 1979, Peng initially emphasized the role of the Party in providing overall supervision for the legal system. This is evident in his persistence in espousing the importance of following the "four basic principles"—the most basic of which is the leadership of the Chinese Communist Party.[70] Thus in his speech to the first session of the Chinese Legal Studies Society, Peng stressed that "the work of the Legal Studies Society is to uphold the four basic principles."[71] Among the tasks he enumerated at the July 1982 National Conference on Political–Legal Work was that of strengthening the leadership of basic-level Party organizations in the campaign against economic crimes.[72]

Despite his promotion of overall Party supervision, however, Peng cautioned that Party officials should not get involved in individual cases, so as to avoid arbitrary intervention. He told an audience at the Central Party School that

> The leadership of the Party Committee to which we speak does not mean that it examines and approves concrete cases. . . . If [the Party Committee] has a hand in every case, surely it will be picking up sesame seeds and ignoring the watermelon, foolishly concentrating on minor issues while neglecting important matters.[73]

Although Peng's comment seems to contradict the concept of Party leadership, in fact it merely indicates that such leadership should take on a new form of indirect supervision. For Peng also stated that instead of involving itself in concrete cases,

> the Party Committee should lead, supervise, and support public security, procuracy, and judicial organs in the independent conduct of their duties. . . . When [these organs] are right the Party Committee should support them, when they make mistakes the Party Committee should criticize and correct them and when necessary take on some of their duties.[74]

Peng declined to enact an all-embracing prohibition on direct Party involvement, as indicated by the absence in the final draft of the constitution of any prohibition on Party interference in the handling of cases.[75] In explaining the process of constitutional revision, Peng stressed the importance of the Party leadership.[76] Thus, Peng saw the threefold process of Party approval of legislation, interpretation of statutes, and appointment and supervision of Party personnel as the preferred way to ensure Party control over the legalization program, without incurring the costs that direct supervision of cases might bring. Although Peng's emphasis on CPC leadership began to change as his political fortunes came to be associated with the NPC, Peng's legacy as a Party organizer remained an important component of his individual character—and indeed may have contributed to his ability to take on the role of lawgiver so effectively.

The Lawgiver

Max Weber saw the lawgiver as one who has been assigned the responsibility of systematically codifying or reconstituting particular laws.[77] The features of the lawgiver are not derived from the circumstances of legislators imbued with attributes of democratic liberalism. Rather, in Weber's view, it is the lawgivers' purported access to divine wisdom that empowers them to issue authoritative formal norms articulated through specialized terminology to govern social behavior. In the context of the PRC, where access to divine wisdom can be read as reception of Party ideology and policy, Peng fits the typology particularly well. Throughout his career, Peng was charged with codification of law based on Party ideology and policy—in the context of CPC history, surely an accepted substitute for divine inspiration.

Peng's experience and expertise in organizational matters in Jin Cha Ji and Yan'an served him well in his responsibilities as the Party official in charge of legal system after 1949. During the state-building period of the 1950s, Peng guided the establishment of China's legal system from an instrumentalist perspective, using law to ensure implementation of Party policies. For example, in his discussion both of the 1951 regulations on counterrevolutionaries and the 1952 regulations on the *san fan/wu fan* campaigns, Peng emphasized that these measures were aimed at ensuring Party control over the mass movement and preserving central control over local levels.[78] Peng's discussion of the 1954 Constitution emphasized the need to use it and the laws to meet the needs of the Chinese people under the leadership of the Party.[79] Throughout his speeches on law during the early and mid-1950s, Peng repeatedly returned to this instrumentalist theme: Law must serve specific policy objectives, as these are set out by the Party.[80]

Peng resumed this role as lawgiver after his rehabilitation in early 1979, through his positions on the Legislative Affairs Committee, the

Bills Committee, and later the Committee for Revising the Constitution. In his explanation of the policy basis for various substantive laws, Peng emphasized that such legislation was designed to serve the regime's policies of economic modernization.[81] Thus, the 1979 Criminal Law Code was aimed at maintaining social stability in order to facilitate the Party's policies of socialist modernization.[82] These policies were also dominant in the drafting of the Economic Contract Law, as indicated by Peng's speech to the third session of the Fifth NPC Standing Committee in September 1980.[83] Under Peng's guidance, the drafting of the 1982 Constitution also gave vent to Party policies supporting economic modernization, expanded support for intellectuals, and family planning.[84]

Peng's instrumentalist approach to lawmaking also revealed support for legislative restraint. During his tenure as chair of the NPC Standing Committee, he cautioned against entrenching parochial policy views in legislative articulations of Party policy:

> We must avoid subjective, one-sided attempts to formulate a multiplicity of all-embracing laws and must not allow our laws to become too complicated and elaborate for our cadres and people to learn and apply.[85]

Although some have suggested that Peng's caution masked a broader effort to forestall reform efforts associated with Deng Xiaoping and Zhao Ziyang,[86] Peng also seemed to call for a broader consensus in the expression of Party policy. Thus, despite the potential problems of divergent interpretations and application,[87] Peng's view that law should serve as a tool of policy enforcement mandated the use of broadly worded enactments that would permit the Party to maintain maximum control over interpretation and allow maximum flexibility in using law to exercise control over society.

Thus, Peng Zhen's character reveals a complex mix of personae. As an individual, Peng Zhen exhibited traits of toughness, intelligence, and affability. As a politician, Peng took on the role of the aggressive functionary who could be counted on to apply his considerable abilities to achieving assigned policy goals while maintaining a sharp focus on his own political advancement. Peng's career was strongly influenced by his role as a Party organizer. Although this derived from his early experiences in the Communist underground, Peng later used his organizational positions and ideology to pursue his own political interests. Peng's emphasis on Party organization and the use of formal rules and procedures for the exercise of institutional authority allowed him to confine policy debate within institutional channels where he had significant influence. As lawgiver, Peng Zhen stood for several clearly identifiable principles. First, that law should be an instrument of policy. Second, laws and regulations should reflect policy consensus. And finally, formal laws should be imbued with sufficient flexibility to permit policy changes, but not be so malleable as to be devoid of authority. In sum, Peng Zhen was a complicated person. His personal characteristics as an individual, politician, Party organizer, and lawgiver often complemented each other, but sometimes, they seemed to operate in contradiction. This perspective on Peng Zhen's personae provides important context for his evolving views on law and authority.

CHAPTER 2

The Pre-Liberation Period: Discipline and Revolution

DURING THE PRE-LIBERATION period, Peng Zhen was an archetypal Leninist revolutionary: committed to the controlled articulation, dissemination, and enforcement of Party policy. This phase in Peng's career serves as a baseline from which to view subsequent developments. Peng began his path to power in the Communist Party of China (CPC) hierarchy during this period, and his experiences laid the groundwork for the emphasis on organizational discipline that was to characterize so much of his subsequent career. During this period, the perilous life of underground Party work made discipline a paramount goal, one that took precedence over other considerations. The policy-making process was a flexible mixture of directives from the Party elite tempered by vague notions of democratic centralism. Once policy was decided, it was the province of organizations to ensure dissemination and rigid enforcement. Political and legal institutions were not vehicles for popular participation and institutional restraint, but rather were to be mechanisms for policy enforcement by the Leninist vanguard Party. These views informed Peng's participation in the December 9th Movement, his leadership of the Jin Cha Ji Border Region, and his role in the Yan'an rectification campaign. As an implementer of Party policies, Peng's growing mastery of the dynamics of discipline made him increasingly valuable to higher-level leaders and laid a foundation for his rise in the Party hierarchy.

Discipline and the Underground Party: The December 9th Movement

The December 9th Movement erupted in 1935 in response to perceived capitulation by the Nationalist government and local warlords to Japanese demands to create an "autonomous" region comprising the five northern Chinese provinces of Hebei, Shandong, Shanxi, Chahar, and Suiyuan.[1] The uprising provided an opportunity for the CPC to strengthen its internal organization and to expand its influence over the myriad of political activists in the area. There had been a history of serious disagreements between the CPC Central Committee and the local Hebei CPC Committee over political strategy, particularly over the role of workers' unions in the revolution.[2] Indeed, the Hebei Provincial Committee had attempted in May 1935 to supplant the Beiping Municipal CPC Committee with its own "CPC Beiping Municipal Work Committee" (*Zhonggong Beiping shi gongzuo weiyuanhui*) to organize underground work, particularly among high school and university students.[3] However, the Hebei committee itself was far from unified and had been beset by internal factional problems that hampered its effectiveness as an instrument through which to pursue the CPC's revolutionary goals—not to mention resulting in the death and arrests of many of its members.[4] Peng Zhen had apparently been involved in the internal bickering within the Hebei cell but was gradually drawn under the influence of Liu Shaoqi and the CPC Centre.

Pursuant to the August 1, 1935, directive issued by the CPC Central Committee,[5] Party strategy had come to concentrate on attacking Japanese aggression. This provided a useful basis for establishing links with the students in Beijing by catering to their hostility toward Japanese encroachments and their impatience with the Nationalists' policies of accommodation. Although contemporary observers claimed otherwise,[6] later analysis suggests heavy involvement by the CPC in the movement from the outset.[7] The Party's policies were clearly evident in official statements by patriotic organizations such as the National Salvation Association and the North China Liberation Association. Thus, the manifesto of the Association called for (1) punishment of traitors and confiscation of their property; (2) rights to assembly, organization, and free speech; and (3) action to organize the Chinese people in support of these policies, whereas the program of the North China Liberation Association included specific references to tolerance for political parties other than the Kuomintang (KMT) and specific criticism of the Nationalist capitulation.[8] Indeed, a main concern within the Party was over which committee should be responsible for liaison with the Beiping Student Union during the movement.[9] Police searches became more frequent and seemed targeted against underground Communists, whereas the students seemed more vigorously noncooperative with police inquiries about Communist activities.[10]

On the other hand, although CPC members were clearly active in the December 9th Movement, and perhaps in its instigation, there was a clear lack of organizational and policy discipline within the movement. Given the rather fractured state of the Hebei provincial committee at the time, this was not surprising. However, the uprising did provide an opportunity for the CPC Centre to strengthen its activities and recruitment. With the appointment of Liu Shaoqi to head the North China Bureau in spring 1936, the Party Centre's involvement began in earnest. Peng Zhen and Lin Feng were transferred from the Tianjin CPC Committee (where they were seen as "being on the right track") to the North China Bureau.[11] Peng Zhen's prior involvement in the Hebei provincial committee allowed him to play an important role for Liu in gathering information and reporting back to the bureau in Tianjin. Peng's activities were secretive, however. Even Yao Yilin, who as secretary of the CPC Tianjin Committee and was prominently involved in the movement, was unsure as to the nature of Peng's activities.[12] Zhang Youyu (appointed by Liu to direct political education under the North China Liaison Department[13] and later *mishu* to Peng Zhen) recollected that many of the movement's participants in Beijing were kept in the dark about Liu's activities.[14] Lu Ping (appointed party secretary at Peking University before the Cultural Revolution) recollected that although many were aware that the CPC had representatives in the Beijing underground, no one seemed to know the identity of these individuals.[15] Whether such secrecy was motivated by security concerns vis-à-vis the Japanese and the warlord government of Yan Xishan or by internal concerns for accurate reporting is unclear, although it was consistent with Liu Shaoqi's generally secretive approach to Party work in the White Areas[16] and was mandated by CPC policy on the strict separation of open and secret work.[17] But in the end, it must have been grating on the movement leaders, particularly after Peng authored a withering report criticizing the movement's tendencies toward "closed doorism" (*guanmen zhuyi*) and "capitulationism" (*touxiang zhuyi*).

Peng's report incorporated Liu Shaoqi's critique of the movement, although Liu apparently dropped the latter charge in favor of the milder critique of adventurism (*maoxian zhuyi*).[18]

Although the differences between Liu and Peng regarding the problems of the movement were not inconsequential, each reflected a concern with discipline. Although Liu seemed worried that the students were simply acting recklessly, without regard to the effect of their actions on the long-term goals of the revolutionary movement, Peng's charge of capitulationism was aimed more specifically at issues of leadership, in particular the concern that the students were insufficiently loyal to CPC directives. For Peng, the movement could be successful only to the extent that it furthered the Party's immediate goals, and this required subservience to CPC leadership. Liu took a somewhat broader view that the movement could contribute to the Party's long-term revolutionary goals, but only if the students acted responsibly and did not alienate popular support. Although Peng was later attacked during the Cultural Revolution for allegedly acting on behalf of Liu Shaoqi to stifle the movement,[19] this was largely an effort to reinterpret Liu's and Peng's efforts to bring discipline to the movement in an effort to restrain the revolutionary enthusiasm of the participants.

Their minor differences of approach notwithstanding, Liu and Peng both saw that CPC guidance of the movement was critical, and the North China Bureau continued its efforts to influence the student nationalists. Yu Qiwei (Huang Jing), later to become secretary of the CPC Beiping Bureau in late 1936 and ultimately the mayor of Tianjin, acted as the Party's major channel to the National Salvation Associations (*jiuguohui*)[20] and the emergent National Liberation Vanguard of China (*Zhonghua minzu jiefang xiangfengdui*)—the NLVC.[21] Peng's ties to the movement were elevated to the context of broader intra-Party organizational matters. He was appointed director of the North China Bureau's Organization Department in mid-1936 and was closely involved with reorganizing the Beiping CPC Committee. Peng was also appointed to represent the CPC's North China Bureau in leading the student movement and was credited with promoting the alliance of various movements for national salvation and resisting Japan in North China.[22]

After the disastrous March 31 incident in which numerous students were arrested after what was later viewed as an ill-conceived and reckless (in Liu's words, "adventurist") confrontation with police, Beiping Party secretary Li Xuefeng was replaced by Li Baohua and took over the local organization department.[23] Peng Zhen took over Li Baohua's previous responsibilities as CPC representative for Eastern Hebei, although this was only a temporary arrangement and Peng soon returned to Tianjin and the North China Bureau.[24] The Hebei committee itself was also criticized,[25] although some, such as Luo Fu (Zhang Wentian), called for leniency and criticized the labeling policy errors as errors of political line.[26]

Peng was sent yet again to Beijing in mid-1936, not merely to collect information and report back to Liu, but also to resolve specific problems.[27] Peng's activities ranged from the specific task of bringing stability to the Party cell (*dangzhibu*) at Qinghua University, to conducting a general review of Party activities. This review was published as an article on "Examining Work in Beiping Based on the Party's New Tactics" (*Genju dang de xin celue lai jianguo Beiping gongzue*) for the Party's internal journal *Huoxian* (*Fireline*).[28] Peng was appointed to manage CPC control over the NLVC[29] and directed the creation of various subcommittees for education, agriculture, and culture aimed at carrying out Party policies in these areas.[30] Peng organized the first national congress of the NLVC in February 1937 and saw to the appointment of CCP candidates to most of the high positions.[31] Official histories of the period now portray the NLVC after 1937 as the primary link by which the CPC led the national anti-Japanese patriotic youth.[32] Although Party directives gave ample attention to the importance of pursuing the united front strategy, equally clear was the commitment to achieving domestic political goals of carrying out class struggle and seizing political power.[33] Thus, at an expanded Politburo meeting convened in March 1937, Zhang Wentian reviewed the Party's underground work and concluded that new approaches were necessary which emphasized (1) open lawful activities, (2) strengthening Party leadership, (3) working on a national scale, and (4) relying on "cadres who can work independently."[34] Having shown his abilities in the context of the student movement, Peng clearly fell into this category, and he subsequently participated in the White Areas Work Conference held May 17–June 10 in Yan'an, as well as the CPC Politburo meeting that convened at the same time.[35] Peng is described in his official biography as having supported the basic policies and strategic principles put forward to the conference by Liu Shaoqi, and he may well have contributed to the preparation of Liu's "Party Work with the Masses in the White Areas."[36]

The December 9th Movement provided Peng Zhen an entry into central-level politics. Peng's role in CPC underground work had developed from a role as project operative to one where his ties with the student movement became but one component of Peng's larger responsibilities for intra-Party organizational matters. Although the day-to-day tasks may not have changed much, because student activism in Beijing and Tianjin remained the focus of CPC work, the change in Peng's organizational position had broader implications for his rise in the Party ranks. Although Liu appointed many subordinates to deliver working reports on local conditions,[37] Peng's reporting must have had a particular impact. Liu chose to cultivate the young Peng, and as his own stature rose, so too did that of his protégé. When Liu made his triumphant return to Yenan in 1937,[38] Peng accompanied him to deliver a report to the Politburo on work in the White Areas.[39] Peng's association with Liu's work in the White Areas was subsequently affirmed through Peng's inscription of calligraphy for a major posthumous volume on Liu Shaoqi.[40]

Discipline and Party Building: The Jin Cha Ji Program

The Jin Cha Ji (Shanxi-Chahar-Hebei) Border Region was considered an ideal locale for guerrilla warfare because although it was nearly surrounded by the Japanese, the interior of the area was largely free of Japanese control.[41] However, the situation was chaotic, with anti-Japanese activities left mainly to roving bands of guerrillas that were often little more than bandit gangs.[42] The Party's influence was not particularly strong—its main claim to authority lay in its assertion of leadership in the resistance to Japan.[43] Peng Zhen's role in Jin Cha Ji reflected a broader process of building Party power that evolved from an initial institution-building effort to a process of consolidation, then culminated the formalized declaration of CPC policy for the region.

Building the Organizations of Party Power

The opening of the Jin Cha Ji People's Government in January 1938 was a culmination of several months of preparatory work.[44] In September 1937 Deng Xiaoping conveyed a directive from the North China Bureau to Zhao Zhensheng (a pseudonym for Li Baohua, who had worked with Peng Zhen as secretary of the Beiping CPC Committee in late 1937) to establish a CPC Committee for Jin Cha Ji with Wang Ping and Liu Xiufeng and in coordination with the Eighth Route Army. The Jin Cha Ji military district was established in November under the leadership of Nie Rongzhen, and shortly thereafter, the Jin Cha Ji CPC Committee was established, chaired by Yu Qiwei (Huang Jing), who also had worked with Peng during the December 9th Movement.[45] The preparatory organs for the People's Government were set up in early December.[46] The formal establishment of the Border Region at a congress of military, political, and civilian representatives in January 1938 saw the creation of quasigovernmental institutions, whereas the Second United Front and the general absence of KMT authority permitted many Party activities to be carried out openly.[47] The institutions of rule included the representative congress; a provisional administrative committee chaired by Song Shaowen with Hu Renkui as vice chair and five subdepartments for civil affairs, finance, education, industry, and commerce, and secretariat; and the law courts.[48] Formal edicts were issued on such matters as reducing interest rates and quartering resistance troops, as well as on topics such as wasteland recovery and agriculture and water management, all of which comprised the various responsibilities of villages.[49] Formal regulations were also used to articulate Party policies on the punishment of traitors; control of corruption; mediation of disputes; elections; organization of various administrative and judicial bodies; and management of economic activity.[50]

Peng Zhen was dispatched to Jin Cha Ji in February 1938 to represent the North China Bureau, and in March he was designated the bureau's resident representative.[51] In this capacity, Peng acted as a channel for conveying policies and decisions from the Party Centre. He had carried out the same task in Ji Yu Jin, where he spoke on Party strategy and policies to the provincial committee in February 1938.[52] Not surprisingly, therefore, there was a close correlation between the content of Peng's speeches and the focus of various instructions emanating from the Party Centre and the North China Bureau. Neither was Peng operating wholly unsupervised—Liu Shaoqi made numerous visits to Jin Cha Ji, as did other top leaders such as Zhu De.[53] Upon his appointment, Peng was given specific instructions for consolidating and expanding the border area, including (1) winning over traitors, ruffians, bandits, and other undesirables who had entered various parties and political, popular, and especially military groups, and resolving the many unprincipled disputes that were going on within these groups; (2) investigating and purging ruffians, bandits, and other undesirables; (3) restoring order in the region; (4) improving Party organization; (5) building mass organizations; and (6) pursuing ongoing administration of government affairs.[54] Peng was also directed to establish governmental organizations to restore order to the struggle against Japan and protect the interests of the masses while recruiting competent activists and purging (*xishua*) incompetent corrupt elements.[55] These instructions were in line with the decisions of the August 1937 Lochuan conference, where Liu Shaoqi had criticized leftist tendencies within the Party that were manifested in opposition to the United Front policies of cooperation with the Nationalist KMT.[56] Later on, during the Cultural Revolution, Peng was criticized by Red Guards for supporting United Front policies too vigorously, although clearly this was the mandate of CPC policy at the time.[57] Moreover, the CPC views on the United Front being articulated by Peng in 1938 emphasized the importance of independent autonomy (*duli zizhu*) in the CPC's political and economic activities, even while the Party formally acknowledged the United Front in its relations with the Guomindang.[58]

During his tenure in Jin Cha Ji, Peng grappled with new challenges in an uncertain setting. In addition to the general remoteness and backwardness of the region, local elites remained hostile to CPC policies and personnel, and the Japanese Army was a constant threat.[59] In response, the CPC worked to establish mass organizations to strengthen its power in Jin Cha Ji.[60] As he engaged in organizing resistance against Japan during this period,[61] Peng Zhen's primary role was in expanding Party power through organizational and popular front work.[62] Local armed brigades were established at the subdistrict (*fen qu*) level, some of which engaged in military operations against the Japanese, although most were confined to building goodwill through local civil works.[63] Patriotic associations for resisting Japan and saving the nation (*kang Ri jiu guo hui*) were brought under CPC control in a way reminiscent of the December 9th Movement strategy.[64] Associations of workers, peasants, women, and youth were also convened to disseminate CPC policies.[65] The newspaper *Kang di bao* (Resist the enemy) was established in December 1937 by the political department of the Jin Cha Ji Military Region and later became the *Jin Cha Ji Daily*, a major vehicle for dissemination of CPC pronouncements and a source of many of Peng Zhen's subsequent political associates such as Deng Tuo.[66] These organizational activities continued throughout Peng's term in Jin Cha Ji,[67] but at least by the time the Border Region was formally established in early 1938, the Party had developed the beginnings of a mass base upon which to build its institutions of governance.

Although the process of institution building proceeded apace, there were significant problems with the quality of Party members and hence the effectiveness of governance in Jin Cha Ji. Nie Rongzhen noted the need for better coordination of military and civilian work;[68] Peng Zhen himself called attention to problems of corruption and the need to raise political consciousness.[69] The first Jin Cha Ji representative Party congress was convened in Shanxi's Wutai county in April 1938 as a vehicle for bringing military units, political power, and popular groups under Party control.[70] Peng was dispatched by the North China Bureau to lead the congress and convey the policies of the Party Centre.[71] The policies adopted at the congress focused on the task of reforming Party organization, strengthening Party leadership, and enacting specific rules on Party rectification, as follows:[72]

> (1) Improving Party leadership work and establishing systems for reporting, investigating, and assessing the relations among transmission organs; introducing Party members and the opening and closing of Party files; and restoring Party files and renewing membership. (Here the focus was on the mechanics of Party administration of information and personnel.)
>
> (2) Renewing registration and periodically straightening out of Party members. (This point concerned the process for weeding out undesirable members.)
>
> (3) Inspecting and evaluating cadres, regulating investigations by the Regional CPC Committee down to the county level, conducting investigations by the county committees down to the district level, conducting investigations by the district committees down to the committee level, and assessing the need to wipe out traitors and transfer capitulators. (This policy reflected the ongoing problem of supervising officials at various levels of the CPC organization and getting rid of those with uncertain loyalties.)
>
> (4) Renewing, in accordance with policies of the Party Centre and the North China Bureau, the investigation of Party members who have resumed their relationships. (Here again, the matter at issue is the investigation of politically suspect CPC members.)
>
> (5) Establishing Party training offices and stipulating the basic materials for education of Party members. (In the wake of reexamination and purging of suspect Party members, this policy was aimed at preventing the recurrence of problems of political reliability.)

These provisions were formalized in subsequent regulations on the conduct of Party members.[73] Although there were criticisms of the scope of the rectification,[74] the effort to tighten up Party administration and improve the quality of Party members was to be a constant theme throughout Peng's tenure in Jin Cha Ji.[75]

Peng also attended to organizational matters. In his October 1938 speech "On political authority in the Jin Cha Ji Border Region," he focused on specific institutional mechanisms for achieving the goals of destroying the enemy's political power and building up the CPC.[76] Peng specifically addressed the role and jurisdiction of the Jin Cha Ji administrative council in maintaining social and economic order and establishing leadership over the masses—both in resisting Japan and in gaining independence from the old system. The links between the administrative council and the local people's councils was critical in this respect, and Peng's discussion foreshadowed the election reforms that followed and ensured CPC dominance in the local people's councils.

Organizational changes were also carried out regarding the relationship of Jin Cha Ji to the CPC Centre. In November 1938 the Party Centre established the Jin Cha Ji Subbureau of the North China Bureau, with Nie Rongzhen, Peng Zhen, Guan Xiangying, and Cheng Zihua as commissioners and Peng appointed as secretary.[77] Under this central organization, subregional organs were established, the most important of which was the Jizhong (Central Hebei) District, where Huang Jing (Yu Qiwei) was appointed secretary and put in charge of coordinating activities among Party, political, military, and civilian organizations.[78] The Jin Cha Ji Subbureau was intended to bring the region under unified Party leadership that would also unify the organization of military units, organs of political power, and mass organizations.[79]

However, in a decision that reflected the shrinking fortunes of the CPC in North China as well as an effort to tighten central control over the Jin Cha Ji area, the Jin Cha Ji Subbureau was renamed the North China Subbureau of the Party Centre—again with Peng as secretary and Nie, Guan, and Cheng as commissioners.[80] In effect, this decision eliminated Liu Shaoqi's North China Bureau as an intermediary organ between the Party Centre and Jin Cha Ji. Three regional CPC committees were established under the North China Subbureau:[81] (1) the Jin Cha Ji Regional CPC Committee under Secretary Liu Lantao, which was to be the headquarters responsible for all three provinces within the region; (2) the Central Hebei (Ji Zhong) Regional CPC Committee;[82] and (3) the Ji Re Cha Regional CPC Committee under Ma Huizhi, responsible for Pingxi, Pingbei, and East Hebei (Ji Dong) districts. An administrative commission of the North China Subbureau that included Liu Lantao and Zhao Zhensheng (Li Baohua) was responsible for day-to-day operations.[83]

In line with these organizational developments, significant attention was paid to establishing more Party organizations and to wresting political power away from the local traditional elites. In May 1939 Peng and Nie Rongzhen issued a formal directive to Xiao Ke and the East Hebei CPC Committee urging renewed work to implement the decisions of the January 1939 North China Subbureau Congress, particularly with respect to accelerating Party building among the masses as a basis for guerrilla warfare.[84] In Central Hebei (Jizhong), there were ongoing problems of failure to comply with policies of the Centre regarding the need to pursue Party building and consolidation of political authority even while participating in the United Front.[85] The CPC's organizational efforts were so problematic that the Party Centre had to fend off a KMT attempt in mid-1939 to incorporate Central Hebei into the Nationalist-controlled Hebei Province.[86]

Consolidating the Party's Leadership

Despite these difficulties, however, by late 1939 the focus shifted from Party building to consolidation. In August–September 1939, the second Jin Cha Ji CPC representative congress was convened in Fouping county to review the August 25 decision of the CPC Politburo "Decision on Consolidating the Party," which directed internal rectification of thought, politics, and organization.[87] This was presented as an essential component of the fight against Japan and was mandated by Mao Zedong's directive of April 1938 on consolidating tasks in the Border Region and his directive of May 1938, "Problems of Strategy in Guerrilla War Against Japan."[88] Although problems of continued leftism were noted by the North China Bureau in August 1938, of greater importance was the apparent willingness of local cadres wrapped up in the struggle against Japan to overlook the struggle against landlords and the need to improve the livelihood and political involvement of the "basic masses."[89] This was exacerbated by the problem of local elites attempting to use United Front policies to protect their own political and economic interests against CPC reforms.[90]

The congress heard a report reviewing Party work over the previous 20 months, which noted a number of problems, including (1) improper recruiting and irresponsible purges of Party members; (2) continued problems with opportunists (*touji fenzi*) joining the Party; (3) inefficient methods of transmitting instructions; (4) corruption; (5) inappropriate handling of mistakes through open attacks at large meetings rather than education and small-group critiques; and (5) generalized problems of education and training.[91] The report set forth several areas of important future work, including (1) adjusting recruiting practices to account for target locales, class background, local conditions, scope, and careful screening of applicants; (2) building local CPC committees and managing elections to local councils; (3) strengthening leadership; (4) improving quality of cadre personnel and performance; (5) strengthening educational activities in the service of Party building; (6) improving work style; (7) attending to matters of secrecy; (8) strengthening control over guerrilla activities; and (9) building intra-Party unity. Although the document was careful to note the successes achieved in Jin Cha Ji, its tenor overwhelmingly implied that was that more work was needed to increase the Party's effectiveness in the area. Indeed, the Party Centre was compelled to issue a directive in September 1939 urging the North China Subbureau and the Jin Cha Ji area to give serious attention (*da da zhuyi*) to the problem of improving the quality of cadres in political authority.[92]

After the congress, the North China Bureau convened an organization work conference (the Jingshan Conference) in November–December 1939 to plan implementing the congress's decisions. Among the speakers were Guan Xiangying, Zhao Zhensheng (Li Baohua), Peng Zhen, He Long, and Huang Jing (Yu Qiwei).[93] Peng's speech to the Conference dutifully reiterated the directives of the August 25 Politburo decision that emphasized Party consolidation overexpansion while also touching on various themes that would recur later in his career.[94] In discussing the need for continued struggle against capitulationists and spies within the Party,[95] Peng went on to note that as a result of the problematic influence of landlords and capitalists on newly recruited Party members, "many subjectively faithful communists still harboured anti-Party sentiments."[96] Peng's conceptualization of "capitulationism," which had come up during the December 9th Movement four years earlier, focused on organizational discipline and subservience to the Party, rather than on ideological purity. Peng suggested that even those who devoutly accepted the ideology of communism should be struggled against if they harbored doubts about the CPC and its leadership. Thus, Peng Zhen revealed once again his commitment to using organizational discipline to ensure compliance with CPC policies and directives, although this also gave evidence of the "sectarian tendencies" later attributed to Peng by his mentor Liu Shaoqi.[97]

Peng's speech to the Jingshan Conference also devoted considerable attention to the problem of materials and methods for training Party cadres—focusing in particular on matters of class struggle, the exposure of capitulationists and spies, and the use of Party rules and regulations to impose iron discipline. These remarks foreshadowed the Centre's decision, taken in February of the following year, directing the various regions to establish party schools[98] and was a precursor to Peng's subsequent role as deputy director of the Central Party School in Yan'an. Finally, Peng addressed Party organizational work specifically, spelling out in detail how the tension should be resolved between promoting a democratic work style while still imposing iron discipline: A democratic work style was to be promoted in order to break down the power of established traditional local leaders, but once CPC cadres had assumed positions of authority, there should be strict compliance with Party directives. This approach would later become a central theme when Peng was made director of the CPC Central Organization Department.

Peng Zhen reiterated these policies at a North China Subbureau expanded cadres' meeting in April 1940.[99] In his speech at the meeting, Peng stressed the importance of ensuring that the struggle against internal opponents (diehards and capitulationists) be linked to the resistance war against Japan.[100] Although conceding that some landlords and capitalists had been labeled unfairly as diehards and capitulationists, Peng stressed the overwhelming importance of the struggle against these elements generally. This had been dictated by the February 1 decision of the Party Centre that noted that the conflict between "the orientation toward capitulation by the big bourgeoisie and the tendency toward resistance by the communists and petite and middle bourgeoisie had become increasingly obvious and serious" and directed the use of democratic dictatorship to attack all plots against the Japanese base areas and the liquidation of traitors and anti-Communist elements.[101] Peng also noted the need to indoctrinate the military with a fuller understanding of the counterrevolutionary nature of these elements and the extent to which they obstructed the fight against Japan. This was part of a broader effort to assert political control over military activities after the Jingshan meeting.[102]

Formal Articulation of Party Policy

The most complete statement of Jin Cha Ji policies under Peng's administration is contained in the "Current Administrative Program Concerning the Jin Cha Ji Border Region," also referred to as the "Twenty-Point Program" (*shuang shi gangling*) issued August 30, 1940, by the North China Bureau.[103] Peng delegated a group of cadres to conduct research and prepare discussion points as a basis for his own drafting work.[104] The program summarized Party policy regarding such issues as establishing organizations for resisting Japan, creating economic and tax policies, ensuring property rights, addressing education and culture, and establishing measures for the punishment of "traitors";[105] in addition, the bases for these policies to be carried out under the direction of local Party committees were also created.[106] This localized strategy emphasized the role of rural organization and was later interpreted as a repudiation of the urban strategy attributed to Wang Ming and returned "Bolshevik" students.[107] Although many of the attendant policies had been articulated as early as 1937 with Mao's statements of policies for resisting Japan,[108] the Twenty-Point Program was the first attempt to implement them on a region-wide basis.[109]

The Twenty-Point Program also detailed the organizational steps to be taken in the realization of these policies. Article 5 set forth the so-called three-thirds system (*san san zhi*) by which Party dominance of popular and administrative organizations was to be achieved.[110] All popular and government bodies were to reserve one-third of their membership for the Chinese Communist Party, leaving two-thirds to be made up of "other parties resisting Japan together with independent persons." Article 11 also established the three-thirds system for a variety of specialized bodies for such tasks as disaster relief, cooperation among nationalities, mutual aid among the peasants, and the improvement of health and hygiene. This system was aimed at increasing local support for Party policies—particularly the "double reduction" policy regarding rents and interests that had been enacted in regulations in early 1939,[111] but which continued to face stiff resistance from landlords and continued apathy by the peasantry.[112] Not only did this approach ensure Communist representation in the village councils, but when linked with the one-third guaranteed to leftist "non-Party" representatives, it gave the Party effective control. Thus, the process helped build the Party's links to local communities[113] and effectively deprived the landlord and rich peasants of their political power while inducing their grudging compliance with the economic reforms.[114] The Program also included provisions for actively repressing enemies, traitors, anti-Communists, and diehards—thus providing a basis for the elimination of potential opponents to Party rule.[115] And in contrast to the organizational framework established for the enforcement of Party dominance, there existed no such framework for the protection of personal and property rights.[116]

The Twenty-Point Program provided Peng with an opportunity to reiterate policies toward intellectuals, which had been articulated in the Party Centre's 1939 decision, "Vigorously Recruit Intellectuals" (*Daliang xishou zhishi fenzi*):

> We have all along protected and cultivated the broad mass of intellectuals, we prize elementary school teachers who are young intellectuals, and we make every effort to raise their status and improve their lives and we spare no efforts to safeguard them; in the same way we esteem and revere scholars and specialists and emphasize giving them favourable treatment.[117]

Peng also gave personal attention to putting arts and culture in the service of Party policies.[118] After his appointment as secretary of the Party Centre's Jin Cha Ji Subbureau, he arranged to remove the performance activities of the Northwest Front Service Group from the Jin Cha Ji Military Region to the Jin Cha Ji Subbureau.[119] Peng's interest in personally directing the arts extended to a decision to bring the Jin Cha Ji performers to Yan'an after his appointment to the Party School in 1941.[120]

Peng elaborated at some length on the Twenty-Point Program in a speech to a North China Subbureau expanded cadres' meeting in September 1940.[121] In this speech, Peng summarized virtually all relevant policy matters being addressed in Jin Cha Ji. After noting changes in the international situation, particularly the agreement of the United States, Great Britain, and France to give priority to the war in Europe, Peng noted that the increased intensity of Japanese advances in the area should not be taken as justification for permitting the struggle against Japan to supplant CPC goals of class struggle and revolution. In matters of Party organization and conduct, Peng noted problems of "leftism," such as indiscriminate labeling of diehards and capitulationists, failing to comply with CPC policies such as the three-thirds system, uncontrolled taking of private property, and not following CPC instructions concerning alliances with intellectuals and non-CPC cadres. Rightist errors were also mentioned, such as creating unprincipled alliances with class enemies under the guise of the United Front, failing to follow CPC policy in attacking diehards and traitors, and confusing the KMT Three People's Principles with Communism; in addition, problems of corruption and bureaucratism were discussed. Peng stressed the need for more education on the link between united front and class struggle, indicating that many CPC cadres, as well as members of the population at large, remained relatively apathetic politically and were more concerned with resisting Japan than in fulfilling CPC objectives. In this respect, Peng drew upon the Party Centre's directives that the various regions establish Party Schools in order to strengthen Marxist training for CPC cadres as a basis for consolidation and development of the Party.[122] Peng gave further attention to explaining the basic policies of the Border Region and to the critical task of implementation. Finally, Peng focused on the linkage between seizing political power and completing economic transformation.

Implementation of the Twenty-Point Program was taken up at a major work conference convened by the North China Bureau in January 1941.[123] Particular attention was given to overcoming previously identified problems in United Front work of leftism (undue attention to class struggle) and rightism (permitting the resistance of Japan to overcome the tasks of enforcing Party policies against landlords and for the benefit of the "basic masses"). In light of the deteriorating military circumstances, the conference also provided particular attention to military matters, focusing on strengthening Party control over mobile military units while adopting slogans calling for the Party to study the army and the militarization of Party members.[124]

Peng gave three speeches to the work conference, addressing in turn consolidating the Party, finance and production, and culture.[125] In his speech on Party consolidation work, Peng contended that although some aspects of the consolidation policy had been accomplished, there were deficiencies in the areas of cadre promotions, Party discipline, education in political theory, and separation of leading cadres from production, as well as problems of political work, ranging from coercive orders and the remnants of the household head system to undisciplined and excessive democracy among petite bourgeois intellectuals and peasants, and capitalistic selfishness by Party cadres. Peng cautioned that the consolidation program should carefully differentiate between dissidents and traitors, noting that the processes of investigation and testing should take precedence over actual purges and acknowledging the right of individuals to appeal purge decisions.[126] In addressing finance and production issues, Peng touched on several issues that would become recurring themes later in his career, including the need for leading cadres to participate in production (a policy issue that would resurface during Peng's drafting of the Latter Ten Points in the Socialist Education Campaign of 1962–1966),[127] the need to establish a wage arbitration commission and labor contract system (presaging Peng's efforts subsequently to develop legal institutions through which Party policies could be implemented in the economy and elsewhere), and the importance of not permitting human rights concerns to obstruct the campaign to eliminate traitors (in this case, something of a departure from his speech on Party consolidation, but consistent with his later role during the campaign against counterrevolutionaries and other class enemies during the early 1950s). In addressing cultural work, Peng emphasized the importance of bringing cultural work into the service of CPC policies, which, together with his statement in the speech on finance and production concerning the need to cultivate young intellectuals in the service of the CPC program, heralded his ongoing ties with cultural workers and intellectuals, which continued up through the Cultural Revolution.

Peng summarized his experience at Jin Cha Ji in a "Report on Party Work and Concrete Policies in Jin Cha Ji Border Region," delivered informally to Mao and the CPC Politburo at a meeting running from June 4–August 21, 1941[128] and issued as an internal Party document at Yan'an in September.[129] The report is divided into two main sections, addressing, respectively, "Various Concrete Policies" and "Party Building." The policy section provides an overview of political conditions in the Border Region and discusses at length the matter of political authority before going on to address economic policy, land, labor, and finance.[130] Of particular note in the discussion of political conditions is the attention paid to the "anti-CPC high tide," in which Peng summarizes the policy detailed in his report to the North China Subbureau expanded cadres conference of the previous September on the need for an anti-Japanese alliance with landlords and capitalists. Yet Peng's report to the Politburo was more frank about the use of united front rhetoric to coopt as many landlords and capitalists as possible once the CPC began to attack "local tyrants" (*tuhao*) and to redistribute land.[131]

In discussing economic policy, Peng elaborated on the September 1940 report with regard to the handling of individual enterprises. Although these were to be tolerated, the general policy of increasing material and financial resources and of directing all economic activities for the common benefit mandated gradually bringing these small producers under the ambit of production, sales, and consumers' cooperatives.[132] Peng's report to the Politburo was somewhat more permissive: Whereas the September 1940 report cautioned that satisfying public welfare and military requirements was a precondition for permitting private production and trading activities, Peng's report to the Politburo argued more directly that private production and trading formed the bases for satisfying public and military requirements.[133] Cultural revolution Red Guards later seized on this as an indication of Peng's ambivalence toward the role of capitalism in China.[134]

The most extensive passage in the policy section of Politburo report contains Peng's discussion "Building Political Power," which he describes as the "fundamental issue of all revolutions."[135] Here again, Peng elaborates on the September 1940 report, although he skips over much of the theoretical discussion of class dictatorship contained in his report to the North China Bureau meeting of the previous year—presumably because his Politburo audience would have been fully familiar with this line of discourse. Instead, Peng discusses at some length the stages of building political power in Jin Cha Ji, including (1) an initial period before the establishment of the Border Region when political authority rested in the old political institutions dominated by landlord and capitalist interests and in newly emergent popular patriotic organizations such that two separate systems coexisted; (2) a period of decentralized political authority vested in elected village heads; (3) a period of reform in political institutions through the use of representative congresses; and finally (4) a period of revolution in political power.

Peng's Politburo report also omitted reference to a penultimate stage discussed the previous September that involved the establishment of political organs of the popular will (*minyi jiguan*) such as the administrative council, moving instead directly from the reform stage to revolution and dispensing with the question of organs of popular will as a flaw of "extreme democracy."[136] This meant that the three-thirds system was to take on greater permanence. Because the period of revolution in political power had not yet arrived, of particular importance during Peng's tenure was the transition from decentralized authority under the village head system to the use of representative congresses.[137] These popular organizations would in turn serve as the pool from which officials in administrative organs would be drawn.[138] Peng explained that the reason for this system of indirect representation was the need to prevent "the stealthy deprivation of the people's real democratic rights under extreme democracy." Distinguishing between the concepts of political power (*zheng quan*) and the power of rule (*zhi quan*), Peng argued that the political power of the people did not include the powers of direct election and recall of officials.[139] In essence, Peng was seeking to ensure the Party's control over the processes of selection of local officials—by undermining the traditional village heads, elevating the role of Party-controlled popular organizations, and then using these bodies as a basis for strengthening Party control over elected government positions. Peng also sought to loosen the prerequisites for candidacy to administrative office, so as to facilitate the appointment of inexperienced but politically favorable individuals.[140] Peng noted a number of deficiencies in implementing the program, particularly the problem of traditional elites holding on to power even under the new system. Although Peng's comments in this regard were later interpreted by Cultural Revolution Red Guards as attempts to "beautify the landlord class" and protect landlords during the process of building political power,[141] Peng's speech set out an ambitious, albeit gradual, program of transition by which the CPC established and maintained a legitimate position of political leadership at the local level.

Although issues of Party building were of course related to political power, Peng's report addressed them separately.[142] Of particular importance was the question of Party consolidation, which had been taken up the previous year by the CPC Politburo and in several North China Subbureau meetings. Peng's report makes reference to the decisions made at these meetings and then addresses the question of implementation. Noting that Party influence remained incomplete in many areas, Peng urged a rigorous program of investigation of cadre performance and appraisal of cadre ideology and attitudes as a way to improve CPC performance and influence.[143] Peng also addressed the problem of purging Party members, indicating that on the basis of the experience of purges in Central Hebei and Beiyu,[144] this was going to be a long-term problem—due in part to the haphazard recruiting processes of past years that had permitted KMT spies, Trotskyites,[145] landlords, merchants and rich peasants, and all manner of other undesirables to join the Party. Although Peng's approach to Party consolidation work was consistent with the views Peng expressed in his speech on Party consolidation to the January 1941 North China Subbureau meeting, his attitude toward purges was more strident—absent were the conciliatory notes of January on overextending the purges or on rights of appeal.

Peng's discussion of discipline and democracy also sounded a stricter note. Cautioning that the CPC had been accused of being able to talk but not act (*neng shuo bu neng xing*), Peng argued that disciplined performance of Party plans and policies was essential to protecting the reputation of the revolutionary movement. Although noting the basic policy of democratic centralism, Peng explicitly gave priority to the centralist aspects required by wartime conditions. Peng cautioned that notions of democracy were subject to abuse by dissidents and separatists.

Although these views were broadly consistent with those expressed the previous January to the North China Subbureau, Peng's report to the Politburo evidenced a more strident tone—particularly with regard to dissidents (*yijifenzi*) whom Peng had previously distinguished from traitors but who now were lumped together with speculators and swindlers.[146] Moreover, Peng suggested that all Party members were potentially subject to the doleful influence of both bureaucratism from semifeudal socioeconomic and political relations and undisciplined independence and anarchy from lifestyles of capitalists, intellectuals, and even the peasantry.

Peng's report to the Politburo reflected a change in focus that accompanied his recall to the Centre. With his appointment to the Central Party School in September 1941, Peng was able more easily to articulate a purist position unfettered by local concerns. Moreover, Peng was soon to be in charge of a looming rectification campaign at the Party School, a position that would require a steely determination not swayed by subjective circumstances. Despite the noticeable hardening of Peng's position upon his recall to the Centre, the record of his pronouncements in Jin Cha Ji reveals a pattern of priorities. First, Peng was preoccupied with ensuring disciplined dissemination and enforcement of Party policies. Second, Peng devoted significant attention to problems of purity within the Party, a trait born of the haphazard CPC recruitment campaigns of the late 1930s—but one that would continue to feature prominently in Peng's career, and indeed, one that contributed significantly to Peng's advancement in the CPC hierarchy. Finally, Peng was concerned with the use of public political institutions for the exercise of Party power.

Jin Cha Ji provided Peng Zhen with an important opportunity to solidify his reputation as a Party organizer and administrator. The war against Japan allowed the destruction of structures of political institutions that had existed previously, and also allowed the consolidation of Party power. The needs of revolution mandated that the Party attend to its external relations and build its influence in the context of changing political institutions. Peng played a critical role in this process. Although Liu Shaoqi's patronage, together with the collective responsibility of the North China Subbureau, made it unlikely that Peng would fail, his subsequent posting to the Central Party School confirmed that Peng's performance in Jin Cha Ji met with general approval from higher levels. Although conditions in the region were far from perfect, and certain that Peng's adversaries were not above criticizing them in an effort to undermine his position, Peng was largely able to deflect criticisms of his performance.[147] During this period, Peng also began to cement the personal and political relationships that would surround his subsequent career—powerful cadres such as Liu Shaoqi and Nie Rongzhen became important patrons, and lesser officials such as Deng Tuo, An Ziwen, and Cheng Zihua became important supporters. It should also be noted that Peng began to make his fair share of enemies during this period. Chen Boda, for example, apparently never forgave Peng for purportedly referring to him as an ignorant bumpkin (*huli hutu*) in conversations with Nie Rongzhen[148] and later would have the opportunity for retaliation during the Cultural Revolution.

In any event, by early 1941 the situation in Jin Cha Ji had become increasingly perilous. The Eighth Route Army's "Hundred Regiments Offensive" was launched in August 1940, and despite initial victories, it led to a vicious and effective Japanese counterattack.[149] The "Three Alls" (burn all, kill all, loot all) campaign severely threatened the Border Region.[150] Although these disasters were not of Peng's making—indeed, he is hardly mentioned in the military correspondence of the period—his posting to Yan'an, first to attend the planned Seventh CPC Congress and then to assume the vice directorship of the Central Party School in June 1941, was almost certainly determined in part by the military reversals in Jin Cha Ji; a valuable cadre such as Peng simply could not be left in such a vulnerable forward position. But equally importantly, Peng's work in Jin Cha Ji solidified his reputation as an effective administrator and Party builder, and these easily justified his appointment to the Central Party School in Yan'an.[151]

Discipline Inside the Party: From Jin Cha Ji to Yan'an

Peng Zhen's handling of discipline and Party building in Jin Cha Ji—particularly his attention to the problems of investigating, appraising, and, where necessary, purging CPC cadres—made him a natural choice to head the rectification campaign at the Central Party School. The aggressive expansion of the CPC during the late 1930s and early 1940s had resulted in large numbers of newly recruited cadres with little education, few skills, and a woeful ignorance of Party ideology. As Peng had noted in Jin Cha Ji, problems with the quality of CPC cadres threatened the reputation of the Party and the success of its programs. Although problems with cadre training had been evident since at least

1940 when the Centre issued its instruction on the creation of Party Schools,[152] the organizational and ideological focus of rectification at the Central Party School in Yan'an had begun to emerge in late 1941.

In September, Mao spoke out against factionalism (*zongpai zhuyi*) and subjectivism (*zhuguan zhuyi*) to an expanded meeting of the CPC Politburo.[153] He repeated the theme in a speech to the Second Shen-Gan-Ning Border Region congress, chastizing Party members who failed to carry out democratic cooperation with non-Party elements in the course of the United Front.[154] The Centre's decision of December 1, 1941, regarding on-site cadre education made specific reference to the problems of subjectivism (*zhuguan zhuyi*), factionalism (*zongpai zhuyi*), and dogmatism (*jiaotiao zhuyi*), and the Centre urged a comprehensive and theoretically driven approach to cadre training.[155] The Centre decision of December 17 gave particular responsibilities for cadre education to the Central Propaganda Department, which was to be responsible for the Yan'an Cadre School.[156] However, the Politburo's decision of February 28, 1942, reorganized the Central Party School to accommodate the rectification campaign, with jurisdiction given to the CPC Secretariat, and Mao was named director.[157] Mao's lack of confidence in the Propaganda Department was evident in his speech "Oppose Formalism" (*Fandui dang bagu*) given to a propaganda work conference held jointly by the Central Propaganda Department and the Central Publishing Bureau on February 8, 1941,[158] in which Mao criticized the overly formalized styles of Party documentation and writing.

Peng Zhen's appointment to the Central Party School in 1941 gave him charge of the training and ongoing indoctrination of Party members. As deputy director and director of education, and with responsibility for political study, Peng was in charge of all-around work in the day-to-day activities of the school.[159] Peng was later accused of supporting Wang Ming and Zhang Wentian (Luo Fu), who had been director of the Marxism-Leninism Institute since its establishment in 1938.[160] However, it seems more likely that he was brought to Yan'an to support Mao's challenge to the Wang Ming line, although no doubt he was also working to represent Liu Shaoqi's interests as well. Peng's experience and reputation in both urban (December 9) and rural (Jin Cha Ji) underground work would have lent credibility to Mao's challenge against Wang Ming's rejection of peasant-led revolution and support to the policy documents on underground work being prepared with the assistance of military leaders such as Chen Yi and Tao Zhu.[161]

Peng was primarily responsible for political education while his colleagues on the Party School Organization Management Committee, Deng Fa and Lin Biao, handled teacher administration and military education, respectively.[162] Peng was given specific responsibility for conducting the rectification campaign at the Central Party School.[163] Mao had been critical of subjectivism at the school, and apparently he looked to Peng to clean house.[164] Peng attended the September 1941 Politburo meeting at which Mao articulated the initial goals of the program.[165] Peng's "Plan for the Party School," which was issued jointly with Mao Zedong and Ren Bishi in late 1941, provided an organizational framework for the rectification that was to come.[166] Given the general brevity of the document (five pages in all), it is remarkably detailed. The plan revealed Peng's emphasis on the use of Party organs to control the selection and training of cadres. The plan provided that students were to be recruited from cadre ranks nominated by local Party organs. Students were to be classified on the basis of educational (cultural) levels, and the distribution of incoming students was to be based on origins in central, county, and district departments. Student entrance to the school was to be directed by the Party Secretariat and recorded with the Organization Department. The plan also contained provisional arrangements for students from the central departments pending the completion of a military–political institute. Detailed provisions for the staffing of the school were also made, in some cases specifying who would be in charge of teaching specific topics, and in some cases merely specifying that such matters as procedures for appointment of school director would be made by the central leadership. Peng even attended to such minutiae as the number of sheets of paper and ink sticks per student, as well as matters of subsidies and living arrangements. The provisions of the school plan were amplified through additional measures, such as the "Regulations on Qualifications of Newly Admitted Students to the CPC Central Party School"[167] and the Politburo decision on organization and training methods.[168]

Peng produced several written documents in connection with the rectification. Indeed, under a directive issued by Mao in September 1942, Peng had a quota obligation to produce 15,000 characters per month, mainly on the subject of Party building.[169] First among these was his May 14, 1942, article, "The Spirit and Practice of the Twenty-Two Documents Issued by the Leadership Council," in which Peng summarized the documents that were required reading for cadres and students in the campaign.[170] Peng's article is still considered to be the authoritative guide on how to study these documentary foundations for the rectification.[171] Although he appeared to support Mao's approach toward the rectification, Peng also subtly suggested allowing somewhat greater leniency in implementing campaign goals. Thus, he emphasized the more palatable of Mao's instructions, namely to reform errors through killing the disease and saving the patient, and to focus on changing attitudes rather than attacking individual persons. And although Peng reiterated Mao's policy of opposing subjectivism—which in essence entailed a license to attack virtually anyone in the Party, regardless of their previous political status and contributions—he also stressed the need to take into account the different concrete circumstances of the campaign and its victims.[172] Thus, at this early point in the rectification campaign, Peng seemed to act as a tempering force.

Yet Peng was also engaged in establishing administrative arrangements at the Central Party School that would support the rectification movement. Thus, he determined the process by which students at the Central Party School were to undergo rectification in study groups organized, basing it on an appraisal of the students' education level, rather than their organizational status.[173] The students were not to continue their studies in the conventional curriculum until they completed the rectification and a determination was made as to their conditions of thought and politics, their abilities for study and work, and their political development levels. Completion meant passing an examination that asked questions such as, "What is dogmatism (*jiaotiao zhuyi*) in the Party's style of study?" or "What is experientialism (*jingyan zhuyi*) in the Party's style of study?"[174]

But Mao soon began to accelerate the effort to eliminate all real and suspected challengers. At a Politburo meeting March 16, 1943, Mao tied the rectification campaign directly to the elimination of petit bourgeoisie ideology and counterrevolution, an effort made necessary by the increased numbers of newly recruited military, students, and party members and in light of KMT policies of using spies (*tewu*) against the CPC.[175] At an April 28, 1943, Politburo meeting, Mao called for efforts to eliminate hidden traitors (*nei jian*) and a special "Committee to Struggle Against Hidden Traitors" was established under Liu Shaoqi, Kang Sheng, Peng Zhen, and Gao Gang.[176] Although Kang Sheng has been most publicly identified with the "Rescue Campaign" taking on the features of a full-fledged inquisition,[177] Mao's speech to the Party School of August 8, 1943, confirmed his imprimatur for the campaign.[178] Kang was in overall charge of the investigation of cadres, but specific cases were investigated by Li Kenong, Wang Dongxing, Wu De, Li Mianmin,

Wang Shoujiang, Mao Cheng, and others through open-ended questions such as, "How did you come to Yan'an?" and "What did you come to do in Yan'an?", as well as in-depth reviews of personal backgrounds.[179]

There is some evidence that Peng Zhen supported the rescue campaign,[180] and such support would have been mandated by Peng's position on the Committee to Struggle Against Hidden Traitors, as well as Peng's repeated attacks on spies at Jin Cha Ji. Political motives may have played a role as well, and indeed, Peng was later to be accused of colluding with Liu Shaoqi to attack Ke Qingshi (later the Shanghai CPC secretary and an intimate of Kang Sheng) as a KMT spy.[181] But once Mao and the Party Centre lost their enthusiasm for the campaign, the politician in Peng changed course as well. With their blessing and support, Peng organized a summary of the experience of the "Rescue Campaign," which concluded that it was harmful and brought it to a close.[182] Ultimately, the Party Centre concluded that 99 percent of the verdicts rendered were in error, and with the August 15, 1943, "Decision on Investigating Cadres," the Party Centre signaled its opposition to expanding the movement and curtailing Kang's activities.[183] In January 1944, the Party Centre formally issued Mao's directive ending the campaign.[184]

Peng's work on rectification in the Party School was described more fully in his speech of July 18–19, 1944, to the entire school assembly, entitled "Questions About Methods of Thinking."[185] In this speech, Peng elaborated on his ideas about discipline within the Party. He acknowledged that intra-Party conflict was virtually unavoidable in light of the many different kinds of new members being admitted (indeed, it was Peng's responsibility to reeducate many of these newly admitted cadres). He reiterated the Maoist dictum of attacking the disease while saving the patient, and he noted that this might mean harming an individual's "face" while cautioning against harming their positivism.[186] As he had in his previous speech on the 22 Documents, Peng adopted a rather tempered stance toward the rectification. Indeed, he seemed almost apologetic over Mao's preoccupation with subjectivism, sectarianism, and formalism. Although he noted that the effort to eliminate these ills was a revolution in thought and work styles within the Party, he ascribed little significance to them other than that the campaign had brought on considerable debate that at times elicited excitement and quarreling by the participants (*you shi zheng de mian hong er chi chaojia*).[187]

Instead, Peng focused on the class implications of the debates over egalitarianism.[188] Although he belatedly acknowledged the validity of criticisms of a very few special people with high living standards, Peng concentrated his attack on those who gave vent to unacceptable sentiments of individualism or had misplaced expectations that socialism meant the banal equality of egalitarianism.[189] Although Peng devoted extensive attention to the virtues of Mao's prescriptions for rectification, he still argued for attention to specific conditions and the need for nuanced assessment of Party members. Drawing examples by distinguishing between the instincts of bees and the purposeful thinking of humankind, or by noting that a watermelon could not be fully described merely by making reference to its green color, Peng argued that the true essence of a person's political stance required a deeper examination.[190]

Peng's views on internal discipline required subordinating individual concerns to the broader interests of the Party. In the Party's external relations, Peng indicated that institutions, policies, and laws were to be used to strengthen the Party's political power and to restrain its enemies.[191] Ancillary matters such as economic development and the war with Japan were considered important primarily to the extent that they could be channeled to the service of the Party's political ascendancy. Within the Party, the emphasis was on the purity and depth of commitment by Party members. Such commitment could not be taken for granted but had to be constantly tested and refined. In part because he was aware of the diversity of views and backgrounds of the new Party members being subjected to education at the Central Party School, Peng was committed to ridding them of their preconceptions and ideas.

Peng's role in the Yan'an rectification campaign underscored his role as the vehicle for imposing discipline within the Party. No doubt mindful of his experiences during the December 9th Movement and in Jin Cha Ji, where ensuring disciplined compliance with Party dictates was difficult at best, Peng was a vigorous proponent of orthodoxy while at the Central Party School. Indeed, Peng's effectiveness was such that Mao considered him to be a model example for training cadres to be sent to guerrilla areas.[192] As the rectification campaign wound down, Peng took over operations at the Party School from Mao.[193] He was appointed acting director (*daili buzhang*) in March 1944 and held this position more or less constantly until May 1948, when he was appointed full director.[194]

Although Peng was still primarily a functionary, rather than a driver of policy, his star was clearly on the rise. He participated in drafting the report on revisions to the Party constitution, along with Deng Xiaoping and Liu Shaoqi.[195] Peng was included on a committee organized by the CPC Secretariat to prepare an official resolution on the Party's history, to be presented to the Seventh CPC Congress in 1945.[196] Although he did not play a central role in drafting the history resolution—most of the work was done by Hu Qiaomu—Peng's inclusion on the drafting committee with the likes of Liu Shaoqi, Kang Sheng, Zhou Enlai, Luo Fu (Zhang Wentian), and Gao Gang attest to Peng's rising status. Peng also gave an important speech to the congress, reiterating many of the provisions on building political power from his 1941 Jin Cha Ji policy report.[197] In addition, Peng served as chair of the Credentials Committee for the congress—evidence not only of his increasing importance, but also of the fact that his work at the Yan'an Central Party School and during the rectification campaign, as well as his portfolio in the Organization Department, made him an invaluable source of personal information on CPC cadres.[198]

The Revolutionary Disciplined: Peng's Failure in Manchuria

After the defeat of Japan, the Chinese Communists turned their attention to Manchuria, where decisive battles loomed with the Nationalist government for control of China's industrial heartland. The CPC Centre sent four Politburo members (Peng Zhen, Chen Yun, Gao Gang, and Zhang Wentian) and more than one-fourth of the membership of the Central Committee to accelerate Party work in Manchuria.[199] In September 1945 the Politburo established a Northeast Bureau headed by Peng Zhen as secretary and including Chen Yun, Cheng Zihua, Wu Xiuquan, and Lin Feng as deputies.[200] On the military side, the CPC Centre also established a Northeast Autonomous People's Army under the command of Lin Biao, with Peng Zhen as first political commissar, Luo Rongdan as second political commissar, and Cheng Zihua as deputy political commissar.[201]

Although this posting presented Peng with an important opportunity to solidify his military contacts and to expand his reputation as a skilled Party organizer yet further, problems emerged almost immediately. Rather than comply with the Centre's instructions to focus on control of the railroad lines and permit the Soviet Union's Red Army to take control of Changchun, Peng argued that the Northeast campaign should focus on retaking the major cities.[202] For example, Peng gave a speech to the Northeast Bureau on political power building in December 1945 in which he focused on the need to accelerate local organizational work in the small and medium cities as a basis for building political power in the Northeast.[203] Peng held to this position well into 1946, asserting that the formula that had worked so well in Jin Cha Ji—namely, linking up with and gradually dominating the local masses (petite bourgeoisie and students as well as peasants and workers) as a step toward securing a monopoly on political power—could and should be replicated in Manchuria.[204] Peng called for a specific plan on mobilizing the masses and determining the attitudes of various classes toward the CPC and the Nationalists, and also on identifying the needs of peasants and workers and addressing conflicts arising from land reform.[205] Apparently confident in the success of the filtered democracy approach that he used successfully to build and legitimate Party power in Jin Cha Ji, and in furtherance of the Centre's directives on establishing representative assemblies and provisional administrative committees for the region, Peng also attempted to establish a representative congress system in Liaoning and in Shenyang.[206]

Peng's position was justified in part by the Centre's instructions of the previous year that gave emphasis to *both* retaking the cities (including large cities) and controlling the major lines of communication.[207] The directive had urged cadres not to permit their rural experience to lead them to ignore the importance of the cities. Mao's discussion of the tasks for 1945 specifically linked the objectives of retaking the cities and the transportation system from the Japanese as part of the strategy for expanding the liberated areas.[208] And indeed, Peng had taken up these themes in his speech to the Seventh National CPC Congress in May 1945, where he argued in favor of recapturing the cities and linking up with underground organizations there.[209] It is virtually inconceivable that Peng would have articulated these views without a significant degree of support from the highest levels of the leadership. Indeed, there was a degree of support for Peng's opposition to Lin Biao's proposal to establish multiple rural base areas in the Northeast and his counterproposal favoring the taking of the cities of Pan Yang, Changchun, and Harbin.[210] However, in December 1945 the Centre issued formal directives ordering the Northeast Bureau to establish rural base areas[211] and to adopt a strategy of leaving the high road alone and seizing the land on two sides (*rangkai dalu zhanling liangxiang*) that in effect required withdrawal from cities such as Shenyang.[212] Delays in implementing these directives were later the focus of Cultural Revolution charges that

Peng had opposed Mao's directive on building base areas.[213] Ultimately, Liu Shaoqi was moved to rebuke Peng and the Northeast Bureau for failing to attend to a rural base area strategy.[214] In one of Liu Shaoqi's "confessions" during the Cultural Revolution, he acknowledged delaying support for Lin Biao's leadership in Manchuria, suggesting that Lin retained long-standing animus against Liu for supporting Peng Zhen in the dispute until the last possible moment, when it became clear that Mao was soon to intervene.[215] Peng's belated acknowledgment of the Centre's directives in April was too little, too late,[216] and in June 1946 Lin Biao replaced Peng as secretary for the Northeast Bureau.[217] Although Peng was permitted to hold a place as deputy secretary, it was clear that he was through as far as the Manchurian campaign was concerned.

Peng's failure in Manchuria can be ascribed to the fact that at this stage in the war, military concerns were considered more important than Party organizing. The CPC Centre was not prepared to sacrifice the strategy of maintaining control over the communications infrastructure and avoiding direct confrontation with an enemy superior in numbers and equipment—an approach that had worked quite well against the Japanese. Thus, despite the important political factors supporting the urban strategy—not only was Peng in favor, but even the senior leader Chen Yun was to be in charge of the recapture of the Northeastern cities[218]—military strategy was given priority.

A second factor involved relations with the Soviet Union. Shortly after arriving in Manchuria, Peng spoke out about the need for autonomy from the Soviet Union and seemed unabashedly hostile to Soviet attempts to direct the civil war.[219] Thus, when Soviets claimed that their treaty obligations required them to permit the Nationalists to enter Shenyang after the withdrawal of the Japanese, Peng resisted to the point where the Soviets threatened the use of tanks to remove People's Liberation Army troops from the city.[220] Peng got into a shouting match (*chao le yi jia*) with the Soviet commander and backed off only when ordered to do so by the Party Centre.[221]

Finally, Peng's removal must have been motivated at least in part by the realization that Peng stood ready to interpret policy ambiguities in favor of his own prerogatives—if not to ignore altogether directives from the CPC Centre. Although Liu Shaoqi may well have protected Peng from more serious consequences from the Manchurian affair, it is clear that Liu had had enough. During the course of the Chongqing negotiations in late 1945, Liu noted that Peng (and Lin Biao) had not responded to an instruction from the Centre directing the work of the

Northeast Bureau away from Changchun and toward the rural areas—an instruction with which Peng clearly disagreed.[222] In yet another exchange, Liu rebuked Peng for his continued insistence on an urban strategy, contrary to instructions from the Centre.[223] Although Cultural Revolution attacks on Peng's performance in the Northeast (described as "political capitulationism" and "military adventurism") were no doubt overexpressed,[224] it does seem clear that Peng skirted the line between disciplined discussion of policy and insubordination.

Peng's removal from Manchuria was a potentially serious blot on his career. The consummate Party organizer and discipline man had himself been disciplined. Peng would never again be given military responsibilities of any significance. He is alleged to have been ordered by Mao in January 1954 to prepare a self-criticism (*jiantao*) regarding his errors in the Northeast.[225] Reportedly, Peng argued that his errors did not constitute "right opportunism" and its implied charge of defiance of orders from the Centre, but rather that they were merely errors of policy. Peng was reportedly urged by Liu Shaoqi to rewrite the self-criticism, and with the assistance of Liu Ren and Zheng Tianxiang, he submitted a revised report admitting to more serious errors. However, in the clouded atmosphere of the fourth session of the Seventh CPC Congress in February 1954 and the preoccupation with the Gao Gang question, Peng apparently was able to persuade Mao and Lin Biao to limit the description of Peng's errors to ones of policy only. The significance of these events was amply demonstrated by Peng's attempt nearly forty-five years later to get the last word, through a 1988 article on his experience in Manchuria.[226]

Despite the setback in Manchuria, and probably as a result of the influence of Liu Shaoqi, Peng's career as a whole was not seriously undermined by the Manchurian affair. Rather, the debacle in the Northeast seemed to focus Peng's work on the more specialized tasks of Party organization. Indeed, even though Deputy Director An Ziwen had taken over Peng's substantive duties in the CPC Organization Department, Peng resumed an active role after returning from the Northeast in 1946.[227] Party organization work also permitted Peng to play a significant role in the land reform campaign in North China in the late 1940s and led to his playing a major role in the retaking of Beiping.

With the defeat of the Japanese, the attention of the Communist movement turned to civil war. In an effort to solidify ties among the local peasantry, land reform policies were adopted that first attempted to reach accommodation with compliant rich peasants and even some landlords. Thus, the Centre's May 4th Directive of 1945 had called for careful distinctions to be drawn among different types of landlords and urged restraint in the seizure of land from rich peasants. However, by 1947 KMT military advances had made such restraint impossible, and the land reform movement became radicalized.[228] In September 1947 Peng was sent back to Jin Cha Ji under orders from Mao to oversee the land reform campaign—scant consolation, perhaps, for his setback in the Northeast, but also an indication of Mao's continued confidence.[229] Peng's speech to the Jin Cha Ji Border Region Land Conference held in October–November 1947 reflected this change: he argued for confiscation of lands owned by landlords and rich peasants and for equal distribution of land throughout the rural areas.[230] Peng adopted the same theme in his explanation of the October 1947 Agrarian Law (*Zhongguo tudi fa dagang*) to the Jin Cha Ji Peasants Association.[231]

The civil war also mandated continued attention to internal discipline, in an effort both to ensure correct implementation of land reform and to protect against KMT infiltration, which was made much easier by the withdrawal of the Japanese and the consequent proximity between Communist and Nationalist lines.[232] Peng took up the theme of rectification as well. In his speech to the 1947 Jin Cha Ji Land Conference, he called for the use of government institutions and courts to ensure thorough implementation of the Agrarian Law and land reform policies.[233] Noting that a fair number of landlord and rich peasant elements had sneaked into the Party, Peng stressed organizational purity, ideological struggle, and education to ensure that Party cadres maintained correct attitudes toward the policies.[234] This distinction between political institutions from internal Party discipline matters had characterized Peng's approach to governance in Jin Cha Ji, and it served as a harbinger of Peng's views on the relationship of law and Party organization after the establishment of the PRC.

In his handling of the Party's external and internal relations during the pre-Liberation period, Peng exhibited classic Leninist traits emphasizing organization and discipline as the bases for political authority. In Beiping during the December 9th Movement, he was instrumental in conveying the views of an increasingly disenchanted North China Bureau to radical students who seemed increasingly immune to CPC influence. In Jin Cha Ji, Peng once again served as a conduit for instructions from the Party Centre, although here he had significant opportunity to place his own imprimatur on local policies. At Yan'an,

Peng played an organizational role, building mechanisms for implementing the rectification campaign. Discipline remained a major feature in Peng's writings and speeches. The revolutionary role of the vanguard Party required external discipline through the oppression of class enemies and the manipulation of public institutions to facilitate the building of the Party's political power. Internally, discipline was also necessary in order to ensure consistent enforcement of Party policies. And although Peng's performance in Manchuria suggested that he was not above departing from these principles when his own policy choices were at stake, this emphasis on discipline continued in Peng's thought after liberation. What was to become new in Peng's thinking after the establishment of the PRC was the transition from revolution to governance.

CHAPTER 3

State Building: Discipline and Governance

THE COMMUNIST PARTY of China's (CPC) successes in the civil war against the Nationalists soon required a return to political organizing and power building in the cities. In May 1948 the North China Bureau was reconstituted through the merger of the Jin Cha Ji and Jin Ji Lu Yu (Shanxi, Hebei, Shandong, Henan) Bureaux, with Liu Shaoqi as first secretary, Bo Yibo as second secretary, and Nie Rongzhen as third secretary and commander of the North China Military District.[1] Although Peng Zhen did not take a prominent position in the Bureau, he was consulted by Liu Shaoqi about the proposal, and later, on orders from Mao, he participated in the organizational meetings that gave rise to the creation of the Bureau.[2] In September 1948 the North China People's Government (NCPG) was established with Dong Biwu as chair and Bo Yibo as deputy.[3] In mid-February 1949 the NCPG moved its offices to Beijing,[4] and in March the Party Centre and the military leadership moved in as well.[5] The key question was political power building, and a series of planning meetings was held in which Peng Zhen, Dong Biwu, Bo Yibo, and other CPC cadres, along with military leaders Lin Biao and Nie Rongzhen, participated to discuss linking up with local non-Party democratic personages through whom CPC political authority could be entrenched.[6]

Although he maintained his position at the Centre as Director of the CPC Organization Department,[7] Peng Zhen was given more direct control over the work of preparing for the recapture of Beijing—in late 1948 he was appointed secretary general of the city with Ye Jianying as mayor and chair of the Military Committee.[8] As a senior, albeit second-echelon, leader with responsibility for Party organization work and experience in underground work throughout North China, Peng was a logical choice to play a major role in the preparatory work for solidifying Party rule in Beijing and the other cities in the region. Peng's ties in Jin Cha Ji were particularly important here, because during the period of Japanese occupation, underground work in Beijing and Tianjin was directed by the urban work department of the Jin Cha Ji Border Region under Liu Ren (later Peng Zhen's vice mayor in Beijing).[9]

Peng continued to hold significant positions in the CPC Centre and in the central government, posts that complemented his position in the Beijing administration. He retained his position on the CPC Politburo, gained in 1945 at the Seventh National CPC Congress. Following the establishment of the PRC in October 1949, the Party Centre established a Politics and Law Commission in the Central Administrative Council under Dong Biwu, with Peng Zhen appointed vice chair and deputy secretary of the Commission's Party Office.[10] He was replaced as head of the CPC Organization Department by An Ziwen in 1950. Throughout the 1950s Peng had significant responsibilities at both of the centers of government in Beijing. These provided him ample opportunity to voice policy positions on law and political authority.

From Revolution to Regulation: Peng Zhen During the State-Building Period (1949–1956)

Peng's views on governance were articulated in the context of his responsibilities for governance in Beijing, his position at the Politics and Law Commission, and his leadership of the National People's Congress (NPC) Standing Committee. Each of these roles required attention to challenges of institutionalizing political authority, and Peng's official statements during this period revealed a gradual change in thinking from emphasis on revolution to emphasis on governance. This entailed a transition from attention to campaign-style attacks on the obstacles to Communist power to calls for more regularized systems of rule.

Peng and the Beijing Municipal Administration

Peng Zhen's appointment as CPC Secretary for Beijing gave him tremendous authority initially, and in 1951 he was made mayor.[11] Peng's first priority in Beijing was to consolidate the political authority of the new regime, and in pursuit of this, he emphasized three basic tasks: eradicating the old political order; carrying out economic construction; and transforming the educational system so as to train a new cohort of political, cultural, and military cadres.[12] First, however, Peng had to deal with the immediate problems of securing social order, improving military administration, eliminating bandits, and improving living standards. Campaigns against counterrevolutionaries, the urban bourgeoisie, and cadre corruption provided the forum within which to pursue these aims—hence Peng's apparent enthusiasm for the *sufan* and *san fan/wu fan* campaigns that characterized the early years of the PRC.

Municipal administration also required that Peng turn his attention to building Beijing's commercial and industrial base. Under the policy slogan "production first, production second, production third" (*di yi shi shengchan, di er shi shengchan, di san hai shi shengchan*), Peng directed a five-year development plan that gave priority to existing heavy industry.[13] The plan focused on new factory construction and socialist transformation of commercial enterprises and individual handicraft enterprises. As chief of the Beijing municipal Party apparatus, Peng used the Party's organizational mechanisms to ensure Party control over the economic sphere. Peng used his position as chair of the Beijing municipal Federation of Trade Unions (*zong gonghui*) to issue directives to the mining operations in Western Beijing on establishment of Party-run unions; and he used his position as municipal secretary to direct the activities of the local mining bureau.[14]

Peng's speech to the First Beijing Representative Congress in 1954 served as a summary of the city's development during the first five years after Liberation.[15] When Peng noted the achievements of the first five years, he signified that much of the task of revolution and social transformation had been accomplished. On the other hand, Peng cautioned that the elimination of the poisons of the old society required a long-term struggle, and he specifically criticized what he termed rightist thinking, which was seen to belittle the need for continued vigilance against counterrevolutionaries, class enemies, and spies. Serious struggle was to be waged against recalcitrant capitalists who continued to resist collectivization. These doctrinaire positions were then put into practice: in January 1956 Peng reportedly oversaw the complete transformation of Beijing's private enterprises over a period of twelve days—a pace that was then taken by Mao as a model for socialist transformation over the more cautious approach favoured by Chen Yun.[16]

Although Peng could hardly be characterized as dismissive of the continued need for attacks on class enemies, what he criticized most was the lack of leadership in thought and politics. In particular, Peng suggested that there was insufficient professionalism among leadership cadres who were not sufficiently demanding of either their own performance or of the performance of subordinates and the masses. Peng also criticized as inadequate the process by which experience was summarized and formalized into regulations. In surveying the tasks ahead, Peng returned to this theme, arguing that more attention should be given to state planning and the role of formal laws and regulations. This concern with regulatory systems was then extended to the economy, where Peng reviewed the application of the First Five-Year Plan to Beijing's developing industrial economy; to education, where Peng argued in favor of strengthened technical training for cadres and specialists; to health care, where Peng stressed the need to regularize the "patriotic health movement" and to improve health care in heavy industry; and to urban construction, where Peng discussed the capital construction plans for Beijing municipality. In each of these areas, Peng suggested that the voluntarist nature of past campaigns should give way to a more formally regularized system. These themes, articulated in the First Beijing Representative Congress, were reiterated in subsequent speeches on propaganda work and leadership work styles.[17] Speaking to the first Beijing Municipal CPC representative congress in June 1956, Peng called for appointment of cadres to be based on expertise as well as morality, and he suggested that veteran cadres give way to younger, better-educated candidates in Party appointments.[18]

By the late 1950s Peng's work in Beijing had largely been taken over by Vice Mayor Liu Ren. Peng's appointment as Secretary for the CPC Secretariat, although a disappointment because he might legitimately have expected to be appointed CPC General Secretary,[19] nonetheless brought him significant central-level policy responsibilities. Liu Ren had served with Peng in Jin Cha Ji, and he had effective charge of the city while Peng was occupied with matters at the Secretariat.[20] Nonetheless, Peng's position as mayor and CPC secretary of Beijing gave him a solid political base that complemented his other political appointments. Peng's status rose steadily during the 1950s, particularly after the purge of Gao Gang.[21] Indeed, Peng attempted to establish Beijing as a model city, replicating on a municipal level many of the commemorative efforts adopted at a national level to glorify the accomplishments of the PRC.[22] His power base in Beijing continued right up to 1966[23] and ultimately frustrated Mao's attempts to control Peng's activities and attitude.[24]

Peng Zhen and the Politics and Law Commission

Although Peng Zhen was nominally subordinate to Dong Biwu on the Politics and Law Commission and indeed did not attend the Commission's first plenary session because of his responsibilities in the Beijing administration, he played a major role in the Commission's day-to-day activities.[25] Among the challenges facing Peng in his role as a political-legal official was the question of abolishing old Kuomintang (KMT) laws, for which the PRC had little in the way of replacements. Although the newly installed PRC government as one of its first acts abolished the Nationalists' *Complete Book of the Six Laws* (*Liu fa quan shu*), in fact, many of these laws continued to be relied on.[26] Peng was also active in the Commission's Party Committee and in 1950 was designated to serve as acting chair of both the Commission and its Party Committee when Dong took medical leave.[27] Peng became full deputy secretary of the Party Committee in January 1951 and was appointed party secretary in March 1953.[28] By this time, Peng was appearing regularly as coauthor of Dong Biwu's reports to Premier Zhou Enlai on the work of the Commission, and when Dong left the Commission in 1954 to take over as chief of the Supreme People's Court, he left everything in Peng's hands.[29]

The pattern of interaction between Dong Biwu and Peng Zhen in the Politics and Law Commission reflected disagreements between them on various aspects of the use of law for political ends. It appears that Peng won the upper hand. Thus, Dong's periods of inactivity, particularly in November 1950, when Dong took medical leave, and December 1951–May 1952, when he repeatedly issued reports to the Government Administrative Council (a precursor to the State Council) under joint authorship with Peng Zhen, corresponded with the CPC campaign against counterrevolutionaries of late 1950 and the *san fan/wu fan* campaigns of late 1951 and early 1952, in which Peng played a significant role. In early 1950 Peng had served as deputy to Liu Shaoqi on a General Study Committee (*Zongxuewei*) in charge of the campaign to root out counterrevolutionaries in various departments, which paved the way for his prominent role in the expanded campaign later in the year.[30] In the anticounterrevolutionary campaign, Peng took a hard line and argued against permitting leniency in the handling of counterrevolutionaries.[31] Peng supported a policy of "harshness first, leniency later, target higher ups first and subordinates later" (*xian wu hou wen, xian shang hou xia*).[32] Although he adopted a somewhat more lenient approach in the *san fan* campaign against corruption within the Party, he was still fairly hard line in the *wu fan* campaign against the urban bourgeoisie.[33] In each of these efforts, Peng took an unabashedly instrumentalist approach to subordinating the role of law and legal institutions to CPC policy dictates. This must have rankled Dong Biwu and may well have contributed to his reduced participation in CPC political–legal work, while Peng's support for the mass movement on judicial reform and its critique of "old" judicial principles cemented Dong's displacement.[34]

The campaign against counterrevolutionaries afforded Peng an opportunity to articulate a view of law as a vehicle for political repression. Peng cautioned against enacting regulations that were too detailed and that might "shackle the masses."[35] Indeed, before the official launching of the campaign, Peng asserted that the mandate for law and governance in China was to serve the greatest interest of the greatest number,[36] thus permitting the CPC to define the public interest in a way that suited its own political and ideological goals. Law would serve first as a statement of these goals and then as an organizational framework for carrying them out. Thus, the regulations on counterrevolutionaries were viewed as a legal weapon for repressing "those who collude with imperialism," "inciters," "tempters," "officials receiving bribes," "traitors," and "those using arms to cause disruption of the masses" without providing significant definitional detail.[37]

On the other hand, the regulations were also intended to provide an organizational framework that, while allowing anyone to denounce counterrevolutionaries to the People's Government, ensured that the power of individuals and groups to apply sanctions was subject to the control of the Party / state.[38] Speaking to the first national judicial work conference in August 1950, Peng asserted that law should apply not just to counterrevolutionaries but also to workers, peasants, cadres, and others who violate the law, no matter how good they might be.[39] Peng underscored the role of the regulations on counterrevolutionaries in providing standards for judicial personnel.[40] In the context of suppressing counterrevolutionaries, the new measures were to augment the instructions of the Common Program of 1949 on preventing leftist (overly harsh) and rightist (overly lenient) errors.[41] Noting the lack of trained legal personnel, Peng called for the establishment of political–legal committees "responsible for directing and linking up the work of organs concerning civil affairs, public security, judicial affairs, bureaux of investigations, law courts, and supervision as well as for the disposal of mutual relations between organization and work."[42] These committees would serve to control further mass participation in the campaign against counterrevolutionaries. In a similar vein, Peng's October 1951 Chinese People's Political Consultative Congress (CPPCC) speech on resisting America and aiding Korea focused on the role of "patriotic pacts" (*aiguo gongyue*) as both a formalized articulation of individual loyalty, and a mechanism for the state to require such articulation and to identify and punish unreliable elements who resisted.[43]

Peng expressed similar views about the role of law during the subsequent *san fan* campaign. On the basis of instructions from Mao, who had been alarmed by reports on corruption from Deng Xiaoping, the CPC Centre issued a decision on December 1, 1951, to launch a campaign against cadre corruption, waste, and bureaucratism.[44] The initial impetus stemmed from reports of malfeasance by Hebei officials Liu Qingshan and Zhang Zishan but soon expanded into a general campaign.[45] Peng was designated the Beijing delegate to the initial meetings ordered by Mao to examine the problem of corruption, and he took particular responsibility for the campaign in Beijing.[46] The Supreme People's Court established a special tribunal to hear cases, and a public trial was held in Beijing for prominent offenders.[47] Despite the intensity of the campaign and Mao's attachment to it, Peng took a somewhat restrained tack regarding the objects of struggle, perhaps because he was reluctant to pursue charges against Beijing officials with whom he had existing or potential political alliances. Peng noted that the problem of corruption in the PRC was limited in comparison with the record of the Nationalist regime, and he suggested that the vast majority of cadres had the support of the people and that the problem of corruption could definitely be resolved.[48] In contrast to the unremittingly harsh treatment to be meted out to counterrevolutionaries, Peng noted that the struggle against corruption and theft was one between two work styles, and thus it was a matter subject to the popular democratic united front that should be handled pursuant to the conciliatory themes of the Common Program.[49] Indeed, Peng's political competitor from Shanxi, Bo Yibo, speaking in his capacity as chair of the Central People's Government Conservation Inspection Committee (*Jieyue jiancha weiyuanhui*), was moved to complain in January about the relative inactivity among Beijing units involved in the campaign: "while the situation at a few departments that are implementing the campaign is relatively good, in most units the important significance of the campaign is not fully understood, and consequently they are still not able to implement directives concerning the movement on a grand scale."[50]

Although his substantive views were more lenient, Peng's approach to the role of formal regulations was similar as with the campaign against counterrevolutionaries: law served first as a statement of policy ideals and then as the basis for an organizational framework for implementation. For example, in a speech to a meeting of the Beijing CPC Committee, the Beijing committee of the CPPCC, the Beijing municipal government, and mass organizations held December 20, 1951, Peng noted that the reason for the ongoing problem of corruption was that there had not been "systematic and wide ranging linking of activists and masses in eliminating corruption and adopting systemic punishments."[51] Peng sought to routinize the anticorruption campaign by formalizing the sentences to be handed out for corruption under the rubric of "consolidating the victories of the *san fan/wu fan* campaign."[52] This involved establishing a framework of judicial organizations and administrative units to decide cases involving corruption and to impose reasonable punishments in cases where imprisonment had been improperly imposed.[53] Specific provisions were enacted to determine sentencing based on such factors as the amount paid in bribes.[54] In an effort to protect middle-level cadres, Peng argued in favor of fairly high offense thresholds for imposition of the death penalty, claiming that 15 to 30 million yuan was too low to justify such a harsh sentence.[55] As was the case with the campaign against counterrevolutionaries, the regulations permitted investigatory organs significant flexibility and discretion in carrying out their tasks, although overall Party control was to be maintained through a system of Party committees.[56]

Peng also sought to bring greater organizational discipline to the performance of courts and police organs. Speaking to the issue of judicial independence, Peng noted that this did not mean independence of individual judges—and in fact permitted supervision from local People's Congresses and their standing committees, higher-level courts, or other organizations, as well as Party organs.[57] By using the occasion of national procuracy work conferences in 1954 and 1956, Peng addressed the need for the procuracy and the courts to reduce incidences of wrongly decided cases.[58] Peng attacked the attitude of "officials never retract decisions" that purportedly characterized the KMT regime, and he suggested that the system of procuracy review of public security bureau arrests, court trial of procuracy cases, and appellate court review was a necessary step toward eliminating incorrect arrests and judgment.

Speaking to public security officials in 1956, Peng argued that collectivization and transformation of private enterprises reflected the emergence of new conditions in China and required greater attention to formal legal procedure and reform of old police work styles.[59] In noting that the application of law should limit the discretion of local officials, Peng seemed to be influenced by the views of Wu Han, his colleague from Jin Cha Ji whose 1944 article on the "Rule by Man or Rule by Law" included a call for broader democracy in the application of state-led legal rules.[60]

Peng's support for the use of formal law and regulation to control local officials was also evident in the slogan "all citizens are equal before the law" (*gongmin zai falu mianqian ren ren pingdeng*), which was ultimately included in the 1954 PRC Constitution.[61] During the Cultural Revolution Peng was attacked for his use of the doctrine "all are equal before the law" to oppose class struggle and proletarian dictatorship.[62] However, in fact, Peng's views on equality before the law focused on the problem of special privileges, which he identified specifically with privileges not sanctioned in law (*falu zhiwai de tequan*).[63] Criticizing those who claimed past "meritorious service" (*gong lao*) or "difficult service" (*ku lao*) as grounds for immunity from the application of law, Peng argued that the illegal acts even by Party members with strong revolutionary credentials should be handled not merely through internal policy measures, but through formal legal sanctions. The slogan emerged at the same time that Peng and others were suggesting the need to bring greater formality to governance. Although Peng suggested that in China's popular democracy led by the working class, legal equality for citizens should be recognized,[64] the notion of equality before the law did not necessarily require a diminution of the Party/state's political power. Rather, it required consistency in enforcement of laws and regulations according to their terms—in effect limiting the discretion of local officials to interpret and enforce rules.[65] The ideal of equality before the law still permitted the Party/state to enact provisions for differential treatment and even repression of particular individuals or groups. For example, Peng oversaw the enactment and implementation of regulations on repressing counterrevolutionaries in the late 1950s, without any apparent contradiction with his prior views on equality before the law.[66] Equality before the law did not preclude laws and regulations treating differently situated groups differently; it simply required that singular statutory provisions be enforced consistently. Peng was to return to this theme after his rehabilitation in 1979.[67]

Peng's changing views on law and political authority drew on conclusions about changing social conditions. Peng noted as early as 1953 that the three great enemies of the revolution had been eliminated, and therefore the current challenges were to strengthen the legal system and perfect the laws in order to safeguard the smooth development of socialist construction.[68] This view was reiterated in Peng's reports to the Second National Judicial Work Conference in April 1953 and the Second National Organization Work Conference in September, to the effect that the basic challenge of class struggle had largely been accomplished.[69] Peng's Cultural Revolution critics later accused him of promoting class reconciliation and using law to undermine proletarian dictatorship.[70] Although Peng's views no doubt were influenced by the policy preferences of his mentor Liu Shaoqi,[71] Red Guard critics conveniently overlooked the fact that these views were also consistent with those of Mao Zedong at the time. Mao was quoted in Liu Shaoqi's speech on the 1954 Constitution as saying a bourgeois republic could not exist in China,[72] with the implication being that hostile classes had largely been eliminated. Mao was also on record in support of the need for formal institutions for managing the transition to socialism.[73]

What set Peng apart was that even after Mao began to doubt the relaxation of class struggle, Peng continued to emphasize the role of formal legal institutions as the basis for exercising state coercion. Thus, even in the late 1950s and early 1960s, when Mao's concerns over the continued existence of "remnant" bourgeois classes caused him to revisit the necessity of class struggle,[74] Peng continued to support the use of formal institutions and procedures in managing social and political relations. In speeches to the Third National Judicial Work Conference (March 1956) and a national meeting of united front department heads (April 1956); in an article published in July 1956 on national issues; and in preparations for the political report to the Eighth CPC Congress, Peng was said to assert that class struggle had largely been resolved.[75]

This theme was articulated in the section of Liu Shaoqi's 1956 political report to the Eighth CPC Congress addressing the "Political Life of the State," which Peng reportedly drafted.[76] This section was apparently added to the third draft of Liu's report to cover a series of policy issues (such as the people's democratic dictatorship, the democratic united front, minority nationalities) that had been included in earlier drafts under the heading of people's democratic dictatorship and to bring in new issues (such as policy on counterrevolutionaries, bureaucratism, and the legal system) that had not been included in prior drafts.[77] The report repeatedly referred to the "people's democratic dictatorship," an alternative formulation that downplayed the role of class struggle in comparison to the more radical term "dictatorship of the proletariat." Although the "dictatorship of the proletariat" presumed the centrality of class struggle and hence the need for ongoing dictatorship exercised by a singly proletarian class, the "people's democratic dictatorship" suggested that class struggle within the people was diminished and thus dictatorship could be exercised through more democratic means. The underlying presumption of the "people's democratic dictatorship" was that the main task of repressing counterrevolutionaries and other class enemies had been accomplished. Thus, the report argued that whatever further struggle was required should accordingly be carried out to legal processes by the duly authorized legal institutions of the public security bureaux, procuracy, and people's courts. After the Eighth CPC Congress and the political positioning on class struggle and development policies that accompanied it were concluded, Peng continued to assert the theme of the end of class struggle.[78] Conclusions on the decline of class struggle also meant that more attention should be paid to formality of law and legal institutions without concern that such formality would weaken class dictatorship. This suited Peng Zhen's political imperatives by legitimizing a greater role for the formal *zheng-fa* institutions and procedures for which he was responsible, and by permitting an extension of Peng's political–legal activities to the legislative realm.

Peng Zhen and the NPC Standing Committee

Peng Zhen was appointed secretary of the First NPC Standing Committee in 1954. In light of Peng's career as a Party organizer and functionary, the appointment revealed the extent to which the Party leadership viewed the legislative process as an appendage of Party rule. Thus, in light of his prominence in the Party's *zheng-fa* apparatus, Peng's formal role was to ensure that legislation remained a vehicle for the expression and enforcement of CPC policy. However, the inclusion of a parliamentary role to Peng's existing portfolios also created a political and organizational interest for him to expand the authority and interests of the NPC. As well, the NPC Standing Committee appointment permitted Peng to expand his administrative experience from the limits of Beijing municipality to the national context.

In reporting on the work of the 1955 NPC Standing Committee at the conclusion of its first year of operation, Peng emphasized the Committee's role in the work of legal interpretation, to the extent of issuing a formal opinion on interpretation of legal questions that established separate and distinct areas of jurisdiction for the NPC Standing Committee (authorized to decide on the limitation and supplementation of existing law); the Supreme People's Court (authorized to decide on concrete legal issues arising in the course of adjudication); and lower-level agencies such as the Academy of Science and the *People's Daily* editorial departments (authorized to issue nonbinding interpretation of technical or day-to-day legal questions).[79] Peng's speech to the 1956 NPC also addressed legislative interpretations.[80] Legislative interpretation work extended to questions such as (1) whether membership in local people's committees (*renmin weiyuanhui*) must be limited to members of the local people's representative congresses; (2) the rules for filling vacancies in local political positions (including provincial governors, mayors, and court judges) during the course of local representative congress meetings; (3) whether local chief judges and chief procurators could also serve as members of the local representative congress; (4) the handling of secret trials; and (5) the appointment of defense counsel for persons deprived of political rights.

Peng's 1956 report also spoke to expanded NPC involvement in administrative enactments, including (1) rules on illegal publications, (2) a decision on handling war criminals from the Japanese invasion, (3) a decision granting the chair of the NPC Standing Committee authority to receive foreign diplomats during times when the chairman and vice chairmen of the PRC were on leave, (4) regulations on agricultural cooperatives, (5) regulations on the cultural amusement tax, and (6) a decision on the timing for local People's Congress elections and candidate lists. The nature of these enactments revealed the extent to which central administrative fiat was becoming important as an instrument of rule, as well as the degree to which central administrative rulings were required to resolve procedural matters that might otherwise be addressed through local legislation. Subsequent reports on the work of the NPC Standing Committee reflected these themes.[81]

Extending the NPC Standing Committee's authority to include interpretation and enforcement of legislation and issuance of administrative regulations permitted Peng Zhen to further his political–bureaucratic purposes while serving the Party's goal of maintaining continued control over the institutions and edicts of governance. Peng's Party credentials, especially his prominence in the CPC's *zheng-fa* apparatus, lent legitimacy not only to his chairmanship of the NPC Standing Committee, but also to entrenching its authority to interpret legislation and issue administrative rules. Peng's focus on Party leadership over broad issues of programs and policies rather than direct administration strengthened his policy-making authority.[82] As long as Peng remained a faithful vehicle for the transmission of Party policy, increased NPC authority entrenched the Party's control over the operation of state government. Peng's personal political purposes were also served by expanding the authority and reach of the institution with which he was affiliated.

Peng's reporting on the work of the NPC revealed policy preferences and political realities in the operation of legal institutions and processes during the early years of the PRC. In contrast to the NPC Standing Committee's authority to interpret legislation, the courts were granted little power in this regard and instead were relegated to deciding issues directly before them in adjudication. Although this was broadly consistent with the civil law tradition from which the PRC legal system was drawn, it also served the political interests of the Party to prevent the emergence of alternate power centers. In contrast to the surfeit of administrative regulations, formal legislation was limited—particularly in broadly applicable areas of doctrine and principle. Although Peng is said to have given priority to drafting such laws of general application as codes of civil and criminal law and procedure,[83] success in completing these laws was elusive. Although he directed the drafting of legislation and regulations on organization of the people's courts, the procuracy, and municipal and local street committees and residents' associations,[84] his reporting on major laws was limited to narrowly applicable measures such as the Arrest and Detention Act and the Military Service Law.[85] And although Peng noted ongoing legislative drafting work on the criminal and civil law codes, formal enactments were not forthcoming. For example, despite repeated drafting and revision of a criminal code (twenty-two by 1957 and thirty-three by 1963), ongoing review by the Secretariat, the Politburo Standing Committee, and Mao himself did not result in final agreement on the legislation.[86]

Although Peng's emphasis on the need for regularity in the exercise of government authority suited the CPC's policy priorities of the day and also reflected Peng's own administrative preferences, he also can be seen seeking to expand his political position by supporting an expansion of the NPC's authority. Peng oversaw the relocation of the NPC offices out of the Party Centre at Zhongnanhai and into the Great Hall of the People in September 1959,[87] with the symbolism of the move as an expression of the NPC's expanding role taking on equal, if not greater, importance than its suggestion about the need for more office space. Ultimately, however, the NPC Standing Committee remained a limited forum, continually subordinate to the CPC Secretariat and (despite efforts by Peng and Liu Shaoqi) the State Council. Thus, to a large extent, Peng's efforts to support the NPC Standing Committee as a mechanism for greater regularity in the institutions of rule were an exercise in backing the wrong horse—particularly while Mao was Party chairman. Peng's pursuit of a similar strategy in the post-Mao era was more successful, perhaps reflecting changes in the personalities and political gamesmanship of Mao's successors.

After victory in the civil war, the CPC faced the challenge of managing a transition from revolution to governance. Peng Zhen was a central figure in this task because it entailed a transition from discretionary edicts and mass campaigns to formally articulated rules and a semblance of institutionalized procedures as the bases for the exercise of political authority. Regularizing the articulation of Party policy required building institutions that would be fundamentally different from the underground organs with which Peng and many of the CPC leaders were familiar. During the state-building period of the early 1950s, Peng Zhen continued to emphasize the role of law as an instrument of Party policy aimed at consolidating political power through internal and external discipline. The disciplining power of law was aimed primarily at hostile forces outside the Party, as indicated by the campaigns against counterrevolutionaries and the urban bourgeoisie. However, internal discipline was also stressed in the *san fan* campaign against official corruption.

Yet the forms through which such discipline was enforced had begun to change as the needs of governance required increased institutionalization. This had implications for those wielding political authority—for if the targets of revolution were largely eliminated and the needs of governance required increased routinization in institutions and rules, what then was to be made of the power and authority of political leaders?

Discipline and Political Conflict: The Hundred Flowers and Anti-Rightist Campaigns 1956–1958

The gradual regularizing of political authority in the PRC and the emergence of more formal institutions of rule made for a range of policy conflicts among the top leadership. Although these differences came to the fore during the early and mid-1950s in the context of the Gao Gang–Rao Shushi affair and also in the case of Hu Feng, a semblance of consensus still characterized the top leadership. The ideal of the Yan'an round table (if not its actual operation) seemed adequate to resolve differences of policy and politics within the ruling elite. Yet the collective leadership consensus gradually began to break down, and the Hundred Flowers Campaign and the Anti-Rightist Campaign that followed represented the beginning of a tortuous process of disintegration in the elite consensus.[88] The Hundred Flowers Campaign made obvious to many the extent of popular doubts about the regime, whereas the Anti-Rightist Campaign seemed merely to confirm the venality of the Party's dictatorship and worked to cow those few who had remained untouched by politics.[89] Peng Zhen played a significant role in these campaigns, and although there is much debate as to what his exact positions were, his public statements reflected an ongoing tension between the need to protect the Party from its external critics on the one hand—a theme that characterized Peng's political career from the December 9th Movement through the early 1950s—and the need to regularize the mechanisms of Party and state rule on the other—a theme that had become increasingly evident in Peng's writings and speeches from 1954 onward.

Mao Zedong's call for "blooming and contending" made in May 1956 in a statement to the Supreme State Conference initially passed largely unnoticed, despite ongoing preparatory work by the propaganda bureaucracy under the direction of Lu Dingyi that emphasized the need for such blooming and contending.[90] Mao's speech at the Eighth CPC Congress in September 1956 attacking bureacratism and factionalism and calling for increased inner-Party ideological education failed to stimulate the program.[91] Gradually, however, driven by alarm over unrest in Eastern Europe in the wake of Khrushchev's anti-Stalin speech, a consensus began to emerge at the Centre giving the campaign a note of political urgency. Although he had hardly touched on the subject in his political report to the Eighth CPC Congress in September,[92] Liu Shaoqi, speaking at the second session of the Eighth CPC Politburo in November, called for a rectification to purify Party work and to avoid the emergence of a new aristocracy.[93] In December the Politburo formally called for a program of inner Party rectification, although the role for comments and criticisms from non-Party elements and intellectuals was still limited. Criticism from outside the Party was soon given greater importance, however, and Mao's February 1957 speech on contradictions among the people provided important ideological guidelines for submitting the Party to external critique. But it took until late April for Mao to secure Politburo support for expanding the reform effort from a limited program aimed at attracting technical talent to the service of the regime, into a wide-open campaign of political rectification involving criticism from outside the Party.[94]

There is substantial disagreement in the scholarly community over Peng Zhen's position on the question of the Hundred Flowers Campaign. One authoritative view holds that Mao's call for non-Party members to voice criticisms of the Party encountered significant resistance from Liu Shaoqi, Peng Zhen, and others.[95] And indeed there is substantial evidence to suggest Peng Zhen was reluctant to support the "blooming and contending" called for by the Hundred Flowers Campaign.[96] Rather than actively soliciting criticism from the masses and intellectuals and urging rectification on the part of CPC cadres, organizations under Peng's control emphasized the need for continued ideological and propaganda work to improve attitudes and behavior among intellectuals and masses. For example, a propaganda work conference sponsored by the Beijing CPC Committee in March–April 1957 called for strengthening ideological work in order to ensure that intellectuals maintained a "Marxist-Leninist outlook" and to learn from the masses, while also criticizing the masses themselves for pursuing personal parochial benefits.[97] To the extent that cadres should be the focus of examination and criticism, Peng called for the rectification campaign to avoid dogmatic and unrestrained critiques, and he suggested that it instead take on the character of "mild wind and gentle rain"—further evidence of his doubts about encouraging popular criticism of the Party.[98]

Other observers have concluded that Peng was not as strongly resistant as it may have appeared.[99] Peng Zhen's public appearances and statements after late April's Politburo endorsement seemed to support the campaign.[100] Many of the Hundred Flowers criticisms lodged against the conduct of campaigns against counterrevolutionaries focused on legal officials ignoring or being ignorant of law and regulatory procedure were consistent with Peng's own comments on the subject.[101] And as early as August 1956, Peng had criticized bureaucratic Party work styles.[102] Peng's oft-cited speech to the Beijing propaganda work conference in April 1957 even as it suggested a tempered approach, still called for more blooming and contending.[103]

A third interpretation, one that offers a way to reconcile conflicting conclusions about Peng's position in the matter, holds that although Peng had reservations initially, he was ultimately persuaded to support Mao's initiative.[104] Although by training and personal experience Peng was apprehensive about opening the Party to criticisms from non-Party outsiders, he was at the same time fully aware of many shortcomings in the Party's leadership at the basic level. He was frequently critical of the heavy-handed attitude of local Party cadres and of the chronic problems of incompetence and inefficiency, which were the target of much of the criticism during the Hundred Flowers movement.[105] Peng's views on the need for rectification were no doubt also influenced by his visit to Eastern Europe in November 1956–February 1957, when he saw firsthand the consequences of pent-up popular frustration with Soviet rule. Peng's report on the visit revealed his concern over the potential in China for social upheaval.[106] The report referred specifically to worker unrest born of contradictions with capitalists and suggested that unity among socialist countries required the elimination of domestic discord. Although the visit may well have impressed on Peng the need for continued repression of dissent, it might just as easily have convinced him of the need to improve relations between Party cadres and their subjects. These factors probably convinced Peng to overcome his innate reluctance and to acquiesce to Mao's call for open-door rectification.

Yet Peng's gradual (and perhaps reluctant) agreement to permit criticism from non-Party members once again revealed his readiness to use the accepted rhetoric of the moment in support of his own political goals. For just as Peng's support for the rhetoric of "equality before the law" coincided with his efforts to strengthen his political resources in the *zheng-fa* system, so too by subscribing to themes of cooperation with non-Party members did Peng act to bolster his political resources in the NPC.[107] The theme of cooperation with non-Party elements had been included in Mao's 1956 speech on the Ten Great Relationships. Liu Shaoqi had reiterated the point in his speech to the Second Plenum of the Eighth CPC Central Congress in May 1958[108] and his speech at the tenth anniversary of the founding of the PRC.[109] Peng Zhen also held that cooperation between Party and non-Party sectors was a necessary and beneficial component in the regime's development program.[110] But it was the institutional implications of these policies that held significance for Peng. The call for cooperation with non-Party elements had the potential to raise the political prominence of the NPC, whose

Standing Committee Peng Zhen chaired. In contrast to the CPC Secretariat, where Peng held a secondary position, and the State Council, where Peng held no position of consequence, the NPC offered a platform from which Peng could strengthen his position within the Chinese political elite—perhaps even claiming a place on the Politburo Standing Committee. Indeed, it was reported that Peng had plans for a series of NPC permanent committees to supervise government work,[111] which would have enabled Peng to use the theme of cooperation with non-Party elements as a basis for solidifying his own political stature within the Party. Thus, Peng's support for the rhetoric of cooperation between Party and non-Party members, although on the one hand consistent with norms of the moment and with Peng's own conclusions about conditions in Chinese society, also served his own personal political interests.

Whether he was unalterably opposed to the Hundred Flowers initiative, supportive from the start, or a gradual convert, Peng continued to emphasize the importance of organizational controls. In his April 1957 speech, Peng stressed the role of Party committees at all levels, indicating that the criticism campaign should be confined to existing organizations.[112] In his May 1957 speech to the Beijing CPC Committee, Peng urged CPC cadres to solicit opinions and reform their work styles, but he stressed as well that the campaign should begin at the level of the municipal CPC standing committee and leading cadres before moving gradually to lower levels.[113] This would permit the campaign to be effectively controlled by higher levels, both directly through issuing instructions based on their experiences to lower levels and also indirectly through leading by example. Thus, Peng's concern about the conduct of "blooming and contending" focused on the mechanics of soliciting criticism of the Party rather than on the principle of whether criticism was due.[114] And to the extent that open-door rectification and the receipt of criticisms from non-Party elements had become unavoidable, Peng's emphasis on Party control over the process would serve to limit the effect of critiques from outsiders. This was consistent with the Party's handling of Hu Feng.[115] Thus, although Peng may have been persuaded to support the Hundred Flowers Campaign of rectification, even one that solicited views from outside the Party, he still maintained that regimented control should be exercised to keep the campaign within the bounds of Leninist discipline.

It was this emphasis on organizational discipline that also helps to explain Peng's attitude toward the Anti-Rightist Campaign. As the crescendo of criticism was reaching its zenith in May 1957, the Party was evidently having second thoughts. Gone were the organizational controls that would permit disciplined rectification while maintaining the political authority of the CPC. Mao's first formal indication of reprisal came in his May 15 article "Circumstances are Changing" (*Shiqing zhengzai qi bianhua*), circulated to high-level Party cadres for review, in which he suggested that although some criticism of the Party was correct, some of the most savage rightist criticism of the Party coming from the democratic parties and institutions of higher education should be repressed.[116] From mid-May to early June, the Politburo and Secretariat were in continuous session discussing the forthcoming campaign against "rightists." The *People's Daily* editorial of June 8, 1957 ("What Is This About?") publicly signaled that the Party was about to retaliate.[117] Distinguishing between legitimate criticism of Party work styles and rightist opposition to socialism, the editorial suggested that some had abused the Hundred Flowers Campaign in order to attack the leadership of the Party.[118] A central directive issued June 26 set forth the outlines of the campaign of attacking "capitalist rightists."[119] The initial focus was on literary critics such as Ding Ling and Feng Xuefeng, who had come under suspicion as early as the 1955 campaign against Hu Feng; Zhou Yang's intense attack during the fifty-day meeting of July–September 1957 exemplified this effort.[120] Continued expansion of the targets of the campaign extended to those who had voiced criticism of the Party[121] and later to opponents of the Party's agricultural collectivization policy.[122]

As is the case with Peng Zhen's role in the Hundred Flowers Campaign, there is significant disagreement over his role in the Anti-Rightist backlash. There is ample evidence to suggest that Peng Zhen was an active proponent of attacks on rightists.[123] Certainly, Peng would have vigorously resisted suggestions from critics in the Hundred Flowers Campaign that the Party yield its monopoly on political power.[124] In light of Mao's June 19 instruction specifically noting that conditions were particularly suitable for the campaign to begin in Beijing,[125] the politician in Peng could hardly have resisted an aggressive campaign. Peng's speech to the Beijing Representative Congress in August 1957 called for continued deepening of the campaign against "rightists" and echoed Mao's line that the struggle was over the very survival of socialism.[126] As well, however, there is substantial evidence to suggest that Peng urged limits on the anti-rightist attack. Red Guard attacks during the Cultural Revolution repeatedly charged that Peng opposed

Mao's call for retaliation against rightists.[127] Peng made several public speeches arguing against "expansion" (*kuodahua*) of the campaign,[128] which were consistent with the views of Liu Shaoqi.[129] Although Peng articulated these views after the campaign had largely run its course, they were given well before the 1959 campaign against "Right Opportunism" linked to criticism of Peng Dehuai, and they suggest that although Peng may have accepted the need to strike back at many of the Party's critics, he did not want the campaign to go on indefinitely.[130] Even Peng's support for the use of a quota system for targeting rightists is amenable to interpretation as an effort to limit the scope of the campaign. In fact, Peng's 5 percent quota was among the lowest set during the campaign.[131] Finally, although analysis indicating that Peng supported the Anti-Rightist Campaign may fairly be grounded in conclusions that he opposed open-door rectification under the Hundred Flowers rectification, in fact, as discussed above, Peng's views on the rectification campaign were mixed.

The conflicts in the evidence suggest that Peng's own role was conflicted. Those elements of Peng's persona that gave primacy to political advancement through ruthless pursuit of policy goals would certainly have driven him to at least acquiesce to, if not vigorously support, the campaign against the rightists. However, there are tempering factors as well. First, Peng's attitudes toward the Anti-Rightist Campaign would certainly have been influenced by conclusions articulated by Liu Shaoqi at the Eighth CPC Congress and elsewhere concerning the conclusion of the revolution and the general elimination of hostile classes, which would have militated in favor of tempering attacks on alleged rightists.[132] Peng's political characteristics would also have driven him to minimize attacks on intellectuals and legal cadres drawn from the institutions upon which Peng relied for political support. Despite some interpretations that Peng harbored lingering animus toward intellectuals generally,[133] Peng also had a long history dating back to Jin Cha Ji of cultivating intellectuals in the service of Party policy and of Peng's own political goals.[134] During the Anti-Rightist Campaign, he reportedly acted to protect intellectuals such as Wu Han and Deng Tuo with whom he had institutional or personal links.[135] Similarly, when legal specialists came under fire for allegedly advocating the role of an independent judiciary in China,[136] Peng's response was twofold. First, he reportedly acted to protect those jurists with whom he had institutional or personal links. Thus, when Beijing court chief Wang Feiran was sacked for alleged rightism, Peng reportedly secured him a position at the Beijing library.[137] Second, Peng sought to construct the notion of judicial independence in a way that permitted *zheng-fa* institutions a greater role while still subjecting them to the dictates of Party policy. Thus, Peng articulated a view of judicial independence that was dependent on the PRC Constitution, which only insulated the courts from interference from administrative organs; it did not provide any guarantees of independence from the Party.[138] Thus, Peng supported a greater degree of administrative autonomy for the officials and institutions for which he was responsible, but this was autonomy from intrusion by departments outside the *zheng-fa* system. Internal discipline still required continued subservience by lower levels to dictates from superiors within the same administrative system. Moreover, legal officials and institutions remained subject to Party control, thus affording Peng significant supervisory authority in his role as Party leader of the *zheng-fa* system. Thus, whereas Peng might well have supported a campaign that reminded Party and non-Party intellectuals and legal specialists alike of the centrality of the CPC's leadership role, it seems unlikely that he would willingly have gone along with an effort that would weaken, if not depopulate, the very institutions that he was using as a political base.

During the state-building period of the 1950s, Peng Zhen articulated views on law and political authority that reflected changes in the material conditions under which the newly established PRC operated. Peng saw the CPC as no longer confined by the requirements of underground revolution—and moreover as bearing responsibility for bringing greater regularity to the exercise of governance. Peng, active in attacks against perceived enemies of the Party, particularly during the course of campaigns against counterrevolutionaries and in the *wu fan* campaign, nonetheless called for greater regulatory order in these mass movements. As the transition from revolution to governance proceeded, Peng came to emphasize institutional processes even more heavily.

To a large degree, Peng's views held that the function of law in the exercise of political authority was contingent on current conditions. Law was not an absolute norm for regulating public or political affairs. Instead, the role of law depended on conditions of class struggle, and as class conflict receded, law could play a greater role. Conclusions about the decline of class struggle warranted a greater role for legal institutions and doctrines of legal equality. Thus, in his speeches on political–legal work, Peng argued that although internal and hostile contradictions should be treated differently, they both should be handled by political–legal organs.[139] Speaking to public security organs in 1961 in the context of a renewed campaign of rectification, Peng argued against the use of methods of dictatorship and in favor of criticism, persuasion, and education to address nonantagonistic contradictions among the people.[140] Yet when hostile elements threatened, Peng was prepared to permit significant departure from strict procedural requirements, even when legal institutions were involved. Thus, his 1962 address to a national political–legal work conference extolled the role of *zheng-fa* organs but stressed the importance of Party leadership and the use of reform through labor regulations in attacking counterrevolutionaries.[141]

Still, Peng's political personae remained always in evidence, at once motivating him to promote and protect officials and institutions where he had political interests, but also calling him to reiterate the centrality of the Party in the operation of the legal system. Changing social conditions might require greater procedural regularity and greater clarity in the substantive norms of legal rules, but Peng still held to the requirements of Leninist discipline that all institutions of political authority, including those in the judicial realm, should remain subject to Party control.

CHAPTER 4

The End of Discipline: The Lead-up to the Cultural Revolution

ALTHOUGH THE HUNDRED FLOWERS and Anti-Rightist Campaigns fractured the governing consensus within the Chinese political elite, the Great Leap Forward and the disastrous famine that followed shattered the last vestiges of unity. For Peng Zhen, this meant that his role as a policy implementer would gradually give way to one as a political combatant. Although of course these two aspects of Peng's persona overlapped continually, during the period beginning with the Great Leap Forward and culminating in the Cultural Revolution, we see Peng more closely involved in efforts to challenge Mao's leadership. As Peng's role changed, so too did the focus of his thinking change from discipline to political struggle. And it was the nature and consequences of that struggle that laid the foundation for Peng's thinking about the role of law in the post-Mao age.

The Great Leap Forward and Its Aftermath

Although the Hundred Flowers and Anti-Rightist Campaigns seemed—on the surface, at least—to focus on the broad theme of Party leaderships, economic policy remained a core issue.[1] Mao's pursuit of cooperativization in agriculture in mid-1955 had been hotly disputed, most notably by Deng Zihui,[2] although Liu Shaoqi also came in for criticism from Mao through the now-famous "women on bound feet" (*xiao jiao nu ren*) analogy.[3] Although Mao had apparently endorsed Deng's call for "opposing rash advance" (*fan mao jin*) in 1953, by 1956 the slogan was associated with a conservative approach to cooperativization that Mao opposed, and later still, it became a target for expansion of the Anti-Rightist Campaign under the rubric of "right opportunism."[4] Problems in industry and the urban economy also persisted.[5]

Peng Zhen's attitude toward collectivization was undoubtedly influenced by his experience at the time of Liberation with land reform in the suburban agricultural areas surrounding Beijing, and by the policies of 1954–1955 on forming Agricultural Producers' Cooperatives. Noting the intensity of private ownership ideals among the peasantry during a series of investigation and regulation efforts concerning agricultural land use in the Beijing suburbs in 1949, Peng focused on land held by landlords and rich peasants and protected middle peasant land holdings from redistribution.[6] In summarizing conditions in the rural areas surrounding Beijing in early 1955, Peng had noted the potential for peasant resistance to profit sharing and the collective use of draft animals and tools; he suggested that long-term education would be necessary to overcome problems of the "private attitudes" (*siyou guannian*).[7] Peng asserted that the Centre's policies on cooperatives had only been "basically implemented" (*jiben guanche*), meaning that problems and deficiencies remained. He urged consolidation: a word of caution suggesting that a firmer foundation for the Agricultural Producers' Cooperatives still needed to be established before new policy initiatives were considered.

Peng articulated a similar theme in his comments on Mao's report on agricultural cooperatives (*Guanyu nongye hezuohua wenti*), issued July 31, 1955, to a meeting of provincial, municipal, and regional Party Secretaries.[8] Peng noted once again the extent to which individual profit seeking and petit bourgeois practices existed even among poor peasants. Although he suggested that socialist transformation could not be achieved without eliminating problems of private ownership and conducting class struggles against rich peasants, Peng drew upon his *wu fan* experience with the urban bourgeoisie and suggested that transformation of peasant attitudes generally would require a more thoroughgoing effort. Peng suggested the traditional forms of production for poor peasants were incompatible with collectivization. Transforming these practices and attitudes would be no small feat. Peng seemed under no illusions as to the difficulty of the task, and he noted that many Party officials were not even sure of its urgency. Although he deployed the rhetoric of class struggle to describe the requirements and conditions for collectivization, Peng's effort to note the difficulty of the task seemed a plea for moderation. During the Cultural Revolution, Peng's caution was held against him. He was charged with organizing a critique of the cooperativization policy and soliciting materials critical of the program from Hebei and Shanxi.[9] Although the charge that Peng had said "exploitation is good" (*boxue you li*)[10] seems unfounded, clearly he was uncertain about the capacity of the peasantry to sustain further collectivization efforts.

Notwithstanding these and other calls for caution, Mao was ultimately able to secure support for his Great Leap Forward program. The Third Plenum of the CPC Central Committee in September 1957 announced a twelve-year "Draft Program for Agricultural Development," thus paving the way for the formal decision in May 1958 by the second session of the Eighth CPC Congress launching what was later termed the Great Leap Forward.[11] Newly appointed Politburo member Tan Zhenlin would take charge of the Great Leap in agriculture, announcing plans for increased agricultural production.[12] Mao's summer 1958 inspection tour moved him to declare the benefits of the People's Communes, and whatever restraints might have existed previously fell away.[13]

Despite his expressed reservations, Peng spoke out in his role as an implementer of Party policy on the role of institutions in implementing the Great Leap policies. By 1958 the Secretariat had largely surpassed the State Council as the locus for policy making. Chair Deng Xiaoping served as the channel for conveying top leadership views to the Secretariat, and Peng served as the link between the Secretariat's policy makers and the implementation process by lower-level organs.[14] Indeed, Deng Xiaoping reportedly referred to Peng as in fact the "Assistant General Secretary" on whom the work of the Secretariat depended.[15] During the period of the late 1950s, Peng apparently attended meetings of the Politburo Standing Committee, even though he was not formally a member.[16] Peng may have had doubts about the Great Leap, but he was still responsible for ensuring that CPC official policy was carried out by the agencies under his jurisdiction. Thus, at the Seventh National Procurators' Work Conference in February 1958, Peng (who was still responsible for law and public security matters) gave "important instructions" and called for procuracy organs to support the Great Leap Forward.[17] In particular, he directed that procuracy work should focus on problems of falsifying reports on agricultural production, theft of materials, waste, and other manifestations of resistance to Great Leap policies.

After an initial period of enthusiasm, however, uncertainty emerged among the leadership over Great Leap policies mandating collectivization in agriculture and increased industrial production targets. Despite the façade of consensus at the Beidaihe meetings of August 1958, by the end of the year, both the scope of the campaign and the conduct of local cadres implementing it were the subject of close scrutiny and debate.[18] Peng Zhen's editorial in the November 1958 inaugural edition of the Beijing CPC Committee journal *Qianxian* (Frontline) identified a range of problems in the way cadres were conducting the campaign. Under the rubric of criticizing the doctrine of the mean ("*zhongyong zhuyi*"), middle-of-the-road–ism ("*zhongyou zhuyi*"), and the practice of finding fault ("*chuimao qiu ci*") with the masses, Peng argued that CPC cadres needed to be more active in ensuring that the implementation of policy accorded with local conditions.[19] Although the article seemed on the surface to support the Great Leap Forward, the emphasis on attending to local conditions and the critique of cadres who simply passed on central directives without regard for local needs and without soliciting opinion from the masses suggested that the Great Leap policy was itself increasingly under fire. Peng's editorial echoed Liu Shaoqi's call for decentralization of policy making and implementation, rather than the commandism of central dictates,[20] a theme Peng later repeated in his April 1959 report on the work of the National People's Congress (NPC) Standing Committee.[21]

While the Zhengzhou meetings of November 1958 resulted in a tempering of Great Leap policy on the communes, further retrenchment was being considered.[22] Peng Dehuai's criticisms of the Great Leap Forward, made quietly at the April 1959 Seventh Plenum in Shanghai and then more openly at Lushan in July, were emblematic of sentiments held elsewhere in the leadership.[23] In late June, just before the Lushan meetings, Peng Zhen, presumably in his role as Secretary for the Secretariat, reportedly called a meeting of participants to discuss some eighteen questions tied to a possible retreat from to the Great Leap Forward.[24] The document called for allowing greater flexibility on the issues of communal mess halls; restoring the "three fixed" (*san ding*) policy on agricultural production, procurement, and sales; restoring agricultural markets; and establishing the production team as an accounting unit. Although Mao apparently approved the questions as an agenda for Lushan,[25] he resisted further retrenchment and singled out Peng Dehuai, Zhang Wentian, Huang Kecheng, and Zhou Xiaozhou for retribution for questioning the Great Leap Forward and by extension challenging Mao's leadership.[26]

After the upheavals of the Hundred Flowers and Anti-Rightist Campaigns, the disaster of the Great Leap Forward and the purge of Peng Dehuai raised unprecedented questions about the Party's economic policies and thus its political legitimacy.[27] Adjustments to the Great Leap policies had been suggested in the Twelve Articles issued in November 1960, while the Sixty Articles on Agriculture issued March 1961 and then revised in June signaled a more obvious retreat.[28] The Guangzhou Work Conference held in March 1961 saw Mao give approval to rural investigation work by central, provincial, and local Party organs,[29] which led to a series of policy papers offering a thorough review of the Great Leap Forward and its consequences.[30]

Peng Zhen was an important player in this policy review process. Beginning in April 1961, purportedly at Mao's direction, Peng organized subordinates on the Beijing Party Committee, including Liu Ren, Wang Hanbin, and Chao Fan, to conduct investigation visits to nearby rural areas near Beijing such as Fengtai and Huairou to investigate problems of egalitarianism in the commune system.[31] Peng's Huairou report is alleged to have had a significant impact on the Centre's correcting of "leftist errors" in the Sixty Articles on the People's Communes.[32] Parallel investigations of industrial policy were also alleged to have been conducted by Peng associates Liu Ren and Zheng Tianxiang (later to head the Chinese Supreme People's Court in the early 1980s).[33] Informed by the results of his investigations, Peng indicated his concerns with the hardships brought on by the Great Leap Forward, suggesting that the suffering was due to inadequate study of local conditions before implementing the Great Leap policies.[34]

One consequence of the investigation work on the Great Leap Forward done by Peng Zhen and others was the report of the Changguanlou meetings of November–December 1961, at which some fifty six documents were assembled and studied under the auspices of the Beijing CPC Committee, allegedly in an effort to prepare a critique of problems with the Great Leap Forward.[35] Although the Changguanlou meetings might have appeared consistent with the broader review of the Great Leap Forward organized by the CPC Secretariat,[36] Peng seems to have gone further with the Changguanlou effort than Mao had anticipated when he authorized wide-ranging investigations of the Great Leap Forward as a way to help the Party learn from the disaster. Not only were the meetings allegedly held in secret, but this was in effect a provincial-level organization purporting to review national-level policies.[37] Organizational work was handled mainly by Deng Tuo and Xiang Ziming, with Song Shuo and Liao Shuzun playing prominent roles. Peng was later charged with acting under the direct instructions of Liu Shaoqi and Deng Xiaoping.[38] Zheng Tianxiang and Wan Hanbin (who was to serve as Peng's deputy in the NPC Standing Committee's Legal Affairs Committee in the early 1980s) also participated. The meetings resulted in a report of some 13,000 characters delivered to Zheng Tianxiang for conveying on to Peng Zhen. The conclusions reached at the meeting generally criticized the Great Leap Forward as ill-considered: the slogan "greater, faster, better, and more economical" was challenged as internally contradictory, the elevated production targets of the Great Leap Forward were seen as excessive and beyond the capacity of the peasantry, the communes were attacked as premature, and the Great Leap policy in general was criticized as having been carried out without use of formal rules and regulations.[39] Not surprisingly, the substantive policy points raised at the Changguanlou meetings were generally consistent with statements attributed to Peng Zhen opposing the "three red banners" and supporting policies of limited private agricultural production, such as *san zi yi bao* (three extensions—one guarantee) foreshadowed by the Sixty Articles on Agriculture.[40] As well, the Changguanlou meetings raised questions about the permanence of class struggle, reflecting the views of Peng Zhen and Liu Shaoqi about the decline of class struggle and the emergence of socialism. Finally, the critique of the failure during the Great Leap Forward to rely on formal regulations was emblematic of Peng's ongoing concern with formalization of rules and procedures.

Although the Changguanlou report and the materials from the various associated investigations might well have been used effectively to challenge Mao's policies, an open conflict was forestalled by Mao's self-criticism at the 7,000 Cadres Conference in January 1962.[41] After Liu Shaoqi delivered a sobering report on conditions after the Great Leap Forward,[42] Peng gave a speech on the preparation of the work report, in which he noted that Mao himself was not free from mistakes ("*Mao zhuxi ye bu shi shenme cuowu dou meiyou*").[43] Peng challenged the participants to overcome what he termed a tendency in the Party not to raise opinions or investigate errors. Despite being challenged himself, by Chen Boda directly and Deng Xiaoping indirectly in their speeches, Peng, with support from Bo Yibo, pressed on and called for investigation of Mao's mistakes. Ultimately Mao made his famous self-criticism—less than what was required, perhaps, but sufficient to at least delay further attacks.[44]

Socialist Education

The political conflicts of the early 1960s stemmed from unprecedented policy crises facing the regime and the concomitant challenge to CPC legitimacy stemming from the failure of the Great Leap Forward. Among the consequences was a climate of general liberalization in culture and ideology.[45] As China was suffering what may have been the worst famine in its history, Chinese intellectuals were speaking out in unprecedented numbers. Under the leadership of the Beijing Municipal CPC Committee and its propaganda and cultural arms, veiled allegorical criticisms of Mao were emerging, the best-known of which were Beijing vice mayor Wu Han's play *Hai Rui Dismissed from Office* (*Hai Rui ba guan*), Deng Tuo's "Evening Chats at Yan Shan," and the "Notes from a Three Family Village" issued by Deng Tuo, Wu Han, and Liao Mosha.

Wu Han's *Hai Rui Dismissed from Office* was staged in early 1961 and echoed a broad pattern of literary criticism on the Hai Rui theme dating back to 1959, including *Hai Rui Scolds the Emperor* (*Hai rui ma huang di*), *The Story of Hai Rui* (*Hai rui gushi*), and *Hai Rui the Qing Official* (*Qing guan Hai rui*).[46] The work emerged out of the context of general dissatisfaction with the Great Leap Forward and a more specific concern with supporting upright officials who could pursue virtuous policies within the CPC system.[47] Inspired by the work of Wu Han (referred to as the daring vanguard—*jixianfeng*), Liao Mosha (United Front director for the Beijing CPC Committee) published a piece in the January 20, 1961, Beijing *Evening News* (*Beijing wanbao*) containing a veiled call for criticism of Mao and began urging Wu Han to be more open in his critique.[48] Three months later, Deng Tuo (secretary for the Beijing CPC Secretariat and a long-standing Peng Zhen associate from the Jin Cha Ji base area) published a series of *zawen* entitled "Evening Chats at Yan Shan" (*Yanshan ye hua*), under the pen name Ma Nancun, in which he challenged conventional formulations of Chinese Marxism, many of which were closely associated with Maoist policies.[49] Deng organized Wu Han and Liao Mosha to join him in a regular column, "Notes from a Three Family Village," starting just as Mao was calling for assessments of the Leap policies. Deng, Wu, and Liao were attacked during the Cultural Revolution for their continued allegorical—and often humorous—criticism of Mao and his policies.[50]

As these allegorical critiques emerged in the context of the broader policy debates over the Great Leap Forward and the famine, inevitably, more overt political machinations came to the fore. By 1962 conditions in China had worsened to the point where the central leadership began to be concerned about social stability. The ruinous famine of 1960–1962 had already killed millions, and although the retrenchment policies aimed at restoring agricultural production were beginning to have an effect, the general state of affairs was poor.[51] In December 1962 Peng Zhen gave a speech to the fourth administrative session of the All China Federation of Trade Unions, in which he suggested that he recognized the depth of the problem. Noting the seriousness of the current difficulties despite the implementation of the "eight-character policy" of retrenchment, Peng cautioned that the Party stood in danger of losing the support of the workers.[52] As he had so many times before, Peng favored organizational solutions. Harkening back to his earliest years of political activism, Peng extolled the role of the labor union system in ensuring Party control over the workers. As the primary link between Party leadership and the working classes, the union system was crucial to implementing Party policies of increasing production and conserving materials.

Peng's call for strengthening the Party's union work also had implications for the political struggle for control over Party policy. Peng noted that the workers were important elements of the working class that could complement (and by implication perhaps substitute for) the peasantry as the instrument of socialist dictatorship. The union system would be a major vehicle for educating workers in internationalism, patriotism, and socialism. In the combative atmosphere of the early 1960s, this suggested that Peng was speaking to the question of political struggle and the search for allies. Conceding Mao's identification with the peasantry, Peng was not only suggesting that this represented a partial and perhaps inadequate representation of China's working class, but also that worker allegiance could be developed as a counterweight to Mao's affiliation with the peasantry.[53] The effort to strengthen Party leadership in the industrial sector may also have been a factor in Peng's support for an effort to create an administrative system of industrial "trusts" that would have overall control over particular industries.[54]

Peng's interest in building political alliances was evident in his calls for expanded cadre training.[55] Noting that the majority of cadres had joined the Party before liberation, Peng called for increased attention to recruiting, training, and promoting new cadres. Calling bluntly for old cadres to make way for new recruits, Peng suggested that an infusion of new cadres would benefit the Party as a whole. In the context of the times, Peng's remarks suggested a strategy to limit Mao's influence by gradually isolating and retiring those Mao loyalists who had entered the Party before 1949 and bringing in new ranks who could be trained and indoctrinated through the institutions controlled by the Party's central apparatus under Liu Shaoqi, Lu Dingyi (Propaganda Minister), An Ziwen (CPC Organization Department), and Peng Zhen himself in his role as secretary of the CPC Secretariat. Peng pursued a similar approach in higher education, where Party organization work could ensure a support corps of graduates.[56] In this vein, Peng also called for greater attention to be paid to studying the classics of Marxist ideology and less to the study of Mao's contributions,[57] which of course had political and organizational implications in that Peng would then be in a better position to influence cadre training through use of his own personal and institutional resources.

Peng Zhen's reliance on organizational vehicles was also evident in his ongoing work in the legal sphere. Speaking to a national political-legal work conference in November 1962, Peng stressed the importance of Party leadership over the police, the procuracy, and the courts.[58] After a seemingly half-hearted effort to identify counterrevolutionary enemies outside the Party as targets for political–legal organs, Peng devoted the bulk of his remarks to the question of relations among judicial organs and the importance of law and procedure in the handling of criminal suspects. Peng was later criticized for using the letters and visits system to undermine the dictatorship of the proletariat when he launched internal investigations of the public security organs in response to letters from prisoners seeking redress.[59] Peng insisted that the law be followed throughout the criminal process—from arrest and detention through adjudication and reform through labor. Party leadership should be strengthened so as to ensure that the functions and work styles of the police, procuracy, and courts were coordinated and harmonized. Peng argued in favor of reliance on established structures and norms of governance—contrasting these explicitly with the voluntarist informality preferred by Mao and typified by the Great Leap Forward. In particular, Peng's support for formal *zheng-fa* organs stood in obvious contradistinction to Mao's views on the relative unimportance of legal formalities and procedures compared with the role of administrative and informal mechanisms for decision making.[60] In this context, Peng represented the establishment wing of the Party that already controlled the institutions of power and was insistent that these institutions retain their monopoly on authority and the exercise of power.

But Mao remained determined to regain control over these institutions. Mao's call at the Tenth Plenum in September 1962 that the Party should "never forget class struggle" served notice to intellectuals and their supporters that ideological orthodoxy would henceforth be required.[61] This was Mao's first public warning to Peng Zhen and his Beijing-based allies. But it would take nearly four more years for Mao to complete his assault on Peng's Beijing propaganda machine. The following year, the Four Cleans Campaign, nominally aimed at rural work practices but actually an attempt at a broad-based review of current policies on politics, economy, and organization, revealed Mao's intent to reassert the need for ideological purity in virtually all aspects of Chinese life. Whether motivated by the personal need to retain unchallenged authority or by a genuine concern over the restoration of capitalism in China, Mao seemed committed to continual reappraisal and reform among intellectuals and the Party elite.[62] Under the theme of cadre reform, the Socialist Education Campaign was Mao's final effort to pursue his political agenda from within the Party.[63] Consistent with his position leading up to and following the Tenth Plenum on greater orthodoxy among intellectuals, Mao called as well for reform in the arts and in Party work.[64] In the area of cadre reform, Mao issued his First Ten Points in May 1963 as a directive for the conduct of the campaign, emphasizing the importance of poor and lower-middle peasant organizations as the main force for mobilizing popular participation.[65] Although Peng Zhen is said to have worked on the initial drafting, this would have been in his secretarial capacity at the Secretariat.[66] Peng was closely supervised by Mao, and final revisions were made by Chen Boda.

The Latter Ten Points issued in September was more reflective of Peng's views. The document was based on Peng's report on his investigation of local Party organizations in Hebei, Jiangxi, Hunan, Guangxi, Yunnan, Guizhou, Sichuan, and Shaanxi in May and June in which he concluded that with some exceptions local officials should drive the campaign.[67] Although the Latter Ten Points allowed work teams to replace "bad" officials in some instances, in general, the document supported local officials and confined higher-level Party work teams to the role of support staff.[68] Consistent with his political practices of protecting subordinates, Peng was particularly careful to protect local officials in Beijing from work team interference—indeed, during the Cultural

Revolution, Liu Shaoqi actually accused Peng of expelling the Four Cleans work teams from Beijing.[69] Peng's restrained view of the work teams was ultimately disapproved in Liu Shaoqi's Revised Latter Ten Points issued in September 1964, which urged that work teams sent from higher levels were to take charge of local Party reform.[70]

Peng's willingness to protect local officials from work team interference was strengthened by personal political interest. Thus, he moved to replace Zhang Panshi as head of a Central Propaganda Department work group sent to Beijing University in July 1964 on directions from Kang Sheng, when Zhang continued to press criticism against Peng's associate Lu Ping, head of the school's Party Committee.[71] The next year, Peng would again come to the defense of Lu Ping, convening a work conference at the International Hotel in Beijing, stacking it with Lu supporters, and ensuring that Lu remained insulated from work team attacks.[72] Peng's vice mayor in Beijing, Liu Ren, when confronted with questions about classification of rich peasants, purportedly evinced a similar view, permitting local officials to handle the problem and resisting interference from work teams.[73] However, Peng's exercise of political expediency in protecting his personal networks of political supporters was grounded in formal rules and procedures. Peng's Latter Ten Points established concrete regulations for officials' participation in labor in place of vague generalizations issued earlier.[74] Peng thereby made lower-level officials accountable, but he also set standards for evaluating their behavior. This issue also revealed his concern with practicality, for although Mao explained these labor activities as a way of building symbolic ties with the masses, Peng viewed the process as an important method by which officials could gain a more complete understanding of local conditions. Peng used the instrument of formal regulation both to insulate his political allies from interference and to control their behavior.

The issue of the treatment of landlords in these documents also reflected divergent views on the development of Chinese society. Mao's "points" emphasized the need for ongoing class struggle and advocated reliance on poor and lower-middle peasants in establishing proletarian dictatorship over hostile elements, thus authorizing a broad attack on a rather poorly defined enemy.[75] Peng, by contrast, tended to downplay the threat posed by "bad" elements, admonishing against broadening the scope of attack against them and setting out procedures for their treatment that would ensure that establishment Party organs with which Peng was associated remained in control.[76] This approach was justified by the view that because the Party had already seized and consolidated political power, the impact of the preexisting bad classes was diminished, and with it the need for the kind of flexible voluntarism that Mao preferred to be driven by his own preferences rather than by organizational routine. Moreover, Peng did not share Mao's frequently expressed concerns with the restoration of capitalism in China; he continued to emphasize behavior rather than class origin in determining the political qualities of individuals.[77] The Latter Ten Points explicitly noted that the sons and daughters of landlords and rich peasants could break from their class backgrounds and criticized the practice of applying parents' class labels to their children.[78] Peng came back to this theme repeatedly, supporting policies of cooptation (*shumai zhengce*) and stressing the capacity of the bourgeoisie to accept Party leadership and transform themselves.[79]

Peng's approach was rejected, however, in Liu Shaoqi's Revised Latter Ten Points, which flatly stated that "Children of landlords and rich peasants should be barred without exception from taking positions of local basic-level teaching cadres."[80] As he had previously when Peng had overstated the problems with the December 9ers, and again when Peng overstepped the bounds of acceptable dissent in Manchuria, Liu seemed willing to let his protégé test the ideological and policy parameters before stepping in with corrective measures. Ultimately, Liu was not prepared to defend Peng's position in the face of strong resistance from Mao, but instead he acquiesced to policies that discriminated against children of bad classes—which after all entailed little more than acknowledgment of well-established practices. The Revised Latter Ten Points also placed significant emphasis on the role of work teams to correct problems of local cadres, another rejection of Peng Zhen's proposed approach. Nonetheless, Peng ultimately checked and approved the document; the politician in Peng ensured that he would be loyal to his mentor's effort and was reconciled with Mao's preferences on rural political reform.[81]

A compromise position was articulated in the Twenty-Three Articles, which expanded the campaign from its original focus on rural work style to a more broad-based Party rectification effort, even as it backed away from the most severe attacks on local cadres.[82] The Twenty-Three Articles represented something of a vindication for Peng—indeed, he is reported to have drafted the document.[83] Speaking in January 1965, Peng praised the Twenty-Three Articles as a document against left deviation.[84] Peng Zhen's efforts to resist Mao's policy preferences in the

Socialist Education Campaign, first through the Latter Ten Points and later in the Twenty-Three Articles, reflected increased tensions between the two men and set them on a course toward a final breaking point.[85]

Peng's slogan "Everyone Equal Before the Truth" (*zhenli mianqian ren ren pingdeng*), which became particularly prominent during the Socialist Education Campaign, seemed to be a direct challenge to Mao's efforts to leverage his stewardship over ideology into a restored position of policy leadership.[86] The reference to "everyone" reflected Peng's views on collective decision making and organizational discipline; the reference to "truth" reflected in turn his belief in the power of objective rationality.[87] Peng's use of the rhetoric of "equality" implied a denial of Mao's class-based analysis,[88] whereby all perceptions of conditions are colored by class, and thus the accuracy or appropriateness of differing views could be determined not by reference to their content and application to specific conditions, but rather based on the class nature of their proponent or proponents. Of course, Mao's approach could also be used to impose class labels on proponents of policy positions with which he disagreed. Instead, Peng called for collective decision making that was based on "objective" assessments of conditions. By arguing that policies should be evaluated on the bases of content and results, rather than on the basis of the purported class features of their proponents, Peng suggested that class might not determine all aspects of perception and policy preference after all. Peng's faith in "objective laws" (*keguan guilu*) that could be discerned by rational analysis and then be implemented in practical terms had been evident in his public pronouncements and policy style since the days of Jin Cha Ji.[89] With the failure of the Great Leap Forward and the subsequent debates over economic policy, Peng and others stressed the importance of respecting objective truth even more than before.[90]

By questioning Mao's view that everything has a class nature, Peng was implicitly rebuking Mao for his refusal to heed the advice of his colleagues on economic policy because, in the view of Peng and others, objective truth was arrived at through an involved process of mutual consultation and rational discussion. Claiming that all are equal before the truth (and by implication no one, including Mao, had a monopoly on correct interpretation of events), Peng argued that criticism must have a target and it must be reasoned—an oblique critique of Mao's penchant for continuous struggle and criticism.

Whereas during the revolutionary and early state-building periods the focus of Peng Zhen's public pronouncements was discipline—the discipline of revolution and the discipline of governance—this was a discipline imposed on the objects of rule. Whether outside the Party altogether or merely working at lower levels in the hierarchy, the subjects of rule were to be the targets of discipline and control, first through informal mechanisms of revolution, then gradually through increasingly formal structures of state and Party authority. With the crises of the late 1950s and early 1960s, however, Peng's focus turned to the sources of political authority, and he began to articulate ideas about the need for procedural constraints on the exercise of political power.

The Final Straw: Peng Zhen and the Reform of Culture

By 1965 Peng Zhen (and others in the CPC leadership) were in increasingly open conflict with Mao. Indeed, the extent to which Peng's resistance to Mao during 1965 contributed to Peng's downfall was evident when on May 12, 1966, the Centre and the North China Bureau obtained from the Beijing CPC Committee copies of six major speeches given by Peng between January 1965 and January 1966; four days later, the expanded meeting of the Politburo voted through the May 16 Circular that effectively ended Peng's political career for the time being.[91] The story of the fall of Peng Zhen and the onset of the Cultural Revolution has been discussed elsewhere and need not be repeated in detail here.[92] A summary of these events, however, is useful to set the context for Peng Zhen's subsequent views on law and political authority.

After expressing his dissatisfaction with Zhou Yang's handling of initial reforms in the propaganda and culture bureaucracies that had been sought by Mao at the expanded Politburo meetings of May 1963, Mao called for a renewed effort.[93] In December Mao called for more wide-ranging reform in the cultural sphere.[94] After Propaganda Chief Lu Dingyi declined, Peng accepted Mao's charge to head up the "Five-Person Group" in mid-1964 to oversee reform in culture.[95] How enthusiastic Peng was to take on this task remains uncertain. Reportedly he volunteered,[96] although he could hardly have been unaware of the dangers of taking responsibility for implementing Mao's instructions to identify political significance in art and culture when these were precisely the discourses for which Peng had tolerated, if not encouraged, critiques of Mao and his policies.[97] Although Peng favored keeping intellectuals in check,[98] his tacit support for the critical polemicism of Deng Tuo and Wu Han in the early 1960s suggested that he wanted to harness intellectuals for his own political purposes. But to do this effectively, Peng had to protect members of his intellectual stable from the kind of wide-ranging attack suggested by Jiang Qing's comments that "the cultural front consists almost entirely of demons and monsters" and "the cultural front is headed by very bad people, they are our reactionaries, in the past we relied on them too much."[99] The chairmanship of the Cultural Revolution Small Group provided Peng with a potentially useful opportunity to limit the campaign and protect his allies while still carrying general measures to ensure political compliance from intellectuals.

Peng's approach to reforms in the cultural sphere contributed to tensions with Jiang Qing, particularly over reforms in Peking opera, which Mao had mandated as early as 1963.[100] Jiang considered reform of opera to require nothing less than adopting a "modern theatre" that was unsullied by the forms and values of the feudal past.[101] Peng challenged Jiang's views as not representing either the Centre or Mao himself,[102] and he sought to revise the terms of cultural reform while appearing to go along with calls for fundamental changes in the liturgy called for by Mao. Whereas Mao said Peking opera was emblematic of class struggle, Peng argued that reform of opera should serve politics and the development of productive forces, indicating as he had previously that China was already in a stage of socialism.[103] Peng also supported retaining the basic form of Peking opera, which Mao and Jiang had critiqued as feudalistic, and even went so far as to criticize those who would "attempt to use Peking opera to transform the world."

Peng's conflicts with Jiang Qing also extended to his efforts to protect Wu Han and the Three-Family Village, which had been a thorn in Mao's side at least since the 1962 Tenth Plenum. Almost immediately after Peng took charge of the Cultural Revolution Small Group in 1964, he began fending off criticisms of Wu Han's political reliability from Jiang Qing and Kang Sheng, who viewed Wu's *Hai Rui ba guan* as confirmation of his anti-Maoist views.[104] As chair of the Group of Five in charge of cultural reform, Peng was charged by Mao, but with the agreement of Liu Shaoqi, to head up the investigation and criticism of Wu Han.[105] As with the case of his responsibility for cultural reform generally, Peng had been placed in a position where he likely would have to choose between loyalty to Mao and pursuit of his own political agenda. Apparently confident that he could weather the storm protected by Liu Shaoqi and other allies, Peng tried to sideline the attacks on Wu Han.[106] In meetings with Mao Zedong, Peng openly voiced his frustration with Jiang Qing over her preoccupation with Wu Han and

Hai Rui.[107] A telling commentary on Peng's deteriorating relationship with Jiang Qing comes from a report on a meeting between Peng and Zhou Enlai in November 1965, where Peng is said to have apologized for arriving late to a meeting on account of running into "that woman."[108] Zhou did not need to inquire further as to whom Peng was describing.

Peng's increasingly personalized battles with Jiang Qing had broader implications. Jiang's patron Kang Sheng had personal reasons to strike out at Peng, who had been instrumental in curtailing Kang's "Rescue Campaign" at Yan'an. Peng's opposition of Jiang's radicalism also came perilously close to challenging Mao himself. Less than a month before Mao spoke out against the potential for revisionism within the Party at the Central Economic Work Conference of September–October 1965,[109] Peng addressed a meeting of cultural office (*ting*) and bureau (*ju*) directors and challenged a number of radical themes. He called for the separation of art from politics, he challenged the notion that "destruction is justified" (*you po you li*), and he reiterated the theme of equality before the truth.[110] Whether these conflicts increased Peng's gradual isolation from Mao or were simply a product of such isolation, it seems clear that by late 1965, little was left of the closeness that had earlier characterized relations between the two men. Indeed, by October Peng's reporting to Mao on reform in literature and art took the form of comments while sharing the rostrum at the National Day celebrations, suggesting that Peng had lost confidence that his formal written reporting was being submitted to or read by the Chairman.[111]

The appearance in *Wen Hui Bao* on November 10, 1965, of Yao Wenyuan's article criticizing *Hai Rui Ba Guan* raised an open challenge to Peng's handling of the investigation of Wu Han. Yao's attack on Wu Han also challenged Peng's network of linkages with establishment intellectuals in Beijing.[112] Peng would come to use all of his political and organizational talents to ensure that the Wu Han inquiry would not devolve into a political investigation of one of his primary constituencies. If accepted, the charge that Wu Han had sought a reversal of verdicts on Peng Dehuai would have constituted a violation of Party discipline with extremely serious consequences for Wu, who was, after all, only recently enrolled as a Party member. Aside from Peng's direct interest in protecting his vice mayor, he also had an interest in muting criticism of efforts to rehabilitate Peng Dehuai, regardless of whether Wu Han originally intended *Hai Rui* to be a plea for Peng's return. Peng Zhen had apparently already been involved in an effort among the ruling elite in early 1965 to persuade Mao to allow Peng Dehuai back into the fold.[113] And earlier, at a 1959 Politburo Standing Committee meeting convened immediately after the Lushan Plenum, Peng had attempted to place Peng Dehuai's case in historical context, citing principles of leniency associated (officially, at least) with the Party's handling of the Yan'an rectification and the investigation of the Ping Jiang Uprising.[114] Nonetheless, Peng attempted to use personal persuasion to convince Mao there was no organizational link between Wu Han and Peng Dehuai[115] and to use his organizational authority over the Group of Five to prevent discussion of the possible links between *Hai Rui* and Peng Dehuai.[116]

Peng also had an interest in protecting his bureaucratic and organizational authority. As chair of the Cultural Revolution Small Group, Peng was incensed that Yao's article had been printed without his approval. Peng correctly saw the piece as a veiled attack on himself and his handling of cultural reform.[117] Peng succeeded in blocking publication in Beijing for a time, in part by insisting that all critiques of Wu Han by name must be approved by the Beijing CPC Committee, which approval Peng was not prepared to grant.[118] After Jiang Qing complained of Peng's intransigence, Mao was moved to raise his oft-cited critique that Peng was creating an independent kingdom in Beijing.[119] Ultimately, Peng was compelled to permit publication of the critique of *Hai Rui*, but he insisted on including a commentary limiting the scope of Yao's attack. Peng also insisted that the word "comrade" (*tongzhi*) be used before Wu's name, thus attempting to ensure that the conflict remain within the discourse of internal contradictions and academic issues, rather than a question of class struggle and political conflict.[120] However, before publication, Zhou Enlai added two lines to the commentary that expressed Mao's view that if Wu Han's play raised issues of anti-Marxism, these could be debated.[121]

Once he was compelled to permit open discussion of *Hai Rui*, Peng tried to manipulate the terms of the criticism of Wu Han, in part by insisting that the review of *Hai Rui* be conducted by Peng's Beijing Party apparatus. Speaking to Liu Ren and Deng Tuo after Yao's article had been released in Shanghai, Peng reportedly said, "No matter who issued the article, this is not the final summation. The final summation is determined by the [Beijing Party Committee] organization."[122] Peng also worked to ensure publication of alternative critiques, such as Deng Tuo's piece linking the Hai Rui debate to the inheritability of virtue.[123] Through his position as chair of the Cultural Revolution Small Group,

Peng attempted to define the situation with Wu Han as a nonantagonistic contradiction and directed that discussion of *Hai Rui* should include discussion of broader issues of governance and Party rule, as well as the issue of upright and corrupt officials.[124] Peng imposed three specific prohibitions (*san bu zhun*) on the investigation of Wu Han, which proscribed (1) discussing the questions of the target (*yao hai wenti*) of the play thus blocking discussion of links between *Hai Rui* and Peng Dehuai, Huang Kecheng, and other victims of the Lushan Plenum; (2) discussing the issue of Wu Han opposing the Party and opposing socialism; and (3) elevating the discussion of Wu Han to the political realm, rather than confining it to academic issues.[125] In response to radical Wang Li's efforts to prod the Group of Five to discuss links between *Hai Rui* and Peng Dehuai, Peng averred, "When briefing the Chairman, some people obstinately insist on linking *Hai Rui Ba Guan* with Peng Dehuai. This confuses the boundaries between academics and politics."[126]

In addition to these procedural maneuvers, Peng also attempted to attack Yao Wenyuan directly. Soon after the publication of Yao's article, Peng reportedly ordered Liu Ren to conduct an investigation into Yao's background in anticipation of the need for political retaliation.[127] Peng also was at least perceived as attempting to use his relations with Zhou Yang and others to mobilize the CPC Propaganda Department against Yao.[128] During the course of Politburo discussions of Wu Han's alleged errors, Peng repeatedly suggested that Yao's article also contained errors that should be investigated, and through the Group of Five, he organized the collection of materials prepared by Qi Benyu, Guan Feng, Zhang Chunqiao, and Yao Wenyuan containing leftist errors.[129]

Mao's position in this debate appeared to evolve as the political positions taken by his contentious subordinate, and their implications, became clear. Mao is said to have initially disagreed with Kang Sheng's assertions that *Hai Rui* was about the Lushan Plenum and the purge of Peng Dehuai.[130] On the other hand, he could not have been pleased with Peng Zhen's increasingly open disagreements—even criticisms—of Jiang Qing's views on cultural reform, which clearly bore Mao's imprimatur.[131] During the Beijing CPC Committee's work conference of mid-December 1965, Peng reportedly expanded the discussion of "errors" to include mistakes by Mao and others, thus attempting to minimize whatever mistakes might be ascribed to Wu Han.[132] Reportedly this got back to Mao, possibly via Red Flag reporter Cheng Hong, no doubt contributing to the chairman's increased irritation at Peng.

Speaking with Chen Boda and other radicals on December 20, Mao indicated that *Hai Rui* was indeed a political matter, particularly the phrase "*ba guan*," which implied the unjust dismissal of Peng Dehuai.[133]

Although Mao remained somewhat obtuse,[134] in keeping with his practice of playing subordinates off against each other while retaining for himself greater freedom of action and initiative, he steadily distanced himself from Peng's position. Whereas earlier Mao had assured Peng Zhen regarding Jiang Qing, "we are two different people—she is she, I am I, she does not represent me,"[135] in his subsequent meeting in Hangzhou on December 25 with Peng and Kang Sheng, Mao pointedly did not intervene during their argument over the political significance of the phrase "*baguan*."[136] Mao averred that perhaps (*yexu*) Peng's view was correct that *Hai Rui* was not a political question, but then he urged Peng to heed the views of opponents such as Zhang Chunqiao. Later, in Shanghai, Mao told Peng publicly at a banquet for leading municipal officials that he should "learn from the Shanghai comrades, and deepen the struggle to criticize *Hai Rui ba guan*," and following a particularly acrimonious exchange between Peng and Zhang Chunqiao on the issue of *Hai Rui*, Mao pointedly failed to support Peng—reportedly telling the disputants in effect, "You work it out; for the moment, let's eat."[137]

The 1966 "February Outline" issued by the Group of Five reflected Peng's policy conclusions on the significance of Hai Rui and revealed his efforts to control the substance and process of the investigation.[138] Drafted with the assistance of vice ministers of propaganda Xu Liqun and Yao Zhen,[139] the report formally restricted the campaign to the academic issue of Wu's historiography and ignored the general issue of political class struggle in the sphere of culture, terming the matter one of academic struggle between bourgeois and proletarian ideologies. While noting the importance of struggling against the ills of the bourgeois ideology, the document also called for "opening wide," a reference to continuing the loosening of orthodoxy in academic discussion that had characterized the early 1960s, and by implication supporting those who took advantage of this loosening to lodge critiques of Mao's policies. The outline reiterated the dictum "equality before the truth" and specifically criticized those who would "overwhelm people with their power," additional oblique references that tolerated, if not encouraged, doubts about the chairman.

Peng reportedly met several times with Mao to explain the Feburary Outline.[140] After discussion of the document at a Politburo Standing Committee meeting convened by Liu Shaoqi in Beijing on February 5,

Peng, together with Lu Dingyi and Xu Liqun, met Mao in Wuhan on February 8.[141] Mao was apparently quite relaxed (*kuan*) about the document and agreed to its distribution. He raised only two points: first, that there need not be a political summation after two months; and second, that criticisms of Guo Morou and Fan Wenlan, whose allegedly bourgeois writing on the Hai Rui theme had been a focus of criticism from the Group of Five, should be handled through self-criticism and that they could continue to work in the cultural sphere.[142] Peng reported by telephone to Liu Shaoqi in Beijing on February 10, and he apparently responded to Liu's specific question as to whether Mao had any objections by saying Mao had voiced no objections (*Mao Zedong zai tingqu huibao shi . . . meiyou tichu shenme fouding de yi jian*).[143] On February 12 the document was circulated within the Party after its approval by the Politburo Standing Committee.[144]

Despite Peng Zhen's efforts to control debate on Wu Han, the February Outline was not the last word on the subject. In hindsight, Mao's standing silent in the face of open challenges to Peng's handling of the Wu Han affair, and his suggestion that Peng should reconsider his position suggested Mao was increasingly dissatisfied with Peng's efforts. Thus, when meeting with Peng in Wuhan in early February, Mao's query as to whether the issue of Wu Han was a political matter was not an open question, but rather a test of Peng's position when Mao's mind on the question had already been made up.[145] The exchange between Mao and Peng on the question whether Wu Han was anti-Party and antisocialist is instructive.[146] Peng's initial response that this depended on whether Wu was among those dismissed from office by the PRC reflected his reliance on organizational procedures that he controlled as the basis for discipline over personnel. Mao's rejoinder that Wu had not been dismissed as vice mayor ("*hai zhaodang ta de shizhang*"), although implying agreement, also seemed to cast doubt on this formalistic standard for assessing Wu's political fate. In the larger context of Mao's differences with Party traditionalists, Mao can be seen maneuvering Peng into a position where his responsibility for cultural reform would force a choice between loyalty to Mao and protection of longtime political allies and associates.[147]

Although Mao apparently agreed to allow the February Outline to be distributed, he reserved disagreement with its contents. The mildness of Mao's queries to Peng Zhen, Lu Dingyi, and Xu Liqun when first presented with the document, and his refusal to let the focus of criticism from the Group of Five shift to relative small fry like Guo

Moruo, suggested that he had already dismissed the relevance of the February Outline except as a basis for criticizing Peng Zhen. According to Group of Five member Wang Li, Mao lost his temper when informed that the Standing Committee had unanimously approved the document—"That may agree, but I do not"—and went on to criticize the Outline and its authors.[148] Mao was undoubtedly aware that with authorization from Lin Biao, Jiang Qing's radical group had sponsored a Military Forum on Literature and Art in Shanghai that began February 2 and was to run through February 20.[149] Kang Sheng, who had participated in meetings of Peng Zhen's Group of Five and thus knew of the content of the February Outline, assisted in organizing the Military Forum. Kang helped prepare a Forum Summary (*Zuotanhui jiyao*) that served as a direct counterpoint to Peng's February Outline. Despite his misgivings, Peng could not prevent the Forum Summary from being circulated through the Secretariat, although he did oppose distribution of a second edition that emphasized the significance and importance of the Great Proletarian Cultural Revolution.[150]

Although the Forum Summary did not address the issue of *Hai Rui* directly, it took a position completely contrary to that in the February Outline regarding reform of culture—namely, that since 1960 a sharp class struggle between socialism and capitalism was taking place in the field of culture. This struggle was seen as exemplified in the effort (by Jiang Qing's estimation, a failure) to reform Peking opera—thus drawing Peng Zhen yet further into the ambit of criticism. Jiang's outline also attacked Luo Ruiqing for failing to promote cultural reform in the military, thus laying the foundation for identifying a clique of Peng, Luo, and Lu Dingyi (who was already implicated by virtue of his support for Peng in the Group of Five). The charge of revisionism was also made, linking cultural reform in China to the Khrushchev reforms in the Soviet Union, setting the stage for attacks on Peng as a revisionist. The Forum Summary closed with a call for renewed cadre education—suggesting the failure of the Socialist Education Campaign, and by implication critiquing Peng, who had played such an important role in undermining Mao's First Ten Points. This renewed criticisms that had been lodged without effect in 1964 by Chen Boda that Peng Zhen had undermined the success of the Four Cleans (*siqing*) Campaign in Beijing.[151] The Forum Summary also urged the reorganization of the cultural corps—a further critique of Peng's handling of the *Hai Rui* matter.

Peng had been outmaneuvered and was in serious political trouble.[152] The February Outline had not achieved its desired objective of defusing the political attacks on Peng's subordinates in the Beijing CPC Committee. When contrasted with the Shanghai "Forum Summary" issued by the radicals, the February Outline now provided an ample basis for direct attacks on Peng himself. Emboldened by Mao's support for the Forum Summary, a Cultural Revolution Document Drafting Group composed of Chen Boda, Kang Sheng, Jiang Qing, and Zhang Chunqiao prepared a Central Committee circular that became the basis for the May 16 Circular attacking Peng Zhen.[153] After a last-ditch effort by Zhou Enlai to persuade Peng to save himself by retracting the February Outline, Peng faced the Secretariat in Beijing April 9–12, 1966, and learned of Mao's direct criticism of the February Outline.[154] The enlarged Politburo met for the second time in Hangzhou. The formal meetings started on April 19, with informal talks beginning several days earlier. Peng's political fate was already evident: Mao refused to meet with him, and Peng found himself ostracized at the dining hall of his guest house.[155] The formal critique of Peng Zhen begun by the Cultural Revolution Document Drafting Group was largely finalized during these mid-April meetings. In the face of direct criticism from Mao, Peng expressed loyalty to the chairman and directed the Beijing CPC Committee to criticize the errors of Wu Han, Deng Tuo, and Liao Mosha.

But it was too little, too late. Under Liu Ren's direction, and with the assistance of Wang Hanbin, the Beijing Committee disseminated seven sets of documents received from Mao on the question of Peng Zhen being anti-Party. On April 27 Peng reportedly told a meeting of the Beijing CPC Secretariat attended by Liu Ren, Zheng Tianxiang, Wan Li, and Chen Kehan that the Centre had criticized Beijing's parochialism (*benwei zhuyi*) and indicated that he would no longer be responsible for Beijing affairs.[156] Peng left Beijing for Hangzhou, where he was placed under house arrest a few days later.[157] Despite a rather half-hearted attempt by Deng Xiaoping to spread the blame for the February Outline, the Secretariat followed the lead of an expanded Politburo meeting of May 5 and denounced the February Outline and its primary proponent Peng Zhen.[158] On May 11, acting on instructions from Mao, the CPC's North China Bureau assigned Propaganda Minister Huang Zhigang the task of leading the work of reorganizing the Beijing CPC Committee.

The Secretariat's May 16 Circular sealed Peng's downfall. The Circular termed the February Outline a revisionist document and blamed its errors squarely on Peng, charging that he had not consulted with others on the Five-Person Group or elsewhere in the leadership.[159] The May 16 Circular was buttressed by the "May 7 Directive," purportedly drafted by Lin Biao, which summarized Mao's ideological program for the Cultural Revolution.[160] The veracity of these charges is in some doubt in light of evidence that Peng convened at least one formal meeting of the Five-Person Group to discuss the Outline and had indeed sought Mao's approval for it,[161] although it seems equally clear that Peng used his considerable powers of persuasion to push the document through over the objections of others. Peng was publicly attacked a few days later,[162] and in what was to become a pattern of routinized oppression, the Politburo established a case examination committee to handle Peng's file.[163] Decisions on reorganization of the CPC Beijing Committee were more or less finalized at a May 23 meeting of the Politburo, and on June 3 Peng was stripped of his posts in the Beijing CPC Committee, with Li Xuefeng reassigned from the CPC North China Bureau to become Beijing's first secretary, and Wu De brought in from the Jilin Provincial CPC Committee to be second secretary. Tao Zhu took over as standing secretary for the CPC Secretariat and head of the Propaganda Ministry, and Ye Jianying took Peng's position as secretary for the CPC Secretariat.

Peng was denounced throughout the summer of 1966 as having supported revisionism in the former Beijing CPC Committee.[164] In July, Kang Sheng accused Peng of plotting a mutiny in Beijing in February.[165] At the Eleventh Plenum in August, Peng was dismissed from his Politburo position and from his post on the Secretariat. He was formally arrested in December, and in what must have been the ultimate degradation, he was paraded through the streets of Beijing before being sent off to political oblivion. A campaign of denunciation against Peng continued well into 1967, with the charges being expanded from revisionism to include plotting a coup d'état in consultation with Lu Dingyi, Luo Ruiqing, and Yang Shangkun;[166] carrying out counterrevolution—justified largely by references to the 1961 Changguanlou meetings;[167] and even working in league with foreign imperialists.[168] Even after his formal dismissal, Peng was periodically dragged out to struggle sessions—the duration of the criticism against him reflecting a lingering fear by the Maoists that only the most thorough repudiation could prevent his regaining power and the capacity for retribution.[169] By mid-1967 Peng Zhen's role as a champion of Leninist discipline and Party organization, as the chieftain of Beijing, and as a vigorous and generally effective political infighter appeared to be over.

The fall of Peng Zhen has given rise to countless debates over Mao's strategy and objectives. Some suggest that the attack on Peng was part of larger strategy aimed at Liu Shaoqi; others viewed Mao as using Peng to test Liu Shaoqi's loyalty and suggested that Mao remained willing to permit Liu to survive.[170] In explaining why Mao would put Peng and later Liu in charge of the early stages of the Cultural Revolution when it was obvious Peng and Liu doubted the Chairman on the underlying policy issues, some have suggested that Mao did so in order to test their loyalty, then purged them when they failed. Others suggest that the assignments of Peng and Liu were aimed to legitimize attacks already planned by Mao against recalcitrant colleagues—that is, Mao knew they would fail because their hearts weren't in it.[171] But regardless of Mao's motives, as Peng fell, the discourse of law and the political authority that he had articulated also fell into disgrace. Although his influence continued to be felt as a negative example of a failed policy extolling the role of formal organizations and procedures in the exercise of political authority, it appeared that Peng Zhen and his approach to the role of law as a basis for discipline and political authority would be erased from the public expressions of Chinese elite legal culture.

The period leading up to the Cultural Revolution saw significant transformation in Peng Zhen's views on discipline and political authority. With the revolutionary period largely completed, the emphasis on external discipline was diminished and increasingly complemented by an articulated need for discipline within the Party's disciplinary process. This was of a character wholly different from the internal disciplinary efforts at Jin Cha Ji and Yan'an, or even during the *san fan* campaign, where internal discipline was mainly exercised against newly recruited Party members and cadres. By the late 1950s Peng Zhen saw the need for discipline extend to the Party elite. This was driven in no small part by Peng's political loyalties, which bound him to the organizational establishment within the Party. But Peng could also justify the need for greater procedural regularity in government decision making by reference to the obvious calamities that were resulting from the Chairman's experiments. Thus, the insistence on rigid discipline for the subjects of rule was gradually being complemented by the requirement for discipline amongst the sources of rule. The Chairman and his supporters were increasingly admonished to comply with some of the same principles of discipline that were imposed on China's masses.

Peng supported procedural restraints on government decision making largely out of political interest. Mao's policy positions were not widely shared in the government and would have been avoided had a more democratized decision-making system been in place within the ruling elite. Thus discipline among the sources of rule would require that individual initiatives such as Mao was pursuing must be subordinate to the will of the collective—a principle that obviously complemented Peng's position as a member of the majority in the leadership who opposed some of Mao's policy initiatives. The transition in Peng's thinking on discipline—from discipline imposed on society by the Party in pursuit of goals of revolutionary transformation to include discipline accepted by the Party in pursuit of collective decision making—was driven primarily by political considerations. By promoting collective decision making, Peng sought to ensure that the policy preferences with which he and Liu Shaoqi were associated remained in effect and undiluted by the minority viewpoint associated with Mao and his supporters. The Cultural Revolution saw the temporary failure of these approaches, as Peng found himself fighting for his political life and grasping at whatever variety of organizational and personal resources he could find.

The Cultural Revolution saw the end of the model of Leninist discipline that had characterized many of Peng Zhen's doctrinal expressions on law and political authority. Mao's ultimate refusal to participate in consensual decision making at the Centre effectively destroyed the key prerequisite for requirements of strict adherence to central dictates. Without some measure of collective decision making, in which even those participants whose views were not adopted could subscribe to the final decision and thus promote its enforcement, the motivation for, and indeed the legitimacy of, rigorous enforcement was lost. For Peng and many other traditionalists in the central leadership, this meant that the decision-making process needed to be reformed and some measure of collective policy process restored. This also meant that some degree of permanence, or at least stability, had to be brought to policy decisions once they were made. Finally, the ravages of the Cultural Revolution, and particularly the violence and upheaval wrought by the popular masses unconstrained by organizational channels, raised the specter of chaos (*da luan*) that would haunt the survivors of Mao's last great initiative. The norms of collective decision making, a modicum of policy stability, and the imposition of organizational channels on popular behavior were not alien to the model of Leninist discipline. But when the

Chairman removed himself from the limits imposed by these norms, the informal and often ad hoc nature of the Leninist discipline system had to be reconsidered. This had implications for the role of law, and thus it was not surprising that once rehabilitated, Peng embarked on an effort to establish a system of socialist legalism in the post-Mao era.

CHAPTER 5

The Post-Mao Period: From Leninist Discipline to Socialist Legalism

WITH HIS REHABILITATION in early 1979, Peng Zhen resumed his previous role in the center of Chinese elite politics, as once again he was given charge over the political–legal (*zheng-fa*) regime. In the immediate post-Mao period, Peng's role in law building followed a path similar to the one he followed during the early 1950s. But although many of Peng's themes for PRC law during the early post-Mao period echoed his previously held views, new elements were introduced in the areas of legislation and the Party's role. Peng also called for increased attention to formality and generality in the content and operation of law.

Rehabilitation and Resumption of *Zheng-fa* Activities

After his rehabilitation from Cultural Revolution disgrace,[1] Peng Zhen was appointed chair of the Legal System Committee (*Fazhi weiyuanhui*) of the National People's Congress (NPC) Standing Committee in February 1979.[2] In this capacity, he oversaw revisions to laws on such matters as elections and government organization and led the drafting work in areas of criminal justice and foreign investment. Aided by his effort to read continuously on law and policy issues while in exile,[3] Peng assumed the chair of the Communist Party of China (CPC) Central Committee's Politics and Law Committee in 1980 and was made the person responsible for the leading group in charge of the trials of Lin Biao and Jiang Qing. In September 1980 Peng was appointed Vice Director of the Committee for Revising the Constitution and took de facto charge of the committee's work.

At the time of Peng Zhen's return to power, the political environment within which legal reform was developing was characterized largely by the struggle between Deng Xiaoping's reformist coalition and the Cultural Revolution holdover leadership of Hua Guofeng.[4] In February 1978 the National Science Conference proclaimed that intellectuals, so maligned during the Cultural Revolution, would henceforth be considered mental workers and considered members of working classes. This set the stage for the gradual return of specialized experts to the field of law. In April, after the Eleventh Congress of the CPC Central Committee, the Fifth NPC issued its "Decision on Certain Questions of Accelerating Industrial Development" as the basis for industrial reform, and Deng's call for "seeking truth from facts" at the National Military Work Conference in June heralded further emphasis on specialized expertise. The landmark Third Plenum of the Eleventh Central Committee of the CPC in November–December 1978 saw formal announcement of the "Open-Door Policy" encouraging foreign investment and the initial program of economic reform in agriculture. These were accompanied by the call for a program of legal reform explicitly intended to complement the economic reform policies.[5] Legal reform was also seen as essential to strengthening the Party's legitimacy, which had nearly been destroyed by the Cultural Revolution.[6] The political context for economic and legal reform was further entrenched at the Sixth Plenum of the Eleventh CPC Central Committee in June 1981, which approved the Resolution on Party History and replaced Hua Guofeng and his followers with Deng's reform team, including Zhao Ziyang and Hu Yaobang.[7]

Shortly after his formal rehabilitation by a Central Committee edict concluding that Cultural Revolution charges against him had no basis in fact, Peng took over the leadership of the politics and law apparatus.[8] At the outset of the post-Mao legal reform effort, Peng Zhen took a leading role in the areas of legislative drafting, law and politics management, and constitution building as he chaired the NPC's Legal System Committee, took de facto control of the constitution revision process, and led the CPC's Politics and Law Committee. Peng's tasks mirrored many of his assignments during the 1950s and early 1960s, and his commitment to the use of law to enforce policy decisions was familiar to those who had watched his performance during the pre–Cultural Revolution period. For Peng Zhen, instrumentalism remained an essential feature of law—legislation and regulations were aimed primarily, if not exclusively, to implement policy goals, although now these centered on political stability and economic development. Peng's work in the early 1980s also reflected the familiar theme of organizational control. And there was a new component to Peng's doctrinal position as he gradually began to articulate a view of law as a basis for legitimacy.

Law as Instrument

The importance of legislation in the post-Mao reforms was articulated by Deng Xiaoping in his directive on "liberating thought,"[9] which mandated a major legislative effort on criminal and civil law and procedure, and in such needed areas as factory law, labor law, foreign investment law, and laws regulating relations between the state and enterprises.[10] Consistent with this, Peng's pronouncements in the early years after his return underscored that law should remain an instrument of Party policy. Instrumentalist uses of legal forms have long standing in China[11] and are generally consistent with concepts of discipline discussed earlier. Yet the new attention paid to legal forms marked an important departure from the prior discourse of discipline based on Party policy. Although law remained an expression of policy, once stated, it became subject to general scrutiny and discussion in ways that secret Party norms and directives did not. Also, once made public, the law was more difficult to change.

Of particular importance early on was the use of socialist legal reform to strengthen discipline within the Party. Thus, in a speech to the Northeast delegation to a CPC work conference, Peng called for greater democracy within the Party while asserting that the Cultural Revolution marked a departure from this policy.[12] Thus, inner-Party democracy was to be a vehicle for driving policy consensus through winning over or even suppressing dissenting views. Although most of the critique was reserved for Lin Biao, Mao's mistakes did not escape scrutiny, and Peng stressed the error of expanding the targets of the 1957 Anti-Rightist Campaign as an example of ignoring the need for inner-Party democracy. Peng's approach to the work of the NPC's Legal System Committee revealed a similar approach. In a speech to students and officials from the Public Security Bureaux, the Procuracy, and the People's Courts in October 1979, Peng stressed the importance of "rallying round" the Party, the state, and the people and of practicing internal democracy by unifying thought within the Party.[13] The political aspects of this process were thinly veiled. By asserting that institutions and officials in the political–legal area must preserve and strengthen Party character, Peng suggested that their careers depended on loyalty to the new Deng coalition. Politics and law work was to be a tool of unifying Party members and of carrying out the rectification that Deng Xiaoping was using to purge Cultural Revolution holdovers—*zheng-fa* work would assist in clarifying major issues of principle in Party line, reregistering Party members, unifying cadre thought, rectifying leadership departments, and strengthening leadership work.[14]

Peng's October 1979 speech also drew attention to particular features of ideological and policy underpinnings of the reform effort. His reference to the 1954 Constitution emphasized the importance of changing conditions for the norms and procedures of governance. In particular, the end of class struggle was seen as mandating greater attention to the legal system—hence Peng's reiteration of the 1954 dictum on "equality before the law." Peng also made pointed reference to the 7,000 Cadres Conference of 1962, at which Mao had made a self-criticism for his handling of the Great Leap Forward. Of particular importance here was the fact that Peng Zhen had criticized Mao by name at that conference, in effect for disregarding Party norms of collective decision making. Although Peng was ostensibly voicing support for the economic reform policies of the Third Plenum, he was also raising a note of caution about the importance of procedural norms and consensus-based decision making in governance. Thus, the reform policies would herald the prospect of greater formality and equality in the application of law and greater inner-Party democracy in the process of creating policy norms, while still enabling the Party / state to retain its monopoly on power over the economy.

Peng's instrumentalist approach to the role of law was evident as well in his assertion that law and jurisprudence were in essence a single science.[15] For Peng, law was to be the authoritative articulation of political, social, and economic policies, sanctioned by the Party and enforced by the state. In Peng's view, the rule of law presented no conflict with the leadership of the Party because the Party determined the content of law.[16] Law was the instrument of rule through which the Party / state articulated its policies and exercised its political authority. In this sense, law was written in lowercase—it was not "Law" as a Diceyan set of overarching normative standards governing behavior of rulers and ruled alike, but rather "law" as edicts enacted in pursuit of policy goals. So too was jurisprudence then the study of enactments ("law"), not the study of norms ("Law"). Thus the science of law (*faxue*, roughly translated as jurisprudence) was not the philosophy of general principles of law familiar to jurists elsewhere, but rather was the study of law as the embodiment of policy—conceived, articulated, and enforced through the Party / state apparatus.[17] By conflating this concept of law with the study of jurisprudence, Peng suggested that law in the PRC was subject only to the policy concerns of the Party / state and need not be held up to scrutiny by reference to external standards.

This approach affected Peng's view on legislative work as well. In Peng's view, the policy foundations for legislation must be finalized before being enshrined in law. On the issue of economic legislation for example, Peng said in 1980,

> Currently reforms of the economic system are being introduced in our country and conditions are constantly changing. Some major reforms are still at an experimental stage and we are still in the process of accumulating experience. At the same time, we lack experience on economic legislation. Therefore, it takes some time to formulate economic laws.[18]

Peng suggested that before matters were ripe (*chengshu*), legislative work should be limited to outlines, drafts, and initial preparation.[19] Detailed laws would take time to enact if the purpose of the law was to articulate final policy decisions.

Nonetheless, Peng's return to the helm of the CPC's law-making agenda saw a number of legislative accomplishments in quick succession. At the Second Session of the Fifth National People's Congress, seven draft laws were announced, including the Joint Venture Law, Criminal Law, Law on Criminal Procedure, laws on organization of local People's Congresses and Governments, election laws for the NPC and local People's Congresses, and organization laws for the People's Courts and the People's Procuracies. The Economic Contract Law was enacted at the Fourth Session of the Fifth National People's Congress in December 1981. In August 1982 a trademark law was issued, signaling the beginning of efforts to build an intellectual property system. In March 1982 the Civil Procedure Law of the PRC was issued, which recognized personal and property rights to an extent not previously acknowledged. Extensive legislation was also directed toward the foreign business sector as statutes were enacted during the early 1980s on joint venture taxation, special economic zones, labor relations, foreign exchange, and other matters.[20] These were important precursors to the revisions to the constitution, which Peng oversaw. In April the constitution was reviewed in expectation that it would be finally ratified at the year's end. Peng's role in the drafting of these laws was exercised through his role in the NPC Standing Committee.[21]

Although Peng's direct involvement in legislative drafting was probably limited as a result of the range of his political responsibilities, he received and responded to regular reports from his NPC secretaries, including Yang Jingyu, Xiang Chunyi, and Qiao Xiaoyang,[22] and is said to have provided extensive comments guiding legislative language, presumably in furtherance of his policy priorities. Peng directed—and on some issues (such as joint ventures, contracts, and state-owned enterprises) personally participated in—investigation work on local conditions that would inform the content of legislation.[23] But his primary responsibility was to ensure that the enacted laws reflected Party policy. Speaking on the so-called Seven Draft Laws (including criminal law and procedure, court and procuracy organization, taxation, and joint ventures), the Civil Procedure Law (draft), and the General Principles of Civil Law (GPCL), for example, Peng provided specific guidance on the policy foundations for these enactments.[24] Peng's role as policy steward for the legislative process was critical not only for those measures such as criminal law and procedure and contract law, where the contours of the policy consensus were driven by familiarity with (if not necessarily full agreement on) local conditions and needs, but also in areas of foreign economic relations where a concrete policy line had not yet fully emerged.[25] In overseeing drafting of the Sino–Foreign Joint Venture Law, the Foreign Economic Contract Law, and the Wholly Foreign-Owned Enterprise Law, Peng is credited with ensuring that these enactments remained consistent with existing provisions on government authority and economic planning.[26] At this early point in his political comeback, Peng remained generally supportive of Deng's reform agenda, which was reaffirmed at the Twelfth National CPC Congress in September.

Zheng-fa *and Organizational Discipline*

If law was to be an instrument of policy, one use to which it would be put was to ensure Party control over the mechanisms and processes of state power. In contrast to the devolution of power to Red Guards and revolutionary committees during the Cultural Revolution, Peng viewed the role of law in the early post-Mao period as a basis for ensuring that the Party / state maintained its monopoly on coercion. Speaking about the Seven Draft Laws, for which he played a key role in either drafting or revising, Peng emphasized the link between effective democracy and the socialist legal system.[27] This was not popular liberal democracy, but rather was to be a disciplined process whereby limited diversity of views within the political elite would be tolerated within specific ideological parameters. In addressing the new Criminal Law in particular, Peng stressed that its main task was to use "criminal sanctions to struggle against all counterrevolutionary and other criminal activities."[28] The law was to "ensure that the personal, democratic and other rights of citizens are not infringed by any person or institution in violation of law."[29] The emphasis here was not on limiting state action, for the Party / state could always enact laws to permit its intrusion into personal affairs of citizens—indeed, Peng's NPC Committee was instrumental in deleting the Four Freedoms (speaking out freely, air views fully, hold great debates, and write big-character posters) from the PRC constitution.[30] Rather, Peng's focus was on reasserting the Party / state's monopoly on coercion. By articulating a doctrinal basis for ensuring that coercive force remained the exclusive province of the Party / state, Peng served the Deng coalition's goals of preventing a return to the use of extrainstitutional coercion that had characterized the Cultural Revolution. Deng and his associates controlled the institutions of the Party / state and sought to use law to protect such control. Peng argued not that law was to serve as a general source of external norms binding the state as well as the society, but rather that law should express the policies of the Party / state and should serve as a mechanism for monopolizing enforcement of normative prescriptions for the economy and society.

Peng's service of Deng Xiaoping's political agenda was also evident in his handling of the prosecution of Lin Biao and Jiang Qing. Peng served as chair of the Centre's leading committee on the Lin and Jiang cases, and according to committee member Liu Fuzhi, he was closely involved in all the committee's work.[31] Speaking to the Politburo Standing Committee, Deng specifically approved Peng's approach to limiting the jurisdiction of the special court to counterrevolutionary crimes of the Lin and Jiang group, and specifically excluding issues of errors within the Party.[32] Peng echoed this theme in his speech to the special court, at once attacking the crimes of the Lin-Jiang group and also sending a message to Cultural Revolution collaborators that they would be spared a full purge in exchange for loyalty to Deng's program.[33] In suggesting a programmatic agenda of learning from the experience of the Cultural Revolution, Peng also served notice of the Deng leadership's views on the role of law. Peng contrasted the errors of illegal, secret, and militant methods of political struggle with the benign attributes of legal, open, and cultured approaches that would implicitly characterize the Deng regime's exercise of political power.[34] Thus, it was not the conduct of political struggle itself but rather the use of extrainstitutional mechanisms that was objectionable. Of course, because Deng's coalition controlled the avenues for legal and open discourse, the outcomes of such discourse could be controlled as well.

With the only permissible venue for political action limited to existing political institutions, the focus shifted in turn to internal organizational discipline, and so Peng renewed his previous attention to the need for local compliance with central Party directives.[35] The Party could change the law, but once the law was formally enacted, Party officials could not violate it openly. In discussing the Criminal Law and Criminal Procedure Law, Peng's references to the need to do things according to law were not necessarily aimed at protecting individual rights, but rather to ensure that the Party's policy dictates were followed. Thus, in presenting revisions to the Criminal Law, Peng noted that criminal sanctions should be aimed at preserving social and economic order. Peng urged that the law should be strictly enforced and that it be applied strictly according to its terms based on the familiar principle of "equality before the law."[36] Similarly, the Criminal Procedure Law provided rules for judicial work while ensuring Party leadership over the work of the courts, procuracy, and public security organs.[37]

The centrality of Party discipline in Peng's views on rebuilding the NPC itself was reminiscent of his work in the 1942 Rectification Campaign at the Party School in Yan'an. Peng focused on attitudes and work style as the bases for ensuring compliance by lower-level officials. In a major speech on NPC work in 1979, Peng emphasized the need for democratic centralism in the course of seeking truth and correcting mistakes.[38] This meant, in effect, that subordinate People's Congresses would be expected to adhere to instructions received from higher levels. In the context of Peng's later efforts to use the NPC Standing Committee as a political platform, much of Peng's speech seems to suggest an effort to bend to his will the Legal System Committee (and perhaps the NPC as a whole). In addition, Peng was laying the groundwork for subsequent challenges to Deng Xiaoping's authority. For although the speech resonated with Deng's slogans (*tifa*) on seeking truth from facts and practice being the sole criterion for truth, the call for democratic centralism also suggested that Deng must listen to voices other than his own.

Peng held that politics and law organs should exercise democratic dictatorship through leadership of the Party.[39] Their duties were to provide investigation and research assistance, organizational work, and secretariat work—in other words, to assist in supporting Party leadership initiatives and to implement those initiatives.[40] Speaking to public security officials in Guangdong in early 1980, Peng emphasized the importance of Party leadership in anticrime campaigns.[41] The behavior of police and other political–legal workers in particular required proper coordination and compliance with regulations on such matters as arrest and detention—regulations that were enacted at the Centre and then handed down for enforcement.[42] Peng sought to strike a balance between requiring adherence to minimal procedural standards (mainly to ensure compliance with higher-level directives) and the discretion to respond to local concerns appropriately. Thus, in a 1980 speech to central-level officials of the Supreme People's Procuracy, the Supreme Court, the Public Security Bureau, and the Ministry of Justice, Peng called for detailed inquiry into the facts of difficult cases and criticized indiscriminate arrests, while also recognizing the need to avoid tying the hands of local cadres and judicial personnel.[43]

Peng expressed a similar theme in a major speech to a symposium of security officials from five major cities (Beijing, Tianjin, Shanghai, Guangzhou, and Wuhan).[44] Focusing yet again on public security matters, Peng noted continued conditions of public dissatisfaction with conditions of public order. After reviewing a series of policy measures to be followed, including organizational reform, the establishment of police academies, relations between the Public Security Bureau and the People's Armed Police, funding issues, youth crime, and administration of the death penalty and special cases, Peng devoted the bulk of the speech to the need to solidify Party leadership over local public security organs. Peng's insistence that prosecutions and criminal convictions be handled according to law and based on proper evidence reflected his long-standing concern with ensuring that the power of local officials was restrained to the service of Party policies.[45] Two years later, the theme was the same, albeit in the context of substantively different issues: in Sichuan, Peng asserted that such issues as rural public security, economic crime, and the relations between Chinese and foreigners required stronger basic-level organizations but should still be subject to rigorous Party leadership and discipline.[46] The importance of addressing local issues through a national system of political–legal workers remained a central component of Peng's proposals for responding to problems of economic crime, declining public order, and other challenges brought on by economic reforms.[47]

Peng's views on the organization of local political–legal organs were summarized in a speech to an expanded meeting of the CPC's Politics and Law Committee in October 1982.[48] Peng called for a system of direct reporting to central and State Council offices by local *zheng-fa* organs (public security bureaux, civil affairs departments, and judicial organs). Noting that the Cultural Revolution had undermined local reporting procedures by requiring that local reporting be reviewed and approved by politics and law small groups (*zheng-fa xiaozu*), Peng called for better unification of thought between Centre and locality, and he urged local organs to follow decisions of the central Secretariat and Politburo Standing Committee. These new approaches were described as doing things according to law, and the procedures were extended as well to the review of Cultural Revolution cases and internal Party investigations. The message here was that the new legal reforms required local subservience to central authority, not only in an attempt to ensure consistency, but also to prevent local abuses and the "settling of accounts."

The theme of local institutions working under the leadership of central departments was also evident in Peng's statements on the role of administrative punishments such as reform and reeducation through labor. Peng argued that petty crime did not require the full weight of the criminal justice sanctioning apparatus, but rather should be handled through administrative initiatives under the authority of local reform-through-labor officials.[49] The activities of these local departments would of course be subject to national regulations that would serve as broad parameters within which local administration could be carried out.[50] Although these views were in part an attempt to balance the conflicting demands of central and local departments in handling the increasing problem of social order, Peng's support for the *laojiao* and *laogai* systems is heavily implicated in the abuses these systems permitted in repressing dissent and depriving criminal defendants of a modicum of due process.

Asserting that the basic task was to serve the socialist economic base, Peng noted that the Open-Door Policy had led to deteriorating public security conditions locally, and he held that the focus of political–legal work should be to strike at economic crimes and crimes against socialist spiritual civilization.[51] Organizationally, Peng directed that political–legal work be intensified at the local level through the neighborhood and security committees, and that political–legal committees be established at the provincial level to oversee local efforts. Although the courts and other judicial organs were also to participate in this effort, the key for Peng at this stage was to establish and strengthen a vertically integrated administrative system for enforcing public order. This was the operational side of the *zheng-fa* paradigm, which was to be extended to civil affairs as well, as Peng reiterated the theme of Party leadership and policy control in resolving civil disputes.[52] The issue was one of building local organizations with the authority to enforce policy imperatives, but subject to sufficient institutional discipline to ensure that such enforcement complied with central Party goals.

Law and the Legitimation of Political Authority

Although his emphasis on instrumentalist and organizational approaches to the role of law was familiar, Peng's approach to political-legal work in the post-Mao era was not merely a repetition of his 1950s efforts, but instead reflected subtle yet important changes of perspective. Peng's expanded responsibilities during the late 1950s and 1960s permitted him a broader appreciation of changing political, social, and economic conditions in China and their consequences for law. Peng's downfall during the Cultural Revolution alerted him to the dangers of political leadership unfettered by institutional restraints. Of course, Peng did not become a libertarian, and in fact, he argued consistently in favor of political orthodoxy. However, his doctrinal views expressed during the post-Mao period reflected the recognition that governance in the PRC required relatively formal and effective institutions and processes of law and political authority. Peng also seemed to appreciate the potential for socialist law to lend legitimacy to the post-Mao regime.

At a national work conference for public security, procuracy, and judicial workers in July 1979, Peng weighed the issue whether law or the Party Committee should be taken as primary and concluded that law was the greater of the two ("*fa da*") because it was the final articulation of Party policy.[53] In a major speech to the Party School in November 1979 (later reprinted in the CPC's theoretical journal *Hongqi*) Peng called for greater systematization in the operation of the legal system.[54] Under the rubric of "all are equal before the law," Peng called for eliminating special privileges. In the same vein, he called for efforts to lend greater stability to the text of legislation, and while supporting Party leadership over the legislative and judicial processes, he argued against direct Party review of judicial decisions on grounds that this would undermine the authority of the courts.

Complementing this approach was Peng's support for efforts to build up local people's representative congresses.[55] Peng's explanation of the newly revised legislation for elections to the NPC and local People's Congresses emphasized the need to expand the number of candidates standing for election and to ensure that the number of candidates exceeded the number of electoral vacancies.[56] Peng reiterated this view in his 1980 report on the work of the NPC Standing Committee, in which he noted the importance of local elections as "an important foundation for democratic centralism. Holding direct elections at the county level enables people to exercise direct control over the county People's Congress."[57] In the context of the larger political issues of Deng Xiaoping's political battles with Cultural Revolution holdovers, the move to hold carefully supervised elections at the local level would also have the effect of removing local officials who were obstructing the Centre's economic reform policies. Peng's support for local-level elections was driven in part by concerns about the decline in CPC prestige and popularity in the aftermath of the Cultural Revolution. And indeed, Peng was publicly identified as one of the central leadership figures with a serious interest in ensuring that local political officials did not obstruct the process.[58] Peng retained influence in this sector of activity even after his formal retirement.[59]

However, Peng's support for local elections did not mean tolerance for unrestricted political diversity. Once formed through the protodemocratic process permitted by the new law, local People's Congresses were still subject to the general requirements of Party leadership and national organs of political authority.[60] In this respect, Peng's work during the post-Mao period was reminiscent of his underground work in Jin Cha Ji during the 1930s and early 1940s.[61] Education and propaganda work were critical:

> To implement the election law properly . . . it is necessary to conduct universal propaganda and education among the cadres and the people on socialist democracy and the legal system and to make good preparations in all fields, including the ideological and organizational fields and including technical and administrative preparations for the elections.[62]

But as Peng's longtime colleague from Jin Cha Ji, Cheng Zihua, noted in his 1981 report on nationwide county-level elections, electoral activities would not be tolerated that practiced ultraindividualism and openly opposed the Four Basic Principles (which included Party leadership and the socialist road).[63]

The early period of Peng Zhen's return to the apex of Chinese politics saw him reengage in the political–legal work that had dominated his career during the 1950s and early 1960s. Attention to legislation was combined with an emphasis on political control over the content and implementation of legislation. Legal institution building was also used to promote political discipline, even as it served as a mechanism for building legitimacy. The role of law was viewed primarily as the formal expression of policy conclusions already reached within the Party's decision-making apparatus. And Peng himself pursued much the same personal career path that had won him such high standing two decades earlier: a functionary whose diligence and command of the politics and law administrative system made him invaluable to top-level patrons. However, Peng's attributes were also threatening, and he was ultimately denied a seat on the Politburo Standing Committee. This served as the basis for a major reorientation in Peng's work and ideas about law, as his "exile" to the NPC Standing Committee resulted in major strengthening of China's legislative institutions. Peng's position as chair of the NPC Standing Committee provided him with both a political interest to promote legislative institutions and processes, and a platform from which to pursue that interest.

New Approaches to Law and Political Authority

The vigorous reforms of 1979–1982, while signaling dramatic reversals of Maoist policies on the economy, also created problems of their own.[64] Although some reforms continued—in April 1983, for example, state enterprise reforms were begun with the policy of remitting taxes instead of direct profits (*li gai shui*)—retrenchment was inevitable, and in June the Sixth National People's Congress announced the curtailing of credit and delayed implementing a number of foreign investment and domestic development projects. In September, the Second Session of Sixth NPC called for strict sanctions for "economic crimes" such as speculation and profiteering, and in October the Second Plenum of the Twelfth CPC Central Committee launched an attack on "spiritual pollution." Clearly the government was grappling with the new challenge of spurring economic growth while ensuring that the resulting entrepreneurial implications remained under control. It was during this period that Peng Zhen was particularly visible in calling for caution and restraint in the area of legislation. Some legislative activity was pursued, although largely in areas dominated by foreign interests. In March 1984, for example, the Fourth Session of the Sixth NPC Standing Committee enacted the PRC's first patent law. In March 1985 a foreign economic contract law was enacted by the Tenth Session of the Sixth NPC Standing Committee.

To a large degree, however, the formal articulation of economic reform policies remained the province of CPC Central Committee documents and departmental regulations rather than formal legislation. Thus, in January 1983 expansion of the new contracting system, particularly in agriculture, was the focus of CPC Document No. 1, rather than legislation.[65] In January 1984 the CPC's Document No. 1 called for expanding rural reforms through land-use contracting and permitted broader autonomy in labor and capital management. In May regulations were issued on a responsibility system for factory managers—regulations made necessary by the NPC's reluctance to enshrine enterprise reform proposals into legislation. In October the Third Plenum of the Twelfth CPC Central Committee endorsed the policy of a "socialist commodity economy" and attacked previous commitments to lifetime employment under the "iron rice bowl." In 1985 policy enactments continued to take precedence over legislation in economic reform activities, as CPC Document No. 1 called for further decollectivization and privatization of agriculture. In April the CPC Central Committee called for further wage and price reform. Even in the foreign investment sector, administrative regulations were predominant—as issuance in 1986 of the all-important "Provisions on Encouragement of Foreign Investment" (often referred to as the "Twenty-Two Articles") was left to the state council.

Although to a certain extent Peng and the NPC Standing Committee had successfully resisted the efforts of the Deng reformists to entrench their policy preferences into formal legislation, this also tended to marginalize the NPC from the policy process. There were exceptions, however. The NPC passed the GPCL in January 1986, and in August the NPC reluctantly endorsed the PRC's first bankruptcy law, although formal enactment was two years away. Foreign business matters remained a dominant component of the NPC agenda: the Wholly Foreign-Owned Enterprise Law was enacted in April 1986. Throughout this period, Peng's approach reflected themes of legislative restraint, more independence for the legislature, and limits to the Party's role in day-to-day administration.

Legislative Restraint

Although his statements on law as a basis for policy enforcement and organizational discipline suggested otherwise, Peng insisted that his was not a simply utilitarian approach. In an "important speech" at the founding session of the China Law Society (*Zhongguo faxue hui*) in 1982,[66] Peng stressed that the law must not be conceived in the abstract as a basis for changing social and economic conditions. Rather, it should proceed from existing conditions of social development and development of the economic base. Peng suggested that in light of China's actual conditions, law should work to protect socialist public ownership and to ensure implementation of the planned economy. This approach was justified by reference to Deng Xiaoping's dictum of the Four Basic Principles,[67] although Peng was in effect using Deng's words against him. By arguing that law should be formulated in response to China's basic conditions and according to the guiding norms of Party leadership, the socialist road, the dictatorship of the proletariat, and the leadership of Marxism–Leninism–Mao Zedong Thought, Peng was questioning whether Deng's reforms and the laws proposed to entrench them satisfied these criteria.

Casting aspersions on the market-oriented policies of reform, Peng suggested that although foreign ideas about law could and should be borrowed to pursue socialist modernization, the borrowing should take place only when it served China's actual conditions. And in an oblique critique of the Academy of Social Sciences, which under economist Ma Hong was then serving as the think tank for Deng's reform policies, Peng suggested that research work was all too often divorced from reality. Peng used this opportunity to argue that even though it had its own legal structure that must be respected, legislation should proceed from reality. In Peng's view, "We cannot simply have a brainstorm and then carelessly enact some law" (*buneng lingji yi dong xiang gao shenme fa jiu caoshuai di gao shenme fa*).[68] In addressing the issue of economic legislation in particular, Peng suggested that important economic laws and regulations to serve the needs of the four modernizations should be enacted only in a "well-planned and gradual manner."[69] Some have suggested that this permitted Peng to delay the enactment of laws with which he disagreed,[70] although Peng's views can also be interpreted as embodying principled resistance to efforts by competing factions to have their policy preferences entrenched through legislation. Peng's support for articulating general principles in advance of specific legislation may well have been an attempt to ensure that by entrenching his policy preferences in general principles, he could influence the content and meaning of subsequently enacted laws and regulations. In addition, Peng's long experience in Party organizational matters would have made him well aware of the practice of competing factions attempting to entrench their views in formal expressions of policy, the form for which had now become law and regulation. Peng would also have been acutely aware that conceptual inconsistencies among laws and regulations, born of policy conflicts among the agencies charged with preparing these enactments, would undermine the effectiveness of the system as a whole.

A noteworthy example of Peng's cautious approach to legislating policy preferences with which he disagreed concerned the Bankruptcy Law.[71] Peng was unhappy with the provisions of the draft statute, and he succeeded in subjecting the draft to a seemingly interminable series of symposiums and conferences. Because of its implications for resolving problems of moribund state enterprises, the Bankruptcy Law came to be linked closely with the fate of the State Enterprise Law, which Peng also opposed. Ultimately, the lobbying of supporters such as Cao Siyuan succeeded in pushing the Bankruptcy Law through the NPC Standing Committee at the end of 1986, although its implementation remained dependent on passage of the State Enterprise Law. The State Enterprise Law was delayed further, ostensibly at the insistence of Peng Zhen, and was not finally passed until April 1988.

Peng's views about the need for caution in legislation were also evident in his discussion of civil law. Although the draft Civil Procedure Law had been seen as a necessary element of judicial reform, the GPCL raised sensitive issues concerning the tension between the conventional (and still dominant) public law paradigm that espoused Party / state leadership of social and economic relations under the rubric of economic law, and an emerging private law discourse that contemplated greater autonomy for civil law relations in the economy and society.[72] The GPCL presented Peng Zhen with a difficult dilemma. Here was precisely the kind of broad statement of principles that Peng had repeatedly said he favored over narrowly drafted topical laws. Yet Peng signaled his disagreement with many of the principles being proposed for the GPCL, especially the very notion that civil relations in society might be arranged independently of the state's regulatory oversight. In a speech on the drafting of the GPCL, Peng urged that legislation must proceed from China's conditions, that a variety of different opinions must be considered, and that civil law was an independent category of law requiring special care.[73] The reference to China's current conditions clearly suggested doubts as to whether the GPCL principles of private property, party autonomy in contracts, and a diminished role for the state were consonant with existing conditions in China. In a sense, Peng saw the GPCL as in conflict with current conditions, whereas the promoters of the law saw it as a necessary step toward a changed future. Peng's reference to considering different opinions was clearly intended to caution supporters of the law that merely because they represented the predominant reformist view did not relieve them of the responsibility to heed opposing views. Finally, Peng's reference to civil law being an independent category of law suggested that the civil law paradigm, embodying increased autonomy for property and contract relations in society, was merely an addition to, rather than a replacement for, the economic law paradigm with its presumptions about state intervention in the economy.

Yet such caution could not go on indefinitely, and Peng was ultimately compelled to push the legislation through, reportedly after having been told by Japanese business officials that their investments in China could not by expanded until China enacted a civil code. Peng's personal intervention in moving the drafting group to resolve its internal differences and move toward completion of the legislation seemed to belie Peng's well-publicized emphasis on the importance of formal legislative processes. Yet Peng was politically astute enough to spread responsibility for the GPCL broadly—in reviewing the drafting process, Peng described in detail the numerous meetings and expert consultations that were required in preparing the draft.[74]

Peng's 1983 speech on implementation of a new constitution revealed starkly his approach to the role of law as a broad statement of general principles.[75] Peng had overseen the 1980 amendment that had deleted the "four big freedoms," but a more wide-ranging revision seemed to be warranted. The decision to revise the constitution yet again came in September 1980, proceeding apace with the preparation of the CPC's Resolution on Party History and in the midst of the final campaign to unseat Hua Guofeng and the remaining Cultural Revolution holdovers. The 1978 Constitution had reflected an uneasy compromise between emergent reformers and those Cultural Revolution appointees who had survived the purge of the Gang of Four, and as such contained many inconsistencies on such matters as class struggle, China's progress toward socialism, and property relations.[76] The proposed revisions were aimed at resolving these differences in favor of a clear commitment to reforming the economic system. Predictably, the scope of the revisions gave rise to policy conflicts over the extent of economic reform, which in turn delayed the process.[77] Peng's preliminary report of April 1982 noted the importance of ensuring that the constitution conformed to the reform policies enacted at the Third Plenum of the Eleventh CPC Central Committee in December 1978, but he went further to argue that the constitution's main purpose was to preserve and develop the socialist system.[78] Although acknowledging the reform discourse that socialist transformation had largely been accomplished and as a result greater attention could be paid to development of productive forces without undue concern about exploitation—indeed, Peng had been associated with this view for nearly twenty-five years—he still held that public ownership should remain the foundation of the economy.

Peng also gave prominence to the influence of the 1954 Constitution that he had helped draft. Of particular importance was the dictum "all are equal before the law," which has been included in the 1954 document and then resuscitated for the 1982 revisions. Although the concept of equality before the law incorporated into the 1982 Constitution admitted the possibility of unequal treatment of citizens through legislated inequality, it did require statutes to be enforced according to their terms.[79] The issue then was not so much the protection of citizens from the state; rather, it was to ensure that the state acted in accordance with set procedures and policies rather than the preferences of individual leaders.

Subject to these qualifications, equality before the law nonetheless signaled important conclusions about the changing character of class struggle and the transition to a rule-based system of governance that would replace the campaign style of rule associated with Mao and the doctrine of permanent revolution. In this regard, the rights of citizens were made dependent on behavior rather than class, and the notion of class struggle itself came to be reconstructed. As Peng himself noted in 1981, the family and class situation of offenders of public order varied, yet the marshaling of institutions of legal coercion against such offenders was still characterized as class struggle.[80] The 1982 campaign against economic crime formalized the notion that economic crime was a matter of class struggle, thus establishing that behavior was the talisman for identifying hostile elements rather than family history or socioeconomic class background.[81] Thus, in contrast to the essentially preemptive approach of the Maoist years, which assumed that certain class backgrounds would inevitably lead to aberrant behavior, the government's punitive apparatus was now reactive. Law was to be directed toward specific conduct, as the class origins of thought had come to be replaced by behavioral manifestations of class as the focus of state coercion.

With the reinterpretation of class struggle, the constitution shifted focus to the role of productive forces rather than the relations of production.[82] This in turn permitted greater emphasis on economic growth policies recognizing private property, material incentives (including intellectual property rights for innovation), and the pursuit of profit. Because the policies of the post-Mao period represented a continuation of sorts of the policies and programs associated with the Eighth Party Congress of 1958,[83] these were reflected in the revised constitution. So too did the thrust of Peng's explanation of the draft draw on his own previously expressed viewpoints. In a statement echoing his views on state building during the early 1950s, Peng noted with regard to the 1982 Constitution, "From head to tail, this draft of the Constitution sets forth one basic principle: Serve the greatest interests of the greatest number of people."[84] With class struggle no longer the primary focus of political concern, the function of law was now to attend to the needs of economic development, while at the same time recognizing the rights and status of members of society on a more or less equal basis, uncomplicated by class difference.

The draft constitution presented in April was not adopted but was instead sent back for further revisions, particularly in the area of economic relations. Peng Zhen's "Explanation" of the subsequent revisions (and what was ultimately to be the final version) noted the role of collective and individual economic sectors in addition to the sector of ownership by the whole people. This was a significant expansion on the previous draft's approach and signaled Peng's begrudging acceptance of the Deng policies on economic diversification.[85] The final version also underscored the importance of the transition from the conditions of class struggle that necessitated a "dictatorship of the proletariat" to conditions of socialism which permitted a "people's democratic dictatorship." Although the struggle against decadent ideas that threatened China's socialist spiritual civilization would continue, the basic philosophy of rule would involve a more inclusive formulation and one which permitted a higher degree of intervention of legislative institutions. Thus, Peng's "Explanation" of the new draft expressly drew on the inspiration of the 1954 Constitution. Peng gave significant emphasis to equality before the law and stressed the need for broader popular education about law and the need for legality in governance.

By the time the revisions to the constitution were nearing completion, Peng realized that his future at the highest reaches of the Party would be limited. Not only did this influence his approach to the NPC and the local People's Congresses, but it also drove him to attempt to limit the influence of the Party on constitutional language. In a speech after the NPC's tentative endorsement of the revised constitution in early 1982, Peng suggested that the revised constitution should be based on opinions from various local People's Congresses, and that whereas debate would be carried out under Party leadership at various levels, the issues under debate in the Politburo Standing Committee were not the only issues for discussion.[86]

Peng's approach to legislative restraint was tied to his belief that law building should be a long-term process requiring not only strong policy consensus but also significant attention to public education.[87] Peng's views on the role of law in articulating final policies were particularly evident in the discussion of economic policy. The mid-1980s saw reformist efforts to accelerate the move away from state planning as the basis for the economy. Peng was less than enthusiastic. Speaking to the Zhejiang Provincial People's Congress Standing Committee, Peng acknowledged that economic restructuring was a basic policy mandated by the constitution, but suggested that in light of the lack of consensus on how to carry out these policies, legislation should proceed slowly.[88] Noting the problems of enforcement of legislation, Peng suggested that before going ahead with legislative initiatives, it was necessary to do research and take account of experiences in order to produce useful laws. To the extent that legislation should be enacted to support economic reforms, Peng suggested that it should also include regulations governing supervision of policy enforcement by Party and administrative organs.[89] Peng was also concerned that legislation not entrench premature decisions about developing a market economy in China. Referring to Marx's "Critique of the Gotha Program," Peng suggested that China's economy was not so well developed as to permit decentralized distribution of commodities; rather, it still required state planning to coordinate relations between state, collective, and individual enterprises.[90] Peng was also prepared to use provisional regulations as stopgap measures pending full legislation and also to devolve significant lawmaking powers to the localities, on the theory that different conditions warranted variations in legislative schemes.[91] Thus, legislation should uphold the Four Basic Principles (including the primacy of socialism), but must recognize that the establishment of socialism was a long-term process, that could be threatened by precipitous action.

Peng's cautious approach to legislative action was motivated not only by his personal policy disagreements but also by a rather fundamental sense of what legislative procedure required. Decrying the past practices of "one-man rule" (the reference was to Lin Biao saying Mao's words were the highest directive, but a clear parallel was drawn to Deng Xiaoping), Peng suggested to a class at the Training Institute for Legislative Cadres that there must first exist a collective consensus before a legal system can be built (*di yi yao kai jiti di er yao you fazhi*).[92] Peng also asserted that having a legal system was not merely having law to follow; it meant doing things according to procedures and building consensus before formalizing Party policy in legal enactments. Although Peng acknowledged that this meant devoting considerable resources to cadre training (not only to build appreciation of the need for consensus but also to drive the consensus itself), he suggested this was a necessary aspect of the long-term effort to build a legal system.[93]

Peng also saw these attributes as essential to building effective compliance with legal rules. Speaking on the NPC Standing Committee's "Decision on Basic-Level Legal Knowledge for Citizens," Peng argued that popularizing legal knowledge was essential to ensuring enforcement of the regime's norms of "all citizens are equal before the law" and all organs and individuals "must respect the law and the Constitution."[94] Peng viewed such popular knowledge as important in permitting citizens to supervise the behavior of Party cadres. In Peng's view, legislation adopted though a formal legal process could be presented more easily as a standard for government and Party behavior.[95] For Peng, the process of legislative enactment was an important contributor to effective enforcement of enacted law.[96] As well, the role of legislative and legal educational activities in forging closer links between the subjects of law and the sources of law were in Peng's view reminiscent of the Yan'an spirit of collaboration, which he saw as an ideal for managing state-society relations.[97]

A New Role for the NPC

The enactment of the 1982 Constitution was a culmination of sorts in Peng's career. However, unlike the experiences of other senior leaders,

Peng's successful handling of his task did not result in further promotion. Indeed, before formal passage of the constitutional revisions, it was clear that Peng would not be elevated to the Politburo Standing Committee. Thus it was not surprising to see the expanded legislative and administrative powers of the Standing Committee provided for in the 1982 Constitution preparing the way for Peng's use of the NPC Standing Committee as a power base.[98] Whereas previously the NPC Standing Committee had mainly served to relay agenda items already decided by the CPC Politburo and to organize full meetings of the NPC, the 1982 Constitution authorized the Standing Committee to enact laws and also to supervise the work of the State Council and other administrative bodies.[99] As others have observed, this led to a significantly expanded role.[100] Although these changes certainly worked to Peng's advantage after his appointment to chair the NPC Standing Committee, they also paralleled Peng's approach to the work of the NPC from the late 1950s.[101]

Although Peng's ideological preferences mandated legislative restraint, Peng's organizational interests as head of the NPC system drove a new perspective on the place of legislative institutions in Chinese politics. Promoting the role and importance of the NPC was a natural result of Peng's appointment as chair of the NPC Standing Committee, as Peng's position gave him a direct interest in promoting the institution of which he was in charge. However, in the process, Peng also strengthened the place of the constitution and the law as foundations for political and organizational arrangements. Through the period of his tenure as chair of the NPC Standing Committee, Peng consistently argued in favor of a stronger role for the NPC and the lower-level People's Congresses. This was linked directly to the constitution, which Peng suggested authorized the NPC to play a greater role in government activities—his call for greater collective decision making was in essence a call of resistance to the political primacy of Deng Xiaoping's narrow policy circle.[102] Peng also suggested that the constitution had increased the powers and authority of the local People's Congresses to enact local laws and regulations and handle economic legislation.[103] In discussing the role of local village committees, Peng acknowledged the importance of Party leadership, but also suggested that the principles of democracy and constitutional authority might permit local organs of governance significant autonomy from Party secretaries.[104] Although subject to general supervision by the NPC Standing Committee, the local People's Congresses also were granted greater autonomy under a principle of noninterference by the NPC Standing Committee.[105]

Peng's NPC responsibilities and interests drove him to promote law and legal knowledge as specialized and newly privileged elements of political discourse. He called on officials and delegates in the NPC system to study law as well as theory so as to understand better the implications of legislative work.[106] He asserted that the NPC Standing Committee must work according to the legal authority given it, even if this caused conflicts with other Party / state organs.[107] In Peng's view, governance should not be the product of the immediate policy preferences of a particular elite group, but rather should reflect a broader consensus within the political leadership as a whole. In many ways, the reforms brought about by the Deng coalition in the early and mid-1980s were experiments to no less a degree than were Mao's experiments in commune building during the late 1950s. And to a large extent the policy preferences of Deng's leadership coalition held no greater a claim to legitimacy than did those of the Maoist radicals two decades earlier—both groups had gained ascendancy for their programs through hardball political infighting supported by military connections. Viewed from this perspective, one that was certainly shared by many in the post-Mao leadership like Peng Zhen, whose revolutionary credentials and experience were arguably as strong as those of Deng Xiaoping, the push to enact laws based on temporary policy preferences would have seemed an inappropriate use of the legislative mechanism. The view that Peng Zhen was obstructing the reform process[108] is probably correct. But although the reasons may have derived from a combination of political and organizational interests, Peng's support for a new degree of independence for the NPC added a new discourse of principled support for the independence of the legislature. This added a new dimension to the dynamic of elite politics and provided an important foundation for further development of the Chinese legal system.[109]

Evolving Views on Party Leadership: Separating Political and Legal Work

Peng's changing responsibilities led him to an evolving view on the primacy of Party leadership. Deng Xiaoping's 1980 speech to the CPC Politburo has set the tone for a gradual reordering of the Party's role in day-to-day administrative affairs,[110] and Peng Zhen took up the theme in the context of constitutional requirements. Peng's long career as a

Party functionary, as well as his consistent view that law should follow Party policy,[111] gave his views on Party compliance with the constitution particular power and legitimacy. Peng did not denounce the importance of Party leadership. Instead, he held that the constitution authorized local political organizations—particularly local neighborhood and village councils—to take a leading role in public affairs.[112] Functions such as resolving disputes, maintaining public order, and making representations to the people's governments on behalf of citizens, which previously had been dominated by local Party secretaries, were to be handled by local popular committees. Although he described the separation of political from social life (*zheng she fenkai*) as necessary to strengthen the relationship between basic-level Party organs and organs of political authority under the rubric of democratic centralism, the clear message of Peng's approach was to diminish the role of the Party in day-to-day administration. This view appeared, for example, in Peng's statements on reform of the factory manager responsibility system in state enterprises, where Peng noted that although the general principle of Party leadership remained sacrosanct, many specific aspects of factory work were beyond the expertise of the Party committee and should be left to the manager's authority.[113]

In Peng's view, the Party's role should remain one of moral and ideological leadership, rather than administrative management.[114] During the Anti-Spiritual Pollution Campaign of 1982–1983, Peng stood with those who called for strict enforcement of socialist orthodoxy in order to prevent the CPC's socialist ideals from being destroyed by an emerging liberalism in intellectual discourse.[115] Law was to play a role here: Peng noted that the core issue of implementation of the PRC constitution was to preserve and develop the socialist system.[116] This meant greater attention to the people's democratic dictatorship (an allusion to the use of coercion to ensure conformity with the traditional socialist ideology); caution regarding market-oriented economic reforms; a more aggressive program of ideological leadership in social life (under the rubric of socialist spiritual civilization); and stronger Party leadership. Thus, Peng called on the constitution for support for his views that modernization not be pursued to the detriment of socialist modernization and spiritual civilization—a view that would hold greater currency in the mid-1990s than when Peng first articulated it in the early 1980s.

Peng's views on the Party's leadership role in ideology were also evident during fall 1986, when he actively participated in attacks on Hu

Yaobang's failure to maintain ideological purity, which led ultimately to Hu's dismissal.[117] Speaking in October 1986, Peng called for stronger Party leadership in building a socialist spiritual civilization, and he made specific reference to the importance of Marxism, Leninism, and Mao Zedong Thought, thus setting the tone for the Anti-Bourgeois Liberalization Campaign that followed.[118] And again, Peng relied on the constitution's entrenchment of the Four Basic Principles as grounds for rebuffing calls for further liberalization.[119] Peng bemoaned the absence of Party leadership over issues of China's socialist civilization, and he argued that the constitution and the legal system should be grounded in principles of socialist democracy subject to the leadership of the working class and the Party. Speaking in March 1987, Peng reiterated these points and noted that Party leadership was crucial to establishing the necessary conditions for the successful operation of socialist democracy and the legal system.[120]

In more concrete areas of work, Peng's approach to Party leadership was closely informed by his political and organizational interests. Although he continued to make reference to the reified discourse of political–legal (*zheng-fa*) work when addressing issues of Party leadership, Peng drew distinctions between political and legal work in practice. Thus, when calling for greater Party attention to major crimes during the anticrime campaign of 1983–1984, Peng carefully separated political dictates (including remarks by Deng Xiaoping) from the ambit of law.[121] The campaign was viewed as a political matter in which Party leadership was needed to ensure consistency in enforcement and in avoiding errors in the treatment and punishment of criminals—issues that were primarily of organization and policy rather than law.[122] After the campaign, Peng continued to treat the issue of Party leadership over the increasingly decentralized public security system as primarily political rather than legal.[123] The training of so-called political–legal cadres was primarily a political matter focusing on the dissemination of centralized administrative and political standards (including social science training), and the work of these cadres was to focus generally on political matters such as resolving disputes and preserving public order.[124] In the context of ongoing anticrime campaigns, Peng called for stricter government administration of expanding market-oriented economic activities in order to combat corruption problems, where the key tasks though were political and organizational, not legal.[125] Peng explained the apparent contradiction by reference to the distinction between long-term efforts to build a legal system and the immediate political tasks of combating crime and economic crime, which were growing to epidemic proportions by 1986.[126] Even as he referred to the role of Party leadership in political–legal work, Peng's repeated references to proceeding on the basis of actual conditions suggested that the time-honored mantra that joined the political and the legal into a single doctrine of *zheng-fa* was itself becoming worn and increasingly inapplicable to describe the development of the legal system.[127] Instead, Party leadership was increasingly being confined in the realm of political and organizational activities, rather than the realm of law.

In the area of institutional relations—particularly where his NPC system was involved—Peng interpreted the role of Party leadership as outside the realm of day-to-day administration. Speaking in 1985 to the Tenth Session of the Sixth NPC Standing Committee and later to the preparatory meeting for the full NPC session in 1986, Peng outlined an approach that separated the spheres of supervisory responsibility among the Party, government, and the judiciary, saying that each of these spheres had its own discipline system and suggesting that none should interfere in the discipline activities of the others.[128] In a speech to responsible officials from the provincial People's Congresses, Peng listed the elements he thought appropriate for Party supervision: (1) thought and work habits; (2) policy; (3) problems of work; (4) morality; and (5) violations of Party discipline. Of particular note is that Peng's list specifically did *not* include supervision over problems of government and administrative discipline.[129] The constitution and the socialist legal system were independent priorities, which, although consistent with the basic norm of Party leadership, would also contribute to improving the Party's work style. By incorporating notions of accountability and the requirements of Party adherence to legal norms, Peng was in essence suggesting that Party leadership might itself be subordinated to the content of the laws that Peng's own NPC Standing Committee was considering. Thus, in the area of legislation, Peng saw Party leadership as critical to the building of long-term principles but not as a basis for direct organizational intrusion or intervention based on parochial policy preferences of the moment.[130]

Peng's changing views on Party leadership complemented his own political interests. In the area of political–legal work, Peng seemed to agree that Party policies should inform the management of short-term campaigns against economic crime and corruption. As the Politburo member responsible for the *zheng-fa* portfolio, Peng was responsible for Party policies in this area and had an interest in their being carried out.

However, on the legislative front, Peng had a considerable political interest in protecting the NPC from the intrusion of immediate policy prerogatives from outside—especially those with which Peng disagreed. Thus, although he continued to extol the role of Party leadership over abstract matters of ideology, he still argued against Party involvement in day-to-day administration.

As he had during the 1950s, after his return to power, Peng expressed the view that the role of law was contingent on current material conditions. During the first decade of the PRC, Peng had noted that changing conditions in Chinese society—notably the suppression of hostile classes and the concomitant decline in the need for class struggle—warranted a greater role for law and notions about legal equality. But he had kept the door open to the use of administrative and extralegal repression should counterrevolutionaries return to threaten the Party's political authority. In the post-Mao period, Peng stood generally in favor of a greater role for law and legal institutions, as these were warranted by changing social conditions, but he also stood ready to dispense with procedural requirements in the face of crisis. Peng's views were informed by his own political imperatives as well. Thus, his approach to legislative restraint was driven in large part by an effort to resist policy initiatives with which he disagreed, while his views on greater independence for the NPC and on changing contours of Party leadership were guided by his organizational responsibilities and interests. Nonetheless, by articulating changing perspectives on legislation, the NPC, and the Party, Peng raised new possibilities for the organization and performance of these institutions that will have a significant impact on the development of the Chinese legal system more broadly.

Peng Zhen, the Senior Statesman: Views on Law as the Basis for Political Reform

By 1986 the institutional relationship between the legislative apparatus and the Party policy system was one of formalized competition. Peng's cautious approach to legislation, although motivated to a significant degree by his disagreement with the content of many reformist policies, was also driven by a concept of law that resisted attempts to entrench immediate policy preferences into formal legislation. Unable to overcome the NPC Standing Committee's resistance, Deng Xiaoping was also unable to ignore the importance of the legislative process, as the legitimacy of his regime had come to depend in part at least on claims to respect the rule of law. The process was compounded by political crises of a different sort as student demonstrations erupted in Shanghai, Beijing, and other cities in December 1986. This saw the removal in early 1987 of Hu Yaobang as Party Secretary at an enlarged meeting of the Central Committee–Politburo and the beginning of a campaign against "bourgeois liberalization." The reformers were not to be denied, however, and in October 1987, the Thirteenth CPC National Congress endorsed further reforms under the conclusion that China had reached the early stages of socialism. In March 1988 the Second Plenum of the Thirteenth CPC Central Committee reiterated the call for a commodity economy.

The Thirteenth CPC Congress also decided that the solution to Deng's problem with his opponents within the regime lay in personnel changes and approved the "retirement from central leading institutions of old comrades who already had accomplished many things" (*nian shi yi gao de lao tongzhi*).[131] Peng Zhen formally retired from his Politburo positions at the Plenum, and his retirement from the NPC was imminent. Nonetheless, Peng continued to speak out actively on political and legal affairs. His was the role of elder statesman, with broad authority to comment on general conditions and policies. Publication of three collections of Peng Zhen's works contributed to the dissemination of his views on law and public affairs.[132] In many ways, Peng's retirement worked to his advantage, as he was able to hold forth on policy matters as a senior statesman without being held responsible for policy failures during the regime's many crises of 1988–1989.

Indeed, Peng had been preparing for this role for some years. In 1986, for example, in a speech to Zhejiang University, he spoke about the debate between Hegel and Feuerback on dialectics and the notion of the "absolute idea" (*juedui guannian*).[133] Peng suggested that success in academic work depended on unity and correctness of ideas. Noting that both the Party charter and the PRC constitution had incorporated the Four Basic Principles, Peng said that among these, Party leadership and socialism were the backbone concepts. But he cautioned that Marxism was not as simple as it might appear to some and must be carefully considered throughout the course of reform and economic restructuring. As he had done many times in the areas of legislation and the need for general referent principles, Peng's Zhejiang speech called for recognition of general principles in the course of reform. This would go well beyond use of the Four Basic Principles as a talisman for reform; rather, it would require continued conceptual reflection of policies and programs. Speeches on spiritual civilization and the Yan'an spirit contained much the same message.[134] Peng returned to the Yan'an theme in 1988, when his preface to a book on the rectification program at Yan'an called for veteran and young cadres to study the Yan'an Party style as a basis for unity in carrying out the reform program.[135] Thus the element of law was added to the recipe for cultivation of Party cadres, which under the Yan'an model had previously been confined to Party policies and ideals. As had previously been the case in Peng's discussions about Party compliance with constitutional requirements, Peng's Party credentials allowed him to include law as a legitimate component of the discourse of Party ideals.

After his retirement, Peng argued that China's changing conditions required changes in the nature of the Party's leadership.[136] The student crisis of spring 1989 provided Peng an important opportunity to speak out on the role of law and the need for reform in the Party. Peng's initial response to the student demonstrations was to call their intentions good but to criticize their methods.[137] Peng's support for the martial law decision seemed rather restrained, as he concluded that "ideas today are relatively chaotic [*luan*]," thus suggesting, in contrast to Deng Xiaoping's assertions, that the movement was not alone as a source of *luan*. Although acknowledging that bourgeois liberal demonstrations would contradict the constitutional requirements of proletarian leadership, his suggestion that everyone must uphold the constitution and the law was a word of caution to the Deng forces that their response must also comply with constitutional and legal procedures.

Although he had provided somewhat tepid support for the declaration of martial law in late May 1989,[138] once the postmortem was under way, Peng returned to familiar themes. Facing the bleak consequences of the military attack in Tiananmen Square, Peng turned his attention to the need for reform within the Party.[139] In what might well have been a summary of Peng's litany of complaints about the direction the Party had taken under Deng's leadership, Peng called for rectification of Party leadership on the bases of (1) the Four Basic Principles—which for Peng Zhen increasingly meant living up to the ideals of socialism, (2) serving the people—a clear reference to the problems of corruption and abuse of power by Party cadres, (3) eliminating factions—a suggestion that collective leadership should be reinstated even to the extent of permitting a degree of dissension from Deng's policies, and (4) establishing the organizational life of the Party—by this, Peng seemed to suggest increased attention to Party discipline through criticism and self-criticism. Peng also called for a program of developing socialist democracy and the legal system, which meant (1) law should replace individuals in governing the country—a not-so-veiled slap at Deng's leadership style, (2) the constitution should be established as the basis for the legal system—here again emphasizing the role of institutional integrity over the policy parochialism of the Deng reformers, (3) upholding the people's democratic dictatorship—a suggestion that the Party needed to move away from its Leninist vanguard leanings and be more responsive to popular concerns, and (4) uphold democratic centralism—again a call for greater consensus-based policy decisions.

Peng also used his position as senior statesman to critique those aspects of the reform policies with which he disagreed. In a speech shortly before his formal retirement, Peng suggested that although some aspects of the reforms in enterprise management could be described as legitimate borrowing of the good experiences from the capitalist West, others were not so benign.[140] Under the guise of explaining the "Mao Zedong Cult" to a group of offspring of senior leaders, Peng cited with approval expressions of disappointment with the corruption in society brought on by the Deng reforms.[141] And even as he referred to Deng's call for socialist self-reflection, Peng went out of his way to criticize the one-man rule associated with Mao (and by implication with Deng as well). Although he agreed that a return to Maoism was untenable, despite pressures for such a move after the Tiananmen massacre and the downfall of the Soviet Union,[142] Peng's critique of Mao's one-man rule and distortions of Marxism were just as applicable to Deng's leadership.[143]

In the aftermath of Tiananmen, Peng renewed his calls for improved Party spirit. Recalling his days as vice president of the Central Party School and director of its Education Department during the Yan'an rectification campaign, Peng was made honorary president of the Society for the Study of the Yan'an Spirit. Speaking at the sixty-ninth anniversary of the founding of the CPC, Peng called for renewed attention to Party building and improving Party work style. His critique of the Deng programs continued: he suggested that "some of our nation's theories have failed to keep pace with practice."[144] At the conference, Peng suggested that the Yan'an spirit should be linked to current issues of Party building, economy, and education—thus calling for greater collective decision making and attention to basic principles in the process of policy making.[145] Peng saw such reforms as essential to the Party's capacity to conduct effectively the political–legal work necessary to eradicate "peaceful evolution."[146]

Peng's suggestions on political reform even went so far as to advocate the intrusion of law into the affairs of the Party. Previously, Peng had consistently held to the view that although the basic norms of behavior between Party, government, and the populace were the same, different discipline systems governed breaches of these norms. However, in a letter to the CPC Central Committee in 1991, Peng called for legal rules publicizing the political financial and work situation of leading cadres and their families.[147] The obvious target of Peng's remarks was the problem of high-level corruption in the Party. The implication of Peng's remarks was that the barriers that separated the Party's internal discipline system from the public law regime should come down. Much as he had when discussing the importance of institutionalized procedures in law making, Peng relied on a legitimation argument, claiming that public legal regulation of the Party would show "the degree of self-confidence of the Communist Party" and would be a "measure for increasing the Party's reputation."[148] Peng viewed corruption as an inevitable result of the economic reforms, but one that was manageable if the Party devoted itself to strengthening political and ideological work.[149] Peng's conclusions that legal reform must extend to the Party were expressed once again from his hospital bed to a delegation of senior leaders that included Jiang Zemin and Li Peng.[150]

Peng's call for Party accountability to legal rules and institutions was nearly unprecedented and set the tone for subsequent efforts in the area of legal reform. However, there was considerable irony in this approach, as it had been voiced in the early 1950s by the then–Politburo politics and law Chair Dong Biwu, who was then shouldered aside by Peng Zhen himself. But times were different, and what was politically and ideologically unacceptable to Peng during the period of socialist transformation had become a necessity forty years later—a socialist legal system in which the Party was subject to rather than exempt from the rules of law.

New Directions for PRC Law: Socialist Legalism

Peng's views on the nature of the Party's ideological leadership but the limits of its administrative intervention were also based on conclusions that the exigent circumstances of the war of liberation and the struggle for power had already passed on, and with this had passed on the need for unfettered Party discretion.[151] In the new period of reform after the 1978 Third Plenum of the Eleventh Central Committee, Peng came to conclude that China could be governed according to formal laws and a constitution that expressed Party policies but that should not arbitrarily be brushed aside with changing political alignments. Peng's commitment to this view seemed resilient even to the crisis of Tiananmen. Peng's speech after the Tiananmen crisis focused on need for the Party to rectify its leadership—implying that the authoritarian discretion of the Party Centre was no longer suited to current conditions.[152] Law and procedural formality were to replace individual officials and arbitrary discretion in governance. Peng's emphasis on the constitution as the basis for law and Party compliance with law offered the possibility that the Party could accept legal regulation without violating the norm of Party leadership under the Four Basic Principles. As Peng had pointed out earlier, the Party's leadership could extend to complying with law.

In emphasizing the role of the people's democratic dictatorship, Peng stressed the transition from dictatorship of the proletariat to democratic dictatorship, a transition that further diminished the role of class and class difference. As Peng had noted previously, the decline of class struggle permitted greater attention to law as the basis for governance. Finally, Peng noted the importance of democratic centralism, a return to the themes of inner-Party democracy that characterized his critiques of Mao's domineering leadership two decades earlier. Peng's speech seemed to suggest that the answer to the dilemmas of Leninist discipline lay in the application of socialist law to a society where class struggle and inequality are seen as gradually but steadily diminishing. Peng's response to the Tiananmen disaster represented something of a culmination of the transition from Leninist discipline to socialist law. With the revolution completed, the needs of governance and economic development required increased attention to institutional and procedural limits on Party power.

This effort was emblematic of the transition in Peng's thinking from emphasizing Leninist discipline to emphasizing the role of socialist legalism. The premises of Leninist discipline were that the vanguard Party must lead China's masses to revolutionary victory and ultimately to socialism. This entailed a struggle against hostile classes that required discipline both within and without the Party and that permitted Party directives to be conceived and enforced through a rather flexible policy process that focused on control of outcomes rather than procedure. With the attainment of victory in the revolution, and through socialist transformation, these needs changed. The decline of hostile classes in particular entailed the possibility of increased equality in the governance of society. This in turn would permit and perhaps mandate greater formality in the process and content of law, and leave less room for arbitrary intervention by the Party.

Peng's appreciation of the interrelationships between the mechanisms for rule and China's changing historical conditions was of long standing. Even as early as his tenure at Jin Cha Ji, Peng had suggested that China's revolutionary conditions were changing and giving way to new socioeconomic circumstances where class enemies were not nearly as important as the need to institutionalize Party rule.[153] During the 1950s, Peng had echoed Liu Shaoqi's conclusions that classes and class struggle were no longer of primary importance and held that governance should follow the constitution and the laws.[154] These views had also been evident in Peng's discussion of the treatment of landlords during the Socialist Education Campaign and his resistance to injecting class-struggle themes into Peking opera before the Cultural Revolution.

By the 1980s, Peng Zhen indicated that China's changing conditions meant the decline of hostile classes and required a reordering of class struggle toward a focus on behavior and away from socioeconomic status. Although this seemed to justify a turn away from the Leninist discipline norms of Party behavior, the alternative that Peng supported reflected a combination of his ideological dispositions and political ambitions. Ideologically, Peng was still wedded to traditional socialist principles and remained apprehensive about economic reform. Thus, in a May 1985 speech explaining the linkage between socialism and the economic reform policies, Peng explained that the socialist legal system was to be deployed to serve the goals of economic restructuring while also ensuring that the economic reforms remained true to socialist principles.[155] Peng's speech to the NPC earlier the same year sounded similar themes.[156] Peng's concerns about economic reform stemmed from the same source as his confidence in a greater role for law, namely the decline of exploitive classes. Just as market-oriented economic reforms might permit the return of exploitation, so too might the continued adherence to a socialist economic program inhibit the return of exploitive classes and thus permit greater equality and formality in the operation of the legal system.

Yet Peng also expressed support for increasingly formal legislation rather than ad hoc Party directives as the source of norms of governance.

As chair of the NPC Standing Committee, Peng had a strong political interest in expanding its legislative functions, and to justify such expansion by reference to China's changing conditions. Thus, in his March 13, 1984, speech to representatives of local People's Congresses, Peng emphasized the transition from revolution to state building and the concomitant need to consolidate the achievements of socialism as grounds for increased reliance on the constitution and the laws.[157] This entailed increased recognition of the independent authority of local legislative organs. Thus Peng's 1984 speech on relations between the NPC Standing Committee and local People's Congresses stressed the importance of noninterference—indicating that although there existed a legal duty of supervision, changing social and economic conditions in China mandated granting greater discretion to local legislative organs.[158] This was in significant contrast with the views in Peng's 1954 speech on Party organization, which stressed the obedience of lower-level organs even if higher levels still must take into account local circumstances.[159] It is not surprising that this change of view satisfied Peng's own institutional and political interests in building a national constituency for the NPC and its Standing Committee, but the argument held a logical integrity of its own.[160]

But what kind of law and legal institutions did Peng have in mind for socialist China? First, Peng viewed law as a mechanism to achieve policy goals of socialism, particularly the centrality of the Party / state and the importance of public ownership in the economy. The Party / state should play a significant role in managing economic life and in guiding the cultural and civil affairs of society. Central to Peng's socialist ideology was the suspicion that if left uncontrolled, Chinese society would quickly devolve into the vicious state of laissez-faire capitalism that seemed to characterize Nationalist China in the 1920s and 1930s. Peng saw socialism as a mechanism that could protect Chinese society from its own worst tendencies. Thus, the Party / state was to ensure that the benefits of economic production were distributed widely, even if somewhat inefficiently. The Party / state should also see to it that whatever limited degree of private economic activity might be required to meet the needs of society did not result in severe disparities in wealth and consumption. And the Party / state was to control the reigns of cultural life in order to ensure that people retained a collective ethic, one that would ensure continued fealty to the state even as its primary goal was social welfare. This was the socialism of the CPC traditionalists in the post-Mao era, and Peng supported it wholeheartedly. Peng's continued reverence for socialist ideology was evident throughout the reform period, as he continually questioned and in some cases obstructed the entrenchment of Deng Xiaoping's quasicapitalist programs. Even while supporting gradual economic reform, Peng held fast to traditional socialist tenets of public property and central economic planning. In contrast to the charismatic socialism associated with Mao Zedong, however, Peng espoused a bureaucratic vision of socialism by which policies and operations would be approved and carried out through a formal system of institutions and procedures.

The legal system that was to pursue these goals embodied three broad characteristics—formalism, generality, and punishment. Peng continued to rely on the punitive force of law, noting on several occasions that law's role as an instrument of policy was to serve as a basis for punishing violators. Peng's emphasis on punishment in the context of anticrime campaigns in the early 1980s[161] continued later in the decade.[162] Law was to be a weapon (*wuqi*) of policy and was to use punishment as the basis for policy enforcement.[163] Peng also argued that law should apply to rulers and ruled alike—the Party itself should do things according to law.[164] Although Peng conceded that the Party should play an important role in the policy-making processes on which specific legislation was based, he held that once enacted, legislation must be enforced generally—clearly indicating that Party officials were not beyond the purview of the law.[165] The goals of generality could be achieved in part by expanded formality in the processes by which law was created and implemented. Peng had noted repeatedly that laws were the formal articulation of policy. Laws were to be written down as formal statements of official norms, and legal institutions were to act according to formally enacted rules. In contrast to the largely secret nature of Party norms and edicts, law was drafted and enacted with formal participation by an increasingly wide circle of actors. These features of formalism, generality, and punishment reflected Peng Zhen's political imperatives. The policy implementer in Peng saw the benefits of effective enforcement that might come from penal approaches to regulation. The politician in Peng saw the advantages of promoting as a mechanism of rule legislation formally enacted through the NPC, with which he was closely associated. The lawgiver in Peng found power in the establishment of a legal system over whose rules he had a large degree of control and that would bind other leaders and institutions.

This combination of formalism, generality, and punishment echoed received principles of legalism.[166] The draconian elements of legalism

TABLE 1

Leninist Discipline and Socialist Legalism Compared

	Leninist Discipline	Socialist Legalism
Origins of law	Party ideology and policy	Party ideology and policy
Expression of rules	Informal Party orders	Formal legislation and regulation
Institutions that enforce rules	Party organs	Judicial and *zheng-fa* organs
Basis for coercion	Class status	Behavior
Enforcement of rules	Rectification, persuasion, education, dictatorship based on informal criteria	Punitive sanctions based on formalized criteria
Application of rules	Separate rules for Party and society	Party and society both subject to law
Staffing	Party cadres	Legally trained specialists

are evident in Peng's calls for harsh punishment of wrongdoers—whether through the *zheng-fa* apparatus or through the application of legislation. Just as Han Feizi and Shang Yang were associated with calls for uniform and clear laws and the elimination of the Confucian deference for feudal and scholarly elites,[167] so too did Peng Zhen call for formal rules that were enforceable as a matter of general application. As well, Peng Zhen's doctrinal pronouncements also reflected a formalistic approach to legal procedure consistent with the received views of legalism, with its emphasis on formal procedures, decisions based on accurate and reliable information, and the keeping of proper formal records.[168] Thus, Peng Zhen's stated views on law and political authority in the PRC represent a doctrine of socialist legalism that may well have established the conceptual parameters for the future development of the Chinese legal system (Table 1).

Summary

Peng Zhen's views on law and governance evolved significantly during the post-Mao era. Although initially Peng resumed a commitment to law as an instrument of Party policy and power that paralleled his work during the 1950s, this approach soon changed. Building on conclusions about changing social and economic conditions in China, and driven by new political realities, Peng oversaw the strengthening of the NPC Standing Committee into a legislative apparatus for the enactment of formal and general rules, rather than the passing of particularistic edicts in furtherance of immediate policy priorities.

And although Peng's continued to support the general imperative of Party leadership, his views on rectifying this leadership became increasingly insistent. Peng viewed the CPC as an all-important source of broad norms, but increasing less as an institution empowered to intervene directly in governmental or economic affairs. Peng saw this approach being entrenched into the PRC constitution, which he repeatedly cited in his efforts to resist what he saw as objectionable features of the reform program. That he was disappointed in the Party's apparent inability to fulfill this role seemed only to strengthen Peng's determination to speak out personally as an elder statesman on the need for socialist principles.

By a fortuitous combination of personal circumstances, ambition, and contemplation, Peng Zhen came to articulate a new vision for the role of law in socialist China that combined the traditions of twentieth-century Chinese socialism with those of pre-Han legalism. Driven in part by Peng's own political aspirations, and consistent in many ways with the prevailing Party policies of the time, the notion of socialist legalism associated with Peng Zhen represents a conceptual foundation from which much of the public law in post-Mao China emerged. Although further evolution and change in the Chinese legal system are inevitable, the legacy of Peng Zhen's views on socialist legalism will continue to exert significant influence.

Conclusion

PENG ZHEN LEFT an indelible imprint on the development of the socialist legal system in China. From his earliest days in the Party underground, to his last years when he advocated replacing Party directives with formal legislation, Peng had a singular impact on the official discourse on law and political authority in China. Peng's activities and viewpoints reflected a combination of attributes and interests that guided his perspectives and policies. His individual talents and abilities were brought to bear in his work as a labor organizer and Party disciplinarian in the earliest years of the Communist Party of China (CPC) and gained him important patrons in the Party leadership—particularly Liu Shaoqi. Later, Peng's successful administrative and organizational work in Jin Cha Ji and Yan'an enabled him to build a career in the elite reaches of the Party. During the 1950s, Peng's responsibilities for political–legal work within the CPC Politburo and his work in the National People's Congress (NPC) Standing Committee allowed him to play a significant role in shaping the Party's legal policy during the first decade of the PRC. Peng's views at the time were emblematic of the generation of veteran revolutionaries whose ideas about law were formed before liberation, when the CPC considered law to be little more than a useful way to express, disseminate, and enforce Party policy.

The transition from revolution to governance brought with it changes in responsibilities and perspective. Although the early years of the PRC saw Peng engaged in vigorous attacks on class enemies, real and perceived, he later became increasingly involved in efforts to lend greater regularity and formality to the dynamics of governance. This process was aided by conclusions about the decline of class struggle and the concomitant need for greater institutionalization of law as a mechanism for the exercise of political authority. Policy conflicts in the late 1950s and 1960s contributed to Peng Zhen's emerging insistence on greater procedural order in governance. Institutional formality was needed not merely for the exercise of rule, but also for the processes of decision making within the elite—a view that was supported by the fact that Peng and his patrons and subordinates dominated the formal institutions of state and Party administration. Peng's downfall at the outset of the Cultural Revolution set the stage for further expansion in Peng's support for formal institutions in the dynamic of governance.

The post-Mao period saw Peng Zhen assigned once again to the realm of politics and law. As with prior periods of legal reform in China, whether during the late Qing, when Shen Jiaben and other officials attempted an ambitious program of law drafting, during the Nationalist period when efforts by constitutionalists such as Song Jiaoren and Zhang Shizhao were thwarted by a regime intent on protecting its political control,[1] or during the 1950s, when the newly established PRC government combined legal institution building with campaigns against political enemies, law reform in the post-Mao era expressed the policy preferences of the ruling elite. Peng Zhen played a central role in this process, and by the end of the 1980s he had articulated a view of socialist legalism that supported a greater role for formal legislation and emphasized procedural regularity as replacement for the subjective and arbitrary Leninist discipline that characterized early periods of revolution and state building.

Through a combination of personal circumstances, ambition, and contemplation, Peng Zhen came to articulate a new vision for the role of law in socialist China. Shunted away from the highest levels of the Party elite, Peng's role as chair of the NPC Standing Committee provided an opportunity to build a political base in the legislature. Peng's work to build the influence of the NPC in the policy process that informs law making in China changed the institutional architecture of law and politics in the PRC. Building on conclusions about changing social and economic conditions in China, and driven by political realities that compelled a new emphasis on the NPC and its legislative functions, Peng's focus shifted from the needs of Leninist discipline to those of socialist legalism. He articulated with almost rigid insistence policy preferences supporting socialist principles of public property and state economic planning. Peng's cautious approach to economic reform and

Notes

INTRODUCTION

1. See, e.g., Keith and Lin, *Law and Justice in China's New Marketplace*; Lubman, *Bird in a Cage*.

2. For further discussion of legal culture and its importance to the operation of China's legal system, see Pitman B. Potter, *Chinese Legal System*.

3. See, e.g., "Xuyan" (Preface), in Tian Jiyun, *Zhongguo gaige kaifang yu minzhu fazhi jianshe*, 3.

4. See, e.g., Peng Zhen, "Guanyu difang ren da changweihui de gongzuo," 389.

5. Wu Fumin, "Zou yifa zhiguo lu"; Zhang Zhiming, *Cong minzhu xin lu dao yifa zhiguo*; "Li Peng on Role of CPC in Rule of Law." Also see Tian Jiyun, *Zhongguo gaige kaifang yu minzhu fazhi jianshe*, esp. 412, for emphasis on the discourse of Party leadership and the centrality of Party policy as the basis for law.

6. See, e.g., Peng Zhen, "Guanyu qige falu cao'an de shuoming," 381; Zhu Liyu, *Peng Zhen minzhu fazhi sixiang yanjiu*, 80, 178.

7. *Dangyuan ganbu falu zhishi duben*, 9–11; *Yifa zhiguo he yide zhiguo jiben fanglue xuexi duben*, 144 ff.

8. "Peng Zhen dies at age 95," *Xinhua* (New China News Agency), April 28, 1997.

9. Portions of the following section derive from Potter, "Peng Zhen: Evolving Views on Party Organization and Law." Additional information appears in the authoritative bibliographical summaries, *Peng Zhen nianpu* and CPC Shanxi Party Committee Historical Research Office, *Peng Zhen shengping dashi nianbiao*. Also see the biography of Peng Zhen in Xue Qingzhao et al., *Di yi dai zhongyang lingdao jiti de xingcheng*, 641–42. Unless otherwise cited, information provided in this section comes from these sources.

10. Most authorities agree that Peng came from a poor peasant family. See CPC Shanxi Party Committee Historical Research Office, *Peng Zhen shengping*

dashi nianbiao, 1. During the Cultural Revolution, however, Red Guard criticisms of Peng claimed that his was a rich peasant background. See, e.g., "Counter-Revolutionary Revisionist P'eng Chen's Towering Crimes of Opposing the Party, Socialism and the Thought of Mao Tse-tung" (June 10, 1967). For the majority view, see Klein and Clark, *Biographical Dictionary of Chinese Communism 1921–1965*, 713. Also see "Peng Zhen: From Disgrace to Rehabilitation."

11. Peng attended First Shanxi Provincial Middle School in Taiyuan and later claimed that this is where he was introduced to Communism. See "Peng Zhen Writes Inscription for Middle School."

12. Hebei CPC Committee Party History Research Office and Hebei Academy of Social Sciences, "Peng Zhen tongzhi zai Hebei de geming huodong."

13. Yang Shutang, "Peng Zhen tongzhi de geming jingshen jiang yongyuan jili women qianjin," 447.

14. Shanxi Provincial History Research Institute, "Renmin xinzhong de lishi fengbei," 525; Shi Dongbing, *Zuichu de kangzheng*, 12; "Dadao lao pai da pantu Peng Zhen," 3. Peng was accused of betraying CPC comrades to the Nationalists during this period.

15. Peng's official biography specifically notes that Peng was released in spring 1935 at the completion of his sentence. See Shanxi Party Committee History Research Office, *Peng Zhen shengping dashi nianbiao*, 7. Official Party histories indicate the release of the "61 Cadres" (including Bo Yibo, Liu Lantao, An Ziwen, and Yang Xianzhen) in April 1936 upon the decision of the North China Bureau with approval of the Party Centre. See Central Party School Party History Research Office, *Yi er jiu yundong shiyao*, 115; *An Ziwen zhuanlue*, 21–22; Tai Huaiji, *Tiandi you zhengqi*. Also see Qiu Shi, *Gongheguo zhongda shijian he juece neimu*, 2:443. These reports contradict previous assertions that Peng was one of the so-called 61 Cadres who gained release from prison by renouncing their Party loyalties at the direction of Liu Shaoqi. See "Selected Edition on Liu Shao-ch'i's Counter-Revolutionary Revisionist Crimes" (May 5, 1969), 8; "Dossier of P'eng Chen," 36; Li Yong, *Wenhua da geming zhong de ming ren zhi yu*, 49; Bing Shanxue, *Zhongnanhai fengyun jilu*, 72 ff.

16. Huang Huoqing et al., "Zhuinian jingai de lao lingdao Peng Zhen tongzhi," 13–15.

17. Li Tien-min, *Liu Shao-Ch'i*, 37.

18. Lin Biao's Cultural Revolution attack on Peng over the Manchurian matter is reprinted in "Lin Piao's Most Significant Speech," in Ebon, *Lin Piao*, 252, 269; see esp. 260. Also see Li Tien-min, *Liu Shao-Ch'i*, 115, n. 4.

19. See, e.g., Peng Zhen, "Zuohao tongyi zhanxian gongzuo."

20. Although Peng did not figure prominently in the final report of the Committee delivered by Deng Xiaoping to the Central People's Government, Peng's experience in Jin Cha Ji must have been a factor. In particular, the emphasis in the Election Law on local representative committees as the electoral base for the national legislature was reminiscent of the Jin Cha Ji electoral system established under Peng Zhen. See Deng Xiaoping, "Guanyu [Zhonghua renmin gongheguo

quan guo renmin daibiao dahui difang ge ji renmin daibiao dahui xuanju fa] cao'an de shuoming." Also see "Yonghu xuanju fa, kaizhan xuanju yundong."

21. For a description of Peng's arrest and subsequent struggle session, see *China Quarterly* 29 (1967): 188.

22. Schoenhals, "Bo Yibo Has an Attitude Problem," 124–27.

23. Schoenhals, "Central Case Examination Group."

24. Seymour, "Document No. 49, Peng Zhen," 194; CPC Shanxi Party Committee Historical Research Office, *Peng Zhen shengping dashi nianbiao*, 38. Also see photographs in *Mianhuai Peng Zhen*, xviii.

25. See Seymour, *Fifth Modernization*, 193–94.

26. "Former Officials Attend Beijing Spring Festival Celebration."

27. Bachman, *Chen Yun and the Chinese Political System*, 81.

28. "Peng Zhen to Head New Legal Commission."

29. Bartke, *Who's Who in the People's Republic of China*, 287–89.

30. *Xinhua yuebao* (New China monthly) 6 (1981): 80. Although Peng was nominally subordinate to Ye Jianying on the committee, Ye's state of semiretirement gave Peng de facto leadership.

31. *Zhongguo fazhi bao*, June 7, 1983.

32. For discussion of Leninism in the context of reforms in China, see Friedman, "Theorizing the Democratization of China's Leninist State."

33. Liu Shaoqi, "On Inner-Party Struggle," 1078–79.

34. On legalism, see generally Hulsewe, *Remnants of Ch'in Law*; Bodde and Morris, *Law in Imperial China*, 25–26; Wing-Tsit Chan, *Source Book in Chinese Philosophy* 251–61; Needham, *Science and Civilization in China*, 204–15.

35. See Domes, *Peng Te-huai*, 72.

36. See Yuan Beijing shiwei jiguan Mao Zedong sixiang hongqi bingduan, *Da yexing jia, da yinmou jia*, 18.

CHAPTER 1

1. Shabad, *China's Changing Map*, 234–35. For more on Shanxi, see Goodman, *King Coal and Secretary Hu*.

2. Shao Ding, "Ji He Long," 115.

3. See generally Ladany, *Law and Legality in China*.

4. Teiwes, *Politics and Purges*, 2nd ed., 223n.

5. Ngapoi Ngawang Jigme, "Everlasting Affection for a Good Teacher and Bosom Friend."

6. See, e.g., "Look, These Dogs in the Water Are Not Dead Yet!", 7. Also see Liu Yong, "Tongdao zhongxin aidai de lao lingdao Peng Zhen tongzhi," 258; Li Yong, *Wenhua da geming zhong de ming ren zhi yu*, 47 ff.

7. In attacking Deng Xiaoping's work on the Secretariat, Mao noted that the work of the Secretariat was actually being done by Peng Zhen. See "Selected Edition on Liu Shao-ch'i's Counter-Revolutionary Revisionist Crimes" (April 22, 1969), 1. Liu Shaoqi was attacked for supporting Peng's abilities (38). Also

see "Dossier of P'eng Chen," 35. Peng's intelligence was also noted by Nikita Khrushchev. Talbot, *Khrushchev Remembers*, 281.

8. Klein and Clark, *Biographical Dictionary of Chinese Communism 1921–1965*, 714.

9. This is a debated issue; various Cultural Revolution critics as well as contemporary intellectuals have maintained that Peng read very little. However, the texts of his speeches are replete with classical references and turns of phrase, and the secondary Chinese literature on Peng suggests that at the very least, Peng had intellectual aspirations even if these did not rise to the level of academic scholarship. See generally Shi Dongbing, *Zuichu de kangzheng*.

10. You Lin, "Xuexi Makesi zhuyi de dianfan," 210 ff. Peng reportedly criticized the publication of his own selected works on the basis that older work would be taken as theoretical guidance, even though it had little application to China's current conditions. Gu Anrang, Yang Jingyu, and Song Dahan, "Shou yi zong sheng de jiaohui," 220, 229.

11. Zhang Wenjian, "Xuexi Peng Zhen tongzhi qinfen gongzuo de jingshen," 356.

12. Zhou Weizhi, "Jin Cha Ji bianqu kang Ri genju di wen yi gongzuo huigu," 57–60.

13. See, e.g., "Counter-Revolutionary Revisionist P'eng Chen's Towering Crimes," 24.

14. Cheek, "Honorable Vocation," 246.

15. "Down with Ho Lung," 23.

16. See, e.g., "Peng Zhen deng guizu laoye zai xiangshan." Also see "Counter-Revolutionary Revisionist P'eng Chen's Towering Crimes," 33 ff. Peng's continued affection for opulence has been alleged more recently, in the context of the corruption trial of Chen Xitong. Shao Chongzhu, *Zhong gong fan tan da an zhong an*.

17. CPC Central Party School, *Yi er jiu yundong shiyao*, 111. Liu's report appears as "Suqing guanmen zhuyi yu maoxian zhuyi," in CPC Beijing Party Committee Party History Materials Compilation Committee, *Yi er jiu yundong shiyao*, 66–74, and in China Modern Revolutionary History Materials Series, *Yi er jiu yundong ziliao*, 1–12. For further discussion, see Feng Yi, *Liu Shaoqi geming shijian he sixiang yanjiu*, 87–90. For a chronology of the December 9th Movement, see CPC Beijing Party Committee Party History Materials Compilation Committee, *Yi er jiu yundong shiyao*, 448–89. English-language sources on the December 9th Movement include Israel, *Student Nationalism in China*; Israel and Klein, *Rebels and Bureaucrats*; Freyn, *Prelude to War*.

18. See reminiscence of Zhang Youyu (a noted constitutional law scholar, who served under Liu Shaoqi in the North China Bureau and later as Peng Zhen's deputy in the Beijing CPC Committee during the early 1960s) in Chen Shaochou, *Liu Shaoqi zai bai qu*, 140. For more on Zhang Youyu, see Zhang Youyu, *Zhang Youyu xueshu lunzhu zixuan ji*.

19. Li Xuefeng, "Yi jiu san liu nian yi yue dao yi jiu san qi nian yi yue Zhonggong Beiping dang zuzhi yiqi huodong qingkuang."

20. Chen Shaochou, *Liu Shaoqi zai bai qu*, 179.

21. *Yan'an zhongyang dangxiao de zhengfeng xuexi*, i.

22. Peng Zhen, "Ling hui er shi er ge wenjian de jingshen yu shijian," 32.

23. Peng Zhen, "Ling hui er shi er ge wenjian de jingshen yu shijian," 31.

24. Faligot and Kauffer, *Chinese Secret Service*, 165.

25. Peng Zhen, "Sixiang fangfa wenti."

26. Ladany, *Law and Legality in China*, 63.

27. Peng Zhen, "Guanyu zhenya fangeming he chengzhi fangeming tiaoli wenti de baogao."

28. "Beijing shizhang Peng Zhen san yue ba ri zai zhengwuyuan huiyi shang de baogao," 63.

29. Peng Zhen, "Dangqian zhengfa gongzuo de jige wenti," 219.

30. Peng Zhen, "Zai gongan gongzuo gaige huiyi yubei huiyi shang de jianghua," 341, 367.

31. *An Ziwen zhuanlue*, 37–38.

32. "Exposing the Towering Crimes of Counter-Revolutionary Revisionist Li Ch'i."

33. Peng's record in Jin Cha Ji supported political networks not only in Shanxi but in Hebei as well. See, e.g., "Peng Zhen inscribes name for Hebei Power Plant."

34. Nie Rongzhen continually supported Peng even after Peng was dismissed from his posts in June 1966, affirming Mao's conclusions that during the 1950s and early 1960s Peng was actually doing the work of the Party Secretariat even though Deng Xiaoping was nominally the General Secretary. See "Selected Edition on Liu Shao-ch'i's Counter-Revolutionary Revisionist Crimes" (April 22, 1969), 1.

35. See, e.g., "Zhongyang junwei guanyu muqian xingshi he renwu de zhishi," 283.

36. Nie Rongzhen recalled that Peng was in charge of the anti-Japanese war effort in Jin Cha Ji. Nie Rongzhen, *Nie Rongzhen huiyilu*, 338. However, at the time, this was primarily an underground effort centered on Party organizing, and by 1940–1941, when the "hundred regiment offensive" and the "three alls campaign" entailed more direct military engagement, Peng was increasingly involved with central Party matters in Yan'an. Nie Rongzhen, *Nie Rongzhen huiyilu*, 438; Hartford, "Step by Step," 90–105; CPC Shanxi Party Committee Historical Research Office, *Peng Zhen shengping dashi nianbiao*, 11–12.

37. Shan Siyi, *Zai jiefang zhanzheng zhong fengfu fazhan*, 22–23; Zheng Xiaofeng and Shu Ling, *Tao Zhu zhuan*, 188. In hindsight, Peng's thinking may have been correct—the failure to build underground cells in the Manchurian cities led to appalling losses once decisions were made to take urban centers such as Changchun. See generally Zhang Zhenglong, *Xue bai xue hong*.

38. See Li Ligong, "Peng lao yongyuan huo zai women xinzhong."

39. See "Jin Cha Ji kang Ri genjudi dang, zheng, jun, qun zuzhi xulie."

40. Liu Yong, "Tongdao zhongxin aidai de lao lingdao Peng Zhen tongzhi," 258.

41. Wei Li and Pye, "Ubiquitous Role of the Mishu in Chinese Politics," 934.

42. Franz, *Deng Xiaoping*, 184.

43. MacFarquhar, *Origins of the Cultural Revolution*, 1, 204, citing *Zhengfa hongqi* (Political–Legal Red Flag), October 17, 1967: 5.

44. Red Guard criticisms of the Chang Guan Lou Incident include "Events Surrounding the 'Ch'angkuanlou' Counterrevolutionary Incident"; "Thoroughly Disclosing the Inside Story of Chang Guan Lou Counterrevolutionary Incident"; "Big Exposure of a Conspiracy to Usurp the Party and State Leadership." Also see Lieberthal, *Research Guide*, 176–77.

45. Lieberthal credits Xiao Jia with writing the report (*Research Guide*, 177), although Deng Tuo no doubt played a significant role. The report was allegedly delivered to Peng's deputy on the Beijing Party Committee, Zheng Tianxiang. *Guangming ribao*, August 9, 1967: 3. Zheng later became president of China's Supreme People's Court.

46. Lieberthal, *Research Guide*, 177. Also see Cheek, "Deng Tuo: A Chinese Leninist Approach to Journalism," 105.

47. Bo Yibo, *Ruogan zhong da juece yu shijian de huigu*, 1026.

48. Goodman, *Deng Xiaoping and the Chinese Revolution*, 66–67.

49. Teiwes, *Politics and Purges*, 2nd ed., xxxvii.

50. "Zai tan zhenli you meiyou jiejixing." Also see "Counter-Revolutionary Revisionist P'eng Chen's Towering Crimes." 2.

51. See generally MacFarquhar, Cheek, and Wu, *Secret Speeches of Chairman Mao*, 304–5, 338–39; Schram, *Political Thought of Mao Tse-tung*, 307, 313.

52. See generally MacFarquhar, Cheek, and Wu, *Secret Speeches of Chairman Mao*, 278–86, 320–24.

53. See generally Baum and Teiwes, *Ssu-ch'ing*.

54. The First Ten Points are included as app. B in Baum and Teiwes, *Ssu-ch'ing*, 58.

55. The Latter Ten Points are included as app. C in Baum and Teiwes, *Ssu-ch'ing*, 72. Peng Zhen is widely credited as the author of the Latter Ten Points. Solomon, *Mao's Revolution and the Chinese Political Culture*, 435; Ahn, *Chinese Politics and the Cultural Revolution*, 62.

56. Art. 7, "First Ten Points," and art. 2, para. 4, "Latter Ten Points," in Baum and Teiwes, *Ssu-ch'ing*.

57. Baum and Teiwes, *Ssu-ch'ing*, 29 ff.

58. See generally Lee, *Politics of the Chinese Cultural Revolution*; Ahn, *Chinese Politics and the Cultural Revolution*; Dittmer, *Liu Shao-ch'i and the Chinese Cultural Revolution*.

59. Qiu Shi, *Gongheguo zhongda shijian he juece shilu*, 575–76. Also see Liu Shaoqi, "On Inner-Party Struggle" and "Training of a Communist Party Member"; Dittmer, *Liu Shao-ch'i and the Chinese Cultural Revolution*, 116–18.

60. On this point, see Dittmer, *Liu Shao-ch'i and the Chinese Cultural Revolution*. Also see Huang Zheng, "Injustice Done to Liu Shaoqi."

61. For discussion of Peng's role in transforming the NPC Standing Committee, see Tanner, "Organizations and Politics in China's Post-Mao Law-Making System," 72–76.

62. Peng Zhen, "Jiaqiang minzhu yu fazhi jianshe, Jiaqiang renda changweihui gongzuo," 330, as cited in Tanner, "Bureaucratic and Subcommittee Development in the National People's Congress," 15.

63. Nie Rongzhen, *Nie Rongzhen huiyilu*, 338.

64. Peng Zhen, "Zhonggong zhongyang beifang fen ju guanyu Jin Cha Ji bianqu muqian shizheng gangling," 210–14. For discussion of the drafting process, see Nie Rongzhen, *Nie Rongzhen huiyilu*, 414–18.

65. Nie Rongzhen, *Nie Rongzhen huiyilu*, 387, and Nie Rongzhen, *Kang ri mofan genju di—Jin Cha Ji bianqu*; Beijing Military Region, "Outstanding Contributions and Shining Glory." During the Japanese mopping-up campaigns of early 1940, Peng Zhen, Nie Rongzhen, Lu Zhengcao, and Cheng Zihua were directed by the Party Centre to share their experiences in behind-the-lines work and Party building from Wutai and central Hebei (*Jizhong*) with the Centre, the North China Bureau, and other regions. "Zhongyang junwei guanyu muqian xingshi he renwu de zhishi," 286. Jin Cha Ji policies on self-defense corps and youth brigades were used as models for the development of similar organizations in other border areas. "Zhongyang geming junshi weiyuanhui guanyu kang-Ri genjudi junshi jianshe de zhishi," 216, 221, 226. Also see Hartford, "Step by Step," 61, and "Repression and Communist Success," 94. The lessons of the Jin Cha Ji model are summarized in the "Conclusion" of Beijing Military Region Jin Cha Ji war history compilation group, *Jin Cha Ji junqu kang Ri zhanzheng shi*, 567–80.

66. "Zhongyang dangxiao jihua." This work drew directly on Peng's previous experience as director of the North China Bureau's Party School. See CPC Shanxi Party Committee Historical Research Office, *Peng Zhen shengping dashi nianbiao*, 10.

67. One week before the First NPC session that would approve the 1954 Constitution, the vice chair of the Constitution Drafting Committee, Dong Biwu, asked Peng Zhen and Luo Ruiqing for leave to retreat to Beidaihe and said everything was to be in Peng's hands. *Dong Biwu nianpu*, 440. From the time the Constitution Drafting Committee was formed in January 1953 through to the Constitution's enactment, Dong was in constant contact with Peng Zhen, whose associate An Ziwen was also a vice chair of the drafting committee, thus providing Peng additional contacts with the process. *Dong Biwu nianpu*, 417–42.

68. See, e.g., Peng Zhen, "Gongmin zai falu mianqian ren ren pingdeng."

69. Peng Zhen, "Zai di liu ci quanguo gongan huiyi shang de jianghua."

70. The principles are as follows: (1) Uphold the Socialist Road; (2) Uphold Proletarian Dictatorship; (3) Uphold the Leadership of the Party; and (4) Uphold Marxism, Leninism, Mao Zedong Thought. See Deng Xiaoping, "Jianchi sixiang jiben yuanze," 144. Also see Deng Liqun, "Meiyou gongchandang lingdao jiu meiyou shehuizhuyi xiandaihua jianshe."

71. Peng Zhen, "Fazhan shehui zhuyi minzhu, jianquan shehui zhuyi fazhi," 6.

72. "Quanguo zhengfa gongzuo huiyi zai Beijing juxing."

73. Peng Zhen, "Guanyu shehuizhuyi fazhi de jige wenti," 7.

74. Peng Zhen, "Guanyu shehuizhuyi fazhi de jige wenti," 7.

75. Art. 126, Constitution of the PRC (1982).

76. For discussion of the approval role of the Party Secretariat, see Peng Zhen, "Shiyi renmin zhijie canjia guojia guanli de yizhong zhongyao xingshi," 33.

77. Weber, *Economy and Society*, 442.

78. Peng Zhen, "Guanyu zhenya fangeming he chengzhi fangeming tiaoli wenti de baogao," in which Peng notes that the regulations on counterrevolutionaries were necessary to provide a "legal weapon" for use in suppressing counterrevolutionaries, to provide "standards for the measurement of penalties in adjudicating counter-revolutionary crimes," and "to overcome leftist and rightist tendencies" in the campaign. Also see Peng Zhen, "Guanyu Zhonghua renmin gongheguo chengzhi tanwu tiaoli cao'an de shuoming," in which Peng notes that the *san fan/wu fan* campaign had been conducted under the leadership of the Party and that the regulations were part of this effort to "punish corrupt elements," to "consolidate the victories of the *san fan* and *wu fan* campaigns," and to "wage continued struggle against corruption and theft."

79. Peng Zhen, "Quanguo ren da changweihui jiguan yao wei lifa gongzuo fuwu," in which Peng emphasizes "the leadership of Mao Zedong and the repeated discussions within the Party" as the basis upon which the drafting of the constitution proceeded, and emphasizes that law "represents the will of the ruling class" and should "suit the needs of the Chinese people" (261).

80. See, e.g., Peng Zhen, "Zai quanguo jiancha yewu huiyi shang de baogao."

81. "Peng Zhen tongzhi xiang canjia quanguo gong, jian, fa youguan huiyi de tongzhi zuo zhongyao jianghua," 28.

82. Peng Zhen, "Guanyu xing fa cao'an he xingshi susong fa cao'an de shuoming" and "Guanyu qige falu cao'an de shuoming."

83. "Peng Zhen fuweiyuanzhang zuo ren da changweihui gongzuo baogao he guanyu jige falu cao'an de shuoming." Also see Peng Zhen, "Report on the Work of the Standing Committee of the National People's Congress of the PRC," 98.

84. Preamble and arts. 6, 7, and 25 of the Constitution of the PRC (1982).

85. Peng Zhen, "Zai di liu jie quanguo renmin daibiao dahui di yi ci huiyi shang de jianghua."

86. Sen Lin, "China's Decentralization and Provincial Economic Legislation," 102 ff.

87. See "Resolution on Law Interpretation."

CHAPTER 2

1. See generally Israel and Klein, *Rebels and Bureaucrats*; Israel, *Student Nationalism in China*, 112–56; Freyn, *Prelude to War*. Chinese source materials include the following: Pu Yuhuo and Xu Shuangmi, *Dang de bai qu douzheng shihua*; CPC Central Party School Party History Research Office, *Yi er jiu yundong shiyao*, 109–31; China Modern Revolutionary History Materials Series, *Yi er jiu yundong*

ziliao; Sun Sibai, *Beijing daxue yi er jiu yundong huiyi lu*; *Zhongguo geming shi gangyao*; CPC Beijing Party Committee Party History Materials Compilation Committee, *Yi er jiu yundong shiyao*. Also see Chen Shaochou, *Liu Shaoqi zai baiqu*.

2. Hartford, "Fits and Starts," 150.

3. See Gai Jun, *Baiqu douzheng shi*, 191.

4. Gai Jun, *Baiqu douzheng shi*. Also see Li Tien-min, *Liu Shao-Ch'i*, 35–38.

5. For a text of the directive, see "Zhongguo Su-wei-ai zhongyang zhengfu, Zhongguo gongchandang zhongyang weiyuanhui wei kang ri qiu guo gao quanti tongbao shu."

6. See comments of Huang Hua to the effect that ties between the students and the North China Bureau were insufficiently routinized (*bu gou jingchang*) and inadequate (*you lianxi bu shang*), in Sun Sibai, *Beijing daxue yi er jiu yundong huiyi lu*, 22. A further indication of the CPC's distance from the movement was the December 13, 1935, editorial in Tianjin's *Da gong bao* criticizing the movement (40).

7. Hartford, "Fits and Starts," 162–65; Li Tien-min, *Liu Shao-ch'i*, 63.

8. Freyn, *Prelude to War*, 58–60.

9. See, e.g., "Zhongyang gei beifang ju ji Hebei shengwei de zhishi xing," 66, where the discussion focuses on whether the CPC Western Suburbs Committee (*xijiao qu wei*) or the Hebei Provincial Committee should lead liaison work with the students.

10. Freyn, *Prelude to War*, 59.

11. Gai Jun, *Baiqu douzheng shi*, 222.

12. CPC Central Party School Party History Research Office, *Yi er jiu yundong shiyao*, 116; Yao Yilin, "Yi er jiu yundong huiyi," 328.

13. Pu Yuhuo and Xu Shuangmi, *Dang de bai qu douzheng shihua*, 118.

14. Chen Shaochou, *Liu Shaoqi zai bai qu*, 140.

15. Sun Sibai, *Beijing daxue yi er jiu yundong huiyi lu*, 29.

16. See generally Liu Shaoqi, "On Open and Secret Work."

17. See, e.g., "Zhongyang gei beifang ju ji Hebei shengwei de zhishi xing"; Luo Fu (Zhang Wentian), "Bai qu dang muqian de zhongxin renwu."

18. CPC Central Party School Party History Research Office, *Yi er jiu yundong shiyao*, 111; CPC Beijing Party Committee Party History Materials Compilation Committee, *Yi er jiu yundong*, 10; Pu Yuhuo and Xu Shuangmi, *Dang de bai qu douzheng shihua*, 124. Peng's charge of "capitulationism" (*touxiang zhuyi*) is reported in Shanxi Party Committee History Research Office, *Peng Zhen shengping dashi nianbiao*, 7.

19. Israel and Klein, *Rebels and Bureaucrats*, 111–12.

20. CPC Central Party School Party History Research Office, *Yi er jiu yundong shiyao*, 115–16; Israel, *Student Nationalism in China*, 147–49.

21. CPC Central Party School Party History Research Office, *Yi er jiu yundong shiyao*, 115–16; Israel, *Student Nationalism in China*, 147–49. Also see Israel and Klein, *Rebels and Bureaucrats*, 117–19. An Ziwen also played an important role in facilitating CPC control over the National Liberation Vanguard of China. See *An Ziwen zhuanlue*, 23.

22. Huang Huoqing et al., "Zhuinian jingai de lao lingdao Peng Zhen tongzhi," 15.

23. CPC Central Party School Party History Research Office, *Yi er jiu yundong shiyao*, 116; Li Xuefeng, "Yi jiu san liu nian yi yue dao yi jiu san qi nian yi yue Zhonggong Beiping dang zuzhi yiqi huodong qingkuang."

24. Li Baohua, "Yi jiu san liu nian si yue dao shier yue Zhonggong Beiping shiwei de zuzhi jiankuang."

25. See, e.g., "Zhongyang gei beifang ju ji Hebei shengwei de zhishi xing."

26. Luo Fu (Zhang Wentian), "Bai qu dang muqian de zhongxin renwu." Luo Fu (Zhang Wentian) was also more easily disposed toward permitting social groups to exist and operate free of CPC influence—critiquing, in an implied manner, the effort to bring all patriotic groups under CPC control. Luo Fu (Zhang Wentian), "Bai qu dang muqian de zhongxin renwu," 239–41.

27. Li Xuefeng, "Yi jiu san liu nian yi yue dao yi jiu san qi nian yi yue Zhonggong Beiping dang zuzhi yiqi huodong qingkuang."

28. Zhao Jin, "Peng Zhen tongzhi qi qi shibian qian zai Beijing," 330.

29. Israel and Klein, *Rebels and Bureaucrats*, 129.

30. Li Baohua, "Yi jiu san liu nian si yue dao shier yue zhonggong Beiping shiwei de zuzhi jiankuang."

31. Israel and Klein, *Rebels and Bureaucrats*, 129.

32. *Zhongguo geming shi gangyao*, 200–201.

33. Luo Fu (Zhang Wentian), "Bai qu dang muqian de zhongxin renwu," 231.

34. Gai Jun, *Baiqu douzheng shi*, 227–28.

35. Gai Jun, *Baiqu douzheng shi*, 228–29.

36. Gai Jun, *Baiqu douzheng shi*, 229. Also see Shanxi Party Committee History Research Office, *Peng Zhen shengping dashi nianbiao*, 8.

37. Ren Dongyun, *Gongheguo zhuxi de rong yu ru*, 177.

38. Ch'en, "Communist Movement 1927–1937," 219.

39. CPC Shanxi Party Committee Historical Research Office, *Peng Zhen shengping dashi nianbiao*, 8.

40. Qiu Zhizhuo and Lian Gangsheng, *Liu Shaoqi de jiaoyin*, frontispiece.

41. For a masterful general history of Jin Cha Ji, see Hartford, "Step by Step." Also see Hartford, "Repression and Communist Success."

42. Liu Shaoqi, "Armed Forces Persisting in the War of Resistance Against Japan," 70 ff.

43. The CPC's policies for resisting Japan were set forth in the "Ten-Point Program" proposed at the Lochuan conference in 1937. See Mao Zedong, "For the Mobilization of All the Nation's Forces for Victory in the War of Resistance."

44. See generally *Jin Cha Ji kang Ri genjudi*, 6–14; Liu Lantao, "Jin Cha Ji bianqu dang zuzhi zai zhandou zhong cheng chang zhuang da," 83, 84; Nie Rongzhen, *Nie Rongzhen huiyilu*, 337; Chen Lian, *Kang ri genju di fazhan shilue*, 88; Lu Xiangtou, *Liu Shaoqi he ta de shiye*, 236.

45. "Nie Rongzhen gongbu Zhu De Peng Dehuai guanyu chengli Jin Cha Ji junqu de mingling"; "Zhu De Peng Dehuai, Ren Bishi guanyu Jin Cha Ji junqu jiben renwu he gongzuo fangzhen de zhishi."

46. *Jin Cha Ji kang Ri genjudi*, 3:15–17.

47. "Jin Cha Ji bianqu jun zheng min dibiao dahui tongdian." Also see Johnson, *Peasant Nationalism and Communist Power*, 100.

48. *Jin Cha Ji kang Ri genjudi*, 3:22–25; Beijing Military Region Jin Cha Ji war history compilation group, *Jin Cha Ji junqu kang Ri zhanzheng shi*, 24–27. Liu Shaoqi had also urged creation of law courts with popularly elected judges. Liu Shaoqi, "Various Questions Concerning Fundamental Policies in Anti-Japanese Guerrilla Warfare," 43.

49. *Jin Cha Ji kang Ri genjudi*, 3:28. Most of these measures were based on specific instructions from the Centre. See, e.g., "Guanyu Jin Cha Ji bianqu huobi zhengce de zhishi."

50. For texts of these and other regulations, see Han Yanlong and Chang Zhaoru, *Zhongguo xin minzhuzhuyi geming shiqi genju di fazhi wenxian xuanbian*. Also see Jin Cha Ji Bianqu Xingzheng Weiyuanhui, *Xianxing faling huiji*. For general work on laws and regulations in Jin Chi Ji and other border areas, see Lan Quanpu, *Jiefangqu fagui gaiyao*. Also see Hartford, "Step by Step." Among the measures enacted to consolidate CPC authority were the "Provisional organizational regulations for various levels of counties, districts and villages"; the "Provisional organizational regulations for representational meetings" (*canyi hui*); and the "Provisional election regulations," in which the three-thirds system of reserving seats for CPC and allied organizations was formalized. See "Jin Cha Ji bianqu xingzheng weiyuanhui guanyu shengli wancheng ge ji xuanze de zhishi xing."

51. "Zhongyang guanyu beifang ju lingdao renyuan fengong de jueding." Also see *Jin Cha Ji kang Ri genjudi*, 3:27. There appears to have been some uncertainty as to how long Peng was to remain in Jin Cha Ji. For example, Mao Zedong dispatched a special telegram to Peng Dehuai at the end of July 1938 approving Peng's continued residence in Jin Cha Ji and his work with the provincial CPC Committee. "Mao Zedong, Wang Jiaxiang guanyu He Long, Guan Xiangying, lu bu qu Jizhong he Peng Zhen deng gongzuo anpai wenti fu Peng Dehuai dian."

52. Peng Zhen, "Zai zhonggong Ji-Yu-Jin sheng wei huodong fenzi huiyi de jianghua."

53. Ren Dongyun, *Gongheguo zhuxi de rong yu ru*, 12; Qiu Zhizhuo and Lian Gangsheng, *Liu Shaoqi de jiaoyin*, 264.

54. "Guanyu gonggu yu kuoda Jin Cha Ji genjudi de zhishi." These aspects of Peng's instructions closely followed Liu Shaoqi's views on establishing anti-Japanese base areas. See Liu Shaoqi, "Various Questions Concerning Fundamental Policies in Anti-Japanese Guerrilla Warfare," 35–37.

55. "Guanyu pingyuan youji zhan de zhishi," 505–6.

56. Guo Simin and Tian Yu, *Wo yan zhong de Liu Shaoqi*, 52.

57. "Dadao lao pai da pantu Peng Zhen," 6–7.

58. Peng Zhen, "Zai zhonggong Ji-Yu-Jin sheng wei huodong fenzi huiyi de jianghua."

59. Nie Rongzhen, *Nie Rongzhen huiyilu*, 390–91, in which is discussed the

battles of Ying She Kui and Huang Shi Ling in 1938 where the 120th Army put up resistance to a Japanese offensive that threatened the heart of Jin Cha Ji. Peng Zhen was involved in conferences with He Long, Guan Xiangying, Nie Rongzhen, and Yang Chengwu on resistance plans. Also see discussion of Japanese mopping-up campaigns in central Hebei in Qiu Zhizhuo and Lian Gangsheng, *Liu Shaoqi de jiaoyin*, 234.

60. The importance of building up mass organizations to resist Japan and increase the CPC's influence had been emphasized in Mao Zedong's "Problems of Strategy in Guerrilla War Against Japan," 98–99. Also see Liu Shaoqi, "Some Basic Principles for Organizing the Masses."

61. See, e.g., Nie Rongzhen, *Nie Rongzhen huiyilu*, 338.

62. See, e.g., Carlson, *Twin Stars of China*, 222, where Peng is identified as responsible for the "People's Movement" and this is linked explicitly to efforts to resist Japan.

63. Nie Rongzhen, *Kang ri mofan genju di—Jin Cha Ji bianqu*, 10–12.

64. Nie Rongzhen, *Kang ri mofan genju di—Jin Cha Ji bianqu*, 14–15. Also see *Jin Cha Ji kang Ri genjudi*, 3:23.

65. *Jin Cha Ji kang Ri genjudi*, 3:28. Also see Li Bo, *Jin Cha Ji bianqu yinxiang ji*, 70–71.

66. See generally *«Jin Cha Ji ribao»da shi ji*. Also see Cheek, "Honorable Vocation."

67. Beijing Military Region Jin Cha Ji war history compilation group, *Jin Cha Ji junqu kang Ri zhanzheng shi*, 79–83.

68. Nie Rongzhen, *Kang ri mofan genju di—Jin Cha Ji bianqu*, 7.

69. Carlson, *Twin Stars of China*, 222.

70. *Jin Cha Ji kang Ri genjudi*, 1A:12, 3:31; Lu Zhengcao, *Ji zhong huiyi lu*, 63. Also see Beijing Military Region Jin Cha Ji war history compilation group, *Jin Cha Ji junqu kang Ri zhanzheng shi*, 27–28.

71. Nie Rongzhen, *Nie Rongzhen huiyilu*, 338.

72. See Liu Lantao, "Jin Cha Ji bianqu dang zuzhi zai zhandou zhong cheng chang zhuang da."

73. "Zhonggong Jin Cha Ji shengwei guanyu zai zhengquan jiguan zhong gongzuo de dangyuan bixu zunshou de tiaoli."

74. Liu Lantao, "Jin Cha Ji bianqu dang zuzhi zai zhandou zhong cheng chang zhuang da," 87, where Liu Lantao suggests that the campaign purges targeted some who did not deserve it, although he concludes that the effort ultimately strengthened the Party in Jin Cha Ji.

75. See, e.g., "Guanyu zhan sheng di dui Jin Cha Ji bianqu de weigong de zhishi," in which specific directions are given to oppose opportunists and purge traitors even in the midst of military instructions on strategy for resisting the Japanese encirclement effort. This policy was consistent with Mao's critique of liberalism, which he saw as a manifestation of opportunism and selfishness. See Mao Zedong, "Combat Liberalism," 31–33. As indicated by Mao's speech to the Sixth Plenum of the Sixth CPC Central Committee in October 1938, careful screening of Party members was motivated by the attack on Zhang Guotao and

his supporters and the effort to resist infiltration of CPC organs by "traitors, Trotskyites, and pro-Japanese elements." See Mao Zedong, "Role of the Chinese Communist Party in the National War."

76. Peng Zhen, "Lun Jin Cha Ji bianqu kangri genjudi de zhengquan" (On political authority in the Jin Cha Ji border region anti-Japanese base area) (October 13, 1938), *Jin Cha Ji kang Ri genjudi*, 1A:208.

77. Chen Lian, *Kang ri genju di fazhan shilue*, 89. Also see *Jin Cha Ji kang Ri genjudi*, 3:54; Beijing Military Region Jin Cha Ji war history compilation group, *Jin Cha Ji junqu kang Ri zhanzheng shi*, 75–76.

78. Lu Zhengcao, *Ji zhong huiyi lu*, 63.

79. Lu Zhengcao, *Ji zhong huiyi lu*, 62–63.

80. Chen Lian, *Kang ri genju di fazhan shilue*, 89. Also see *Jin Cha Ji kang Ri genjudi*, 1A:15, 3:58.

81. *Jin Cha Ji kang Ri genjudi*, 1A:15.

82. The Central Hebei Region was the most militarized of the three, such that in December 1938 the Centre dispatched He Long and Guan Xiangying to the region with parts of the 120 Division, and a military–political committee was established in January 1939 to govern central Hebei under the command of He Long and Lu Zhengcao. See *Jin Cha Ji kang Ri genjudi*, 1A:15–16. Cheng Zihua was dispatched from his post under Peng Zhen in the Jin Cha Ji Subbureau to Central Hebei to act as political commissar for the local military district and the Third Column (*di san congdui*). Lu Zhengcao, *Ji zhong huiyi lu*, 113; Apter and Saich, *Revolutionary Discourse in Mao's Republic*, 53. The Third Division under Zheng Weishan (with Hu Yaobang as political commissar) was later to play a critical role in the taking of Shijiazhuang from the Japanese. Yang Chengwu, *Yang Chengwu huiyilu*, 123.

83. Liu Lantao, "Jin Cha Ji bianqu dang zuzhi zai zhandou zhong cheng chang zhuang da," 88.

84. "Nie Rongzhen, Peng Zhen guanyu Ji Dong, Pingxi gongzuo de yijian," 263.

85. "Zhonggong zhongyang beifang fenju dui Jizhong gongzuo de zhishi xing."

86. "Zhonggong zhongyang guanyu fandui quxiao Jin Cha Ji Bianqu he Jizhong guihuan Hebei deng qitu de zhishi."

87. *Jin Cha Ji kang Ri genjudi*, 3:78. Also see Liu Lantao, "Jin Cha Ji bianqu dang zuzhi zai zhandou zhong cheng chang zhuang da," 88; Beijing Military Region Jin Cha Ji war history compilation group, *Jin Cha Ji junqu kang Ri zhanzheng shi*, 76–79. The Politburo instruction was influenced in part by Liu Shaoqi's seminal work, "How To Be a Good Communist," in which are discussed the origins, manifestations, and recommended responses to a variety of incorrect attitudes by Party members.

88. Beijing Military Region Jin Cha Ji war history compilation group, *Jin Cha Ji junqu kang Ri zhanzheng shi*, 78.

89. For discussion in the context of Central Hebei, see Beijing Military Region Jin Cha Ji war history compilation group, *Jin Cha Ji junqu kang Ri zhanzheng*

shi, 95–97. The point is made with regard to the Jin Cha Ji experience more generally on 571–72. Also see "Zhonggong zhongyang shujichu guanyu Jizhong gongzuo de zhishi." The importance of integrating class struggle with the anti-Japanese resistance effort had been a central feature of CPC policy in the White Areas. See Liu Shaoqi, "Policies in Anti-Japanese Guerrilla Warfare," 31, 35–37; Luo Fu (Zhang Wentian), "Bai qu dang muqian de zhongxin renwu," 227.

90. Beijing Military Region Jin Cha Ji war history compilation group, *Jin Cha Ji junqu kang Ri zhanzheng shi*, 95–97.

91. "Zhonggong zhongyang beifang fenju guanyu er shi ge yue lai dang de gongzuo zongjie baogao tigang." Although the report was issued by the North China Subbureau as a whole, it almost certainly was drafted by Peng Zhen. Not only would Peng have had responsibility for this work in his capacity as CPC secretary, but the report contains a number of Peng's favorite aphorisms, such as his critique of "*chui mao chiu ci*" (nitpicking) in reviewing the work of Party cadres (at Outline, art. 3(e)).

92. "Zhonggong zhongyang dui Jin Cha Ji gongzuo de zhishi."

93. Liu Lantao, "Jin Cha Ji bianqu dang zuzhi zai zhandou zhong cheng chang zhuang da," 89. Also see *Jin Cha Ji kang Ri genjudi*, 1A:17, 3:83–84.

94. Peng Zhen, "Zai zhonggong zhongyang beifang fenju zuzhi gongzuo huiyi shang de jielun," 296.

95. This work had been mandated by a directive from the Party Centre, issued immediately before the organization meeting. "Zhongyang guanyu Jizhong gongzuo de zhishi," 187.

96. Peng Zhen, "Zai zhonggong zhongyang beifang fenju zuzhi gongzuo huiyi shang de jielun," 300.

97. "Selected Edition on Liu Shao-ch'i's Counter-Revolutionary Revisionist Crimes" (April 22, 1969), 39.

98. "Zhongyang guanyu banli dangxiao de zhishi." For discussion of progress in the work of the party school in the Shan Gan Ning border area, see "Zhonggong Shen Gan Ning bianqu zhongyangju dangxiao gongzuo baogao tigang."

99. Peng Zhen, "Zai zhonggong zhongyang beifang fenju kuangda ganbu huiyi shang de jielun."

100. Peng's speech was clearly influenced by Mao's attack on Wang Jingwei's effort to conclude a separate peace with Japan in late 1939. See Mao Zedong, "Overcome the Danger of Capitulation and Strive for a Turn for the Better" and "Unite All Anti-Japanese Forces and Combat the Anti-Communist Die-Hards."

101. "Zhonggong zhongyang guanyu muqian shiju yu dang de renwu de jueding," 261.

102. Beijing Military Region Jin Cha Ji war history compilation group, *Jin Cha Ji junqu kang Ri zhanzheng shi*, 152–56. Also see "Zhongyang junwei guanyu Jixinan shijian ji women de fangzhen de zhishi"; "Mao Zedong, Wang Jiaxiang guanyu Jixinan shijian yu women fangzhen de buchong zhishi"; "Zhongyang guanyu Jixi shibian jingguo ji jieshi fangzhen de zhishi," in which is discussed

the conflict between the CPC's Eighth Route Army and the army elements of warlord Yan Xishan over anti-Japanese resistance policies.

103. The original published text appears in Jin Cha Ji Bianqu Xingzheng Weiyuanhui, ed., *Xianxing faling huiji*, 1:1–5. Also see Peng Zhen, "Zhonggong zhongyang beifang fen ju guanyu Jin Cha Ji bianqu muqian shizheng gangling." Although the original version of this report is unavailable, the veracity of the reprint is suggested by the accuracy of the reprint of the "Current Administrative Program for the Jin Cha Ji Border Region," contained in the same volume. For discussion of the origins of the term "*shuangshi gangling*" to describe the twenty-point program, see Peng Zhen, *Guanyu Jin Cha Ji bianqu dang de gongzuo he juti zhengce baogao*, i–ii. Also see Peng Zhen, "Zhonggong Jin Cha Ji bianqu zhi gezhong zheng ce" (Various CPC policies for Jin Cha Ji border region) (n.p.: Unification Press, 1942) (handwritten notes).

104. Nie Rongzhen, *Nie Rongzhen huiyilu*, 414–18. For discussion of the Program, see *Jin Cha Ji kang Ri genjudi*, 1A:17–18, 3:107–8.

105. Among the sources for Party policy at this time was the February 1, 1940, decision of the CPC Centre, which addressed anti-Japanese resistance policy, the policy of struggle against bourgeois capitulationists, the methods of political control (including democratic dictatorship), and policies toward intellectuals and economic policy (including the "double reduction" program for rents and interest). "Zhonggong zhongyang guanyu muqian shiju yu dang de renwu de jueding." Also see "Zhongyang guanyu cai jing gongzuo de zhishi," in which all regions are directed to prepare specific policies and plans for finance and economic work in their areas and to report back within the month. Matters of budgeting, currency control, and banking were the subject of further instructions from the Centre and the North China Bureau in April 1940. See "Zhongyang guanyu caizheng jingji zhengce de zhishi" and "Beifang ju guanyu caizheng jingji zhengce de zhishi." Also see "Zhongyang dui Jinxibei caijing zhengce de zhishi." For further review of this report, see Saich, "Introduction: The Chinese Communist Party and the Anti-Japanese War Base Areas," 1002; Saich, *Rise to Power of the Chinese Communist Party*, 974–78.

106. For discussion of the role of Party committees in carrying out land policy, see Peng Zhen, *Guanyu Jin Cha Ji bianqu dang de gongzuo he juti zhengce baogao*, 87–101.

107. Dorris, "Peasant Mobilization in North China," 707–8. Also see Nie Rongzhen, *Nie Rongzhen huiyilu*, 345.

108. For discussion of the economic programs to be pursued under the rubric of resisting Japan, see Mao Zedong, "For the Mobilization of All the Nation's Forces for Victory in the War of Resistance," 27; "Policies, Measures and Perspectives for Resisting the Japanese Invasion," 18.

109. See, e.g., discussion of institution building and the need to formalize financial reporting and plans in East Hebei in "Nie Rongzhen, Peng Zhen guanyu Ji Dong, Pingxi gongzuo de yijian." Also see discussion of the use of local elections to cement CPC control in "Zhonggong zhongyang beifang ju jueding Hebei wenti de ba da gangling."

110. "Jin Cha Ji bianqu xingzheng weiyuanhui guanyu shengli wancheng ge ji xuanze de zhishi xing." The three-thirds system was articulated in Mao Zedong, "On the Question of Political Power in the Anti-Japanese Base Areas," 417–19. Also see Hartford, "Step by Step," 284–317; Apter and Saich, *Revolutionary Discourse in Mao's Republic*, 212–16. For discussion of the three-thirds system in the Shen-Gan-Ning border region, see "Zhonggong Shen-Gan-Ning bianqu zhengfu dang tuan guize (cao'an)."

111. "Jin Cha Ji bianqu jian zu jian xi danxing tiaoli." Also see generally Hartford, "Step by Step," 138 ff. Although specific policy of reducing rent and interest was approved by the CPC Politburo at the Lochuan Conference in August 1937 and was included in Mao Zedong's "For the Mobilization of All the Nation's Forces for Victory in the War of Resistance," 27, oblique reference to the policy was made several months earlier in Mao's "Policies, Measures and Perspectives for Resisting the Japanese Invasion," 18, in which improvement in the people's livelihood was discussed as including "reducing rent and restricting usury."

112. An Ziwen noted that even the peasantry was initially reluctant to involve itself directly in the reforms—obviously out of fear of retaliation in the event the Communists were defeated. *An Ziwen zhuanlue*, 37–38. Although Peng's report claimed that participation in the Jin Cha Ji elections averaged 70 percent of eligible voters, the inclusion in this average of high turnout figures for the counties of Ping Shan (99 percent) and Lin Shou (97 percent) suggests that participation elsewhere in the border area was lower. See Xue Qingzhao et al., *Di yi dai zhongyang lingdao jiti de xingcheng*, 103–4.

113. Of particular note in this respect were directives from the Centre in mid-1940 instructing local CPC organs to attend to the mass organization, political power building, and military and guerrilla assistance rather than focus on Party development. See, e.g., "Zhongyang dui Jinxibei gongzuo de zhishi." This directive also criticized leftism (exclusionary attitudes toward non-Party elements), lofty and coercive regulations, and corruption within the Party. The problem was not Jin Cha Ji's alone: similar issues of managing and coopting non-Party cadres were discussed in Shen Gan Ning as well. See CPC Northwest Central Bureau, "Fei dang ganbu wenti."

114. Peng himself noted that despite their initial resistance to the double reduction policy, landlords finally came to support it when they realized that there were few alternatives under CPC policy. See Van Slyke, *Enemies and Friends*, 152.

115. Although these concerns were of long standing, the Party Centre had reiterated their importance in its decision of July 7, 1940, commemorating the third anniversary of the Japanese invasion. See "Zhonggong zhongyang guanyu muqian xingshi yu dang de zhengce de jueding," 423–24.

116. Subsequently, in 1943 and 1944, regulations were enacted pertaining to the Party/state's powers of inspection, search, arrest, and detention. For a discussion of these procedural regulations, see Lan Quanpu, *Jiefangqu fagui gaiyao*, 127–37; Han Yanlong and Chang Zhaoru, *Zhongguo xin minzhuzhuyi geming shiqi*

genju di fazhi wenxian xuanbian, 3:91–97. These regulations, however, were designed primarily to restrict the independent authority of individual officials rather than impose limits on the power of the Party/state over the citizenry generally. Although the arrest of citizens was subject to approval by higher-level organs, supporting evidence could be submitted after the arrest had been carried out. See "Jin Cha Ji bianqu guanyu daibu sousuo zhencha chuli xingshi tezhong xingshi fan zhi jueding," sec. 2, arts. 3–8.

117. Liu Lantao, "Jin Cha Ji bianqu dang zuzhi zai zhandou zhong cheng chang zhuang da," 91, referring to content in Peng's September 1, 1940, speech elaborating on the "Twenty-Point Program." The official reprint of Peng's remarks appears as Peng Zhen, "Zai zhonggong zhongyang beifang fenju kuangda ganbu huiyi shang de baogao." Also see Mao Zedong, "Recruit Large Numbers of Intellectuals."

118. *Jin Cha Ji kang Ri genjudi*, 1A:18.

119. Zhou Weizhi, "Jin Cha Ji bianqu kang Ri genju di wen yi gongzuo huigu," 57–60. Also see generally Nie Rongzhen, *Nie Rongzhen huiyilu*, 426–28.

120. Zhou Weizhi, "Jin Cha Ji bianqu kang Ri genju di wen yi gongzuo huigu," 57–60.

121. Peng Zhen, "Zai zhonggong zhongyang beifang fenju kuangda ganbu huiyi shang de baogao." Also see "Zhonggong zhongyang beifang fenju jiu yue kuangda ganbu huiyi de yiyi yu chenggong."

122. "Zhongyang guanyu banli dangxiao de zhishi"; "Zhongyang xuanchuan bu guanyu jiaqiang ganbu celue jiaoyu de zhishi." Additional instructions on cadre education were issued subsequently by the Propaganda Department. See "Zhongyang xuanchuan bu guanyu tigao Yan'an zai zhi ganbu jiaoyu zhiliang de jueding."

123. *Jin Cha Ji kang Ri genjudi*, 3:120–21; Beijing Military Region Jin Cha Ji war history compilation group, *Jin Cha Ji junqu kang Ri zhanzheng shi*, 207–10.

124. The Party Centre had given instructions the previous summer on the need to increase political work among the various military units involved in the resistance war. See "Zhongyang junwei, zong zhengzhi bu dui yezhan zhengzhi bu zhaoji de zhengzhi gongzuo huiyi ji junqu bu ganbu huiyi de zhishi," 448. These guidelines took on particular significance in light of the South Anhui incident ("New Fourth Army Incident") in which thousands of Communist troops were killed or captured. See Johnson, "Chinese Communist Leadership and Mass Response," 415.

125. Peng Zhen, "Zai zhonggong zhongyang beifang fenju huiyi shang guanyu gonggu dang de jielun"; "Zai zhonggong zhongyang beifang fenju huiyi shang guanyu caizheng shengchan deng wenti de jielue"; "Zai zhonggong zhongyang beifang fenju huiyi shang guanyu wenhua yundong de jielue." As with his report to the September cadres' meeting, much of the content of these speeches was incorporated in Peng's subsequent report to the CPC Politburo. Peng Zhen, *Guanyu Jin Cha Ji bianqu dang de gongzuo he juti zhengce baogao*, 20.

126. For a summary of the views of the CPC Centre on these issues, see

"Zhongyang guanyu shencha ganbu wenti de zhishi." The question of policies on cadre investigation would surface again in the context of the Yan'an rectification campaign and a new set of instructions, significantly less lenient, would be issued. Nie Rongzhen, *Nie Rongzhen huiyilu*, 501–2.

127. The directive that cadres participate in production was included in the CPC Centre's February 1, 1940, directive on finance and economic work. "Zhongyang guanyu cai jing gongzuo de zhishi." The directive expressly denounced egalitarianism, however, and stated the qualification that cadre participation in production not interfere with anti-Japanese resistance work or obstruct cadres' work and study responsibilities. Peng's discussion both in Jin Cha Ji and later during the Socialist Education Campaign contained similar qualifications.

128. Zhu Liyu, *Peng Zhen minzhu fazhi sixiang yanjiu*, 20–21.

129. *Jin Cha Ji kang Ri genjudi*, 3:152. For text, see Peng Zhen, *Guanyu Jin Cha Ji bianqu dang de gongzuo he juti zhengce baogao*. A handwritten version edited in January 1942 is available as Peng Zhen, *Zhonggong Jin Cha Ji bianqu zhi ge zhong zheng ce*. The handwritten transcription omits sections in the 1981 text and abbreviates others. It also contains inconsistencies in subtitling and sequence of discussion. It is possible that the handwritten transcription was taken from Peng's actual remarks and the 1981 text is based on Peng's formal written report. This would be consistent with the practice of Chinese political reporting generally. For discussion of the contents of a 1944 reprint of the report, see Pepper, *Civil War in China*, 246–50. Also see Saich, *Rise to Power of the Chinese Communist Party*, 1011 ff.

130. The 1942 handwritten transcription of Peng's report omits discussion of these latter policy issues, moving directly from the discussion of political authority to the section on Party building. See Peng Zhen, *Zhonggong Jin Cha Ji bianqu zhi ge zhong zheng ce*, 21–22.

131. Compare sect. I.A.3 of Peng Zhen, *Guanyu Jin Cha Ji bianqu dang de gongzuo he juti zhengce baogao*, 16–17, with sect. II.C of Peng Zhen, "Zai zhonggong zhongyang beifang fenju kuangda ganbu huiyi shang de baogao," 413, which omits reference to land reform and attendant class conflict.

132. "Zhongyang guanyu caizheng jingji zhengce de zhishi."

133. Compare sect. I.C.5 of Peng Zhen, *Guanyu Jin Cha Ji bianqu dang de gongzuo he juti zhengce baogao*, 77–78 with sect. V.B of Peng Zhen, "Zai zhonggong zhongyang beifang fenju kuangda ganbu huiyi shang de baogao," 447.

134. "Dadao lao pai da pantu Peng Zhen," 13–14, 18.

135. See sect. I.B of Peng Zhen, *Guanyu Jin Cha Ji bianqu dang de gongzuo he juti zhengce baogao*, 20.

136. Compare sect. I.B.3 of Peng Zhen, *Guanyu Jin Cha Ji bianqu dang de gongzuo he juti zhengce baogao*, 27–28, with sect. V.A of Peng Zhen, "Zai zhonggong zhongyang beifang fenju kuangda ganbu huiyi shang de baogao," 439–40.

137. See sect. I.B.2 of Peng Zhen, *Guanyu Jin Cha Ji bianqu dang de gongzuo he juti zhengce baogao*, 24–25. For the text of the regulations, see "Jin Cha Ji bianqu xian qu cun zuzhi tiaoli."

138. See sect. I.B.3 of Peng Zhen, *Guanyu Jin Cha Ji bianqu dang de gongzuo he juti zhengce baogao*, 27–31. Also see "Jin Cha Ji bianqu xian qu cun zuzhi tiaoli."

139. See sect. I.B.3 of Peng Zhen, *Guanyu Jin Cha Ji bianqu dang de gongzuo he juti zhengce baogao*, 27–28.

140. Sect. I.B.3 of Peng Zhen, *Guanyu Jin Cha Ji bianqu dang de gongzuo he juti zhengce baogao*, 29.

141. "Dadao lao pai da pantu Peng Zhen," 10 ff.

142. Although of course the CPC consistently pursued the goals of ensuring that "political authority at all levels is held firmly in our Party's hands" (see, e.g., "Zhonggong zhongyang dui Jin Cha Ji gongzuo de zhishi"), issues of political authority were seen as but one of many matters of concern and were generally addressed separately from discussion of CPC development and managerial policies.

143. See sect. II.A and II.B.2 of Peng Zhen, *Guanyu Jin Cha Ji bianqu dang de gongzuo he juti zhengce baogao*, 133–43, 146–50.

144. See sect. II.B.4 of Peng Zhen, *Guanyu Jin Cha Ji bianqu dang de gongzuo he juti zhengce baogao*, 158. Problems in this region, in particular Tangxing county, had come to light several years earlier but apparently were still unresolved. Peng Zhen, "Zai zhonggong Jin Cha Ji shengwei zuzhi gongzuo huiyi shang de jielun," 172.

145. Peng had criticized the so-called Trotskyite faction as early as 1938 for their opposition to the United Front and their subsequent opposition to CPC base area policies that called for moderation in dealing with landlords and capitalists. Peng Zhen, "Jin Cha Ji bianqu hanjian Tuopai de mai guo feizhuang."

146. Compare sect. II.1 of Peng Zhen, "Zai zhonggong zhongyang beifang fenju huiyi shang guanyu gonggu dang de jielun," 476, with sect. II.C.4 of Peng Zhen, *Guanyu Jin Cha Ji bianqu dang de gongzuo he juti zhengce baogao*, 172–73.

147. For example, a report by Yao Yilin and Xu Jianguo complained that Party consolidation work in Pingxi and East Hebei noted that the grain supply conditions in the region were nearly catastrophic (a result, it is implied, of the reduction of the "fair burden" system of procurement that Peng had instituted several years earlier). See Yao Yilin and Xu Jianguo, "Guangfan jinxing kang zhan de caizheng dongyuan," 159. Yao and Xu slammed the practice of mimeographing military plans and suggested that the guerrilla effort in East Hebei was inadequate. "Zhonggong zhongyang beifang fenju guanyu Ji Re Cha gongzuo de yijian." In response, Peng argued that although more needed to be done in East Hebei and Pingxi, the region had shown significant achievements under difficult conditions. Peng focused on the successes of building CPC political and military power in the region, thus blunting many of Yao and Xu's criticisms.

148. Nie Rongzhen, *Nie Rongzhen huiyilu*, 103–4.

149. See generally Hartford, "Step by Step," 106 ff. Also see Nie Rongzhen, *Nie Rongzhen huiyilu*, 438 ff.; *Jin Cha Ji kang Ri genjudi*, 1A:20–22.

150. The years 1941 and 1942 were described as the "toughest years of the eight years of war" in the biography of Deng Xiaoping published by his

daughter Deng Rong. See Deng Rong, "'Chapter 49: From Pu Qingying to Zhuo Lin' of the Biography My Father Deng Xiaoping."

151. The extent to which Peng is identified with the successes of Jin Cha Ji is evidenced not merely by the publication of his speeches on Border Region policies (e.g., Peng Zhen, *Guanyu Jin Cha Ji bianqu dang de gongzuo he juti zhengce baogao*), but also by his prominence in retrospective celebrations. See, e.g., Peng's written remarks to a meeting celebrating the publication of Party history materials on the Shen Gan Ning and Jin Cha Ji Border Regions, in "Peng Zhen tongzhi de shumian jianghua." Peng also provided the calligraphy for the Jin Cha Ji history. See *Jin Cha Ji kang Ri genjudi*, 1A:i.

152. "Zhongyang guanyu banli dangxiao de zhishi."

153. See document G4 in Saich, *Rise to Power of the Chinese Communist Party*, 1008–110.

154. Zhang Zhiqing, Sun Li, and Bai Juntang, *Yan'an zhengfeng qianhou*, 99.

155. "Zhongyang guanyu Yan'an zaizhi ganbu xuexi de jueding," 247. Mao had spoken out against "subjectivism" in his May 1941 report to a Yenan cadres' meeting. See Mao Zedong, "Reform Our Study," 20 ff. Also see generally Saich, *Rise to Power of the Chinese Communist Party*, 974; Johnson, "Chinese Communist Leadership and Mass Response," 416–17.

156. "Zhonggong zhongyang guanyu Yan'an ganbu xuexiao de jueding," 258.

157. Apter and Saich, *Revolutionary Discourse in Mao's Republic*, 281; "Zonggong zhongyang guanyu zaizhi ganbu jiaoyu de jueding." The specific appointments were announced by the Secretariat on March 2, 1942. See "Zhongyang shujichu bangongting guanyu zhengzhi ju dui dangxiao zuzhi ji jiaoyu fangzhen zhi xin jueding de tongzhi."

158. Zhang Zhiqing, Sun Li, and Bai Juntang, *Yan'an zhengfeng qianhou*, 104.

159. *An Ziwen zhuanlue*, 45–46. Also see Tian Jiuru, "Peng Zheng tongzhi zai Yan'an," 327.

160. See generally Wu Jiemin, *Yan'an Ma Lie xueyuan huijilu*. Also see Dai Qing, *Wang Shiwei and "Wild Lilies,"* xviii.

161. See, e.g., Jiang Hongwu, *Chen Yi zhuan*, 545–46; Ceng Changming, "Husong Chenyi tongzhi pu Yan'an"; Zheng Xiaofeng and Shu Ling, *Tao Zhu zhuan*, 183.

162. Gao Xinmin and Zhang Shujun, *Yan'an zhengfeng shilu*, 146.

163. Gao Xinmin and Zhang Shujun, *Yan'an zhengfeng shilu*, 146. Indeed, Peng's role in Yan'an was sufficiently important—in hindsight at least—that in 1990 he was appointed honorary chair of the China Society for Research in the Yan'an Spirit. See "Zhongguo Yan'an jingshen yanjiu hui zai Beijing chengli." Peng also took it upon himself to oversee the publication of materials on the rectification at the Party school. See *Yan'an zhongyang dangxiao de zhengfeng xuexi*.

164. Gao Xinmin and Zhang Shujun, *Yan'an zhengfeng shilu*, 145.

165. Mei Jian, *Yan'an mi shi 1937–1947*, 487. Also see Gao Xinmin and Zhang Shujun, *Yan'an zhengfeng shilu*, 74.

166. "Zhongyang dangxiao jihua." Also see Gao Xinmin and Zhang Shujun, *Yan'an zhengfeng shilu*, 146.

167. "Zhongguo gongchandang zhongyang dang xiao zhaoshou xinshen zige guiding."

168. Gao Xinmin and Zhang Shujun, *Yan'an zhengfeng shilu*, 146.

169. Zhang Zhiqing, Sun Li, and Bai Juntang, *Yan'an zhengfeng qianhou*, 134. Others covered by the edict included Chen Boda (12,000 characters per month); Ai Siqi (10,000 characters per month); Zhou Yang (10,000 characters per month); and Wang Zhen (5,000 characters per month).

170. Peng Zhen, "Ling hui er shi er ge wenjian de jingshen yu shijian." In this summary, Peng addresses the concepts and implementation of 22 documents, namely (1) Mao's February 1, 1942, speech to the Party School "On Reforming Party Workstyle"; (2) Mao's February 8, 1942, speech to the Yan'an Cadres' Conference "Oppose Stereotyped Writing (*bagu*)"; (3) Kang Sheng's two reports "Report Made Twice to Cadres' Meetings Concerning Opposing Subjectivism and Factionalism" and "Bitterly Attack Stereotyped Writing (*bagu*)"; (4) Party Central decision on strengthening Party character; (5) Party Central decision on investigation and research; (6) Party Central decision on the Party school; (7) Party Central decision on education of technical cadres; (8) Mao speech to border area participation group; (9) Mao speech on "Transforming Our Thought"; (10) Mao speech on "Opposing Liberalism"; (11) Mao speech on investigation of villages; (12) the Six Articles Summarizing Party History; (13) Stalin's twelve articles on bourgeoisation of the Party; (14) Liu Shaoqi's "The Interest of Individual Party Members Is to Unconditionally Serve the Interests of the Party," "Listing of Various Errors in Ideology and Thought Within the Party," "Attitudes Toward Handling Errors of Ideology and Thought Within the Party," and "Attitudes on Handling Conflict Within the Party," that comprise sect. 2, 3, 4, and 5 of chap. 2 of Liu's "Transformation of Party Members"; (15) Chen Yun's "How to Make a Party Member"; (16) thought of the Ninth Meeting of the Red Fourth Army on incorrect phenomena within the Party; (17) handbook on guiding propaganda; (18) decision of the Central Committee Propaganda Department on discussion of Party Central decisions at Yan'an and Mao's report on rectification; (19) Stalin on leadership and testing; (20) Lenin and Stalin on Party discipline and Party democracy; (21) Stalin on egalitarianism; and (22) G. M. Dimitrov (Jimitekefu) on cadre policy and cadre education policy.

171. Huang Huoqing et al., "Huigu Yan'an zhongyang dangxiao de zhengfeng yundong."

172. Peng Zhen, "Ling hui er shi er ge wenjian de jingshen yu shijian," 32, where Peng notes, "Since we have only one standpoint, while it may definitely be insufficient, nevertheless it still follows different revolutionary stages and differences in specific issues and economic and political conditions, so that in the course of resolving problems these differences are expressed," and "The specific application of these concepts (i.e. objectivism and materialism) should take into account the differences in issues and specific conditions, even though the changes will be endless."

173. "Zhongguo gongchandang zhongyang dangxiao di er qi zhaoshou xinsheng jianzhang."

174. Wang Chongqing, "Dangxiao lishi shang guanche lilun lianxi shiji fangzhen de guanghui pianzhang," 343–44.

175. Mei Jian, *Yan'an mi shi 1937–1947*, 528.

176. Mei Jian, *Yan'an mi shi 1937–1947*, 529.

177. For a discussion of Kang Sheng's role in the salvation movement during the Yan'an rectification, see Byron and Pack, *Claws of the Dragon*; Apter and Saich, *Revolutionary Discourse in Mao's Republic*, 25.

178. Gao Xinmin and Zhang Shujun, *Yan'an zhengfeng shilu*, 378.

179. Li Mianmin, "Canjia Yan'an 'qiangjiu yundong' de pianxu huiyi," 33–35.

180. Teiwes and Sun, "From a Leninist to a Charismatic Party," 354.

181. Yuan Beijing shiwei jiguan Mao Zedong sixiang hongqi bingduan, ed., *Da yexing jia, da yinmou jia*, 8.

182. *An Ziwen zhuanlue*, 45–46. At the time, An was in charge of the School's Second Division (made up largely of relatively well-educated county- and group-level cadres).

183. "Zhonggong zhongyang guanyu shencha ganbu de jueding"; Nie Rongzhen, *Nie Rongzhen huiyilu*, 501–2. Kang apparently attempted to weaken Peng's position during the rectification by attempting to reexamine the matter of the "61 Cadres" (including Bo Yibo, Yang Xianzheng, and others associated with Peng and the North China Bureau) released from a Kuomintang prison in 1936. Chen Chengzhang and Jin Shi, "An Extremely Treacherous Man Assumed a Loyal Look." Kang no doubt never forgave Peng for his role in squelching the Rescue Campaign and wreaked revenge during the Cultural Revolution, when Peng himself was accused of being among the 61 Cadres during the Cultural Revolution. "Selected Edition on Liu Shao-ch'i's Counter-Revolutionary Revisionist Crimes" (May 5, 1969); "Dossier of P'eng Chen," 36.

184. Mei Jian, *Yan'an mi shi 1937–1947*, 544.

185. Peng Zhen, "Sixiang fangfa wenti."

186. Peng Zhen, "Sixiang fangfa wenti," 8.

187. Peng Zhen, "Sixiang fangfa wenti," 16. For discussion of the centrality of "subjectivism, sectarianism and formalism" in the Yan'an rectification, see Saich, *Rise to Power of the Chinese Communist Party*, 978–82.

188. Peng's attack on egalitarianism was intended in part to respond to criticisms such as those from Wang Shiwei that the Party elite's privileges were betraying the revolution. See Dai Qing, *Wang Shiwei and "Wild Lilies."* Also see Cheek, "Fading of Wild Lilies"; Saich, *Rise to Power of the Chinese Communist Party*, 982–85.

189. Peng Zhen, "Sixiang fangfa wenti," 10.

190. Peng Zhen, "Sixiang fangfa wenti," 17.

191. Liu Shaoqi once commented that Peng could be extremely sectarian in his outlook—an indication that Peng's vigilance in controlling non-Party

elements was considered somewhat extreme. See "Selected Edition on Liu Shao-Chi'i's Counter-Revolutionary Crimes," 651 (April 22, 1969): 39.

192. Jiang Hongwu, *Chen Yi zhuan*, 545–46.

193. Apter and Saich, *Revolutionary Discourse in Mao's Republic*, 240.

194. Shanxi Party Committee History Research Office, *Peng Zhen shengping dashi nianbiao*, 15, 19. Authoritative Chinese sources contradict each other in identifying the leadership of the Organization Department during this period. For example, the department's authoritative history suggests that Peng was actually replaced by Rao Shushi in 1946, with Peng returing to his directorship from 1947 until April 1953. See Liu Huafeng and Wang Yuting, *Zhongguo gongchandang zuzhi gongzuo dashiji*, 597–98. On the other hand, Wang Jianying's authoritative *Zhongguo gongchandang zuzhishi ziliao huibian* suggests that Peng was replaced by Kang Sheng from March 1947 to March 1948 and lists Chen Yun as director concurrently with Peng from March to October 1949. Wang indicates that Peng returned to the directorship in October 1949 and was replaced by Rao Shushi in December 1952. Despite these inconsistencies, it seems clear that Peng had major responsibilities in the Organization Department beginning in 1944, that his work was suspended at least informally while he was in Manchuria, and that he resumed these duties upon returning to the Centre. Most sources appear to agree that An Ziwen remained as deputy director throughout the period, suggesting that he handled the day-to-day work of the department.

195. Huang Huoqing et al., "Zhuinian jingai de lao lingdao Peng Zhen tongzhi," 20. Also see Ren Dongyun, *Gongheguo zhuxi de rong yu ru*, 45; Qiu Zhizhuo and Lian Gangsheng, *Liu Shaoqi de jiaoyin*, 260.

196. Saich, "Writing or Rewriting History?", 327. Also see Huang Huoqing et al., "Zhuinian jingai de lao lingdao Peng Zhen tongzhi," 20.

197. Zhu Liyu, *Peng Zhen minzhu fazhi sixiang yanjiu*, 21.

198. Mei Jian, *Yan'an mi shi 1937–1947*, 495–96; Shanxi Party Committee History Research Office, *Peng Zhen shengping dashi nianbiao*, 16.

199. Shan Siyi, *Zai jiefang zhanzheng zhong fengfu fazhan*, 22. Peng Zhen's selection was due in part to his ties with Jin Cha Ji. The Jin Cha Ji Subbureau as well as the CPC committees for Central Hebei (Jizhong) and Ji Re were charged with organizing Manchurian work committees for activists and leaders to become involved in the work of opening up the Northeast. "Zhongyang guanyu kaizhen manzhou gongzuo gei Jin Cha Ji fenju de zhishi." Also see Bachman, *Chen Yun and the Chinese Political System*, 23–25.

200. Liu Huafeng and Wang Yuting, *Zhongguo gongchandang zuzhi gongzuo dashiji*, 305; Lu Xiangtou, *Liu Shaoqi he ta de shiye*, 290. Also see Zhang Zhenglong, *Xue bai xue hong*, 61; Reardon-Anderson, *Yenan and the Great Powers*, 119–26.

201. Zhang Zhenglong, *Xue bai xue hong*, 64. Luo Rongdan soon returned to Yan'an to recover from illness and was replaced by Chen Yi (65).

202. Zhang Zhenglong, *Xue bai xue hong*, 77, 116.

203. Peng Zhen, "Zhangwo zhengquan, fadong qunzhong."

204. See, e.g., Peng Zhen, "Fadong qunzhong fenzai Jiang jun jingong" and "Dangqian xingshi he Harbin shi gongzuo de jiben fangzhen."

205. Han Lefeng, "Peng Zhen tongzhi zai dongbei de ri ri ye ye," 308.

206. Han Lefeng, "Peng Zhen tongzhi zai dongbei de ri ri ye ye," 312–13.

207. "Zhongyang guanyu chengshi gongzuo de zhishi." Also see "Zhongyang guanyu jianli chengshi gongzuo bumen de zhishi."

208. "Yi jiu si wu nian de renqu," 417.

209. Peng Zhen, "Guanyu dizhanqu de chengshi gongzuo."

210. Zhang Zhenglong, *Xue bai xue hong*, 111–16.

211. "Zhongyang guanyu jianli Dongbei changqi yongjiu genjudi gei Dongbei ju de zhishi." At the time, Mao was recuperating from fatigue and Liu Shaoqi was acting on behalf of the Centre. See Shan Siyi, *Zai jiefang zhanzheng zhong fengfu fazhan*, 23.

212. Zheng Xiaofeng and Shu Ling, *Tao Zhu zhuan*, 188. For a discussion of Lin Biao's role, see Nie Rongzhen, *Nie Rongzhen huiyilu*, 538.

213. "San shi san ge fangeming xiuzheng zhuyi fenzi," 207.

214. Zhang Zhenglong, *Xue bai xue hong*, 117; Lu Xiangtou, *Liu Shaoqi he ta de shiye*, 304.

215. Li Tien-min, *Liu Shao-Ch'i*, 115, n. 4.

216. Peng Zhen, "Jue bu yao hulue genjudi de jianshe."

217. Zhang Zhenglong, *Xue bai xue hong*, 187.

218. Bo Yibo, *Ruogan zhong da juece yu shijian de huigu*, 8.

219. Peng Zhen, "Women de renwu shi zhengqu quan dongbei" and "Jin hou gongzuo de xin fangzhen."

220. Zheng Xiaofeng and Shu Ling, *Tao Zhu zhuan*, 187–88. See generally Reardon-Anderson, *Yenan and the Great Powers*, 123–26.

221. Zheng Xiaofeng and Shu Ling, *Tao Zhu zhuan*, 187–88.

222. Zhang Zhenglong, *Xue bai xue hong*, 77.

223. Zhang Zhenglong, *Xue bai xue hong*, 117.

224. See, e.g., Kau, *Lin Piao Affair*, 33. Also see "Lin Piao's Most Significant Speech," 260.

225. Yuan Beijing shiwei jiguan Mao Zedong sixiang hongqi bingduan, ed., *Da yexing jia, da yinmou jia*, 22.

226. Peng Zhen, "Dongbei jiefang zhanzheng de tou jiu ge yue." In this article, Peng doesn't dispute the Centre's decision to abandon the large cities, but rather asserts that the focus was shifted to small and medium cities as well as the rural areas, and that the Northeast Bureau played a critical role in Party building and mass organization. In this sense, Peng's emphasis on political work contrasts with the emphasis of CPC documents of the period that emphasized the military campaign almost exclusively. Peng also contributed his calligraphy to a published photo album on the *War of Liberation in the Northeast* (Jin Cha Ji Arts Research Society, ed., 1993). See "Deng, Peng Zhen Write Titles for Albums."

227. Sullivan, "Biography of An Ziwen." 33.

228. Pepper, *Civil War in China*, 246–50, 303–5.
229. Hebei CPC Committee Party History Research Office and Hebei Academy of Social Sciences, "Peng Zhen tongzhi zai Hebei de geming huodong," 512.
230. Peng Zhen, "Ping fen tudi yu zhengdun duiwu."
231. Peng Zhen, "Ba nongmin duiwu zuzhi hao."
232. Pepper, *Civil War in China*, 312 ff.
233. Peng Zhen, "Ping fen tudi yu zhengdun duiwu."
234. Peng Zhen, "Ping fen tudi yu zhengdun duiwu."

CHAPTER 3

1. *Dong Biwu nianpu*, 308.
2. Bo Yibo, *Ruogan zhong da juece yu shijian de huigu*, 2–3; Shanxi Party Committee History Research Office, *Peng Zhen shengping dashi nianbiao*, 19. The secretary general of the North China Bureau was Zhang Youyu, who was later to become Peng Zhen's secretary and close collaborator in legal matters. See Guo Simin and Tian Yu, *Wo yan zhong de Liu Shaoqi*, 207.
3. *Dong Biwu nianpu*, 314.
4. *Dong Biwu nianpu*, 324.
5. Bo Yibo, *Ruogan zhong da juece yu shijian de huigu*, 9–10.
6. Bo Yibo, *Ruogan zhong da juece yu shijian de huigu*, 9–10; *Dong Biwu nianpu*, 324.
7. *Dong Biwu nianpu*, 309.
8. Bo Yibo, *Ruogan zhong da juece yu shijian de huigu*, 5. Zhang Youyu was sent to Beijing by Liu Shaoqi to serve as deputy mayor in March 1949. See Guo Simin and Tian Yu, *Wo yan zhong de Liu Shaoqi*, 207.
9. "Jiekai panju zai Beijing de Peng Zhen da pantu jituan de heimu," 3. Indeed, Peng continued to use his base in Jin Cha Ji to articulate his views on the importance of an urban strategy of power building in Manchuria even after he left the region. See Peng Zhen, "Zuohao chengshi gongzuo yingjie geming de xin gaochao." Liu Ren took responsibility for municipal industry in Beijing, while others later associated with the Beijing CPC Committee and the Changguanlou meetings in particular, such as Chao Fan and Bao Ke, also played important roles. See "Jiekai panju zai Beijing de Peng Zhen da pantu jituan de heimu," 4–6.
10. Shanxi Party Committee History Research Office, *Peng Zhen shengping dashi nianbiao*, 21; *Dong Biwu nianpu*, 348.
11. Shanxi Party Committee History Research Office, *Peng Zhen shengping dashi nianbiao*, 24; Guo Simin and Tian Yu, *Wo yan zhong de Liu Shaoqi*, 207 ff.; CPC Beijing Municipal Committee Party History Research Office, ed., *Peng Zhen zai Beijing*.
12. Liu Yong, "Tongdao zhongxin aidai de lao lingdao Peng Zhen tongzhi," 255.
13. Beijing CPC Committee, Beijing People's Congress Standing Committee, Beijing People's Government, and Beijing CPPCC Committee, "Shoudu shehui zhuyi xiandaihua jianshe zhuyao dianjizhe weiye yong cun," 485–87.

14. Zhang Qilin, "Peng Zhen tongzhi guanhuai Beijing kuang gong," 335–36.

15. Peng Zhen, "Beijing shi wu nian lai zhengfu gongzuo qingkuang he jinhou gongzuo renwu."

16. Bachman, *Chen Yun and the Chinese Political System*, 60.

17. Peng Zhen, "Xuanchuan gongzuo bixu cong shiji chufa" and "Yi keneng dadao de zui gao biaozhun yaoqiu women de gongzuo."

18. Ma Ju, "Mianhuai Peng Zhen jiaohui, Jiaqiang dang de jianshe," 369.

19. MacFarquhar, *Origins of the Cultural Revolution, 1*, 145–46. Peng's expectations concerning his elevation at the Congress might also have been assisted by the purported actions of An Ziwen to control the voting procedures. Peng was reportedly so upset with Mao at passing him over for promotion that he refused to speak at the Congress—the only member of the Seventh CPC Poliburo not to do so. Yuan Beijing shiwei jiguan Mao Zedong sixiang hongqi bingduan, *Da yexing jia, da yinmou jia*, 31.

20. Red Guard criticisms linked Liu and Peng in building a factional network of old Shanxi colleagues and referred to Beijing as the "kingdom of Peng and Liu." "Counter-Revolutionary Revisionist P'eng Chen's Towering Crimes," 12. Liu Ren was labeled the "No. 2 leader of the counter-revolutionary revisionist clique of the former Peking Municipal Party Committee"; Cheng Hsuan (Zheng Xuan), "Big Exposure of a Conspiracy." For discussion of Liu Ren, see Li Che, *P'eng Chen fan Mao chi-t'uan*, 241–47. Also see Tianjin Dongfang daxue dongfang gongshe cui jiu congdui, "Jiao si Wan Zhang fangeming xiuzheng zhuyi jituan de zhijie houtai Peng Zhen, Liu Ren," app. 1–7; "Jiekai panju zai Beijing de Peng Zhen da pantu jituan de heimu," 12–14.

21. Teiwes, *Politics at Mao's Court*, 135.

22. For discussion of Peng's effort to publish a Beijing Pictorial (*Beijing huace*) to replicate the China Pictorial adopted in 1959 to commemorate the tenth anniversary of the PRC, see "Xiuzheng zhuyi de dazahui «Beijing hauce»," 18–22.

23. For a listing of Peng Zhen's factional associates as of mid-1966 in the Beijing administration, see Li Che, *P'eng Chen fan Mao chi-t'uan*, 228 ff.

24. MacFarquhar, *Origins of the Cultural Revolution 1*, 204, citing *Zheng-fa hongqi* (Political–Legal Red Flag) (October 17, 1967): 5.

25. *Dong Biwu nianpu* 348–51. The first plenary session was held October 19, 1949, but Peng was occupied with preparations to chair the first session of the Second Beijing Representative Congress, which was to begin the following day. See Shanxi Party Committee History Research Office, *Peng Zhen shengping dashi nianbiao*, 21.

26. Li, "Evolution and Development of the Chinese Legal System." During the Cultural Revolution, Red Guards charged that Peng and Liu Shaoqi "openly advocated that law has the nature of continuity" and that "the old laws of the Kuomintang may be continued." Seymour, *China*, 92.

27. *Dong Biwu nianpu*, 360, 384.

28. See Shanxi Party Committee History Research Office, *Peng Zhen shengping dashi nianbiao*, 26. In 1953 Mao had directed that the government organize

specific functional departments and identified Dong Biwu, Peng Zhen, and Luo Ruiqing as responsible for political–legal work. Bo Yibo, *Ruogan zhong da juece yu shijian de huigu*, 310.

29. *Dong Biwu nianpu*, 403, 407, 440.

30. Peng also served as secretary to the Committee's Party organ. Yuan Beijing shiwei jiguan Mao Zedong sixiang hongqi bingduan, *Da yexing jia, da yinmou jia*, 15.

31. Peng Zhen, "Guanyu zhenya fangeming huodong he chengzhi fangeming tiaoli wenti de baogao"; "Zhaokai qu renmin daibiao huiyi de chubu jingyan"; "Zai di er ci quanguo gongan huiyi shang de jianghua"; and "Report on Political and Legal Work." Also see Ladany, *Law and Legality in China*, 62–63.

32. Liu Yong, "Tongdao zhongxin aidai de lao lingdao Peng Zhen tongzhi," 255.

33. Peng Zhen, "Guanyu sifa bumen de gaizao yu zhengdun wenti." Peng was not alone in taking a harsh line against non-Party bourgeois elements. In major cities outside Beijing, capitalist business operators were subjected to repeated and wide-ranging, although often disorganized, attacks. See Gardner, "Wu-Fan Campaign in Shanghai."

34. Chiu Hungdah, "Institutionalizing a New Legal System in Deng's China," 61.

35. Peng Zhen, "Report on Political and Legal Work," 7. Also see Tang, *Communist China Today*, 250.

36. Peng Zhen, "Makesi Liening zhuyi zai Zhongguo de shengli," 23.

37. See arts. 3, 4, and 5 of "PRC Regulations for the Punishment of Counterrevolutionaries."

38. See art. 20 of "PRC Regulations for the Punishment of Counterrevolutionaries."

39. See Yuan Beijing shiwei jiguan Mao Zedong sixiang hongqi bingduan, *Da yexing jia, da yinmou jia*, 6.

40. See Peng Zhen, "Guanyu zhenya fangeming huodong he chengzhi fangeming tiaoli wenti de baogao."

41. Art. 7 of the Common Program of the Chinese People's Political Consultative Conference directly addresses the respective roles of harshness and leniency in handling counterrevolutionaries. Chen Hefu, *Zhongguo xianfa leibian*.

42. Peng Zhen, "Report on Political and Legal Work," 9.

43. Peng Zhen, "Guanyu kang Mei yuan Chao bao jia wei guo yundong de baogao," 2–3.

44. Wang Chaobin, *San fan shi lu*, 51–52. Also see Bo Yibo, *Ruogan zhong da juece yu shijian de huigu*, 139. Director of the CPC Organization Department An Ziwen also played a significant role. *An Ziwen zhuanlue*, 83 ff.; and Sullivan, "Biography of An Ziwen."

45. Qiu Shi, *Gongheguo zhongda juece chutai qian hou*, 1:66 ff.

46. Wang Chaobin, *San fan shi lu*, 54.

47. Wang Chaobin, *San fan shi lu*, 109 ff.

48. See Peng Zhen's reports of December 20, 1951 (to a meeting of Beijing CPC Committee, Beijing Chinese People's Political Consultative Congress Committee, Beijing municipal government, and mass organizations), and December 28, 1951 (to the Third Beijing Representative Congress), in Wang Chaobin, *San fan shi lu*, 55, 56.

49. Peng Zhen, "Guanyu Zhonghua renmin gongheguo chengzhi tanwu tiaoli cao'an de shuoming." Peng's view contrasted pointedly with that of Luo Ruiqing, who argued in December 1951 that the *san fan* campaign "should be a great struggle like that campaign against counter-revolutionaries." Wang Chaobin, *San fan shi lu*, 59.

50. Bo Yibo, "Wei shenru di pubian di kaizhan fan tanwu, fan langfei, fan guanliao zhuyi yundong er douzheng." Bo had also been appointed chair of the *San Fan* Leading Office under the direction of the CPC Secretariat. *An Ziwen zhuanlue*, 83; Sullivan, "Biography of An Ziwen," 87.

51. Wang Chaobin, *San fan shi lu*, 55.

52. Peng Zhen, "Guanyu Zhonghua renmin gongheguo chengzhi tanwu tiaoli cao'an de shuoming."

53. Art. 10 of "Zhonghua renmin gongheguo chengzhi tanwu tiaoli."

54. "Beijing shi renmin zhengfu zai [wu fan] yundong zhong guanyu gongshanghu fenlei chuli de biaozhun he banfa," 60; "Zhonghua renmin gongheguo chengzhi tanwu tiaoli."

55. Teiwes, *Politics and Purges*, 2nd ed., 113.

56. Although the regulations established a hierarchy of sanctions for crimes of varying degrees of seriousness measured by value of loss, there is little in the way of standards for computation or for determining other measures of seriousness. See "Zhonghua renmin gongheguo chengzhi tanwu tiaoli." Also see Peng Zhen, "Guanyu Zhonghua renmin gongheguo chengzhi tanwu tiaoli cao'an de shuoming," 52.

57. Peng Zhen, "Zai quanguo jiancha yewu huiyi shang de baogao," 269, 271.

58. Peng Zhen, "Zai quanguo jiancha yewu huiyi shang de baogao." Also see Peng Zhen, "Faxian cuo an yao jianjue jishi jiuzheng," 299.

59. Peng Zhen, "Zai quanguo gongan ting ju zhang huiyi shang de baogao." Excerpts appear in Peng Zhen, "Renmin jingcha shi renmin de jinwu yuan."

60. Mazur, "Intellectual Activism," 38. Peng was attacked for these views during the Cultural Revolution. See Yuan Beijing shiwei jiguan Mao Zedong sixiang hongqi bingduan, *Da yexing jia, da yinmou jia*, 23.

61. See art. 85 of the 1954 Constitution in Chen Hefu, *Zhongguo xianfa leibian*, 232. Also see "Peng Zhen tongzhi guanghui zhandou de yisheng," 8. The theme of equality before the law was to reemerge in a slightly revised form during the post-Mao period. See Chen Changhang, "'Falu pingdeng' de lixiang, xianshi, lishi." These views were shared and perhaps inspired by Liu Shaoqi, who gave the speech introducing the 1954 Constitution and who, in response to Mao's "Contradictions" speech, disputed the centrality of counterrevolution as a problem for the PRC. See Beijing huagong xue yuan and Mao Zedong sixiang

xuanzhaun yuan, "Dadao dang nei zui da de zou ziben zhuyi daolu dangquanpai—Liu Shaoqi," 13.

62. "Counter-Revolutionary Revisionist P'eng Chen's Towering Crimes," 2; "Peng Zhen zai wuchan jieji zhuanzheng fangmian de fan Mao Zedong sixiang yanlun," 8; "Peng Zhen de fandong heihua de zhaibian," 3.

63. Peng Zhen, "Gongmin zai falu mianqian ren ren pingdeng," 256. The cause célèbre at the time was the case of Huang Yifeng, although the treatment of veteran cadres had caused considerable consternation since 1949. Teiwes, *Politics and Purges*, 2nd ed., 96–98.

64. Zhu Liyu, *Peng Zhen minzhu fazhi sixiang yanjiu*, 59.

65. Wang Hanbin, "Peng Zhen tongzhi dui wo guo shehui zhuyi minzhu fazhi jianshe de zhuoyue gongxian," 29.

66. See, e.g., "Zhonggong zhongyang pijun zhongyang shi ren xiaozu guanyu fageming fenzi he qita huaifenzi de jieshi ji chuli de zhengce jiexian de zanxing guiding"; "Zhonggong zhongyang shi ren xiaozu 'Guanyu fageming fenzi he qita huaifenzi de jieshi ji chuli de zhengce jiexian de zanxing guiding' de buchong jieshi."

67. Chen Changhang, "'Falu pingdeng' de lixiang, xianshi, lishi," 141–49. In his discussion of the "Seven Draft Laws," Peng noted that the pursuit of special privileges would undermine the legal system. Peng Zhen, "Guanyu qige falu cao'an de shuoming." Moreover, continued reference in the same document to the ongoing presence of "leftist remnants" revealed Peng's concern that such remnants in particular would seek to manipulate the judicial system for their own political benefit.

68. Peng Zhen, "Zheng-fa gongzuo de zhuyao renwu." For discussion, see Wang Hanbin, "Peng Zhen tongzhi dui wo guo shehui zhuyi minzhu fazhi jianshe de zhuoyue gongxian," 29.

69. Yuan Beijing shiwei jiguan Mao Zedong sixiang hongqi bingduan, *Da yexing jia, da yinmou jia*, 21.

70. See, e.g., "Dadao lao pai da pantu Peng Zhen," 7–8; "Dadao wuchan jieji zhuanzheng de sidi Peng Zhen," 3; "«Xiuyang»he «Lun dang nei douzheng»shi zhenya geming pai de ruan daozi," 2; Zhongguo renmin jiefangjun houqin xueyuan «xinghuo liaoyuan»geming zaofantuan, "Chedi qingsuan Peng Zhen fandui Mao zhuxi de taotian zuixing."

71. Among Liu's most prominent statements on the need for peaceful means for establishing socialism in China was his speech introducing the 1954 Constitution, in which he acknowledged that class struggle still existed in China but claimed that the elimination of capitalist exploitation could be achieved peacefully. See Liu Shaoqi, "Report on the Draft Constitution of the People's Republic of China," 291–95.

72. Liu Shaoqi, "Report on the Draft Constitution of the People's Republic of China," 284.

73. In his Contradictions speech, Mao noted that even the process of attacking class enemies must go through government institutions. Mao Zedong, "On the Correct Handling of Contradictions Among the People," 133. And even in

the course of decrying the role of law in China at the Beidaihe meetings of August 1958, Mao still held to the need for organizational procedures in governance. Mao Zedong, "Talks at the Beidaihe Conference," 423–24.

74. Young, "Mao Zedong and the Class Struggle in Socialist Society"; Womack, "Where Mao Went Wrong," esp. 32–34.

75. Yuan Beijing shiwei jiguan Mao Zedong sixiang hongqi bingduan, *Da yexing jia, da yinmou jia*, 29–31.

76. Teiwes, *Politics and Purges*, 2nd ed., 178; MacFarquhar, *Origins of the Cultural Revolution, 1*, 100. Compare Ren Dongyun, *Gongheguo zhuxi de rong yu ru*, 51. The passage of Liu's report addressing "The Political Life of the State" appears in *Zhongguo gongchandang di ba ci quanguo daibiao dahui wenjian*, 45; and in Liu Shaoqi, "Political Report of the Central Committee."

77. Shi Zhongquan et al., *Zhonggong ba da shi*, 150–69.

78. See Peng Zhen, "Zai quanguo gongan, jiancha, sifa huiyi shang de jianghua," 124, where Peng called for continued reliance on the *zheng-fa* institutions of the public security, procuracy, and judiciary in order to avoid mistakes of leftism and rightism in managing the balance between dictatorship and democracy.

79. See Peng Zhen, "Zhonghua renmin gongheguo quan guo renmin daibiao dahui changwu weiyuanhui de gongzuo baogao" (1955).

80. See Peng Zhen, "Zhonghua renmin gongheguo quan guo renmin daibiao dahui changwu weiyuanhui de gongzuo baogao" (1956).

81. See, e.g., Peng Zhen, "Zhonghua renmin gongheguo quan guo renmin daibiao dahui changwu weiyuanhui de gongzuo baogao" (1956). This report, which studiously avoided discussion of the Hundred Flowers Campaign, which was nearing conclusion or the Anti-Rightist Campaign soon to begin, reviewed work in the areas of foreign affairs (including reference to Peng's April 1957 visit to the USSR and Eastern Europe), extensive regulatory enactments (including decisions on courts deciding cases of counterrevolutionaries, state bond issues, and regulations on policy), and rather minimal legislative activities (drafting work on the criminal law code and civil law code still under way).

82. Zhu Liyu, *Peng Zhen minzhu fazhi sixiang yanjiu*, 67.

83. Wang Hanbin, "Peng Zhen tongzhi dui wo guo shehui zhuyi minzhu fazhi jianshe de zhuoyue gongxian," 31. Reportedly, Peng defied Mao's instructions to delay work on criminal and civil codes, and although these were not enacted, Peng still attempted to vest the NPC with exclusive authority to interpret as well as enact legislation. See Yuan Beijing shiwei jiguan Mao Zedong sixiang hongqi bingduan, *Da yexing jia, da yinmou jia*, 25.

84. Wang Hanbin, "Peng Zhen tongzhi dui wo guo shehui zhuyi minzhu fazhi jianshe de zhuoyue gongxian," 31.

85. Peng Zhen, "Zhonghua renmin gongheguo quan guo renmin daibiao dahui changwu weiyuanhui de gongzuo baogao" (1955).

86. Wang Hanbin, "Peng Zhen tongzhi dui wo guo shehui zhuyi minzhu fazhi jianshe de zhuoyue gongxian," 31.

87. Zhang Wenjian, "Xuexi Peng Zhen tongzhi qinfen gongzuo de jingshen," 356. The fact that Peng oversaw the construction of the Great Hall (along with the other "ten great projects") revealed a certain complementarity in his management of political position. See "Peng Zhen tongzhi guanghui zhandou de yisheng," 5.

88. For the leading work on this point, see MacFarquhar, *Origins of the Cultural Revolution, 1*.

89. For general discussion of the Hundred Flowers and Anti-Rightist Campaigns, see generally MacFarquhar, "Secret Speeches of Chairman Mao"; *Communist China 1955–1959*, 12–16; Domes, *Internal Politics of China*, 58–62; Teiwes, *Politics and Purges*, 1st ed., 249–55, and 2nd ed., 166–260, Solomon, *Mao's Revolution and the Chinese Political Culture*, 264 ff. and chap. 17; Lieberthal, *Governing China*, 100 ff.; Han Suyin, *Wind in the Tower*, chap. 6; Goldman, "Peking University Today"; Meisner, *Mao's China*, chap. 11. For a review of contrasting scholarly views, see Teiwes, "Establishment and Consolidation," 135–37. Also see MacFarquhar, *Politics of China*, 79–80.

90. For discussion of Lu's speech to various prominent intellectuals in May 1956, see *Communist China 1955–1959*, 6. For discussion of Lu's report on the CPC Central Committee's policies regarding the Hundred Flowers Campaign, see Xu Taocheng, "'Yin mou'—1957," 44.

91. Bo Yibo, *Ruogan zhong da juece yu shijian de huigu*, 604.

92. Liu Shaoqi, "Political Report of the Central Committee."

93. Bo Yibo, *Ruogan zhong da juece yu shijian de huigu*, 604.

94. This process is explained and documented at length in MacFarquhar, Cheek and Wu, eds., *The Secret Speeches of Chairman Mao*.

95. MacFarquhar, *Origins of the Cultural Revolution, 1*.

96. For discussion of Peng Zhen's role in supporting *People's Daily* editor Deng Tuo in resisting the campaign, see Cheek, "Deng Tuo: A Chinese Leninist Approach to Journalism." For further discussion of resistance to Mao's call for a general rectification campaign in the Party, see generally Goodman, *Deng Xiaoping and the Chinese Revolution*, 57 ff.; Teiwes, *Politics and Purges*, 2nd ed., 196; *Communist China 1955–1959*, 16; Domes, *Internal Politics of China*. 58; Chang, *Power and Policy in China*, 2nd ed., 37; Chu-yuan Cheng, "Root of China's Cultural Revolution," 1162. Peng's mentor Liu Shaoqi has also been suspected of resisting Mao's call for the Hundred Flowers Campaign. See Teiwes, *Politics and Purges*, 1st ed., 252 ff. Also see Xu Taocheng, "'Yin mou'—1957," 45.

97. For the report from a propaganda work conference held under the auspices of the Beijing municipal CPC committee, see "Propaganda Work Conference in Peking."

98. "Peng Zhen tongzhi tan jianchi hefeng xiyu de fangfa."

99. Teiwes, *Politics and Purges*, 2nd ed., 197–98.

100. "P'eng Chen on Contradictions Within the Ranks of the People." Also see Teiwes, *Politics and Purges*, 1st ed., 251–52. Also see Moody, *Opposition and Dissent*, 159; "Mao's 'Khrushchev Speech.'"

101. Ding Shu, *Yangmou: fan you qian hou*, 123 ff. Compare with Peng Zhen, "Guanyu zhenya fangeming huodong he chengzhi fangeming tiaoli wenti de baogao," 4–6.

102. Peng Zhen, "Kefu guanliao zhuyi zuofeng."

103. "Peng Zhen zai Beijing shi xuanchuan gongzuo huiyi shang de baogao"; "P'eng Chen on Contradictions Within the Ranks of the People"; Shanxi Party Committee History Research Office, *Peng Zhen shengping dashi nianbiao*, 31.

104. Goodman, *Deng Xiaoping and the Chinese Revolution*, 58.

105. See, e.g., Peng Zhen, "Beijing shi wu nian lai zhengfu gongzuo qingkuang he jinhou gongzuo renwu," 28–30; Peng Zhen, "Report on Political and Legal Work."

106. Peng Zhen, "Zhonghua renmin gongheguo quanguo renmin daibiao dahui daibiaotuan fangwen Sulian, Jie Ke Si Luo Fa Ke, Luo Man Ni Ya, Bao Jia Li Ya, A Er Ba Ni Ya, Nan Xi La Fa de baogao."

107. Peng was later to be charged with attempting to use the NPC and the Beijing People's Representative Congress to build alliances with non-CPC democratic parties. See Yuan Beijing shiwei jiguan Mao Zedong sixiang hongqi bingduan, *Da yexing jia, da yinmou jia*, 32.

108. Liu Shaoqi, "Report on the Work of the Central Committee of the Communist Party of China to the Second Session of the Eighth National Congress."

109. Liu Shaoqi, "Victory of Marxism-Leninism in China."

110. In the section on the political life of the state that Peng purportedly drafted for Liu Shaoqi's Political Report to the Eighth National Party Congress, criticism was directed against "some members of our Party who hold that everything should absolutely be of one color, who are unwilling to see non-Party people work in state organs, who do not consult with them when circumstances require, and do not respect the authority that goes with their posts." See *Zhongguo gongchandang di ba ci quanguo daibiao dahui wenjian*; Liu Shaoqi, "Political Report of the Central Committee." Indeed, during the Cultural Revolution, Peng was stridently criticized for advocating tolerance toward capitalists. See "Counter-Revolutionary Revisionist P'eng Chen's Towering Crimes," 38, 39.

111. Teiwes, *Politics and Purges*, 2nd ed., 209.

112. "Peng Zhen zai Beijing shi xuanchuan gongzuo huiyi shang de baogao."

113. "Peng Zhen tongzhi tan jianchi hefeng xiyu de fangfa."

114. Peng Zhen did not dismiss the usefulness of accepting criticism; rather, he criticized "wholly incorrect policies and methods of resolution" regarding the handling of contradictions—i.e., regarding the management of the campaign. See "Peng Zhen zai Beijing shi xuanchuan gongzuo huiyi shang de baogao."

115. Qiu Shi, *Gongheguo zhongda shijian juece shilu*, a:110 ff.

116. Bo Yibo, *Ruogan zhong da juece yu shijian de huigu*, 612.

117. Qiu Shi, *Gongheguo zhongda shijian juece shilu*, 1:225 ff.

118. Moody, *Opposition and Dissent*, 159.

119. Bo Yibo, *Ruogan zhong da juece yu shijian de huigu*, 617. The directive was a somewhat scaled-down version of Mao's June 10 instruction, suggesting that

there was significant resistance at the Centre to Mao's plans to attack the democratic parties, and suggesting that intellectuals in educational institutions as well as former capitalists had been targeted during the *san fan* campaign five years earlier.

120. See generally Ding Shu, *Yangmou: fan you qian hou*. Also see Qiu Shi, *Gongheguo zhongda shijian he juece neimu*, 2:580; Qiu Shi, *Gongheguo zhongda shijian juece shilu*, 2:220.

121. For examples of the consequences for individual victims of the campaign, see, e.g., Whyte, *Small Groups and Political Rituals*, 194–203; Chang Jung, *Wild Swans*; Wu Ningkun, *Single Tear*.

122. Lieberthal, *Governing China*, 100–102; Friedman, Pickowicz, and Selden, *Chinese Village Socialist State*, 209–13; Vogel, *Canton Under Communism*, 203 ff.

123. See, e.g., MacFarquhar, *Origins of the Cultural Revolution, 1*.

124. Ding Shu, *Yangmou: fan you qian hou*, 153 ff.

125. Bo Yibo, *Ruogan zhong da juece yu shijian de huigu*, 617.

126. See "Peng Zhen tongzhi zai Beijing shi renmin dai hui shang chanshu fanyou douzheng de weida yiyi."

127. See, e.g., "Counter-Revolutionary Revisionist P'eng Chen's Towering Crimes," 16; "Dossier of P'eng Chen," 37; "Down With P'eng Chen—Big Party Boss of the Kuomintang," 10; "Peng Zhen zai wuchan jieji zhuanzheng fangmian de fan Mao Zedong sixiang yanlun."

128. See, e.g., Peng Zhen, "Zai quanguo gongan, jiancha, sifa huiyi shang de jianghua," in which Peng cautions against expansion of the movement and urges judicial institutions (public security, procuracy, and courts) to rely on legal processes in avoiding excesses in carrying out the campaign. For a more recent articulation of Peng's opposition to expansion of the Anti-Rightist Campaign, see Peng Zhen, "Zai zhongyang gongzuo huiyi Dongbei zu de fayan." At the time of the campaign, Peng's opposition was echoed by others and portended the eruption of serious political conflict over the Great Leap Forward and subsequent Maoist policies. Bo Yibo, *Ruogan zhong da juece yu shijian de huigu*, 618 ff.

129. Lu Xiangtou, *Liu Shaoqi he ta de shiye*, 421.

130. Ultimately, Peng was attacked for seeking reversal of verdicts for those caught up in the campaign against "Right Opportunism" as well. See, e.g., "P'eng Lu Luo Yang Counter-Revolutionary Revisionist Clique's Crime of Kicking up a Strong Wind of 'Reversal of Verdicts.'" Also see Yuan Beijing shi wei jiguan hongqi bingtuan and Yuan Beijing shi wei jiguangeming zaofan dui, "Chedi qingsuan Liu Shaoqi he Peng Zhen fangeming xiuzheng zhuyi jituan zai renmin lai xin lai fang gongzuo zhong de taotian zuixing," 8, wherein Peng is accused of receiving letters from convicted "rightists" and then supporting reversal of verdicts in these cases. A more benign interpretation of Liu's efforts to rehabilitate both "rightists" is contained in Ren Dongyun, *Gongheguo zhuxi de rong yu ru*, 75–76.

131. Ding Shu, *Yangmou: fan you qian hou*, 280 ff. For discussion of the quota system, see Lieberthal, *Governing China*, 101, and references therein.

132. Liu and Mao were beginning to differ sharply on the question of internal Party contradictions, with Liu opposing Mao's alarmist views about the fundamental contradiction between socialism and capitalism being played out inside the CPC. See Lu Xiangtou, *Liu Shaoqi he ta de shiye*, 433.

133. Li Che, *P'eng Chen fan Mao chi-t'uan*, 12, wherein Peng is quoted as having said in 1929 that although everyone should learn from the working masses, "intellectuals should all undergo proletarian transformation."

134. Cheek, "Honorable Vocation," 249. Also see Yuan Beijing shiwei jiguan Mao Zedong sixiang hongqi bingduan, *Da yexing jia, da yinmou jia*, 26–27, where Peng is accused of proposing better treatment for intellectuals.

135. Yuan Beijing shiwei jiguan Mao Zedong sixiang hongqi bingduan, *Da yexing jia, da yinmou jia*, 36–37. No such protection was forthcoming for intellectuals such as Feng Xuefeng and Ding Ling, who challenged Party demands for political orthodoxy; they were attacked by a senior Ministry of Culture official (probably Zhou Yang) who linked them to Hu Feng. Wen Bi, *Zhonguo [zuo] huo*.

136. Ding Shu, *Yangmou: fan you qian hou*, 330–31; Liao Kuangsheng (Liao Guangsheng), "'Independent Administration of Justice' and the PRC Legal System," 130 ff.

137. Yuan Beijing shiwei jiguan Mao Zedong sixiang hongqi bingduan, *Da yexing jia, da yinmou jia*, 36–37.

138. Peng Zhen, "Zai quanguo gongan, jiancha, sifa huiyi shang de jianghua."

139. Zhu Liyu, *Peng Zhen minzhu fazhi sixiang yanjiu*, 53.

140. Peng Zhen, "Gongan jiguan bu neng yong zhuanzheng banfa chuli renmin neibu wenti."

141. Peng Zhen, "Zai quanguo zheng-fa gongzuo huiyi shang de jianghua jiyao."

CHAPTER 4

1. For the authoritative treatment of circumstances leading up to and surrounding the Great Leap Forward, see MacFarquhar, *Origins of the Cultural Revolution, 3*. Among the many excellent works published on the subject, see Lieberthal, "Great Leap Forward and the Split in the Yenan Leadership"; Bachman, *Bureaucracy, Economy and Leadership in China*; Lieberthal, *Governing China*, 102–8.

2. Teiwes and Sun, "Mao, Deng Zihui, and the Politics of Agricultural Cooperativization." Also see Qiu Shi, *Gongheguo zhongda shijian juece shilu*, 1:141 ff.

3. Tang Tsou, *Cultural Revolution and Post-Mao Reforms*, 71. Also see "Drag Out Liu Shaoqi and Show Him to the Public," 14.

4. "Fan you kuodahua de yingxiang," 1372, 1374. Also see Teiwes, *Politics and Purges*, 2nd ed., 262, 274.

5. See generally *Communist China 1955–1959*, 7 ff.; Eckstein, *China's Economic Revolution*, 54 ff.

6. Chai Zemin and An Pingsheng, "Shishi qiushi de fanli," 7.

7. Peng Zhen, "Ban hao nongye shengchan hezuoshe."

8. Qiu Shi, *Gongheguo zhongda shijian juece shilu*, 1:147, 173 ff.

9. Yuan Beijing shiwei jiguan Mao Zedong sixiang hongqi bingduan, *Da yexing jia, da yinmou jia*. Peng Zhen's subsequent rejection of "*fan mao jin*" in November 1957 was deemed by Red Guards an indicator of his political opportunism.

10. "Chedi maizang yi Peng Zhen wei shou de jiu Beijing shi wei," 303.

11. MacFarquhar, "Secret Speeches of Chairman Mao," 14–18; Goodman, *Deng Xiaoping and the Chinese Revolution*, 59; Teiwes, *Politics and Purges*, 2nd ed., chap. 8; Yuan Beijing shiwei jiguan Mao Zedong sixiang hongqi bingduan, *Da yexing jia, da yinmou jia*, 38.

12. *Communist China 1955–1959*, 18.

13. Solomon, *Mao's Revolution and the Chinese Political Culture*, 344 ff. For discussion of veiled critiques of the Great Leap policies as early as April 1958, see Naughton, "Sun Yefang," 138 ff. For discussion as to whether the Great Leap Forward was primarily Mao's initiative or was derived from bureaucratic processes in the State Planning Commission, see Teiwes, "Leaders, Institutions, and the Origins of the Great Leap Forward"; Bachman, "Response to Teiwes."

14. The growing importance of the Secretariat stood in marked contrast to the relative inactivity of the NPC, which Peng and Liu Shaoqi had championed after 1954. By 1958 the NPC was relegated to the sidelines, enacting hardly any formal legislation and precious little in the way of administrative regulations, focusing instead on issuing routine approvals of local representative congress initiatives. See, e.g., Peng Zhen, "Zhonghua renmin gongheguo quan guo renmin daibiao dahui changwu weiyuanhui de gongzuo baogao" (1959); "Zhonghua renmin gongheguo di er jie quanguo renmin daibiao dahui di si ci hui guanyu di sanjie quanguo renmin daibiao dahui daibiao ming'e he xuanju wenti de jueyi"; "Zhonghua renmin gongheguo di er jie quanguo renmin daibiao dahui fa an weiyuanhui guanyu di san jie quanguo renmin daibiao dahui daibiao ming'e he xuanju wenti de jueyi (cao'an) de shencha baogao," 12, 13.

15. Shi Dongbing, *Zuichu de kangzheng*, 2.

16. Yuan Beijing shiwei jiguan Mao Zedong sixiang hongqi bingduan, *Da yexing jia, da yinmou jia*, 37.

17. "Di qi ci quan guo jiancha gongzuo huiyi."

18. See generally Ahn, "Adjustments in the Great Leap Forward," 259 ff. For discussion of the December 1958 Wuhan Resolution that called for consolidation and some degree of scaling back of the Great Leap Forward, see *Communist China 1955–1959*, 25 ff.

19. Peng Zhen, "Zhan zai geming he jianshe de zui qianxian." Mao called himself a "middle of the roader" at Lushan, although this was in the context of a broader review of the Great Leap policies when Mao was attempting to temper policy reversals on the Great Leap Forward. See Teiwes, *Politics and Purges*, 2nd ed., 306. Peng's critique of middle of the roadism in 1958 was, on the surface at least, consistent with prevailing doctrine.

20. For discussion of the impact of the decentralized approach to the Great Leap Forward in Guangzhou, see Vogel, *Canton Under Communism*, 224–27.

21. Peng Zhen's "Zhonghua renmin gongheguo quan guo renmin daibiao dahui changwu weiyuanhui de gongzuo baogao" (1959).

22. Teiwes, *Politics and Purges*, 2nd ed., 306 ff.

23. Li Rui, "Initial Study of Mao Zedong's Erroneous 'Left' Thinking," 56–59.

24. Li Rui, *Li Rui fan "zuo" wenxuan*, 26.

25. Li Rui, *Li Rui fan "zuo" wenxuan*, 26.

26. For discussion, see Teiwes, *Politics and Purges*, 2nd ed., chap. 9. Also see Saich and Hearst, "Li Rui," 78 ff.

27. For discussion of post-Mao reviews of the mistakes of Party leadership during the Great Leap Forward, see Joseph, "Tragedy of Good Intentions."

28. Teiwes, *Politics and Purges*, 2nd ed., 347; MacFarquhar, *Origins of the Cultural Revolution*, 3, 63.

29. Bo Yibo, *Ruogan zhong da juece yu shijian de huigu*, 905–6. Also see Cheek, *Propaganda and Culture*, chap. 5.

30. Goodman, *Deng Xiaoping and the Chinese Revolution*, 66.

31. Zhang Peng and Zhao Youfu, "Yi Peng Zhen tongzhi de Huairou xian nongcun diaocha," 230. Red Guard reports claimed these investigations were done to oppose Mao. "Jingxin dongbo de 'Gong ting zheng bian' yinmou," 2–3. For a critique of Peng's investigation in Huairou, see Shoudu hong dai hui and Hebei Beijing shiyuan, "Peng Zei 'Huairuo diaocha' shi Liu Deng hei si ling bu yinmou bi ziben zhuyi de yanzhong buzhu." These were not the first investigations to examine mistakes and lessons of the Great Leap Forward. In November 1960, for example, the State Planning Commission held a conference under the direction of Li Fuqun to discuss the Great Leap Forward and debate enactment of the "Eight Character Policy" (*ba zi fangzhen*) of *tiaozheng, gonggu, chongshi, tigao* (retrenchment, consolidation, filling out, and raising standards), which in effect brought the Great Leap Forward to a close. See Bo Yibo, *Ruogan zhong da juece yu shijian de huigu*, 893. Also see MacFarquhar, *Origins of the Cultural Revolution*, 3, 49.

32. Zhang Peng and Zhao Youfu, "Yi Peng Zhen tongzhi de Huairou xian nongcun diaocha," 230–31.

33. "Jingxin dongbo de 'Gong ting zheng bian' yinmou," 3. The results of these investigations probably contributed to the drafting of the "Seventy Articles on Industry" under Bo Yibo's direction. See "Dadao fangeming xiuzheng zhuyi fenzi Bo Yibo," 4.

34. Peng Zhen, "Jianchi diaocha yanjiu he qunzhong luxian," where Peng's call for upholding the mass line suggested oblique criticism of Mao's Great Leap policies that were so destructive of ordinary people's lives; and Peng Zhen, "Gongan jiguan bu neng yong zhuanzheng banfa chuli renmin neibu wenti," where Peng urged restraint among the police in handling popular resistance to Great Leap policies.

35. For discussion of the Changguanlou meetings, see MacFarquhar, *Origins of the Cultural Revolution*, 3, 182–83. Also see Joseph, *Critique of Ultra-Leftism*,

78–79; Lieberthal, *Research Guide*, 176–77; Goldman, *China's Intellectuals*, 25 ff. Red Guard accounts appear in "Events Surrounding the 'Ch'angkuanlou' Counterrevolutionary Incident"; "Thoroughly Disclosing the Inside Story of Chang Guan Lou Counterrevolutionary Incident"; Zheng Xuan, "Cuan dang cuan guo yinmou de da baolu"; "'Chang guan lou' fan geming shijian de qian qian hou hou"; "[Changguanlou] Peng Zhen fadong fan Mao."

36. Goodman, *Deng Xiaoping and the Chinese Revolution*, 66–67.

37. Teiwes, *Politics and Purges*, 2nd ed., 384.

38. See "Jingxin dongbo de 'Gong ting zheng bian' yinmou," 1; "Drag Out Liu Shaoqi and Show Him to the Public," 5.

39. Cheng Hsuan (Zheng Xuan), "Big Exposure of a Conspiracy," 5.

40. For discussion of the policy debates on *san zi yi bao*, see Ahn, "Adjustments in the Great Leap Forward," 270 ff. Peng's support for these policies can be attributed in part to the fact that Liu Shaoqi was behind them. See Ren Dongyun, *Gongheguo zhuxi de rong yu ru*, 47; Yi Ling and Wu Yuan, *Liu Shaoqi*, 9–11. In an effort to institutionalize some of the conclusions of the Changguanlou meetings, Liu supported the West Building Conference (*Xi lou huiyi*) in February 1962 to review the economic situation and reinstate the Finance Small Group under Chen Yun. Ren Dongyun, *Gongheguo zhuxi de rong yu ru*, 75–76.

41. See generally Lieberthal, *Research Guide*, 179. For discussion of the 7,000 Cadres Conference, see MacFarquhar, *Origins of the Cultural Revolution, 3*, 149 ff.

42. Liu's report vindicated many of the criticisms lodged by Peng Dehuai at Lushan, and indeed Liu attempted unsuccessfully to have Peng Dehuai rehabilitated. Bo Yibo, *Ruogan zhong da juece yu shijian de huigu*, 1090 ff.

43. Bo Yibo, *Ruogan zhong da juece yu shijian de huigu*, 1026; MacFarquhar, *Origins of the Cultural Revolution, 3*, 155–58. Also see "Chedi maizang yi Peng Zhen wei shou de jiu Beijing shi wei," 302.

44. The issue of collectivization in agriculture—the focus of Great Leap policies and of the critique of Mao's initiatives—remained unsettled, and Peng continued his involvement in investigation of these problems. In Anhui, for example, the pioneering of a responsible field (*zeren tian*) system was championed by CPC Secretary Zheng Xisheng with tacit approval from Peng Zhen, Deng Zihui, Tan Zhenlin, and the vice director of the Central Committee's Rural Work Department, Wang Guanlian. Mao continued to oppose this policy as well as the associated *bao chan dao hu* responsibility system, and he succeeded in having Deng Zihui purged at the Tenth Plenum of the Eighth CPC Central Committee in September 1962. Zheng Xisheng had been purged earlier in the year, at the 7,000 Cadres Conference. See Bo Yibo, *Ruogan zhong da juece yu shijian de huigu*, 1080 ff.

45. Goldman, "Chinese Communist Party's 'Cultural Revolution'"; Solomon, *Mao's Revolution and the Chinese Political Culture*, 412–19.

46. For discussion of Hai Rui and text of the play, see Ding Youguan, "Lishi ju 'Hai Rui Ba Guan' de fengbo"; Ansley, *Heresy of Wu Han*; *Hai Rui Dismissed from Office* (trans. Huang). Also see Li Che, *P'eng Chen fan Mao chi-t'uan*, chap. 3.

47. Fisher, "The Play's the Thing." Also see Teiwes, *Politics and Purges*, 2nd ed., 374. By contrast, the novel *Liu Zhidan*, published by Liu's sister-in-law Li

Jiantong, was more directly linked to the matter of Peng Dehuai and later was used by Kang Sheng as a basis for attacking Xi Zhongxun and others in the Central Propaganda Department. See Qiu Shi, *Gongheguo zhongda juece chutai qian hou,* 1:257–58. Also see Holm, "Strange Case of *Liu Zhidan*."

48. Li Che, *P'eng Chen fan Mao chi-t'uan,* 87, for this interpretation of Wu Han's epithet, *la gu wu qun cao sheng* (at the twelve moon sound the call and in spring grasses will grow).

49. See generally Cheek, "Politics of Cultural Reform"; "Deng Tuo: A Chinese Leninist Approach to Journalism"; and *Propaganda and Culture.* Also see Qiu Shi, *Gongheguo zhongda juece chutai qian hou,* 1:272 ff.

50. See generally Su Shuangbi and Wang Hongzhi, *Wen ge di yi yuan an.* Cheek, after detailed study of these columns, concludes that they were in essence loyalist Party critiques in line with Peng Zhen's views. Cheek, *Propaganda and Culture,* chap. 5.

51. See generally Becker, *Hungry Ghosts.*

52. See Peng Zhen, "Guanyu gonghui gongzuo."

53. The potential effectiveness of these efforts to strengthen control by Party traditionalists over the labor system was borne out during the Cultural Revolution when the Peng (Zhen)–Lu (Dingyi)–Luo (Ruiqing)–Yang (Shangkun) clique was accused of attempting to carry out a workers' movement in opposition to Mao. See Ch'en Kung-shu, "P'eng Chen fan Mao chi," 19–20.

54. Unger, "Struggle to Dictate China's Administration," 21. Ultimately, Mao did turn his attention to urban workers by asserting in early 1965 that an urban socialist education campaign be carried out along the lines of the rural model that had by then been completed. See Yan Jiaqi and Gao Gao, *[Wenhua da geming] shi nian shi,* 50.

55. See Peng Zhen, "Yao zhuyi peiyang tiba xin ganbu."

56. Peng Zhen, "Zijue di zou lishi biyou zhi lu." Also see Peng Zhen, "Qingnian yeyu zuojia yao yanzhe zhengque de fangxiang buduan qianjin"; "Comrade P'eng Chen Makes on Behalf of the Party Central Committee an Important Report." For a critique of Peng's approach, see "Chronology of Important Events."

57. Hamrin, "Yang Xianzhen's Philosophical Criminal Case."

58. Peng Zhen, "Zai quanguo zheng-fa gongzuo huiyi shang de jianghua jiyao."

59. Yuan Beijing shi wei jiguan hongqi bingtuan and Yuan Beijing shi wei jiguangeming zaofan dui, "Chedi qingsuan Liu Shaoqi he Peng Zhen," 9–10.

60. See, e.g., Mao Zedong, "Talks at the Beidaihe Conference," 424, where Mao is quoted as saying draft resolutions and conferences are equivalent to law.

61. Li Che, *P'eng Chen fan Mao chi-t'uan,* 96. Also see "Zhishi fenzi qianjin de daolu."

62. For discussion of the "restoration of capitalism" question, see Yang, "Cultural Revolution and Revisionism"; Wang Ruoshui, "Mao Zedong yu [Wenhua da geming]."

63. For authoritative discussion of the campaign, see Baum and Teiwes,

Ssu-Ch'ing. Also see Hao Ping, "Reassessing the Starting Point of the Cultural Revolution"; Teiwes, *Politics and Purges*, 2nd ed., chap. 11; Bo Yibo, *Ruogan zhong da juece yu shijian de huigu*, 1105–36; Vogel, *Canton Under Communism*, 308–20; Chang, *Power and Policy in China*, 2nd ed., 158 ff.; Meisner, *Mao's China*, chap. 17; Guillermaz, *Chinese Communist Party in Power*, chap. 27; Ahn, *Chinese Politics and the Cultural Revolution*, 62 ff.; Goldman, "Chinese Communist Party's 'Cultural Revolution'"; Thornton, *China: The Struggle for Power*, 256–68; Domes, *Internal Politics of China*, chap. 9; Solomon, *Mao's Revolution and the Chinese Political Culture*, 435 ff.; Johnson, "Chinese Communist Leadership and Mass Response," 397–437.

64. See generally MacFarquhar, *Origins of the Cultural Revolution, 3*, chap. 12.

65. The First Ten Points appear as app. B in Baum and Teiwes, *Ssu-Ch'ing*, 58.

66. MacFarquhar, *Origins of the Cultural Revolution, 3*, 339.

67. Zhang Wenjian, "Xuexi Peng Zhen tongzhi qinfen gongzuo de jingshen," 357. Also see MacFarquhar, *Origins of the Cultural Revolution, 3*, 343 ff.

68. The Latter Ten Points are included as app. C in Baum and Teiwes, *Ssu-Ch'ing*, 72. Although Liu Shaoqi was accused during the Cultural Revolution of drafting the Latter Ten Points (see "Drag Out Liu Shaoqi and Show Him to the Public," 8), more reasoned analyses conclude that Peng was the author. Solomon, *Mao's Revolution and the Chinese Political Culture*, 434–35; Ahn, *Chinese Politics and the Cultural Revolution*, 62.

69. "Liu Shaoqi's reactionary speeches," 14.

70. Baum and Teiwes, *Ssu-Ch'ing*, 29 ff.; Ren Dongyun, *Gongheguo zhuxi de rong yu ru*, 80–81.

71. Hao Ping, "Reassessing the Starting Point of the Cultural Revolution," 71. Also see Ahn, *Chinese Politics and the Cultural Revolution*, 115.

72. Cheek, *Propaganda and Culture*, chap. 6.

73. "You yi jian chumu jingxin de fangeming shijian," 14. Also see "San shi san ge fangeming xiuzheng zhuyi fenzi," 224–25.

74. First Ten Points, art. 9, and Latter Ten Points, art. 7; Baum and Teiwes, *Ssu-Ch'ing*, 67–69, 88–90.

75. First Ten Points, arts. 3 and 5.

76. Latter Ten Points, arts. 3 and 9.

77. In his January 31, 1965, speech to the second session of the Fourth National Committee of the All-China Youth Federation and the simultaneously held Eighteenth National Students Representative Conference, Peng pointed out that the "Party, in dealing with young people with different family origins and experience, attached importance to their behavior." See "Comrade P'eng Chen Makes on Behalf of the Party Central Committee an Important Report," 1. Also see Rosen, *Red Guard Factionalism*, 85.

78. Latter Ten Points, art. 10.

79. Shi Dongbing, *Zuichu de kangzheng*, 21.

80. Revised Latter Ten Points, art. 10. For discussion of Liu Shaoqi's authorship of the Revised Latter Ten Points, see Dittmer, *Liu Shao-ch'i and the Chinese Cultural Revolution*, 50.

81. MacFarquhar, *Origins of the Cultural Revolution, 3*, 406.

82. Baum and Teiwes, *Ssu-Ch'ing*, 47–48. Also see Ren Dongyun, *Gongheguo zhuxi de rong yu ru*, 80–81.

83. MacFarquhar, *Origins of the Cultural Revolution, 3*, 427.

84. Hao Ping, "Reassessing the Starting Point of the Cultural Revolution," 73.

85. Despite the suggestion by Deng Xiaoping, who chaired the Secretariat meeting at which the 23 Articles were passed, that Mao need not attend, Mao insisted, and he gave a speech focusing on the ongoing contradictions in China between socialism and capitalism. See Ren Dongyun, *Gongheguo zhuxi de rong yu ru*, 80–81. It was also at this point that articles began to appear suggesting the existence of leading authorities in the CPC taking the capitalist road. See Baum and Teiwes, *Ssu-Ch'ing*, 47–48.

86. Peng Zhen, "Guanyu xueshu taolun de jige wenti."

87. For critiques of Peng's view, see "Counter-Revolutionary Revisionist P'eng Chen's Towering Crimes." Also see Chang, *Factional and Coalition Politics in China*, 14; P'eng Shu-tse, *Chinese Communist Party in Power*, 279.

88. For a discussion of Mao's contention that all understanding has a class character, see Schram, *Political Thought of Mao Tse-tung*, 180–85, 190–94. For attacks on Peng's resistance to Mao's class theory, see "'Zhenli mianqian ren ren pingdeng' de yao shan shi fou dingwan wuchan jieji zhuanzheng."

89. See e.g, Peng Zhen, *Guanyu Jin Cha Ji bianqu dang de gongzuo he juti zhengce baogao*, 166–67.

90. These issues were given public prominence in the Beijing Party Committee's journal, *Qianxian* (Frontline). For example, one article took the guise of discussing whether truth had a class character, or whether one could distinguish between objective laws and various class-based theories about those objective laws. See "Zai tan zhenli you meiyou jiejixing." Also see Peng Zhen, "Jianchi diaocha yanjiu he qunzhong luxian." For discussion of *Qianxian* and its significance, see Cheek, "Deng Tuo: Culture, Leninism, and Alternative Marxism."

91. "Beijing shi 'Wenhua da geming' da shiji." The speeches under review included (1) Speech of January 21, 1965, on the Four Cleans Campaign; (2) Speech of January 23, 1965, to an expanded meeting of the Beijing CPC Committee; (3) Speech of January 25, 1965, to four levels of cadres in Tong county; (4) Speech of February 5, 1965, to the Beijing CPC Committee's rural four cleans work conference; (5) Speech of May 4, 1965, to the [rural Four Cleans Campaign] subgroup secretariat meeting; and (6) Speech of February 18, 1965, to rural Four Cleans secretariat. Interestingly, none of these speeches is included in any of the published collections of Peng's speeches, and the meetings at which they were delivered are not mentioned in Peng's official biography.

92. See generally MacFarquhar, *Origins of the Cultural Revolution, 3*. An invaluable compilation of materials on the cultural revolution appears in MacFarquhar, "Teaching Materials on the Cultural Revolution." Among the many useful secondary sources on the Cultural Revolution are Schoenhals, *China's Cultural Revolution 1966–1969*; Teiwes, *Politics and Purges*, 2nd ed.; Tang Tsou, *Cultural Revolution and Post-Mao Reforms*; Rosen, *Red Guard Factionalism*. Among

the most useful works published before 1980 (and thus often not fully incorporating the wealth of Cultural Revolution materials that have become available during the Deng reform period) are Teiwes, *Politics and Purges*, 1st ed.; Lee, *Politics of the Chinese Cultural Revolution*; Ahn, *Chinese Politics and the Cultural Revolution*; Chang, *Factional and Coalition Politics in China*; Dittmer, *Liu Shao-ch'i and the Chinese Cultural Revolution*; Domes, *Internal Politics of China*; Gray and Cavendish, *Chinese Communism in Crisis*.

93. See generally Li Che, *P'eng Chen fan Mao chi-t'uan*, 32–33.

94. Shi Dongbing, *Zuichu de kangzheng*, 1. Also see Goldman, "The Party and the Intellectuals," 462.

95. Shi Dongbing, *Zuichu de kangzheng*, 21. Also see "Da dongluan de niandai," 50, which discusses Peng's role in chairing the five-person group charged with investigating the Ministry of Culture and the group's general inaction. Compare Li Che, *P'eng Chen fan Mao chi-t'uan*, 33, where Peng's appointment is explained by reference to his full Politburo position, in contrast to the alternate member status of Lu Dingyi, Chen Boda, and Kang Sheng. The Group of Five was reportedly made up of Peng, Kang Sheng, Lu Dingyu, Wu Lengsi, and Zhou Yang (often absent because of illness). See Daubier, *History of the Chinese Cultural Revolution*, 36–37; Myers, Domes, and von Groeling, *Chinese Politics*, 192. The February Outline itself separates these individuals (less Zhou Yang, who was absent) from seven others (Xu Liqun, Hu Sheng, Yao Zhen, Wang Li, Fan Rouyu, Liu Ren, and Zheng Tianxiang) who were present at the meeting of February 2, 1966, which adopted the report. See "Outline Report Concerning the Current Academic Discussion of the Group of Five in Charge of the Cultural Revolution." More recent authoritative scholarship indicates that Guo Tianfan attended the meeting, rather than Zheng Tianxiang. See MacFarquhar, *Origins of the Cultural Revolution*, 3, 650, n. 136.

96. Shi Dongbing, *Zuichu de kangzheng*, 21–22.

97. See generally Goldman, *China's Intellectuals*, chaps. 4–5.

98. MacFarquhar, *Origins of the Cultural Revolution*, 3, 386.

99. Shi Dongbing, *Zuichu de kangzheng*, 2.

100. Goldman, "The Party and the Intellectuals," 462.

101. See generally Li Che, *P'eng Chen fan Mao chi-t'uan*, 34 ff. and 41 ff.; Goldman, "The Party and the Intellectuals," 464 ff.

102. Shi Dongbing, *Xuanze tupokou*, 155 ff.

103. Peng Zhen, "Zai jingju xiandai xi guanmo yanchu da hui shang de jianghua," 19.

104. Shi Dongbing, *Zuichu de kangzheng*, 22. Jiang Qing had raised the issue repeatedly since 1962, and in February 1965 he began working closely with Yao Wenyuan on a formal critique of *Hai Rui*. See Qiu Shi, *Gongheguo zhongda shijian he juece neimu*, 1:65.

105. Shi Dongbing, *Xuanze tupokou*, 448 ff.

106. Shi Dongbing, *Shanyu yulai*, 3 ff.

107. See, e.g., Shi Dongbing, *Zuichu de kangzheng*, 22 (Peng criticizes Jiang in meeting with Mao September 1964) and 48 (Peng criticizes Jiang in meeting

with Mao following Politburo Standing Committee session before Mao's departure for the South, late 1965).

108. Shi Dongbing, *Zuichu de kangzheng*, 78.

109. Shi Dongbing, *Zuichu de kangzheng*, 41–42; Shi Dongbing, *Shanyu yulai*, 10–11. The Conference began on September 18, and Mao's remarks were reportedly made a month later, certainly after October 1, National Day.

110. Peng Zhen, "Guanyu xueshu taolun de jige wenti."

111. Shi Dongbing, *Zuichu de kangzheng*, 38.

112. For a general discussion of Peng's ties with the "Beida" administration, see "P'eng Chen, Peking, and Peking University."

113. Domes, *Peng Te-huai*, 116. Also see "From the Defeat of Peng Teh-Huai to the Bankruptcy of China's Khrushchev," 137–38. Although the Khrushchev label is generally interpreted to be a critique of Liu Shaoqi, more recent scholarship suggests that Mao originally used the term to criticize Peng Zhen. See Huang Zheng, "Injustice Done to Liu Shaoqi," 11.

114. Li Rui, *Li Rui fan "zuo" wenxuan*, 46.

115. Shi Dongbing, *Zuichu de kangzheng*, 111.

116. Shi Dongbing, *Zuichu de kangzheng*, 89.

117. Shi Dongbing, *Xuanze tupokou*, 433 ff.

118. Shi Dongbing, *Zuichu de kangzheng*, 58.

119. Shi Dongbing, *Xuanze tupokou*, 483.

120. Shi Dongbing, *Zuichu de kangzheng*, 82.

121. Lin Mohan, "'Wen Ge' qian de jichang wenyi fengbo," 274.

122. Shi Dongbing, *Shanyu yulai*, 36.

123. Shi Dongbing, *Shanyu yulai*, 53.

124. Qiu Shi, *Gongheguo zhongda shijian juece shilu*, 2:572. Also see Shi Dongbing, *Zuichu de kangzheng*, 79.

125. Li Che, *P'eng Chen fan Mao chi-t'uan*, 77.

126. Shi Dongbing, *Zuichu de kangzheng*, 89.

127. Shi Dongbing, *Zuichu de kangzheng*, 58.

128. Qiu Shi, *Gongheguo zhongda shijian juece shilu*, 2:595–96.

129. Shi Dongbing, *Zuichu de kangzheng*, 120, 169.

130. Qiu Shi, *Gongheguo zhongda shijian he juece neimu*, 1:65.

131. Qiu Shi, *Gongheguo zhongda shijian juece shilu*, 2:565–67.

132. Shi Dongbing, *Shanyu yulai*, 56.

133. Shi Dongbing, *Shanyu yulai*, 95 ff. Also see Su Shuangbi and Wang Hongzhi, *Wen ge di yi yuan an*, 173.

134. See generally Teiwes, *Politics and Purges*, 2nd ed.

135. Shi Dongbing, *Zuichu de kangzheng*, 48. Mao's reservations about Jiang Qing were relatively well known, as he was not above suggesting even to officials well below Politiburo rank such as Wang Li that Jiang was somewhat "left." See Wang Li, "First Year of the 'Cultural Revolution.'"

136. Shi Dongbing, *Zuichu de kangzheng*, 111–16. Kang Sheng purportedly claimed that he had raised the link between *Hai Rui* and Peng Dehaui with Mao

as early as 1964, although he did not inform Peng Zhen at the time. See Yang Xianzheng, "Tuzai zhong liang, zhongshen yinzei," 36.

137. Shi Dongbing, *Zuichu de kangzheng*, 119–20.

138. For text of the February Outline, see "February Outline," *Main Documents of the Great Proletarian Cultural Revolution*, ed. Union Research Institute, 3–12. For discussion, see Qiu Shi, *Gongheguo zhongda shijian juece shilu*, 2:601 ff.; Shi Dongbing, *Shanyu yulai*, 134 ff.

139. Gong Yuzhi, "«Er yue tigang»he donghu zhixing," 290.

140. Qiu Shi, *Gongheguo zhongda juece chutai qian hou*, 1:274–75.

141. Qiu Shi, *Gongheguo zhongda shijian juece shilu*, 2:573; Su Shuangbi and Wang Hongzhi, *Wen ge di yi yuan an*, 183 ff.

142. Gong Yuzhi, "«Er yue tigang»he donghu zhixing" 299–300, 295–96.

143. Shi Dongbing, *Shanyu yulai*, 157.

144. Qiu Shi, *Gongheguo zhongda shijian juece shilu*, 2:573.

145. Qiu Shi, *Gongheguo zhongda shijian juece shilu*, 2:188–90. Also see Qiu Shi, *Gongheguo zhongda shijian juece shilu*, 2:587 ff.

146. Gong Yuzhi, "«Er yue tigang»he donghu zhixing," 299–300.

147. See generally Dittmer, *Liu Shao-ch'i and the Chinese Cultural Revolution*.

148. Wang Li, "First Year of the 'Cultural Revolution.'"

149. Shi Dongbing, *Shanyu yulai*, 145 ff. Also see Li Che, *P'eng Chen fan Mao chi-t'uan*, 132 ff. See Qiu Shi, *Gongheguo zhongda shijian he juece neimu*, 1:61 ff.; Qiu Shi, *Gongheguo zhongda juece chutai qian hou*, 1:290.

150. Liu Jianzhi, "Budui wenyi gongzuo zuotanhui jiyao chansheng qianhou," 343.

151. Shi Dongbing, *Xuanze tupokou*, 521.

152. A useful chronology of events is presented in "Beijing shi 'Wenhua da geming' da shiji."

153. Huang Zheng, "Injustice Done to Liu Shaoqi."

154. Shi Dongbing, *Shanyu yulai*, 258 ff. Zhou had intervened with Peng previously in an effort to alert him to the seriousness of the opposition to the February Outline (223 ff.). Having attempted to distract criticism of Peng at the March meeting of the enlarged Politburo in Hangzhou by indicating he had no views ("*wo hai meiyou shenme ganjue*") on Mao's charge that Peng was building an independent kingdom in Beijing, Zhou now attempted to convince Peng of how untenable his position had become. *"Wenhua dageming" zhong de Zhou Enlai*, 25–26. Zhou is portrayed as attempting to protect Peng even after Peng's dismissal, first by opposing his arrest in December 1966 and later by deleting critical references to Peng in a speech prepared for Zhou to deliver to the Beijing Revolutionary Committee in April 1967.

155. Li Xuefeng, "Wo suozhidao de 'Wen Ge' fadong neiqing,"608.

156. "Beijing shi 'Wenhua da geming' da shiji," 8.

157. Shi Dongbing, *Shanyu yulai*, 289.

158. Shi Dongbing, *Zuichu de kangzheng*, 242–43, 272; Shi Dongbing, *Shanyu yulai*, 270. Also see Qiu Shi, *Gongheguo zhongda juece chutai qian hou*, 1:373 ff.

159. "Circular of the Central Committee of the Chinese Communist Party" (May 16, 1966). Also see "Liang ge genben duili de wenjian."

160. Wang Lulin, "«Wu Qi zhishi»chutan."

161. "Beijing shi 'Wenhua da geming' da shiji," 5–6; Li Che, *P'eng Chen fan Mao chi-t'uan*, 131–32.

162. "Dadao Peng Zhen," 5.

163. Yan Jiaqi and Gao Gao, [*Wenhua da geming*] *shi nian shi*, 44. For discussion of the case examination system, see Schoenhals, "Central Case Examination Group." Also see Qiu Shi, *Gongheguo zhongda shijian he juece neimu*, 2:493 ff.

164. See, e.g., "Chedi pipan qian Beijing shi wei yixie zhuyao fuzeren de xiuzheng zhuyi luxian"; "Yi jiang sheng yong zhuijiu kou."

165. Chen Chengzhang and Jin Shi, "An Extremely Treacherous Man Assumed a Loyal Look."

166. See generally Qiu Shi, *Gongheguo zhongda shijian juece shilu*, 2:710 ff.; Qiu Shi, *Gongheguo zhongda juece chutai qian hou*, 1:312. Also see "Chedi dadao Peng Luo Lu Yang fan dang yinmou jituan"; "The P'eng Lu Luo Yang Counter-Revolutionary Revisionist Clique's Crime"; "Drag Out Liu Shaoqi and Show Him to the Public," 9. Although Red Guard materials with Mao's backing had claimed the existence of a Peng–Lu–Luo–Yang clique previously (see, e.g., "Shui fandui Lin Biao tongzhi jiu zalan ta de goutou"), these charges did not receive prominence until later in the year.

167. See, e.g., "Chedi maizang Peng Zhen fangeming xiuzheng zhuyi jituan." For a review of the Changguanlou meetings, see note 35 above.

168. Ren Dongyun, *Gongheguo zhuxi de rong yu ru*, 197; "Drag Out Liu Shaoqi and Show Him to the Public."

169. "Beijing jintian kai dahui zai tuochu Peng Zhen gong shen"; "Look, These Dogs in the Water Are Not Dead Yet!", 7, where Peng is described as unrepentant at his appearance before a struggle session at Peking University on July 24, 1967. Also see "Beijing fenshe chongdang le Peng Zhen fan geming fubi houshe."

170. See, e.g., Dittmer, *Liu Shao-ch'i and the Chinese Cultural Revolution*, 68 ff.

171. Tang Tsou, *Cultural Revolution and Post-Mao Reforms*, 85–86.

CHAPTER 5

1. For a description of Peng's return to Beijing, see Seymour, "Document No. 49, Peng Zhen," 193.

2. "Peng Zhen to Head New Legal Commission." For a general biography on Peng Zhen, see CPC Shanxi Party Committee Historical Research Office, *Peng Zhen shengping dashi nianbiao*. For discussion of his work on the Committee, see Tang Tsou, "Back from the Brink of Revolutionary 'Feudal' Totalitarianism," 73 ff.

3. Zhu Liyu, *Peng Zhen minzhu fazhi sixiang yanjiu*, 11.

4. For discussion of the major events of the transition to Deng's rule, see Davis and Vogel, *Chinese Society on the Eve of Tiananmen*, app.; Harding, *China's*

Second Revolution, chap. 3; Lieberthal, *Governing China*, chap. 5; Ogden, *China's Unresolved Issues*, 64–73; MacFarquhar, "Succession to Mao"; Tang Tsou, *Cultural Revolution and Post-Mao Reforms.*

5. See generally Feinerman, "Economic and Legal Reform."

6. For more on law and legitimation, see Potter, "Riding the Tiger."

7. *Resolution on CPC History (1949–1981).* For discussion, see Secretariat for the Party history materials collection meeting and the academic conference commemorating the CPC's sixtieth anniversary, *Dang shi huiyi baogao ji*; CPC Party History Research Association, *Xuexi lishi jueyi zhuanji.*

8. CPC Shanxi Party Committee Historical Research Office, *Peng Zhen shengping dashi nianbiao*, 39.

9. Deng Xiaoping, "Jiefang sixiang, shi shi qiu shi, tuanjie yizhi xiang qian kan," 136–37.

10. Gu Ming, "You Zhongguo tese de shehui zhuyi jing ji fazhi jianshe de kaituozhe," 143.

11. See, e.g., Yu Xingzhong, "Legal Pragmatism in the People's Republic of China"; Keith, *China's Struggle for the Rule of Law*, 218–21.

12. Peng Zhen, "Zai zhongyang gongzuo huiyi Dongbei zu de fayan."

13. Peng Zhen, "Shixian si hua yiding yao you yi ge shengdong huopo anding tuanjie de zhengzhi jumian."

14. Peng Zhen, "Dangqian zhengfa gongzuo de jige wenti."

15. Peng Zhen, "Shixian si hua yiding yao you yi ge shengdong huopo anding tuanjie de zhengzhi jumian."

16. For summary of Peng's views on this subject, see Huang Huoqing et al., "Zhuinian jingai de lao lingdao Peng Zhen tongzhi," 26. Also see Wang Hanbin, "Peng Zhen tongzhi dui wo guo shehui zhuyi minzhu fazhi jianshe de zhuoyue gongxian," 35.

17. For general discussion of issues in contemporary Chinese legal philosophy, see Gregg, "Modernization of Contemporary Chinese Law"; Keller, "Sources of Order in Chinese Law"; Keith, *China's Struggle for the Rule of Law*; Ladany, *Law and Legality in China*; Lo, *China's Legal Awakening*; Tao-tai Hsia, "Legal Development in the People's Republic of China 1949–1981."

18. "Peng Zhen Reports on the Work of NPC Standing Committee."

19. "Shouci quanguo jingji fazhi gongzuo jingyan jiaoliu hui zai Beijing juxing."

20. See generally Potter, *Chinese Foreign Business Law.*

21. Peng is officially described as having directed (*zhuchi*) the drafting of legislation such as the Economic Contract Law and Foreign Economic Contract Law; the General Principles of Civil Law; organization laws for the courts, the procuracy, and the NPC system; criminal law and procedure; patent law; trademark law; and the 1982 Constitution. See generally *Mianhuai Peng Zhen*, 31.

22. For further discussion of Yang Jingyu, see Li Shaozhuang, *Zhu Rongji ren ma*, 362 ff.

23. Gu Ming, "You Zhongguo tese de shehui zhuyi jing ji fazhi jianshe de kaituozhe."

24. Peng Zhen, "Guanyu qige falu cao'an de shuoming"; "Minshi susong fa qicao zhong de jige wenti"; "Zai quanguo minfa tongze (cao'an) zuotanhui shang de jianghua."

25. Wang Hanbin, "Peng Zhen tongzhi dui wo guo shehui zhuyi minzhu fazhi jianshe de zhuoyue gongxian," 34 ff.

26. Song Rufen, "Mianhuai Peng Zhen tongzhi guangyu jingji lifa de jiaohui," 151–52.

27. Peng Zhen, "Guanyu qige falu cao'an de shuoming." The speech is discussed as well in "Quarterly Chronicle and Documentation," *China Quarterly* 79 (September 1979): 663. Also see Ching, "Current Political Scene in China," 699 ff.

28. "Guanyu qige falu cao'an de shuoming," 372.

29. "Guanyu qige falu cao'an de shuoming," 372.

30. See "NPC Standing Committee Discusses Deletion of the 'Four Freedoms.'" Also see "Peng Zhen Reports on the Work of NPC Standing Committee," C/9.

31. Liu Fuzhi, "Mianhuai wo guo shehui zhuyi fazhi zhuyao dianjiren Peng Zhen tongzhi," 83.

32. Liu Fuzhi, "Mianhuai wo guo shehui zhuyi fazhi zhuyao dianjiren Peng Zhen tongzhi," 83.

33. Peng Zhen, "Dui tebie fating bangting renyuan de jianghua."

34. Peng Zhen, "Dui tebie fating bangting renyuan de jianghua." Also see Peng Zhen, "Zai shixian zhong zongjie jingyan jiaoxun."

35. See generally Liao Kuangsheng (Liao Guangsheng), "'Independent Administration of Justice' and the PRC Legal System," 140–41.

36. Peng Zhen, "Guanyu xing fa cao'an he xingshi susong fa cao'an de shuoming."

37. Peng Zhen, "Guanyu xing fa cao'an he xingshi susong fa cao'an de shuoming."

38. Peng Zhen, "Ren da changweihui jiguan yao you yige hao de sixiang zuofeng."

39. See, e.g., Tanner, *Strike Hard!*, 34–35.

40. Peng Zhen, "Zai zhongyang zhengfa weiyuanhui di yi ci huiyi shang de jianghua jiyao."

41. Peng Zhen, "Zai Guangdong sheng he Guangzhou shi gong-jian-fa huibao hui shang de jianghua yaodian."

42. Peng Zhen was reported to have personally approved the 1983 "Regulations on Arrest and Custody," which remained an administative rather than legislative enactment. Seymour, "Cadre Accountability to the Law," 4.

43. Peng Zhen, "Kaizhan diaocha yanjiu, an shiji qingkuang banshi."

44. Peng Zhen, "Zai wu da chengshi zhian zuotanhui shang de jianghua."

45. Liu Fuzhi, "Mianhai wo guo shehui zhuyi fazhi zhuyao dianjiren Peng Zhen tongzhi," 86; Tao Xijin, "Laoji wei ren jiaohui zuo hao gong an gongzuo," 94 ff.

46. Peng Zhen, "Zai Sichuan sheng zheng fa ge bumen fuze tongzhi zuotanhui shang de jianghua yaodian."

47. Peng Zhen, "Xin shiqi de zheng fa gongzuo"; Peng Zhen, "Fazhan shehui zhuyi minzhu, jianquan shehui zhuyi fazhi."

48. Peng Zhen, "Zai zhongyang zheng fa weiyuanhui kuangda huiyi shang de jianghua yaodian."

49. "Peng Zhen tongzhi guancha Qinghuangdao laojiao suo."

50. "Peng Zhen Reports on the Work of NPC Standing Committee," C/3.

51. Peng Zhen, "Xin shiqi de zheng fa gongzuo." Also see "Quanguo zhengfa gongzuo hui zai jing juxing."

52. Peng Zhen, "Minshi susong fa qicao zhong de jige wenti."

53. "Peng Zhen tongzhi xiang canjia quanguo gong, jian, fa youguan huiyi de tongzhi zuo zhongyao jianghua." Later, in a 1982 interview with foreign reporters, Peng backed off a bit, saying he was not sure between law and policy which was more important. Seymour, "Editor's Introduction," 4.

54. Peng Zhen, "Guanyu shehuizhuyi fazhi de jige wenti."

55. For a collection of excerpts from Peng speeches on local representative congresses, see Minzhengbu jiceng zhengquan jianshe si, *Peng Zhen tongzhi guanyu cunmin weiyuanhui jumin weiyuanhui de zhongyao jianghua.* For discussion of local elections, see generally McCormick, *Political Reform in Post-Mao China,* 134; Nathan, *Chinese Democracy,* chap. 10; O'Brien, "Implementing Political Reform in China's Villages." For a discussion of the consequences the local political empowerment, see Li and O'Brien, "Villages and Popular Resistance in Contemporary China" and "Accommodating 'Democracy' in a One-Party State."

56. Peng Zhen, "Guanyu qige falu cao'an de shuoming." Also see Waller, *Government and Politics of the People's Republic of China,* 118.

57. "Peng Zhen Reports on the Work of NPC Standing Committee," C/2.

58. "Document 32: The Student Movement in Hunan," 219.

59. Shu Si, "CCP Stresses Western Political System Does Not Conform to National Condition," 98, where Peng's views are paired with those of Jiang Zemin on the issue of local People's Congress elections in 1993.

60. Peng Zhen, "Guanyu difang ren da changweihui de gongzuo."

61. Hartford, "Step by Step."

62. "Peng Zhen Reports on the Work of NPC Standing Committee," C/2.

63. Cheng Zihua, "Summary Report on the Work of the Nationwide County-Level Direct Elections," 187.

64. For general discussion of the politics of the Deng reforms, see Davis and Vogel, *Chinese Society on the Eve of Tiananmen*; Fewsmith, *Dilemmas of Reform in China*; Howell, *China Opens Its Doors*; Kau and Marsh, *China in the Era of Deng Xiaoping*; Perry and Wong, *Political Economy of Reform in Post-Mao China*; Shirk, *Political Logic of Economic Reform in China.*

65. See generally Oi, "Fate of the Collective After the Commune," 15; Perry and Wong, *Political Economy of Reform in Post-Mao China,* esp. part 1, "Agriculture."

66. "Fazhan shehui zhuyi minzhu jianquan shehui zhuyi fazhi." Also see "Zhongguo faxue hui chengli dahui longzhong kaimu"; "Zhongguo faxue hui chengli dahui zai jing longzhong juxing."

67. Deng Xiaoping, "Jianchi sixiang jiben yuanze."

68. "Fazhan shehui zhuyi minzhu jianquan shehui zhuyi fazhi."

69. "Shouci quanguo jingji fazhi gongzuo jingyan jiaoliu hui zai jing juxing." Reflecting perhaps a degree of hostility to Peng's cautious approach to economic legislation, the Ministry of Justice newspaper *China Legal System Gazette* did not report on the September 2–9, 1982, meeting until September 24.

70. Sen Lin, "China's Decentralization and Provincial Economic Legislation," 97–98.

71. See generally Tanner, "How a Bill Becomes Law in China"; Chang, "The Making of the Chinese Bankruptcy Law."

72. See generally Epstein, "Evolution of China's General Principles of Civil Law."

73. Peng Zhen, "Zai minfa zuotanhui shang be jianghua."

74. "Zai gaodu minzhu de jichu shang gaodu jizhong lifa gongzuo jianchi lilun lianxi shiji." Also see Peng Zhen, "Zai quanguo minfa tongze (cao'an) zuotanhui shang de jianghua."

75. Peng Zhen, "Jinyibu shishi xianfa, yange anzhao xianfa banshi."

76. Cohen, "China's Changing Constitution."

77. "Peng Zhen xiang wu jie renda si ci huiyi tichu guanyu jianyi tuichi xiugai xianfa wancheng qixian de shumian shuoming."

78. Peng Zhen, "Guanyu Zhonghua renmin gongheguo xianfa xiugai cao'an de shuoming."

79. See, e.g., Tang Tsou, "Party, Masses, and Citizens in Rebuilding the Chinese State," 277, and references therein.

80. Peng Zhen, "Zai wu da chengshi zhian zuotanhui shang de jianghua."

81. Forster, "1982 Campaign Against Economic Crime in China"; Tanner, *Strike Hard!* Also see Peng Zhen, "Xin shiqi de zheng fa gongzuo."

82. For discussion of the importance of the theme of "productive forces," see Van Ness and Raichur, "Dilemmas of Socialist Development."

83. Shi Zhongquan et al., *Zhonggong ba da shi*, esp. 413 ff.

84. "Shi yi renmin zhijie canjia guojia guanli de yi zhong zhongyao xingshi." Compare with Peng Zhen, "Makesi Liening zhuyi zai Zhongguo de shengli," 23. Comparisons to Bentham's utilitarianism (e.g., Bentham, *Introduction to the Principles of Morals and Legislation*), are unavaoidable, although probably unintended by Peng himself. Unlike Bentham, Peng was not concerned with the mechanism for identifying whose interests were to be protected through law. In contrast to Bentham's support for democratic processes, Peng held that the Party remained the repository for determinations of public welfare.

85. Peng Zhen, "Guanyu Zhonghua renmin gongheguo xianfa xiugai cao'an de baogao." Also see "Further Coverage of Fifth Session of Fifth NPC."

86. Peng Zhen, "Renzhi zuzhi quanguo ge zu renmin taolun xianfa xiugai cao'an."

87. "Jiaqiang fazhi xuanchuan shi xinwen jie de zhongyao zhize." Also see "Peng Zhen tongzhi de jianghua."

88. Peng Zhen, "Lifa yao shiying gaige, kaifang de xuyao."

89. Peng Zhen, "Zai di liujie quanguo ren da san ci huiyi yubei huiyi shang de jianghua."

90. Peng Zhen, "Yao nuli xuexi Makesi zhuyi de jiben lilun."

91. "Jingji lifa hen xuyao—tansuo shiyan jieduan bu ke xiao."

92. "Peng Zhen tongzhi zai jiejian lifa gongzuo ganbu peixun xueyuan shi de jianghua yaodian." Also see Yu Wen et al., "Peng Zhen tongzhi shi renmin daibiao dahui zhidu jianshe de daitouren," 112 ff.

93. "Peng Zhen tongzhi zai jiejian lifa gongzuo ganbu peixun xueyuan shi de jianghua yaodian." Also see Peng Zhen, "Dui lifa gongzuo ganbu peixun banxueyuan de jianghua."

94. "Renda changweihui shisan ci huiyi tuanhui" 4. For discussion of Peng's views that education of cadres and masses on the principles of "equality before the law" was essential to effective enforcement of law, see Wang Hanbin, "Peng Zhen tongzhi dui wo guo shehui zhuyi minzhu fazhi jianshe de zhuoyue gongxian," 44 ff.

95. Peng Zhen, "Jiaqiang fazhi jiaoyu, weihu anding tuanjie."

96. "Jinyibu shenyi ji xiang falu cao'an."

97. Peng Zhen, "Zai bufen Yan'an shidai wenyi lao zhanshi zuotanhui shang de jianghua."

98. Ladany, "China's New Power Centre?"

99. Compare Constitution of the PRC (1978), art. 25, with the Constitution of the PRC (1982), art. 67.

100. See generally Tanner, "Organizations and Politics in China's Post-Mao Law-Making System"; O'Brien, *Reform Without Liberalization*; O'Brien, "China's National People's Congress."

101. O'Brien, *Reform Without Liberalization*, 78–79.

102. Peng Zhen, "Tan tan ren da changweihui de gongzuo." Also see Peng Zhen, "Guanyu lifa gonzuo"; Peng Zhen, "Jiaqiang minzhu yu fazhi jianshe, jiaqiang ren da changweihui gongzuo."

103. Peng Zhen, "Zuo hao sheng ji ren da changweihui de gongzuo."

104. Peng Zhen, "Tongguo qunzhong zizhi shixing jiceng zhijie minzhu."

105. Peng Zhen, "Quanguo ren da changweihui he difang ren da changeweihui de guanxi."

106. Peng Zhen, "Guanyu quanguo renda changweihui de gongzuo."

107. Peng Zhen, "Yi bu yao shizhi, yi bu yao yuequan."

108. O'Brien, *Reform Without Liberalization*, 135. Also see Sen Lin, "China's Decentralization and Provincial Economic Legislation," 97–98.

109. Peng's efforts to strengthen the role of the NPC Standing Committee were continued in the 1990s by his successor Qiao Shi, who emphasized the importance of legislative institutions lending a degree of permanence to law making, so as to insulate it from the whims of particular leaders. See "Chairman Qiao Shi Speaks at Closing." Differences between Qiao Shi and Jiang Zemin on questions about Party leadership over the law-making and law-enforcement processes were followed by Qiao's loss of his Politburo seat and his chairmanship of the NPC Standing Committee. See "Qiao Shi's Words on Democracy in China."

110. Deng Xiaoping, "Dang he guojia lingdao zhidu de gaige."

111. Wang Hanbin, "Peng Zhen tongzhi dui wo guo shehui zhuyi minzhu fazhi jianshe de zhuoyue gongxian," 37.

112. See comments of Peng Zhen to national meeting of political–legal work on implementing the Constitution, in "Renzhen xuexi he guanche zhixing xianfa." Also see Peng Zhen, "Zai zhongyang zheng fa weiyuanhui kuangda huiyi shang de jianghua."

113. Peng Zhen, "Guanyu caoyi guoying gongzhangfa de wenti."

114. Fu Yang, "Xin shiqi Peng Zhen de renmin minzhu sixiang," 401.

115. See generally Baum, *Burying Mao*, 8.

116. Peng Zhen, "Jinyibu shishi xianfa, yange anzhao xianfa banshi."

117. Baum, *Burying Mao*, 199–200, 206–8; Tong, "Editor's Introduction," esp. 8, 11; "Comparison of Certain Speeches"; "Decision of the Standing Committee of the National People's Congress on 'Strengthening the Education in the Legal System'"; and "Some Materials Regarding Certain Theoretical Issues." Also see Dittmer, "Patterns of Elite Strife," 415–16; Brugger, "Ideology, Legitimacy and Marxist Theory," 11 ff.; Chang, "Who Gets What, When, and How in China," 58. Peng's role in Hu's dismissal went beyond mere rhetorical attacks, he called up the People's Armed Police in Beijing to ensure that Hu went quietly. Dittmer, "Patterns of Elite Strife," 416.

118. Peng Zhen, "Guanyu shehui zhuyi jingshen wenming jianshe zhidao sixiang de jige wenti."

119. "Decision of the Standing Committee of the National People's Congress on Strengthening the Education in the Legal System and Safeguarding Unity and Stability." Also see Tong, "Editor's Introduction," 11–12.

120. Peng Zhen, "Guanyu zheng fa gongzuo de jige wenti."

121. Peng Zhen, "Yanli daji yanzhong xingshi fanzui huodong yao quan dang xia juexin."

122. Peng Zhen, "Yanli daji xingshi fanzui yao zunshou falu, zhuyi zhengce, jiaqiang zonghe zhili."

123. See, e.g., "Renmin wujing yao tigao suzhi shiying xin renwu," where Peng calls on the People's Armed Police to strengthen political training, uphold the four basic principles, and serve the people, with scant reference to law. Also see "Zhengfa zhanxian tongzhi wei renmin li le gong yi nian duo lai shehui zhixu mingxian haozhuan."

124. Peng Zhen, "Dui sheng, zizhiqu, zhishashi zheng fa lingdao ganbu lunxun banxueyuan de jianghua."

125. Peng Zhen, "Zai quanguo zheng fa gongzuo huiyi shang de jianghua."

126. Peng Zhen, "Zai quanguo zheng fa gongzuo huiyi shang de jianghua."

127. Peng Zhen, "Guanyu zheng fa gongzuo de jige wenti." Also see "Guanzhu jianchi sixiang jiben yuanze zhei ge zonggangling jiaqiang duiwu jianshe ba zhengfa gongzuo gaode geng hao."

128. "Dui gaige jiyaojian ding you yao zhongshi jiejue wenti, Gongzuo jiandu he falu jiandu yao jinyibu jianquan"; Peng Zhen, "Zai di liujie quanguo ren da san ci huiyi yubei huiyi shang de jianghua"; "Peng Zhen zai renda yubei huishang fabiao jianghua"; "Peng Zhen chanshu lixiang minzhu he fazhi."

129. "Peng Zhen weiyuanzhang zai ge sheng zizhiqu zhishashi renda changweihui fuzeren zuotanhui shang de jianghua yaodian"; Peng Zhen, "Zai ge sheng, zizhiqu, zhishashi renda changweihui fuzeren zuotanhui shang de jianghua."

130. Ming Wen, "Peng Zhen fazhi sixiang shulue," 95–96.

131. CPC Shanxi Party Committee Historical Research Office, *Peng Zhen shengping dashi nianbiao*, 52.

132. "Peng Zhen wenxuan jieshao"; Zheng Tianxiang, Liu Fuzhi, and Wang Hanbin, "Qieshi jiaqiang shehuizhuyi minzhu yu fazhi jianshe"; "Selected Works of Peng Zhen Reviewed"; You Lin and Yan Jianqi, "Important Documents for Building Socialist Democracy."

133. Peng Zhen, "Yao shanyu zhangwo makesi zhuyi de zhexue wuqi."

134. Peng Zhen, "Guanyu shehui zhuyi jingshen wenming jianshe zhidao sixiang de jige wenti"; Peng Zhen, "Zai bufen Yan'an shidai wenyi laozhanshi zuotanhui shang de jianghua."

135. "Peng Zhen Writes Preface to Book on Party Style."

136. Peng Zhen, "Zai di liu jie quanguo ren da changweihui di er shi si ci huiyi lianzuhui shang de jianghua."

137. See Peng Zhen, "Yong xianfa he falu tongyi sixiang." Also see "Yi shishi wei genju yi xianfa he falu wei junsheng lai tongyi sixiang"; "Yiding yao jianchi fazhi bu neng gao renzhi shei dou meiyou chaoyue xianfa he falu de tequan."

138. Peng Zhen, "Yong xianfa he falu tongyi sixiang."

139. Peng Zhen, "Zai zhongyang zhengzhi ju kuangda huiyi shang de fayan."

140. Peng Zhen, "Zai di liu jie quanguo ren da changweihui di er shi si ci huiyi lianzuhui shang de jianghua."

141. "Peng Zhen Explains Mao 'Cult' to Cadre Children."

142. "Peng Zhen Attacks 'Leftist' Influence, Ideology."

143. Peng Zhen, "Shishi qiu shi, bu shang kong tan."

144. "Peng Zhen Addresses Forum Marking CPC Founding."

145. "Peng Zhen's Speech at Yanan Forum Viewed."

146. Peng Zhen, "Zai quanguo zheng fa gongzuo huiyi shang de jianghua yaodian."

147. "Peng Zhen Stresses Political Reform by Law."

148. "Peng Zhen Stresses Political Reform by Law," 21.

149. "Deng jinghu tanwu hui dang," 7. Also see "Peng Zhen danxin zhong gong kuan yu tanwu, Deng gongzhu Jiang hua qili zhua jundui."

150. "Peng Zhen Calls for Political Reform."

151. Peng Zhen, "Bu jin yao kao dang de zhengce, erqie yao yi fa ban shi." Also see "Jiaqiang fazhi xuanchuan shi xinwen jie de zhongyao zhize."

152. Peng Zhen, "Zai zhongyang zhengzhi ju kuangda huiyi shang de fayan."

153. Peng Zhen, *Guanyu Jin Cha Ji bianqu dang de gongzuo he juti zhengce baogao*, 51–54.

154. See, e.g., Peng Zhen, "Gongmin zai falu mianqian ren ren pingdeng."

155. Peng Zhen, "Yao nuli xuexi Makesi zhuyi de jiben lilun."

156. Peng Zhen, "Zai di liujie quanguo ren da san ci huiyi yubei huiyi shang de jianghua."

157. Peng Zhen, "Bu jin yao kao dang de zhengce, erqie yao yi fa ban shi."

158. Peng Zhen, "Quanguo ren da changweihui he difang ren da changeweihui de guanxi."

159. Peng Zhen, "Dang de zuzhi gongzuo de jige wenti."

160. Perhaps Peng's most lengthy and articulate defense of his position was presented to a delegation of reporters from Hong Kong and Macao. See "Peng Zhen Meets Hong Kong Macao Reporters."

161. Peng Zhen, "Zai Guangdong sheng he Guangzhou shi gong-jian-fa huibao hui shang de jianghua yaodian."

162. Peng Zhen, "Zai quanguo zheng fa gongzuo huiyi shang de jianghua."

163. Peng Zhen, "Guanyu zheng fa gongzuo de jige wenti."

164. Peng Zhen, "Bu jin yao kao dang de zhengce, erqie yao yi fa ban shi."

165. Peng Zhen, "Lifa yao shiying gaige, kaifang de xuyao."

166. On legalism, see generally Hulsewe, *Remnants of Ch'in Law*; Bodde and Morris, *Law in Imperial China*, 23–27, esp. 25–26; Chan, *Source Book in Chinese Philosophy*, 251–61; Needham, *Science and Civilization in China, Vol. 2*, 204–15.

167. There is some evidence that the legalists in fact recognized the importance of social classes in the differential enforcement of legal rules. See, e.g., Bodde, "Idea of Social Classes in Han and Pre-Han China"; Kroll, "Notes on Ch'in and Han Law." But see Fu Zhengyuan, *China's Legalists*, 61–64, for the received wisdom on legalism. What is important from the standpoint of Peng's thinking is not necessarily the conclusions of painstaking research on the nuances of legalist doctrines, but rather the received wisdom on the basic tenets of legalism.

168. Hulsewe, *Remnants of Ch'in Law*, 183–207.

CONCLUSION

1. Kent, *Between Freedom and Subsistence*, 39–40.

2. "Deng Xiaoping tongzhi sang weiyuanhui mingdan." For an analysis of the consequences of Deng's death, see "Deng Dies."

3. See, e.g., Keith and Zhiqiu Lin, *Law and Justice in China's New Marketplace*; Keith, *China's Struggle for the Rule of Law*.

4. See, e.g., *Ruxue yu falu wenhua*; Zhuo Zeyuan, *Fa de jiazhi lun*; *Jiben falu jiazhi*.

Works Cited

Ahn, Byung Joon. "Adjustments in the Great Leap Forward and Their Ideological Legacy." In *Ideology and Politics in Contemporary China*, edited by Chalmers Johnson, 257–300. Seattle: University of Washington Press, 1973.

———. *Chinese Politics and the Cultural Revolution: Dynamics of Policy Process.* Seattle: University of Washington Press, 1976.

An Ziwen zhuanlue (Biographical sketch of An Ziwen). Taiyuan: Shanxi People's Press, n.d.

Ansley, Clive. *The Heresy of Wu Han: His Play "Hai Rui's Dismissal" and Its Role in China's Cultural Revolution*. Toronto: University of Toronto Press, 1971.

Apter, David E., and Tony Saich. *Revolutionary Discourse in Mao's Republic.* Cambridge, Mass.: Harvard University Press, 1994.

Bachman, David. *Bureaucracy, Economy and Leadership in China.* New York: Cambridge University Press, 1991.

———. *Chen Yun and the Chinese Political System*. Berkeley, Calif.: Institute for East Asian Studies, 1985.

———. "Response to Teiwes." *Pacific Affairs* 66, no. 2 (summer 1993): 254–59.

Bartke, Wolfgang. *Who's Who in the People's Republic of China*. Armonk, N.Y.: M. E. Sharpe, 1981.

Baum, Richard. *Burying Mao: Chinese Politics in the Age of Deng Xiaoping*. Princeton, N.J.: Princeton University Press, 1994.

Baum, Richard, and Frederick C. Teiwes. *Ssu-ch'ing: The Socialist Education Movement of 1962–1966*. Berkeley: University of California Press, 1968.

Becker, Jasper. *Hungry Ghosts: Mao's Secret Famine*. New York: Henry Holt, 1997.

"Beifang ju guanyu caizheng jingji zhengce de zhishi" (Instructions from the North China Bureau on finance and economic policy). *Zhonggong zhongyang wenjian xuanji* (Compilation of CPC central documents) 12 (April 1, 1940): 362.

Beijing CPC Committee, Beijing People's Congress Standing Committee, Beijing

People's Government, and Beijing CPPCC Committee. "Shoudu shehui zhuyi xiandaihua jianshe zhuyao dianjizhe weiye yong cun" (The great cause of the main founder of the capital's socialist construction will live forever). In *Mianhuai Peng Zhen*, 483–99.

"Beijing fenshe chongdang le Peng Zhen fan geming fubi houshe." In *Wenge dazibao jingxuan* (Selections from wall posters from the Cultural Revolution), edited by Tan Fang and Zhao Wumian, 288–91. Flushing, N.Y.: Mirror Books, 1996.

Beijing huagong xueyan and Mao Zedong sixiang xuanchuua yuan (Beijing Chemical Industry Institute and Mao Zedong thought propagandists). *Dadao dang nei zui da de zou ziben zhuyi daolu dangquanpai—Liu Shaoqi* (Strike down the biggest person in power within the Party taking the capitalist road—Liu Shaoqi), 4 (April 10, 1967).

"Beijing jintian kai dahui zai tuochu Peng Zhen gong shen" (Beijing convenes large session today to drag out Peng Zhen yet again for public judging). *Xinsheng wanbao* (New life evening news), May 7, 1967.

Beijing Military Region. "Outstanding Contributions and Shining Glory—Marking Centenary of Our Former Commander Marshal Nie Rongzhen." *Renmin ribao* (People's daily), December 25, 1999, in *FBIS Daily Report—China* FBIS-CHI-1999–1231 (January 2, 2000).

Beijing Military Region Jin Cha Ji war history compilation group, ed. *Jin Cha Ji junqu kang Ri zhanzheng shi* (History of the war against the Japanese in the Jin Cha Ji military region). Beijing: Military Science Press, n.d.

"Beijing shi renmin zhengfu zai [wu fan] yundong zhong guanyu gongshanghu fenlei chuli de biaozhun he banfa" (Standards and methods of the Beijing people's government for different types of punishments in course of the [Five Anti] campaign). *Renmin shouce* (People's handbook) (1952): 60.

"Beijing shi 'Wenhua da geming' da shiji" (Chronicle of events of the Cultural Revolution in Beijing). *Beijing dang shiziliao tongxun* (Newsletter on Beijing CPC history).

"Beijing shizhang Peng Zhen san yue ba ri zai zhengwuyuan huiyi shang de baogao" (Beijing mayor Peng Zhen's report to the Government Administrative Council meeting of March 8). *Renmin shouce* (People's handbook) (1952): 63.

Beijing Xinhua English Service (April 28, 1997).

Bentham, Jeremy. *Introduction to the Principles of Morals and Legislation*. London. Printed for T. Payne, 1789.

Bing Shanxue. *Zhongnanhai fengyun jilu* (Storms at Zhongnanhai). Changsha: Hunan Arts Press, 1993.

Bo Yibo. *Ruogan zhong da juece yu shijian de huigu* (Review of various major decisions and affairs). Beijing: Central Party School, 1991.

———. "Wei shenru di pubian di kaizhan fan tanwu, fan langfei, fan guanliao zhuyi yundong er douzheng" (Struggle to deepen and publicize the movement against corruption, waste and bureaucratism). *Renmin shouce* (People's handbook) (1952): 64.

Bodde, Derk. "The Idea of Social Classes in Han and pre-Han China." In *Thought and Law in Qin and Han China: Studies Presented to Anthony Hulsewe on the Occasion of His Eightieth Birthday*, edited by W. L. Idema and E. Zurcher, 26–41. Leiden: E. J. Brill, 1990.

Bodde, Derk, and Clarence Morris. *Law in Imperial China*. Philadelphia: University of Pennsylvania, 1967.

Brugger, Bill. "Ideology, Legitimacy and Marxist Theory in Contemporary China." In *China: Modernization in the 1980s*, edited by Joseph Y. S. Cheng, 1–34. New York: St. Martin's Press, 1989.

Byron, John, and Robert Pack. *The Claws of the Dragon: Kang Sheng—The Evil Genius Behind Mao—And His Legacy of Terror*. New York: Simon and Schuster, 1992.

Carlson, Evans Fordyce. *Twin Stars of China*. Westport, Conn.: Hyperion Press, 1940.

Ceng Changming. "Husong Chenyi tongzhi pu Yan'an" (Accompanying comrade Chen Yi to Yan'an). In *Hua gong shi ziliao* (Materials on the CPC history), edited by Cultural History Materials and Research Committee of the Chinese People's Political Consultative Congress (CPPCC) National Committee, 4:186–93. Beijing: Cultural History Materials Publishers, 1981.

Central Party School Party History Research Office, ed. *Yi Er Jiu yundong shiyao* (Outline history of the December 9th Movement). Beijing: CPC Central Party School Press, 1986.

Chai Zemin and An Pingsheng. "Shishi qiushi de fanli" (A model of seeking truth from facts). *Beijing ribao* (Beijing daily), February 1, 1999: 7.

"Chairman Qiao Shi Speaks at Closing." *Beijing Xinhua English Service*, March 31, 1993, in *FBIS Daily Report—China* (March 31, 1993): 34.

"'Chang guan lou' fan geming shijian de qian qian hou hou" (The whole story of the Changguanlou counter-revolutionary incident). *Hong se zao fan zhe* (Red resisters) (May 13, 1967): 4.

Chang Jung. *Wild Swans: Three Daughters of China*. New York: Simon and Schuster, 1991.

Chang, Parris H. *Power and Policy in China*. 2nd ed. University Park: Pennsylvania State University Press, 1978.

———. "Who Gets What, When, and How in China: Changes in the CCP Leadership and the Rules of the Game." In *Mainland China After the Thirteenth Party Congress*, edited by King-yuh Chang, 50–65. Boulder, Colo.: Westview Press, 1990.

Chang, Ta-kuang. "The Making of the Chinese Bankruptcy Law: A Study in the Chinese Legislative Process." *Harvard International Law Journal* 28, no. 2 (1987): 333–72.

Chang, Y. C. *Factional and Coalition Politics in China: The Cultural Revolution and Its Aftermath*. New York: Praeger, 1976.

"[Changguanlou] Peng Zhen fadong fan Mao" (Changguanlou, Peng Zhen mobilizes against Mao). In *Peng Zhen fan Mao ji* (Record of Peng Zhen opposing Mao), 50:4. Taipei: Mainland Materials Press, 1967.

"Chedi dadao Peng Luo Lu Yang fan dang yinmou jituan" (Thoroughly attack the anti-Party clique of Peng Zhen, Luo Ruoqing, Lu Dingyi and Yang Shangkun). *Guangming ribao* (Bright daily), August 11, 1967: 4.

"Chedi maizang Peng Zhen fangeming xiuzheng zhuyi jituan" (Thoroughly bury Peng Zhen's counterrevolutionary revisionist clique). *Renmin ribao* (People's daily), July 17, 1967: 1.

"Chedi pipan qian Beijing shi wei yixie zhuyao fuzeren de xiuzheng zhuyi luxian" (Thoroughly criticize the revisionist road taken by some responsible people in the former Beijing municipal committee). *Hongqi* (Red flag) 9 (1966): 31.

"Chedi maizang yi Peng Zhen wei shou de jiu Beijing shi wei" (Thoroughly bury the old Beijing municipal committee headed by Peng Zhen). *Wenge dazibao jingxuan* (Selections from wall posters from the Cultural Revolution), edited by Tan Fang and Zhao Wumian, 301–8, 303. Flushing, N.Y.: Mirror Books, 1996.

Cheek, Timothy. "Deng Tuo: A Chinese Leninist Approach to Journalism." In *China's Establishment Intellectuals*, edited by Carol Lee Hamrin and Timothy Cheek, 92–123. Armonk, N.Y.: M. E. Sharpe, 1985.

———. "The Fading of Wild Lilies: Wang Shiwei and Mao Zedong's Yan'an Talks in the First CPC Rectification Movement." *Australian Journal of Chinese Affairs* 11 (1984): 25–58.

———. "The Honorable Vocation: Intellectual Service in CCP Propaganda Institutions in Jin-Cha-Ji, 1937–1945." In *New Perspectives on the Chinese Communist Revolution*, edited by Tony Saich and Hans van de Ven, 235–64. Armonk, N.Y.: M. E. Sharpe, 1995.

———. "The Politics of Cultural Reform: Deng Tuo and the Retooling of Chinese Marxism." *Chinese Law and Government* 16, no. 4 (winter 1983–1984).

———. *Propaganda and Culture in Mao's China*. Oxford: Clarendon Press, 1997.

Chen Changhang. "'Falu pingdeng' de lixiang, xianshi, lishi" (The ideals, reality, and history of "Everyone Is Equal Before the Law"). In *Lun falu mianqian renren pingdeng* (*On "Everyone Is Equal Before the Law")*, edited by Chinese Academy of Social Sciences Law Institute, 141–49. Beijing: Law Publishers, 1981.

Chen Chengzhang and Jin Shi. "An Extremely Treacherous Man Assumed a Loyal Look—Ripping Off Kang Sheng's Mask." *Xinhua Domestic Service*, December 21, 1980, in *FBIS Daily Report—China* (December 24, 1980): L12, L16.

Chen Hefu. *Zhongguo xianfa leibian* (Compilation of Chinese Constitutions). Beijing: Social Sciences Press, 1980.

Ch'en, Jerome. "The Communist Movement 1927–1937." In *The Cambridge History of China, Vol. 13: Republican China 1912–1949, Part 2*, edited by John K. Fairbank and Albert Feuerwerker, 168–229. Cambridge: Cambridge University Press, 1986.

Ch'en Kung-shu, ed. "P'eng Chen fan Mao chi" (Record of Peng Zhen opposing Mao). In *Talu fei ch'ing yeh shu* (Works on the circumstances of the mainland bandits), 52:19–20. Taipei: Mainland Materials Publishers, 1967.

Chen Lian, ed. *Kang ri genju di fazhan shilue* (Brief history of the development of the resist-Japan base areas). Beijing: PLA Press, 1987.

Chen Shaochou, ed. *Liu Shaoqi zai bai qu* (Liu Shaoqi in the White Areas). Beijing: CPC Party History Publishers, 1992.

Chen, Wing-Tsit. *A Source Book in Chinese Philosophy*. Princeton, N.J.: Princeton University Press, 1963.

Cheng Chu-yuan. "The Root of China's Cultural Revolution: The Feud Between Mao Tse-tung and Liu Shao-ch'i." *Orbis* 11, no. 4 (winter 1968): 1160.

Cheng Hsuan (Zheng Xuan). "Big Exposure of a Conspiracy to Usurp the Party and State Leadership: A Commentary on the 'Ch'ang Kuan Lou' counter-revolutionary incident planned and directed by P'eng Chen." *Survey of China Mainland Press*, no. 4014 (September 5, 1967): 1.

Cheng Zihua. "Summary Report on the Work of the Nationwide County-Level Direct Elections." *Chinese Law and Government* 14, no. 3–4 (fall–winter 1982–1983): 172–92.

China Modern Revolutionary History Materials Series. *Yi er jiu yundong ziliao* (Materials on the December 9th Movement). Vol. 2. Beijing: People's Press, 1982.

China Quarterly, no. 29 (1967).

Ching, Frank. "The Current Political Scene in China." *China Quarterly* 80 (December 1979): 691–715 at 699 ff.

Chiu Hungdah. "Institutionalizing a New Legal System in Deng's China." In *China in the Era of Deng Xiaoping*, edited by Michael Ying-Mao Kau and Susan H. Marsh, 60–97. Armonk, N.Y.: M. E. Sharpe, 1993.

"Chronology of Important Events in the Struggle Between the Two Lines in the Field of Higher Education." *Selections from China Mainland Magazines*, no. 18 (February 26, 1968).

"Circular of the Central Committee of the Chinese Communist Party (May 16, 1966)." In *Chinese Communist Party Documents of the Great Proletarian Cultural Revolution, 1966–1967*, edited by Union Research Institute, 20–28. Hong Kong: Union Research Institute, 1968.

Cohen, Jerome A. "China's Changing Constitution." *China Quarterly* 76 (1978): 794–841.

Communist China 1955–1959: Policy Documents with Analysis. Cambridge, Mass.: Harvard University Press, 1962.

"Comparison of Certain Speeches," in "Party Documents on Anti-Bourgeois Liberalization and Hu Yaobang's Resignation, 1987," edited by James Tong, special issue of *Chinese Law and Government* 21, no. 1 (spring 1988): 47–62.

"Comrade P'eng Chen Makes on Behalf of the Party Central Committee an Important Report at the 2nd Session of the 4th National committee of the All-China Youth Federation and at the Simultaneously-Held 18th National Students Representative Conference." *Selections from China Mainland Press*, no. 3395 (February 11, 1965): 1.

Constitution of the PRC (1978). Beijing: Foreign Languages Press, 1978.

Constitution of the PRC (1982). Beijing: Foreign Languages Press, 1982.

"Counter-Revolutionary Revisionist P'eng Chen's Towering Crimes of Opposing the Party, Socialism and the Thought of Mao Tse-tung (June 10, 1967)." *Selections from China Mainland Magazines* 639 (January 6, 1969): 1, 5, 24, 30.

CPC Beijing Municipal Committee Party History Research Office, ed. *Peng Zhen zai Beijing*. Beijing: Central Documents Press, 2002.

CPC Beijing Party Committee Party History Materials Compilation Committee, ed. *Yi er jiu yundong* (The December 9th Movement). Beijing: CPC Party History Materials Press, 1987.

CPC Central Party School Party History Research Office, ed. *Yi er jiu yundong shiyao* (Outline history of the December 9th Movement). Beijing: Party School Press, 1986.

CPC Northwest Central Bureau. "Fei dang ganbu wenti" (The issue of non-CPC cadres) (October 1, 1942). In *Shen Gan Ning bianqu kang Ri genju di* (The Shen Gan Ning base area for resistance to Japan), 2:583. Beijing: CPC Party History Materials Publishers, 1990.

CPC Party History Research Association, ed. *Xuexi lishi jueyi zhuanji* (Special collection on studying the resolution on history). Beijing: Central Party School Press, 1982.

CPC Shanxi Party Committee Historical Research Office, ed. *Peng Zhen shengping dashi nianbiao* (Chronology of the major events in the life of Peng Zhen). Beijing: Party History Publishers, 1992.

"Dadao fangeming xiuzheng zhuyi fenzi Bo Yibo" (Strike down counterrevolutionary revisionist Bo Yibo). *Qinghua daxue jinggangshan bingtuan dazibao bianweihui* (Big character poster compilation committee of the Jinggang mountains corps at Qinghua University) (January 1967).

"Dadao lao pai da pantu Peng Zhen" (Strike down the old-line traitor, Peng Zhen). In *Wei dong «Hong hai yan»*(Protect the east "Red Swallow"), edited by Nankai Daxue wei dong hong wei bing 5.16 zhendoudui (May 16 fighting force of the Protect the East Red Guards of Nankai University), 3, 6–7, 14–15.

"Dadao Peng Zhen" (Strike down Peng Zhen). *Beijing ribao* (Beijing Daily), May 18, 1967: 5.

"Dadao wuchan jieji zhuanzheng de sidi Peng Zhen" (Strike down the deadly enemy of proletarian dictatorship Peng Zhen). *Renmin ribao* (People's daily), October 15, 1967: 3.

"Da dongluan de niandai" (The decade of chaos). N.d. Mimeographed.

Dai Qing. *Wang Shiwei and "Wild Lilies."* Edited by David E. Apter and Timothy Cheek. Armonk, N. Y.: M. E. Sharpe, 1994.

Dangyuan ganbu falu zhishi duben (Reading text on legal knowledge for Party cadres). Beijing: Central Party School Press, 1996, 1998.

Daubier, Jean. *A History of the Chinese Cultural Revolution*. Translated by Richard Seaver. New York: Vintage, 1974.

Davis, Deborah, and Ezra Vogel, eds. *Chinese Society on the Eve of Tiananmen: The Impact of Reform*. Cambridge, Mass.: Council on East Asian Studies, Harvard University, 1990.

"Decision of the Standing Committee of the National People's Congress on Strengthening the Education in the Legal System and Safeguarding Unity and Stability." In "Party Documents on Anti-Bourgeois Liberalization and Hu Yaobang's Resignation, 1987," edited by James Tong, special issue of *Chinese Law and Government* 21, no. 1 (spring 1988): 39–46.

"Deng Dies." *South China Morning Post*, February 20, 1997: Special Section.

"Deng jinghu tanwu hui dang" (Deng worried that corruption will destroy the Party). *Cheng ming* (Hong Kong) (July 1993): 6–7.

Deng Liqun. "Meiyou gongchandang lingdao jiu meiyou shehuizhuyi xiandaihua jianshe" (Without the leadership of the Communist Party there can be no socialist modernization construction). In *Sixiang jiben yuanze tongsu jiangzuo* (Popular lectures on the Four Basic Principles), 9–15. Beijing: Broadcast Publishers, 1981.

"Deng, Peng Zhen Writes Titles for Albums." *FBIS Daily Report—China* FBIS-CHI-93–125 (July 1, 1993): 17.

Deng Rong. "'Chapter 49: From Pu Qingying to Zhuo Lin' of the Biography My Father Deng Xiaoping." *FBIS Daily Report—China* (December 16, 1993): 47.

Deng Xiaoping. "Dang he guojia lingdao zhidu de gaige" (Reform of the system of party and state leadership). In *Deng Xiaoping wenxuan 1975–1982* (Collected works of Deng Xiaoping 1975–1982), 280–302. Beijing: People's Press, 1983.

———. "Guanyu [Zhonghua renmin gongheguo quan guo renmin daibiao dahui difang ge ji renmin daibiao dahui xuanju fa] cao'an de shuoming" (Explanation of the [PRC Election law for the National People's Congress and the local People's Congresses]). *Xin hua yue bao* (New China monthly) 3 (1953): 6.

———. "Jianchi sixiang jiben yuanze" (Uphold the Four Basic Principles). In *Deng Xiaoping wenxuan 1975–1982* (Collected works of Deng Xiaoping 1975–1982), 2:144. Beijing: People's Press, 1983.

———. "Jiefang sixiang, shi shi qiu shi, tuanjie yizhi xiang qian kan" (Liberate thought, seek truth from facts, look ahead in unity and consistency). In *Deng Xiaoping wenxuan 1975–1982* (Collected works of Deng Xiaoping 1975–1982), 130–43. Beijing: People's Press, 1983.

"Deng Xiaoping tongzhi sang weiyuanhui mingdan" (Name list of the funeral committee for comrade Deng Xiaoping). *Renmin ribao* (People's daily), February 20, 1997: 2.

"Di qi ci quan guo jiancha gongzuo huiyi" (The Seventh National Procurators Work Conference). *Xin hua yue bao* (New China monthly) 9 (1958): 19.

Ding Shu. *Yangmou: fan you qian hou* (Plot: Before and after the Anti-Rightist Campaign). Hong Kong: The Nineties Monthly, 1991.

Ding Youguan. "Lishi ju 'Hai Rui Ba Guan' de fengbo" (The storm over the historical play "Hai Rui Dismissed from Office"). *Mingbao yue kan* (Mingbao monthly) (April 18, 1967): 1–56.

Dittmer, Lowell. *Liu Shao-ch'i and the Chinese Cultural Revolution: The Politics of Mass Criticism*. Berkeley: University of California Press, 1974.

———. "Patterns of Elite Strife and Succession in Chinese Politics." *China Quarterly* 123 (September 1990): 405–30.

"Document 32: The Student Movement in Hunan." In *Wild Lily, Prairie Fire: China's Road to Democracy, Yan'an to Tian'anmen, 1942–1989*, edited by Gregor Benton and Alan Hunter, 217–20. Princeton, N.J.: Princeton University Press, 1995.

Domes, Jurgen. *The Internal Politics of China, 1949–1972*. New York: Praeger, 1973.

———. *Peng Te-huai: The Man and the Image*. London: Hurst, 1985.

Dong Biwu nianpu (Chronology of the life of Dong Biwu). Beijing: Central Documents Press, 1991.

Dorris, Carl E. "Peasant Mobilization in North China and the Origins of Yenan Communism." *China Quarterly* 68 (December 1976): 697–719.

"Dossier of P'eng Chen." In "A Compilation of Dossiers," *Selections from China Mainland Magazines*, suppl. 27, 33–39. July 8, 1968.

"Down with Ho Lung." *Current Background*, no. 859 (August 8, 1968): 23.

"Down with P'eng Chen—Big Party Boss of the Kuomintang." *Selections from China Mainland Press*, no. 4203: 9–13.

"Drag Out Liu Shaoqi and Show Him to the Public." *Survey of China Mainland Press*, no. 3946 (May 25, 1967): 9, 14.

"Dui gaige jiyaojian ding you yao zhongshi jiejue wenti, Gongzuo jiandu he falu jiandu yao jinyibu jianquan" (We must be resolute and must give attention to solving issues required by reform, supervision over work and legal supervision must be progressively perfected). *Renmin ribao* (People's daily), March 22, 1985: 1.

Ebon, Martin. *Lin Piao: The Life and Writings of China's New Ruler*. New York: Stein and Day, 1970.

Eckstein, Alexander. *China's Economic Revolution*. Cambridge: Cambridge University Press, 1977.

Epstein, Edward J. "Evolution of China's General Principles of Civil Law." *American Journal of Comparative Law* 34, no. 4 (1986): 705–13.

"Events Surrounding the 'Ch'angkuanlou' Counterrevolutionary Incident." *Selections from the China Mainland Press*, no. 3187 (June 15, 1967): 23–37.

"Exposing the Towering Crimes of Counter-Revolutionary Revisionist Li Ch'i Against the Party, Socialism, and Mao Tse-tung's Thought." *Selections from China Mainland Magazines*, suppl. 23, 1–3. April 16, 1968.

Faligot, Roger, and Remi Kauffer. *The Chinese Secret Service*. Translated by Christine Donougher. London: Headline Press, 1987.

"Fan you kuodahua de yingxiang" (The effects of expansion of the Anti-Rightist Campaign). In *Zhonggong dang shi dao du* (Directed readings in Chinese Communist Party history), 2:1372, 1374. Beijing: Broadcast Press, 1991.

"Fazhan shehui zhuyi minzhu jianquan shehui zhuyi fazhi" (Develop socialist democracy, perfect the socialist legal system). *Renmin ribao* (People's daily), September 30, 1982.

"Fazhan shehui zhuyi minzhu jianquan shehui zhuyi fazhi" (Develop socialist democracy, perfect the socialist legal system). *Zhongguo fazhi bao* (China legal system gazette) (October 1, 1982): 1.

"February Outline." In *Main Documents of the Great Proletarian Cultural Revolution*, edited by Union Research Institute, 3–12. Hong Kong: Union Research Institute, 1968.

Feinerman, James V. "Economic and Legal Reform in China, 1978–91." *Problems of Communism* (September–October 1991): 62–75.

Feng Yi, ed. *Liu Shaoqi geming shijian he sixiang yanjiu* (Research on the revolutionary experience and thought of Liu Shaoqi). Beijing: History Education Society Press, 1988.

Fewsmith, Joseph. *Dilemmas of Reform in China: Political Conflict and Economic Debate*. Armonk, N.Y.: M. E. Sharpe, 1994.

Fisher, Tom. "'The Play's the Thing': Wu Han and Hai Rui Revisited." *Australian Journal of Chinese Affairs* 7 (1982): 1–35.

"Former Officials Attend Beijing Spring Festival Celebration." *FBIS Daily Report: People's Republic of China*, February 1, 1979: E1–E2.

Forster, Keith. "The 1982 Campaign Against Economic Crime in China." *Australian Journal of Chinese Affairs* 14 (1985): 1–19.

Franz, Uli. *Deng Xiaoping*. Translated by Tom Artin. New York: Harcourt Brace Jovanovich, 1985.

Freyn, Hubert. *Prelude to War: The Chinese Student Rebellion of 1935–1936*. Shanghai: China Journal Publishing, 1939.

Friedman, Edward. "Theorizing the Democratization of China's Leninist State." In *Marxism and the Chinese Experience*, edited by Arif Dirlik and Maurice Meisner, 171–89. Armonk, N.Y.: M. E. Sharpe, 1989.

Friedman, Edward, Paul G. Pickowicz, and Mark Selden. *Chinese Village Socialist State*. New Haven, Conn.: Yale University Press, 1991.

"From the Defeat of Peng Teh-Huai to the Bankruptcy of China's Khrushchev" (*Red flag*, no. 13, 1967 / *Peking Review*, August 18, 1967). In *The Case of Peng Teh-Huai 1959–1968*, edited by Union Research Institute, 137–38. Hong Kong: Union Research Institute, 1968.

Fu Yang. "Xin shiqi Peng Zhen de renmin minzhu sixiang" (Peng Zhen's ideology of people's democracy in the new period). In *Mianhuai Peng Zhen*, 392–403.

Fu Zhengyuan. *China's Legalists: The Earliest Totalitarians and Their Art of Ruling*. Armonk, N.Y.: M. E. Sharpe, 1996.

"Further Coverage of Fifth Session of Fifth NPC." *FBIS Daily Report—China* (November 29, 1982): K1.

Gai Jun, ed. *Baiqu douzheng shi* (History of struggle in the White Areas). Beijing: People's Press, 1996.

Gao Xinmin and Zhang Shujun. *Yan'an zhengfeng shilu* (Record of events in the Yan'an rectification). Hangzhou: Zhejiang People's Press, 2000.

Gardner, John. "The Wu-Fan Campaign in Shanghai: A Study in the Consolidation of Urban Control." In *Chinese Communist Politics in Action*, edited by A. Doak Barnett, 477–539. Seattle: University of Washington Press, 1969.

Goldman, Merle. "The Chinese Communist Party's 'Cultural Revolution' of 1962–64." In *Ideology and Politics in Contemporary China*, edited by Chalmers Johnson, 219–54. Seattle: University of Washington Press, 1973.

———. *China's Intellectuals: Advise and Dissent*. Cambridge, Mass.: Harvard University Press, 1981.

———. "The Party and the Intellectuals: Phase Two." In *The Cambridge History of China Vol. 14: The People's Republic of China Part 1—The Emergence of Revolutionary China 1949–1965*, edited by Denis Twitchett and John K. Fairbank, 432–77. Cambridge: Cambridge University Press, 1987.

Goldman, Rene. "Peking University Today." *China Quarterly* 7 (July–September 1961): 101–11.

Gong Yuzhi. "«Er yue tigang»he donghu zhixing" (The "February Outline" and the events at East Lake). In *Hui dao "Wen Ge"* (Revisiting the "Cultural Revolution"), edited by Zhang Hua et al., 289–318. Beijing: Party History Press, 2000.

Goodman, David S. G. *Deng Xiaoping and the Chinese Revolution: A Political Biography*. New York: Routledge, 1994.

———. *King Coal and Secretary Hu: Shanxi's Third Modernization*. Syndey: Institute for International Studies, University of Technology, 1996. Monograph.

Gray, Jack, and Patrick Cavendish. *Chinese Communism in Crisis: Maoism and the Cultural Revolution*. New York: Praeger, 1968.

Gregg, Benjamin. "The Modernization of Contemporary Chinese Law." *Review of Politics* 55, no. 3 (1993): 443–70.

Gu Anrang, Yang Jingyu, and Song Dahan. "Shou yi zong sheng de jiaohui" (Benefit from a whole life's teachings). In *Mianhuai Peng Zhen*, 217–29.

Gu Ming. "You Zhongguo tese de shehui zhuyi jing ji fazhi jianshe de kaituozhe" (Developer of the socialist economic law system with Chinese characteristics). In *Mianhuai Peng Zhen*, 139–50.

Guangming ribao (Bright daily), August 9, 1967: 3.

"Guanyu gonggu yu kuoda Jin Cha Ji genjudi de zhishi" (Instruction on consolidating and expanding the Jin Cha Ji base area) (From Mao Zedong, Luo Fu, and Liu Shaoqi to Nie Rongzhen, Peng Zhen, Zhu De, and Peng Dehuai, April 20, 1938). In *Zhonggong zhongyang wenjian xuanji* (Compilation of CPC central documents), edited by Central Archives, 11:502. Beijing: Central Party School. Periodical.

"Guanyu Jin Cha Ji bianqu huobi zhengce de zhishi" (Instruction on currency policy in the Jin Cha Ji border area) (August 17, 1938). In *Zhonggong zhongyang wenjian xuanji* (Compilation of CPC central documents), edited by Central Archives, 11:539. Beijing: Central Party School. Periodical.

"Guanyu pingyuan youji zhan de zhishi" (Instruction on guerrilla war in the plains) (April 21, 1938). In *Zhonggong zhongyang wenjian xuanji* (Compilation of CPC central documents), edited by Central Archives, 11:505. Beijing: Central Party School. Periodical.

"Guanyu zhan sheng di dui Jin Cha Ji bianqu de weigong de zhishi" (Instruction concerning military victory over the enemy's encirclement campaign in

Jin Cha Ji) (October 2, 1938, authored by Mao Zedong et al. and directed to local military commanders Zuo Quan, Liu Bocheng, Zhou Shidi, and Gan Siqi). In *Zhonggong zhongyang wenjian xuanji* (Compilation of CPC central documents), edited by Central Archives, 11:545. Beijing: Central Party School. Periodical.

"Guanzhu jianchi sixiang jiben yuanze zhei ge zonggangling jiaqiang duiwu jianshe ba zhengfa gongzuo gaode geng hao" (Seizing and upholding this general program of the Four Basic Principles, strengthening development of corps is improving political–legal work). *Renmin ribao* (People's daily), April 2, 1987: 1.

Guillermaz, Jacques. *The Chinese Communist Party in Power 1949–1976*. Boulder, Colo.: Westview Press, 1976.

Guo Simin and Tian Yu. *Wo yan zhong de Liu Shaoqi* (Liu Shaoqi in our eyes). Shijiazhuang: Hebei People's Press, 1992.

Hai Rui Dismissed from Office. Translated by C. C. Huang. Honolulu: University of Hawaii Press, 1972.

Hamrin, Carol Lee. "Yang Xianzhen's Philosophical Criminal Case." *Chinese Law and Government* 24, no. 1–2 (spring–summer 1991).

Han Lefeng. "Peng Zhen tongzhi zai dongbei de ri ri ye ye" (The days and nights of comrade Peng Zhen in Manchuria). In *Mianhuai Peng Zhen*, 303–21.

Han Suyin. *The Wind in the Tower: Mao Tse-tung and the Chinese Revolution 1949–1975*. Boston: Little Brown, 1976.

Han Yanlong and Chang Zhaoru, eds., *Zhongguo xin minzhu zhuyi geming shiqi genjudi fazhi wenxian xuanbian* (Compilation of documents on base area legal systems during China's new democratic revolution period). 3 vols. Beijing: Chinese Academy of Social Sciences Press, 1981.

Hao Ping. "Reassessing the Starting Point of the Cultural Revolution." *China Review International* 3, no. 1 (spring 1996): 66–86.

Harding, Harry. *China's Second Revolution: Reform After Mao*. Washington, D.C.: Brookings Institution, 1987.

Hartford, Kathleen. "Fits and Starts: The Chinese Communist Party in Rural Hebei 1921–1936." In *New Perspectives on the Chinese Communist Revolution*, edited by Tony Saich and Hans van de Ven, 144–74. Armonk, N.Y.: M. E. Sharpe, 1995.

———. "Repression and Communist Success: The Case of Jin Cha Ji, 1938–1943." In *Single Sparks: China's Rural Revolutions*, edited by Kathleen Hartford and Stephen M. Goldstein, 92–127. Armonk, N.Y.: M. E. Sharpe, 1989.

———. "Step by Step: Reform, Resistance, and Revolution in Chin-Ch'a-Chi Border Region 1937–1945." Ph.D. diss., Stanford University, 1980.

Hebei CPC Committee Party History Research Office and Hebei Academy of Social Sciences. "Peng Zhen tongzhi zai Hebei de geming huodong" (Comrade Peng Zhen's revolutionary activities in Hebei). In *Mianhuai Peng Zhen*, 500–520.

Holm, David. "The Strange Case of *Liu Zhidan*." *Australian Journal of Chinese Affairs* 27 (January 1992): 77–96.

Howell, Jude. *China Opens Its Doors: The Politics of Economic Transition*. Boulder, Colo.: Lynne Reinner, 1993.

Hsia, Tao-tai. "Legal Development in the People's Republic of China 1949–1981." In *China Seventy Years After the 1911 Hsin-Hai Revolution*, edited by Hung-dah Chiu and Shao-chuan Leng, 100–118. Charlottesville: University of Virginia Press, 1984.

Huang Huoqing et al. "Huigu Yan'an zhongyang dangxiao de zhengfeng yundong" (Recalling the rectification movement at the central Party school in Yan'an). *Renmin ribao* (People's daily), July 27, 1986: 5.

———. "Zhuinian jingai de lao lingdao Peng Zhen tongzhi" (Recalling esteemed old leader comrade Peng Zhen). In *Mianhuai Peng Zhen*, 13–27.

Huang Zheng. "The Injustice Done to Liu Shaoqi." *Chinese Law and Government* 32, no. 3 (May–June 1999): 9–12.

Hulsewe, A. F. P. *Remnants of Ch'in Law: An Annotated Translation of the Ch'in Legal and Administrative rules of the 3rd Century* B.C. *discovered in Yun-meng Prefecture, Hu-pei Province, in 1975*. Leiden: E. J. Brill, 1985.

Israel, John. *Student Nationalism in China 1927–1937*. Stanford: Stanford University Press, 1966.

Israel, John, and Donald W. Klein. *Rebels and Bureaucrats: China's December 9ers*. Berkeley: University of California Press, 1976.

Jiang Hongwu. *Chen Yi zhuan* (Biography of Chen Yi). Shanghai: Shanghai People's Press, 1992.

"Jiaqiang fazhi xuanchuan shi xinwen jie de zhongyao zhize" (Strengthening propagandizing of the legal system is an important responsibility of media circles). *Zhongguo fazhi bao* (China legal system gazette) (May 14, 1985): 1.

"Jiekai panju zai Beijing de Peng Zhen da pantu jituan de heimu" (Uncover the inside story of Peng Zhen's group of big traitors illegally occupying Beijing). In *Chedi maizang Liu Shaoqi pantu jituan* (Thoroughly bury Liu Shaoqi's traitor group), edited by Hong dai hui Nankai Daxue wei dong hong wei bing «Hong hai yan»(Nankai University Protect the East Red Guards of the red representative congress), 1–14. 1967. Mimeographed.

"Jin Cha Ji bianqu guanyu daibu sousuo zhencha chuli xingshi tezhong xingshi fan zhi jueding" (Decision of Jin Cha Ji border region on arresting, hunting down, investigating, and dealing with those who commit crimes and serious crimes). Han Yanlong and Chang Zhaoru, *Zhongguo xin minzhu zhuyi geming shiqi genjudi fazhi wenxian xuanbian*, 3:91–97.

"Jin Cha Ji bianqu jian zu jian xi danxing tiaoli" (Unitary regulation of Jin Cha Ji border region on the reduction of rents and interest). In *Jin Cha Ji kang Ri genju di* (The Jin Cha Ji base area for resistance to Japan), 1A:88. Beijing: CPC Party History Materials Publishers, 1988.

"Jin Cha Ji bianqu jun zheng min dibiao dahui tongdian" (Telegraphic communiqué on the military, political and civilian representative congress for Jin Cha Ji) (January 15, 1938). In *Zhonggong zhongyang wenjian xuanji* (Compilation of CPC central documents), edited by Central Archives, 11:835. Beijing: Central Party School. Periodical.

"Jin Cha Ji bianqu xian qu cun zuzhi tiaoli" (Regulations for county, district, and village organizations in Jin Cha Ji border region). In *Zhongguo xin minzhu zhuyi geming shiqi genjudi fazhi wenxian xuanbian*, edited by Han Yanlong and Chang Zhaoru, 2:272–81.

Jin Cha Ji Bianqu Xingzheng Weiyuanhui (Administrative Committee of Jin Cha Ji Border Area), ed. *Xianxing faling huiji* (Collection of current laws and edicts). 2 vols. 1945.

"Jin Cha Ji bianqu xingzheng weiyuanhui guanyu shengli wancheng ge ji xuanze de zhishi xing" (Letter of instruction from the Jin Cha Ji border region administrative council concerning the successful completion of various levels of elections) (June 24, 1940). In *Jin Cha Ji kang Ri genju di* (The Jin Cha Ji base area for resistance to Japan), 1A:351. Beijing: CPC Party History Materials Publishers, 1988.

Jin Cha Ji kang Ri genjudi (The Jin Cha Ji Base Area for resisting Japan). Vol. 1A. Beijing: CPC Party History Materials Press, 1988.

Jin Cha Ji kang Ri genjudi (The Jin Cha Ji base area for resistance to Japan). Vol. 3. Beijing: CPC History Materials Publishers, 1991.

"Jin Cha Ji kang Ri genjudi dang, zheng, jun, qun zuzhi xulie" (Arrangement of party, political, military and mass organizations in the Jin Cha Ji anti-Japanese base area). In *Jin Cha Ji kang Ri genju di* (The Jin Cha Ji base area for resistance to Japan). Vol. 3. Beijing: CPC Party History Materials Publishers, 1991.

«Jin Cha Ji ribao» da shi ji (Chronology of Jin Cha Ji Daily). Beijing: Masses Press, 1986.

"Jingji lifa hen xuyao—tansuo shiyan jieduan bu ke xiao" (Economic legislation is much needed, but the period of discussion and experimentation cannot be shortened). *Renmin ribao* (People's daily), January 24, 1985: 1.

"Jingxin dongbo de 'Gong ting zheng bian' yinmou" (The soul-stirring palace coup plot). *Pi Peng zhan bao* (Militant journal for attacking Peng Zhen), no. 3 (August 1967): 2–3.

"Jinyibu shenyi ji xiang falu cao'an" (Progressively reviewing several law drafts). *Renmin ribao* (People's daily), September 5, 1987: 1.

Johnson, Chalmers. "Chinese Communist Leadership and Mass Response: The Yenan Period and the Socialist Education Campaign." In *China in Crisis I: China's Heritage and the Communist Political System*, edited by Ping-ti Ho and Tang Tsou, 397–437. Chicago: University of Chicago Press, 1968.

———. *Peasant Nationalism and Communist Power: The Emergence of Revolutionary China, 1937–1945*. Stanford: Stanford University Press, 1962.

Joseph, William A. *The Critique of Ultra-Leftism in China, 1958–1981*. Stanford: Stanford University Press, 1984.

———. "A Tragedy of Good Intentions: Post-Mao Views of the Great Leap Forward." *Modern China* 12, no. 4 (October 1986): 419–57.

Kau, Michael Y. M. *The Lin Piao Affair: Power Politics and Military Coup*. White Plains, N.Y.: International Arts and Sciences Press, 1975.

Kau, Michael Ying-Mao, and Susan H. Marsh, eds. *China in the Era of Deng Xiaoping: A Decade of Reform*. Armonk, N.Y.: M. E. Sharpe, 1993.

Keith, Ronald C. *China's Struggle for the Rule of Law*. New York: St. Martin's Press, 1994.

Keith, Ronald, and Zhiqiu Lin. *Law and Justice in China's New Marketplace*. New York: Palgrave, 2001.

Keller, Perry. "Sources of Order in Chinese Law." *American Journal of Comparative Law* 17, no. 4 (1994): 711–59.

Kent, Ann. *Between Freedom and Subsistence: China and Human Rights*. Hong Kong: Oxford University Press, 1993.

Klein, Donald, and Anne Clark. *Biographical Dictionary of Chinese Communism 1921–1965*. Cambridge: Harvard University Press, 1970.

Kroll, J. K. "Notes on Ch'in and Han Law." In *Thought and Law in Qin and Han China: Studies Presented to Anthony Hulsewe on the Occasion of his Eightieth Birthday*, edited by W. L. Idema and E. Zurcher, 63–78. Leiden: E. J. Brill, 1990.

Ladany, Laszlo. "China's New Power Centre?" *Far Eastern Economic Review* (June 28, 1984): 38.

———. *Law and Legality in China: The Testament of a China-watcher*. London: Hurst, 1992.

Lan Quanpu. *Jiefangqu fagui gaiyao* (Outline of laws and regulations in the liberated areas). Beijing: Masses Publishers, 1982.

Lee, Hung Yung. *The Politics of the Chinese Cultural Revolution: A Case Study*. Berkeley: University of California Press, 1978.

Li Baohua. "Yi jiu san liu nian si yue dao shier yue Zhonggong Beiping shiwei de zuzhi jiankuang" (The general situation of the organization of the CPC Beiping committee during April–December 1936). In *Yi er jiu yundong* (The December 9th Movement), edited by CPC Beijing Party Committee Party History Materials Compilation Committee, 349–51. Beijing: CPC Party History Materials Press, 1987.

Li Bo, ed. *Jin Cha Ji bianqu yinxiang ji* (Impressions of Jin Cha Ji Border Region). N.p.: Dushu shenghuo chubanshe, 1939.

Li Che, ed. *P'eng Chen fan Mao chi-t'uan* (Peng Zhen's anti-Mao group). Taipei: China Mainland Research Centre, 1969.

Li Lianjiang and Kevin J. O'Brien. "Accommodating 'Democracy' in a One-Party State: Introducing Village Elections in China." *China Quarterly* 162 (June 2000): 465–89.

———. "Villages and Popular Resistance in Contemporary China." *Modern China* 22, no. 1 (January 1996): 28–61.

Li Ligong. "Peng lao yongyuan huo zai women xinzhong" (Old Peng will live forever in our hearts). In *Mianhuai Peng Zhen*, 99–103.

Li Mianmin. "Canjia Yan'an 'qiangjiu yundong' de pianxu huiyi" (Recollections of participating in the rescue movement in Yan'an). In *Hua gong shi ziliao* (Materials on the CPC history), edited by Cultural History Materials and Research Committee of the Chinese People's Political Consultative Congress (CPPCC) National Committee, 3:29–43. Beijing: Cultural History Materials Publishers, 1981.

"Li Peng on Role of CPC in Rule of Law." *China News Digest*. Available at: http://www.cnd.org (March 7, 2001).

Li Rui. "An Initial Study of Mao Zedong's Erroneous 'Left' Thinking in His Later Years." Edited and translated by Tony Saich and Nancy Hearst. *Chinese Law and Government* 29, no. 4 (July–August 1996): 56–59.

———. *Li Rui fan "zuo" wenxuan* (Compilation of articles by Li Rui opposing "leftism"). Beijing: Central Editions Press, 1998.

Li Shaozhuang, ed. *Zhu Rongji ren ma* (Zhu Rongji's troops). Hong Kong: Xiafeier (So far) Publishers, 1998.

Li Tien-min. *Liu Shao-Ch'i: Mao's First Heir Apparent*. Taipei: Institute of International Relations, 1975.

Li, Victor H. "The Evolution and Development of the Chinese Legal System." In *China: Management of a Revolutionary Society*, edited by John M. H. Lindbeck, 221–55. Seattle: University of Washington Press, 1971.

Li Xuefeng. "Wo suozhidao de 'Wen Ge' fadong neiqing" (What I know of the internal situation underlying the impetus for the "Cultural Revolution"). In *Hui dao "Wen Ge"* (Revisiting the "Cultural Revolution"), edited by Zhang Hua et al., 603–16. Beijing: Party History Press, 2000.

———. "Yi jiu san liu nian yi yue dao yi jiu san qi nian yi yue Zhonggong Beiping dang zuzhi yiqi huodong qingkuang" (The situation with CPC organization in Beiping and other activities from January 1936 through January 1937). In *Yi er jiu yundong* (The December 9th Movement), edited by CPC Beijing Party Committee Party History Materials Compilation Committee, 342–48. Beijing: CPC Party History Materials Press, 1987.

Li Yong. *Wenhua da geming zhong de ming ren zhi yu* (Imprisonment of famous personages during the Cultural Revolution). Beijing: Nationalities Institute Press, 1993.

"Liang ge genben duili de wenjian" (Two diametrically opposed documents). *Hongqi* (Red flag) 9: 25–28.

Liao Kuangsheng (Liao Guangsheng). "'Independent Administration of Justice' and the PRC Legal System." In "Studies on the Constitutional Law of the People's Republic of China," edited by Byron S. J. Weng. *Chinese Law and Government* 16, no. 2–3 (summer–fall 1983): 123–52.

Lieberthal, Kenneth. *Governing China: From Revolution Through Reform*. New York: W. W. Norton, 1995.

———. "The Great Leap Forward and the Split in the Yenan Leadership." In *The Cambridge History of China Vol. 14: The People's Republic of China Part 1—The Emergence of Revolutionary China 1949–1965*, Denis Twitchett and John K. Fairbank, 293–359. Cambridge: Cambridge University Press, 1987.

———. *A Research Guide to Central Party and Government Meetings in China: 1949–1975*. White Plains, N.Y.: International Arts and Sciences Press, 1976.

Lin Mohan. "'Wen Ge' qian de jichang wenyi fengbo" (Various disturbances prior to the "Cultural Revolution"). In *Hui dao "Wen Ge"* (Revisiting the "Cultural Revolution"), edited by Zhang Hua et al., 267–76. Beijing: Party History Press, 2000.

"Lin Piao's Most Significant Speech (Informal Address of Politburo Meeting, 1966)." In *Lin Piao: The Life and Writings of China's New Ruler*, edited by Martin Ebon, 252–69. New York: Stein and Day, 1970.

"Ling hui er shi er ge wenjian de jingshen yu shijian" (The Spirit and Practice of the Twenty-Two Documents Issued by the Leadership Council). In Yan'an Wencui (Collection of documents of Yan'an), edited by Chinese Academy of Social Sciences Information Research Bureau and Chinese Media History Information Office, 1:29–34. Beijing: Beijing Publishers, 1984.

Liu Fuzhi. "Mianhuai wo guo shehui zhuyi fazhi zhuyao dianjiren Peng Zhen tongzhi" (Recalling the main cornerstone of our socialist legal system—Peng Zhen). In *Mianhuai Peng Zhen*, 82–88.

Liu Huafeng and Wang Yuting, eds. *Zhongguo gongchandang zuzhi gongzuo dashiji* (Chronology of major events in CPC organization work). Shenyang: Liaoning People's Press, 1992.

Liu Jianzhi. "Budui wenyi gongzuo zuotanhui jiyao chansheng qianhou" (Before and after the emergence of the summary of the military forum on literature and art). In *Hui dao "Wen Ge"* (Revisiting the "Cultural Revolution"), edited by Zhang Hua et al., 321–50. Beijing: Party History Press, 2000.

Liu Lantao. "Jin Cha Ji bianqu dang zuzhi zai zhandou zhong cheng chang zhuang da" (The party organization in Jin Cha Ji grows up and expands in strength during the war). In *Zhonggong dang shi ziliao* (Party history materials), edited by CPC Central Committee Party History Research Office, 32:82–99. Beijing: CPC History Publishers, 1989.

Liu Shaoqi. "The Armed Forces Persisting in the War of Resistance Against Japan" (July 1, 1938). In *Collected Works of Liu Shaoqi: Before 1944*, edited by Union Research Institute, 65–80. Hong Kong: Union Research Institute, 1969.

———. "How To Be a Good Communist" (July 1939). In *Collected Works of Liu Shaoqi: Before 1944*, edited by Union Research Institute, 151–281. Hong Kong: Union Research Institute, 1969.

———. "On Inner-Party Struggle." In *Three Essays on Party-Building*, edited by Liu Shaoqi, 99–161. Beijing: Foreign Languages Press, 1980.

———. "On Inner-Party Struggle" (July 2, 1942). In *The Rise to Power of the Chinese Communist Party*, edited by Tony Saich, 1077–89. Armonk, N.Y.: M. E. Sharpe, 1996.

———. "On Open and Secret Work" (September 1939). In *Collected Works of Liu Shaoqi: Before 1944*, edited by Union Research Institute, 283–302. Hong Kong: Union Research Institute, 1969.

———. "Policies in Anti-Japanese Guerrilla Warfare" (October 16, 1937). In *Collected Works of Liu Shaoqi: Before 1944*, edited by Union Research Institute, 27–51. Hong Kong: Union Research Institute, 1969.

———. "The Political Report of the Central Committee of the Communist Party of China to the Eighth National Congress of the Party" (September 15, 1956). In *Collected Works of Liu Shaoqi: 1945–1957*, edited by Union Research Institute, 337–407. Hong Kong: Union Research Institute, 1969.

———. "Report on the Draft Constitution of the People's Republic of China"

(September 15, 1954). In *Collected Works of Liu Shaoqi: 1949–1957*, edited by Union Research Institute, 275–316. Hong Kong: Union Research Institute, 1967.

———. "Report on the Work of the Central Committee of the Communist Party of China to the Second Session of the Eighth National Congress" (May 5, 1958). In *Collected Works of Liu Shao-ch'i: 1958–1967*, edited by Union Research Institute, 1–40. Hong Kong: Union Research Institute, 1968.

———. "Some Basic Principles for Organizing the Masses" (May 1, 1939). In *Collected Works of Liu Shaoqi: Before 1944*, edited by Union Research Institute, 99–114. Hong Kong: Union Research Institute, 1969.

———. "Suqing guanmen zhuyi yu maoxian zhuyi" (Eliminate closed doorism and adventurism). In *Yi er jiu yundong* (The December 9th Movement), edited by CPC Beijing Party Committee Party History Materials Compilation Committee, 66–74. Beijing: CPC Party History Materials Press, 1987.

———. "Training of a Communist Party Member." In *Mao's China: Party Reform Documents, 1942–44*, edited by Boyd Compton, 108–55. Seattle: University of Washington Press, 1966.

———. "Various Questions Concerning Fundamental Policies in Anti-Japanese Guerrilla Warfare" (October 16, 1937). In *Collected Works of Liu Shaoqi: Before 1944*, edited by Union Research Institute, 27–51. Hong Kong: Union Research Institute, 1969.

———. "The Victory of Marxism-Leninism in China" (September 14, 1959). In *Collected Works of Liu Shao-ch'i: 1958–1967*, edited by Union Research Institute, 47–72. Hong Kong: Union Research Institute, 1968.

"Liu Shaoqi's reactionary speeches." *Selections from China Mainland Magazines*, suppl. 25, 14. May 13, 1968.

Liu Yong. "Tongdao zhongxin aidai de lao lingdao Peng Zhen tongzhi" (Mourning the deeply beloved old leader Peng Zhen). In *Mianhuai Peng Zhen*, 253–59.

Lo, Carlos Wing-hung. *China's Legal Awakening: Legal Theory and Criminal Justice in Deng's Era*. Hong Kong: Hong Kong University Press, 1995.

"Look, These Dogs in the Water Are Not Dead Yet!" *Survey of China Mainland Press*, no. 4032 (October 2, 1967): 6–7.

Lu Xiangtou, ed. *Liu Shaoqi he ta de shiye* (Liu Shaoqi and his career). Beijing: Central Documents Press, 1991.

Lu Zhengcao. *Ji zhong huiyi lu* (Memoir of the Central Hebei Region). Beijing: PLA Press, 1984.

Lubman, Stanley B. *Bird in a Cage: Legal Reform in China After Mao*. Stanford: Stanford University Press, 1999.

Lun xin Zhongguo de zhengfa gongzuo (On political–legal work in the new China). Beijing: Party Documents, 1992.

Luo Fu (Zhang Wentian). "Bai qu dang muqian de zhongxin renwu" (Main tasks for the Party in the White Areas at present) (June 6, 1937). In *Zhonggong zhongyang wenjian xuanji* (Compilation of CPC central documents), edited by Central Archives, 11:224–64. Beijing: Central Party School. Periodical.

Ma Ju. "Mianhuai Peng Zhen jiaohui, Jiaqiang dang de jianshe" (Recall Peng Zhen's teachings, strengthen Party building). In *Mianhuai Peng Zhen*, 362–71.

MacFarquhar, Roderick. *The Origins of the Cultural Revolution, 1: Contradictions among the People*. London: Columbia University Press, 1974.

———. *The Origins of the Cultural Revolution, 3: The Coming of the Cataclysm 1961–1966*. London: Columbia University Press, 1997.

———. "The Secret Speeches of Chairman Mao." In *The Secret Speeches of Chairman Mao: From the Great Leap Forward to the Cultural Revolution*, edited by Roderick MacFarquhar, Timothy Cheek, and Eugene Wu, 14–18. Cambridge, Mass.: Harvard University Press, 1989.

———. "The Succession to Mao and the End of Maoism, 1969–1982." In *The Politics of China 1949–1989*, edited by Roderick MacFarquhar, chap. 4. Cambridge: Cambridge University Press, 1993.

———. "Teaching Materials on the Cultural Revolution," Fairbank Library, Harvard University. Mimeographed.

MacFarquhar, Roderick, ed. *The Politics of China, 1949–1989*. Cambridge: Cambridge University Press, 1993.

MacFarquhar, Roderick, Timothy Cheek, and Eugene Wu, eds. *The Secret Speeches of Chairman Mao: From the Great Leap Forward to the Cultural Revolution*. Cambridge, Mass.: Harvard University Press, 1989.

Mao Zedong. "Combat Liberalism" (September 7, 1937). In *Selected Works of Mao Tse-tung*, 2:31–33. Beijing: Foreign Languages Press, 1965.

———. "For the Mobilization of All the Nation's Forces for Victory in the War of Resistance" (August 25, 1937). In *Selected Works of Mao Tse-tung*, 2:23–29. Beijing: Foreign Languages Press, 1965.

———. "On the Correct Handling of Contradictions Among the People" (speaking notes). In *The Secret Speeches of Chairman Mao: From the Great Leap Forward to the Cultural Revolution*, edited by Roderick MacFarquhar, Timothy Cheek, and Eugene Wu, 131–90. Cambridge, Mass.: Harvard University Press, 1989.

———. "On the Question of Political Power in the Anti-Japanese Base Areas." In *Selected Works of Mao Tse-tung*, 2:417–19. Beijing: Foreign Languages Press, 1965.

———. "Overcome the Danger of Capitulation and Strive for a Turn for the Better" (January 28, 1940). In *Selected Works of Mao Tse-tung*, 2:385–88. Beijing: Foreign Languages Press, 1965.

———. "Policies, Measures and Perspectives for Resisting the Japanese Invasion" (July 23, 1937). In *Selected Works of Mao Tse-tung*, vol. 2, sect. 2(5), 13–22. Beijing: Foreign Languages Press, 1965.

———. "Problems of Strategy in Guerrilla War Against Japan" (May 1938). In *Selected Works of Mao Tse-tung*, 2:81–111. Beijing: Foreign Languages Press, 1965.

———. "Recruit Large Numbers of Intellectuals" (December 1, 1939). In *Selected Works of Mao Tse-tung*, 2:301–3. Beijing: Foreign Languages Press, 1965.

———. "Reform Our Study." In *Selected Works of Mao Tse-tung*, 3:17–25. Beijing: Foreign Languages Press, 1965.

———. "The Role of the Chinese Communist Party in the National War" (October 1938). In *Selected Works of Mao Tse-tung*, 2:195–211. Beijing: Foreign Languages Press, 1965.

———. "Talks at the Beidaihe Conference" (draft transcript) (August 17–30, 1958). In *The Secret Speeches of Chairman Mao: From the Hundred Flowers to the Great Leap Forward*, edited by Roderick MacFarquhar, Timothy Cheek, and Eugene Wu, 397–442. Cambridge, Mass.: Council on East Asian Studies, Harvard University, 1989.

———. "Unite All Anti-Japanese Forces and Combat the Anti-Communist Die-Hards" (February 1, 1940). In *Selected Works of Mao Tse-tung*, 389–94. Beijing: Foreign Languages Press, 1965.

"Mao's 'Khrushchev Speech.'" *Economist* (May 11, 1957): 485.

"Mao Zedong, Wang Jiaxiang guanyu He Long, Guan Xiangying, lu bu qu Jizhong he Peng Zhen deng gongzuo anpai wenti fu Peng Dehuai dian" (Telegram from Mao Zedong to Peng Dehuai Concerning He Long and Guan Xiangying going to Central Hebei and the work arrangements for Peng Zhen et al.) (July 13, 1938). In *Jin Cha Ji kang Ri genju di* (The Jin Cha Ji base area for resistance to Japan), 1A:177. Beijing: CPC Party History Materials Publishers, 1988.

"Mao Zedong, Wang Jiaxiang guanyu Jixinan shijian yu women fangzhen de buchong zhishi" (Supplementary instruction from Mao Zedong and Wang Jiaxiang concerning the Southwest Hebei incident) (December 9, 1939). In *Zhonggong zhongyang wenjian xuanji* (Compilation of CPC central documents), edited by Central Archives, 12:217. Beijing: Central Party School. Periodical.

Mazur, Mary. "Intellectual Activism in China During the 1940s: Wu Han in the United Front and the Democratic League." *China Quarterly* 133 (March 1993): 27–55.

McCormick, Barrett L. *Political Reform in Post-Mao China: Democracy and Bureaucracy in a Leninist State*. Berkeley: University of California Press, 1990.

Mei Jian, ed. *Yan'an mi shi 1937–1947* (Secret affairs at Yan'an 1937–1947). Vol. 2. Beijing: Red Flag Press, 1996.

Meisner, Maurice. *Mao's China: A History of the People's Republic*. New York: The Free Press, 1977.

Mianhuai Peng Zhen (Recalling Peng Zhen). Beijing: Central Archives Press, 1998.

Ming Wen. "Peng Zhen fazhi sixiang shulue" (Summary of Peng Zhen's thinking on the legal system). *Dangdai Zhongguo shi yanjiu* (Research on contemporary Chinese history) 5 (September 25, 1995): 90–96.

Minzhengbu jiceng zhengquan jianshe si (Ministry of civil affairs office on establishing basic level political authority), ed. *Peng Zhen tongzhi guanyu cunmin weiyuanhui jumin weiyuanhui de zhongyao jianghua* (Important speeches of comrade Peng Zhen on the village committees and neighborhood committees). 1990.

Moody, Peter R., Jr. *Opposition and Dissent in Contemporary China*. Stanford: Hoover Institution, 1977.

Myers, James T., Jurgen Domes, and Erik von Groeling, eds. *Chinese Politics—Documents and Analysis, Vol. 1: Cultural Revolution to 1969*. Columbia: University of South Carolina Press, 1986.

Nathan, Andrew J. *Chinese Democracy*. Berkeley: University of California Press, 1985.

Naughton, Barry J. "Sun Yefang: Toward a Reconstruction of Socialist Economics." In *China's Establishment Intellectuals*, edited by Carol Lee Hamrin and Timothy Cheek, 124–54. Armonk, N.Y.: M. E. Sharpe, 1986.

Needham, Joseph. *Science and Civilization in China, Vol. 2: The History of Scientific Thought*. Cambridge: Cambridge University Press, 1956.

Ngapoi Ngawang Jigme. "Everlasting Affection for a Good Teacher and Bosom Friend." *People's Daily*, May 6, 1998: 12, in "Peng Zhen Remembered for Concern for Tibet." *FBIS Daily Report—China* FBIS-CHI-98–148 (May 28, 1998).

Nie Rongzhen. *Kang ri mofan genju di—Jin Cha Ji bianqu* (A model base area for resisting Japan—The Jin Cha Ji border area). Eighth Route Army, 1939.

———. *Nie Rongzhen huiyilu* (Memoirs of Nie Rongzhen). Reprint, Hong Kong: Ming Pao, 1991.

"Nie Rongzhen gongbu Zhu De Peng Dehuai guanyu chengli Jin Cha Ji junqu de mingling" (Nie Rongzhen issues order from Zhu De and Peng Dehuai to establish the Jin Cha Ji Military Region). In *Jin Cha Ji kang Ri genjudi* (Jin Cha Ji Base Area for Resisting Japan), 1A:59. Beijing: CPC Party History Materials Press, 1988.

"Nie Rongzhen, Peng Zhen guanyu Ji Dong, Pingxi gongzuo de yijian" (Opinion of Nie Rongzhen and Peng Zhen concerning work in East Hebei and Pingxi). In *Jin Cha Ji kang Ri genju di* (The Jin Cha Ji base area for resistance to Japan), 1A:263. Beijing: CPC Party History Materials Publishers, 1988.

"NPC Standing Committee Discusses Deletion of the 'Four Freedoms.'" *Selections from World Broadcasts* FE / 6398 / BII / 1 (April 18, 1980).

O'Brien, Kevin J. "China's National People's Congress: Reform and Its Limits." *Legislative Studies Quarterly* 8, no. 3 (1988): 343–74.

———. "Implementing Political Reform in China's Villages." *Australian Journal of Chinese Affairs* 32 (July 1994): 33–59.

———. *Reform Without Liberalization: The National People's Congress and the Politics of Institutional Change*. New York: Cambridge University Press, 1990.

Ogden, Suzanne. *China's Unresolved Issues: Politics, Development, and Culture*. Englewood Cliffs, N.J.: Prentice Hall, 1989.

Oi, Jean C. "The Fate of the Collective After the Commune." In *Chinese Society on the Eve of Tiananmen: The Impact of Reform*, edited by Deborah Davis and Ezra Vogel, 15–36. Cambridge, Mass.: Council on East Asian Studies, Harvard University, 1990.

"The Outline Report on the Current Academic Discussion Made by the Group of Five in Charge of the Cultural Revolution." In *Chinese Communist Party Documents of the Great Proletarian Cultural Revolution, 1966–1967*, edited by Union Research Institute, 7–12. Hong Kong: Union Research Institute, 1968.

"The P'eng Lu Luo Yang Counter-Revolutionary Revisionist Clique's Crime of Kicking up a Strong Wind of 'Reversal of Verdicts' in People's University Must be Thoroughly Repudiated" (May 15, 1967). *Selections from China Mainland Magazines*, suppl. 19, 14–21. March 4, 1968.

P'eng Shu-tse. *The Chinese Communist Party in Power*. New York: Monad Press, 1980.

Peng Zhen. "Ba nongmin duiwu zuzhi hao" (Organize the peasant contingents well) (Speech at JCJ Peasant Association provisional representative congress, 1947). In *Wei chunjie dang de zuzhi er douzheng* (The organization and struggle for a clean and honest party), 1–3. Hong Kong: Democracy Review, 1948.

———. "Ban hao nongye shengchan hezuoshe" (Do a good job with agricultural producers cooperatives) (February 5, 1955). In *Peng Zhen wenxuan*, 277–85.

———. "Beijing shi wu nian lai zhengfu gongzuo qingkuang he jinhou gongzuo renwu" (Government work in Beijing during the past five years and work tasks for the future). *Xinhua yuebao* (New China monthly) 9 (1954): 28–30.

———. "Bu jin yao kao dang de zhengce, erqie yao yi fa ban shi" (Not only must we rely on Party policy, we must also do things according to law) (March 13, 1984). In *Peng Zhen wenxuan*, 491–96; *Lun xin Zhongguo de zhengfa gongzuo*, 361–66; *Peng Zhen Lun xin shiqi de shehui zhuyi minzhu yu fazhi jianshe*, 218–24.

———. "Dang de zuzhi gongzuo de jige wenti" (On various questions of Party organization work) (April 1, 1954). In *Peng Zhen wenxuan*, 248.

———. "Dangqian xingshi he Harbin shi gongzuo de jiben fangzhen" (The current situation and basic policies on work in Harbin) (July 14, 1946). In *Peng Zhen wenxuan*, 138.

———. "Dangqian zhengfa gongzuo de jige wenti" (Several issues on current political–legal work) (March 15, 1980). In *Lun xin Zhongguo de zhengfa gongzuo*, 219.

———. "Dongbei jiefang zhanzheng de tou jiu ge yue" (The first nine months of the war of liberation in the Northeast). *Dang de wenxian* (Party documents) 1 (January 1, 1989): 3–10.

———. "Dui lifa gongzuo ganbu peixun banxueyuan de jianghua" (Speech to the training academy of cadres engaged in legislative work) (July 1, 1985). In *Peng Zhen wenxuan*, 532; *Lun xin Zhongguo de zhengfa gongzuo*, 383; *Peng Zhen Lun xin shiqi de shehui zhuyi minzhu yu fazhi jianshe*, 284.

———. "Dui sheng, zizhiqu, zhishashi zheng fa lingdao ganbu lunxun banxueyuan de jianghua" (Speech to the institute for theoretical training of political–legal cadres from the provinces, autonomous regions and centrally administered cities) (January 5, 1985). In *Lun xin Zhongguo de zhengfa gongzuo*, 367; *Peng Zhen Lun xin shiqi de shehui zhuyi minzhu yu fazhi jianshe*, 238.

———. "Dui tebie fating bangting renyuan de jianghua" (Speech to the personnel of the special tribunal) (November 17, 1980). In *Peng Zhen wenxuan*, 392.

———. "Fadong qunzhong fenzai Jiang jun jingong" (Mobilize the masses to isolate Jiang's army and attack) (April 16, 1946). In *Peng Zhen wenxuan*, 133.

———. "Faxian cuo an yao jianjue jishi jiuzheng" (Wrongly decided cases that are discovered must be resolved and immediately corrected) (March 31, 1956). In *Peng Zhen wenxuan*, 299.

———. "Fazhan shehui zhuyi minzhu, jianquan shehui zhuyi fazhi" (Develop socialist democracy, perfect the socialist legal system). *Renmin ribao* (People's daily), September 30, 1982: 1. Also in *Faxue zazhi* (Legal system journal), no. 5 (1982): 5–6.

———. "Gongan jiguan bu neng yong zhuanzheng banfa chuli renmin neibu wenti" (Public security organs cannot use methods of dictatorship in handling questions within the people) (July 2, 1961). In *Peng Zhen, Lun xin Zhongguo de zheng-fa gongzuo* (On political–legal work in the new China), 130. Beijing: Party Documents, 1992.

———. "Gongmin zai falu mianqian ren ren pingdeng" (All citizens are equal before the law) (September 17, 1954). In *Peng Zhen wenxuan*, 255–59; *Lun xin Zhongguo de zhengfa gongzuo*, 104–9.

———. "Guanyu caoyi guoying gongzhangfa de wenti" (On issues in the drafting of the state enterprise factory law) (March 23, 1984). In *Peng Zhen wenxuan*, 497; *Peng Zhen Lun xin shiqi de shehui zhuyi minzhu yu fazhi jianshe*, 225.

———. "Guanyu difang ren da changweihui de gongzuo" (On the work of local people's congress standing committees) (April 18, 1980). In *Peng Zhen wenxuan*, 383–91; *Peng Zhen Lun xin shiqi de shehui zhuyi minzhu yu fazhi jianshe*, 56.

———. "Guanyu dizhanqu de chengshi gongzuo" (On urban work in the occupied areas) (May 3, 1945). In *Peng Zhen wenxuan*, 76.

———. "Guanyu gonghui gongzuo" (On labor union work) (December 18, 1962). In *Peng Zhen wenxuan*, 340–45.

———. *Guanyu Jin Cha Ji bianqu dang de gongzuo he juti zhengce baogao* (Report on Party work and specific policies in the Jin Cha Ji Border Region). Beijing: Party School Press, 1981.

———. "Guanyu kang Mei yuan Chao bao jia wei guo yundong de baogao" (Report on the campaign to resist America and aid Korea preserving the family and protecting the country) (October 24, 1951). *Renmin shouce* (People's handbook) (1952): 2–3.

———. "Guanyu lifa gonzuo" (On legislative work) (January 23, 1985). In *Peng Zhen wenxuan*, 503; *Peng Zhen Lun xin shiqi de shehui zhuyi minzhu yu fazhi jianshe*, 244.

———. "Guanyu qige falu cao'an de shuoming" (Explanation of seven draft laws) (June 26, 1979). In *Peng Zhen wenxuan*, 368–82; *Lun xin Zhongguo de zhengfa gongzuo*, 156–70; *Peng Zhen Lun xin shiqi de shehui zhuyi minzhu yu fazhi jianshe*, 1–16.

———. "Guanyu quanguo renda changweihui de gongzuo" (On the work of the NPC Standing Committee) (September 6, 1986). In *Peng Zhen wenxuan*, 560; *Peng Zhen Lun xin shiqi de shehui zhuyi minzhu yu fazhi jianshe*, 332.

———. "Guanyu shehui zhuyi jingshen wenming jianshe zhidao sixiang de jige wenti" (Several questions on constructing a leading ideology for socialist spiritual civilization) (October 28, 1986). In *Peng Zhen wenxuan*, 571.

———. "Guanyu shehuizhuyi fazhi de jige wenti" (On several questions concerning the socialist legal system). *Hongqi* (Red flag) 11 (November 2, 1979): 3–7.

———. "Guanyu sifa bumen de gaizao yu zhengdun wenti" (On transformation and rectification of judicial organs) (June 24, 1952). In *Lun xin Zhongguo de zhengfa gongzuo*, 70.

———. "Guanyu xing fa cao'an he xingshi susong fa cao'an de shuoming" (Explanation of the draft criminal law and the draft criminal procedure law) (June 7, 1979). In *Lun xin Zhongguo de zhengfa gongzuo*, 146–55.

———. "Guanyu xueshu taolun de jige wenti" (On several questions for academic discussion) (September 23, 1964). In *Peng Zhen wenxuan*, 354–57.

———. "Guanyu zheng fa gongzuo de jige wenti" (On various issues in political–legal work) (March 31, 1987). In *Peng Zhen wenxuan*, 598; *Lun xin Zhongguo de zhengfa gongzuo*, 418; *Peng Zhen Lun xin shiqi de shehui zhuyi minzhu yu fazhi jianshe*, 350.

———. "Guanyu zhenya fangeming he chengzhi fangeming tiaoli wenti de baogao" (Report on issues in the regulations on suppressing and controlling counterrevolutionaries) (February 20, 1951). In *Peng Zhen wenxuan*, 206–11; *Lun xin Zhongguo de zhengfa gongzuo*, 13–18.

———. "Guanyu zhenya fangeming huodong he chengzhi fangeming tiaoli wenti de baogao" (Report on issues concerning the regulations on the suppression of counterrevolutionary activities and the control of counterrevolution). *Zhongyang zhengshi gongbao* (Central political affairs bulletin) (1951): 4–6.

———. "Guanyu Zhonghua renmin gongheguo xianfa xiugai cao'an de baogao" (Report on the draft of the revisions to the PRC Constitution) (November 26, 1982). *Renmin ribao* (People's daily), December 6, 1982: 1. Also in *Peng Zhen wenxuan*, 435; *Lun xin Zhongguo de zhengfa gongzuo*, 304; *Peng Zhen Lun xin shiqi de shehui zhuyi minzhu yu fazhi jianshe*, 141.

———. "Guanyu Zhonghua renmin gongheguo xianfa xiugai cao'an de shuoming" (Explanation of the revised draft of the PRC Constitution). *Zhongguo fazhi bao* (China legal system gazette) (April 30, 1982): 1; *Xinhua yuebao* (New China monthly) 4 (1982): 6; *Zhen Lun xin shiqi de shehui zhuyi minzhu yu fazhi jianshe*, 100.

———. "Guanyu Zhonghua renmin gongheguo chengzhi tanwu tiaoli cao'an de shuoming" (Explanation of the PRC Draft Regulations for Punishment of Corruption) (April 18, 1952). *Renmin shouce* (People's handbook) (1952): 52–55. Also in *Peng Zhen wenxuan*, 229–36; *Lun xin Zhongguo de zhengfa gongzuo*, 62–69.

———. "Jianchi diaocha yanjiu he qunzhong luxian" (Uphold investigation and study and the road of the masses) (July 8, 1961). In *Peng Zhen wenxuan*, 318–23.
———. "Jiaqiang fazhi jiaoyu, weihu anding tuanjie" (Strengthen education in the legal system, safeguard stability and unity) (January 21, 1987). *Zhongguo falu nianjian* (China law yearbook) (1988): 610. Also in *Lun xin Zhongguo de zhengfa gongzuo*, 413; *Peng Zhen Lun xin shiqi de shehui zhuyi minzhu yu fazhi jianshe*, 344.
———. "Jiaqiang minzhu yu fazhi jianshe, jiaqiang ren da changweihui gongzuo" (Strengthen the building of democracy and the legal system, strengthen the work of the NPC Standing Committee) (June 27, 1986). In *Peng Zhen Lun xin shiqi de shehui zhuyi minzhu yu fazhi jianshe*, 324–31.
———. "Jin Cha Ji bianqu hanjian Tuopai de mai guo feizhuang" (The criminal situation of the treacherous Trotskyite sell-out in Jin Cha Ji border region) (November 7, 1938). Harvard Yenching Library. Folio.
———. "Jin hou gongzuo de xin fangzhen" (New policies for future work) (November 29, 1945). In *Peng Zhen wenxuan*, 106–10.
———. "Jinyibu shishi xianfa, yange anzhao xianfa banshi" (Progressively implement the constitution, do things strictly according to the constitution) (December 3, 1983). In *Peng Zhen wenxuan*, 482; *Lun xin Zhongguo de zhengfa gongzuo*, 352; *Peng Zhen Lun xin shiqi de shehui zhuyi minzhu yu fazhi jianshe*, 201.
———. "Jue bu yao hulue genjudi de jianshe" (We absolutely cannot overlook the construction of base areas) (April 19, 1946). In *Peng Zhen wenxuan*, 128–30.
———. "Kaizhan diaocha yanjiu, an shiji qingkuang banshi" (Develop investigation and study, handle matters according to the actual situation) (April 26, 1980). In *Lun xin Zhongguo de zhengfa gongzuo*, 226.
———. "Kefu guanliao zhuyi zuofeng" (Overcome bureaucratist work styles) (August 16, 1956). In *Peng Zhen wenxuan*, 303.
———. "Yi keneng dadao de zui gao biaozhun yaoqiu women de gongzuo" (Our work must attain the highest standards possible) (July 3, 1955). In *Peng Zhen wenxuan*, 286.
———. "Lifa yao shiying gaige, kaifang de xuyao" (Legislation should implement the needs of reform and opening up) (February 3, 1985). In *Peng Zhen Lun xin shiqi de shehui zhuyi minzhu yu fazhi jianshe*, 263.
———. "Ling hui er shi er ge wenjian de jingshen yu shijian" (The spirit and practice of the twenty-two documents issued by the leadership council). In *Yan'an Wencui* (Collection of documents of Yan'an), edited by Chinese Academy of Social Sciences Information Research Bureau and Chinese Media History Information Office, 1:29–34. Beijing: Beijing Publishers, 1984.
———. "Lun Jin Cha Ji bianqu kangri genjudi de zhengquan" (On political power in the Jin Cha Ji border region anti-Japanese base area) (October 13, 1938), in *Jin Cha Ji kang Ri genjudi* (The Jin Cha Ji Base Area for Resisting Japan), vol. 1A. Beijing: CPC Party History Materials Press, 1988, 208–16.
———. . *Lun xin shiqi de shehui zhuyi minzhu yu fazhi jianshe* (On the development

of socialist democracy and the legal system during the new period). Beijing: Party Documents, 1989.

———. "Makesi Liening zhuyi zai Zhongguo de shengli" (The victory of Marxism-Leninism in China). *Xuexi* (Study) 4, no. 6–7 (July 1, 1951): 21–24.

———. "Minshi susong fa qicao zhong de jige wenti" (Several questions on the draft civil procedure law) (April 14, 1981). In *Peng Zhen wenxuan*, 400; *Lun xin Zhongguo de zhengfa gongzuo*, 243; *Peng Zhen Lun xin shiqi de shehui zhuyi minzhu yu fazhi jianshe*, 73.

———. "Ping fen tudi yu zhengdun duiwu" (Equal land and rectification of contingents) (October–November 1947). In *Wei chunjie dang de zuzhi er douzheng* (The organization and struggle for a clean and honest party), 4–19. Hong Kong: Democracy Review, 1948.

———. "Qingnian yeyu zuojia yao yanzhe zhengque de fangxiang buduan qianjin" (Young spare-time workers should follow the correct orientation and move forward unceasingly) (December 10, 1965). In *Peng Zhen wenxuan*, 358–63.

———. "Quanguo ren da changweihui he difang ren da changeweihui de guanxi" (On the relations between the NPC Standing Committee and the local People's Congress standing committees) (May 28, 1984). In *Peng Zhen Lun xin shiqi de shehui zhuyi minzhu yu fazhi jianshe*, 231.

———. "Quanguo ren da changweihui jiguan yao wei lifa gongzuo fuwu" (Institutions of the National People's Congress should serve the work of legislation) (October 29, 1954). In *Peng Zhen wenxuan*, 260–65.

———. "Ren da changweihui jiguan yao you yige hao de sixiang zuofeng" (The institutions of the NPC Standing Committee must have good thought and work style) (December 29, 1979). In *Peng Zhen Lun xin shiqi de shehui zhuyi minzhu yu fazhi jianshe*, 47.

———. "Renmin jingcha shi renmin de jinwu yuan" (The people's police are the people's servants). In *Peng Zhen wenxuan*, 301.

———. "Renzhi zuzhi quanguo ge zu renmin taolun xianfa xiugai cao'an" (Conscientiously organize various groups and citizens throughout the country to debate the revised draft of the Constitution) (May 4, 1982). In *Lun xin Zhongguo de zhengfa gongzuo*, 270; *Peng Zhen Lun xin shiqi de shehui zhuyi minzhu yu fazhi jianshe*, 116.

———. "Report on Political and Legal Work." *Current Background* 91 (July 10, 1951): 1–9.

———. "Report on the Work of the Standing Committee of the National People's Congress of the PRC." In *Main Documents of the Third Session of the Fifth NPC*, 86–177. Beijing: Foreign Languages Press, 1980.

———. "Shishi qiu shi, bu shang kong tan" (Seek truth from facts, do not engage in empty talk) (June 27, 1990). In *Peng Zhen wenxuan*, 667.

———. "Shixian si hua yiding yao you yi ge shengdong huopo anding tuanjie de zhengzhi jumian" (Realizing the four modernizations requires a lively, vigorous, stable and unified political line) (October 13, 1979). In *Peng Zhen Lun xin shiqi de shehui zhuyi minzhu yu fazhi jianshe*, 29.

———. "Shiyi renmin zhijie canjia guojia guanli de yizhong zhongyao xingshi"

(An important form by which a billion people directly participate in management of the country). *Xinhua yuebao* (New China monthly) 5: 32–33.

———. "Sixiang fangfa wenti" (Questions about methods of thinking). In *Yan'an zhongyang dangxiao de zhengfeng xuexi* (Studying the rectification of the Yan'an central Party school), 7. Beijing: Central Party School Press, 1987.

———. "Tan tan ren da changweihui de gongzuo" (Discussing the work of the NPC Standing Committee) (January 24, 1984). In *Peng Zhen Lun xin shiqi de shehui zhuyi minzhu yu fazhi jianshe*, 214.

———. "Tongguo qunzhong zizhi shixing jiceng zhijie minzhu" (Through the masses governing themselves carry out basic level direct democracy) (November 23, 1987). In *Peng Zhen wenxuan*, 606; *Lun xin Zhongguo de zhengfa gongzuo*, 426; *Peng Zhen Lun xin shiqi de shehui zhuyi minzhu yu fazhi jianshe*, 366.

———. "Women de renwu shi zhengqu quan dongbei" (Our task is to struggle for and seize all of the Northeast) (October 16, 1945). In *Peng Zhen wenxuan*, 103–5.

———. "Xin shiqi de zheng fa gongzuo" (Political–legal work in the new period) (July 22, 1982). In *Peng Zhen wenxuan*, 425; *Lun xin Zhongguo de zhengfa gongzuo*, 282; *Peng Zhen Lun xin shiqi de shehui zhuyi minzhu yu fazhi jianshe*, 121.

———. "Xuanchuan gongzuo bixu cong shiji chufa" (Propaganda work must proceed from the actual conditions) (January 23, 1955). In *Peng Zhen wenxuan*, 272.

———. "Yanli daji xingshi fanzui yao zunshou falu, zhuyi zhengce, jiaqiang zonghe zhili" (Strictly striking blows against crimes requires strict observance of law, attention to policy and strengthening of comprehensive efforts) (November 15–22, 1983–January 17, 1984). In *Lun xin Zhongguo de zhengfa gongzuo*, 348.

———. "Yanli daji yanzhong xingshi fanzui huodong yao quan dang xia juexin" (Strictly striking against serious criminal activity requires resolve of the whole Party) (July 21, 1983). In *Lun xin Zhongguo de zhengfa gongzuo*, 345.

———. "Yao nuli xuexi Makesi zhuyi de jiben lilun" (We need to seriously study the basic theories of Marxism) (June 7, 1985). *Renmin ribao* (People's daily), August 16, 1985: 1. Also in *Peng Zhen wenxuan*, 525; *Peng Zhen Lun xin shiqi de shehui zhuyi minzhu yu fazhi jianshe*, 276.

———. "Yao shanyu zhangwo makesi zhuyi de zhexue wuqi" (We need to grasp more perfectly the philosophical weapon of Marxism) (January 28, 1986). In *Peng Zhen wenxuan*, 551.

———. "Yao zhuyi peiyang tiba xin ganbu" (We need to pay attention to the training and promotion of new cadres) (April 15, 1962). In *Peng Zhen wenxuan*, 321–23.

———. "Yi bu yao shizhi, yi bu yao yuequan" (First, we cannot forget our duties, second, we cannot exceed our authority) (June 22, 1987). In *Peng Zhen Lun xin shiqi de shehui zhuyi minzhu yu fazhi jianshe*, 360.

———. "Yong xianfa he falu tongyi sixiang" (Use the constitution and the laws to unify thought) (May 26, 1989). *Renmin ribao* (People's daily), May 30, 1989: 1. Also in *Peng Zhen wenxuan*, 655; *Lun xin Zhongguo de zhengfa gongzuo*, 432.

———. "Zai bufen Yan'an shidai wenyi lao zhanshi zuotanhui shang de jianghua" (Speech to a group of old cultural warriors from the Yan'an era) (January 27, 1987). *Hongqi* (Red flag) 10 (1987): 4. Also in *Peng Zhen wenxuan*, 590.

———. "Zai di er ci quanguo gongan huiyi shang de jianghua" (Speech to the Second National Public Security Conference) (October 21, 1950). In *Lun xin Zhongguo de zhengfa gongzuo*, 9.

———. "Zai di liu ci quanguo gongan huiyi shang de jianghua" (Speech at the Sixth National Public Security Conference) (June 9, 1954). In *Lun xin Zhongguo de zhengfa gongzuo*, 96–103.

———. "Zai di liu jie quanguo ren da changweihui di er shi si ci huiyi lianzuhui shang de jianghua" (Speech at the liaison session for the twenty-fourth meeting of the Sixth NPC Standing Committee) (January 20, 1988). *Zhongguo falu nianjian* (China law yearbook) (1989): 733. Also in *Peng Zhen wenxuan*, 612; *Peng Zhen Lun xin shiqi de shehui zhuyi minzhu yu fazhi jianshe*, 373.

———. "Zai di liujie quanguo ren da san ci huiyi yubei huiyi shang de jianghua" (Speech at the preparation meeting for the third session of the Sixth NPC) (March 26, 1985). In *Peng Zhen Lun xin shiqi de shehui zhuyi minzhu yu fazhi jianshe*, 269.

———. "Zai di liu jie quanguo renmin daibiao dahui di yi ci huiyi shang de jianghua" (Speech to first session of Sixth National People's Congress) (June 21, 1983). In *Peng Zhen wenxuan*, 473–81; *Peng Zhen Lun xin shiqi de shehui zhuyi minzhu yu fazhi jianshe*, 186–95.

———. "Zai ge sheng, zizhiqu, zhishashi renda changweihui fuzeren zuotanhui shang de jianghua" (Speech to the symposium of responsible persons from the provincial, autonomous region and centrally administered city representative congresses) (November 24, 1985). In *Peng Zhen Lun xin shiqi de shehui zhuyi minzhu yu fazhi jianshe*, 290.

———. "Zai gongan gongzuo gaige huiyi yubei huiyi shang de jianghua" (Speech to meeting in preparation for meeting on reform in public security work) (April 19, 1983). In *Lun xin Zhongguo de zhengfa gongzuo*, 341.

———. "Zai Guangdong sheng he Guangzhou shi gong-jian-fa huibao hui shang de jianghua yaodian" (Main points of a speech to the meeting for reports from the public security, procuracy and courts of Guangdong province and Guangzhou municipality) (February 1, 1980). In *Lun xin Zhongguo de zhengfa gongzuo*, 212.

———. "Zai jingju xiandai xi guanmo yanchu da hui shang de jianghua" (Speech at performance for fellow artists of the Peking opera's modern drama) (July 1, 1964). *Hongqi* (Red flag) 14 (1964): 18.

———. "Zai minfa zuotanhui shang be jianghua" (Speech at the conference on civil law) (May 27, 1981). In *Peng Zhen wenxuan*, 421; *Lun xin Zhongguo de zhengfa gongzuo*, 264; *Peng Zhen Lun xin shiqi de shehui zhuyi minzhu yu fazhi jianshe*, 95.

———. "Zai quanguo gongan ting ju zhang huiyi shang de baogao" (Report to national meeting of public security department and section chiefs) (April 4, 1956). In *Lun xin Zhongguo de zhengfa gongzuo*, 117.

———. "Zai quanguo gongan, jiancha, sifa huiyi shang de jianghua" (Speech to the national conference on public security, procuracy, and the judiciary) (August 16, 1958). In *Peng Zhen Lun xin shiqi de shehui zhuyi minzhu yu fazhi jianshe*, 124.

———. "Zai quanguo jiancha yewu huiyi shang de baogao" (Report to the National Procurators Conference) (November 21, 1954). In *Peng Zhen wenxuan*, 266; *Lun xin Zhongguo de zhengfa gongzuo*, 109–14.

———. "Zai quanguo minfa tongze (cao'an) zuotanhui shang de jianghua" (Speech at the national conference on the general principles of civil law [draft]) (December 4, 1985). *Renmin ribao* (People's daily), May 15, 1986: 4. Also in *Lun xin Zhongguo de zhengfa gongzuo*, 394; *Peng Zhen Lun xin shiqi de shehui zhuyi minzhu yu fazhi jianshe*, 300.

———. "Zai quanguo zheng fa gongzuo huiyi shang de jianghua" (Speech to the national conference on political–legal work) (January 28, 1985). In *Peng Zhen wenxuan*, 509; *Lun xin Zhongguo de zhengfa gongzuo*, 372; *Peng Zhen Lun xin shiqi de shehui zhuyi minzhu yu fazhi jianshe*, 251.

———. "Zai quanguo zheng fa gongzuo huiyi shang de jianghua yaodian" (Important points of a speech at the national conference on political–legal work) (March 5, 1990). In *Lun xin Zhongguo de zhengfa gongzuo*, 444.

———. "Zai quanguo zheng-fa gongzuo huiyi shang de jianghua jiyao" (Abstract of speech to the national political–legal work conference) (November 12, 1962). In *Lun xin Zhongguo de zhengfa gongzuo*, 132.

———. "Zai shixian zhong zongjie jingyan jiaoxun." In *Lun xin Zhongguo de zhengfa gongzuo*, 240.

———. "Zai Sichuan sheng zheng fa ge bumen fuze tongzhi zuotanhui shang de jianghua yaodian" (Major points of a speech to responsible cadres in the political–legal departments of Sichuan Province) (June 4, 1982). In *Lun xin Zhongguo de zhengfa gongzuo*, 274.

———. "Zai wu da chengshi zhian zuotanhui shang de jianghua" (Speech to conference of five centrally administered cities) (May 21–22, 1981). In *Peng Zhen wenxuan*, 405; *Lun xin Zhongguo de zhengfa gongzuo*, 248; *Peng Zhen Lun xin shiqi de shehui zhuyi minzhu yu fazhi jianshe*, 78.

———. "Zai zhonggong Jin Cha Ji shengwei zuzhi gongzuo huiyi shang de jielun" (June 1938). In *Jin Cha Ji kang Ri genju di* (The Jin Cha Ji base area for resistance to Japan), 1A:172. Beijing: CPC Party History Materials Publishers, 1988.

———. "Zai zhonggong Ji-Yu-Jin sheng wei huodong fenzi huiyi de jianghua" (Speech to CPC activists in the Hebei-Henan-Shanxi provincial committee) (February 1938). *Jinzhong lishi ziliao* (History materials for central Shanxi) 2 (1984): 1, 5.

———. "Zai zhonggong zhongyang beifang fenju huiyi shang guanyu caizheng, shengchan deng wenti de jielun" (Summary at the meeting of the

CPC Centre North China Subbureau on issues of finance, production, etc.). In *Jin Cha Ji kang Ri genju di* (the Jin Cha Ji base are for resistance to Japan), 1B:483.

———. "Zai zhonggong zhongyang beifang fenju huiyi shang guanyu gonggu dang de jielun" (Summary at the meeting of the CPC Centre North China Subbureau on issues of consolidation of the party). In *Jin Cha Ji kang Ri genju di* (the Jin Cha Ji base are for resistance to Japan), 1B:475.

———. "Zai zhonggong zhongyang beifang fenju huiyi shang guanyu wenhua yundong de jielun" (Summary of the culture movement for the CPC Centre North China Subbureau meeting). In *Jin Cha Ji kang Ri genju di* (The Jin Cha Ji base area for resistance to Japan), 1B:490. Beijing: CPC Party History Materials Publishers, 1989.

———. "Zai zhonggong zhongyang beifang fenju kuangda ganbu huiyi shang de baogao" (Report to the CPC Centre North China Subbureau expanded cadres conference) (September 1, 1940). In *Jin Cha Ji kang Ri genju di* (The Jin Cha Ji base area for resistance to Japan), 1A:410–76, 475–76, 483. Beijing: CPC Party History Materials Publishers, 1988.

———. "Zai zhonggong zhongyang beifang fenju zuzhi gongzuo huiyi shang de jielun" (Conclusion on the organizational work meeting of the CPC Centre North China Subbureau) (November 1939). In *Jin Cha Ji kang Ri genju di* (The Jin Cha Ji base area for resistance to Japan), 1A:296–308. Beijing: CPC Party History Materials Publishers, 1988.

———. "Zai zhongyang gongzuo huiyi Dongbei zu de fayan" (Speech to the Northeast group of the central work conference) (April 22, 1979). In *Peng Zhen wenxuan*, 364.

———. "Zai zhongyang zheng fa weiyuanhui kuangda huiyi shang de jianghua" (Speech to expanded meeting of the central politics and law committee) (February 26, 1983). In *Lun xin Zhongguo de zhengfa gongzuo*, 333; *Peng Zhen Lun xin shiqi de shehui zhuyi minzhu yu fazhi jianshe*, 173.

———. "Zai zhongyang zheng fa weiyuanhui kuangda huiyi shang de jianghua yaodian" (Main points of a speech to the expanded meeting of the central politics and law committee) (October 4, 1982). In *Lun xin Zhongguo de zhengfa gongzuo*, 301.

———. "Zai zhongyang zhengfa weiyuanhui di yi ci huiyi shang de jianghua jiyao" (Outline of speech to the first meeting of the central politics and law committee) (February 6, 1980). In *Lun xin Zhongguo de zhengfa gongzuo*, 216.

———. "Zai zhongyang zhengzhi ju kuangda huiyi shang de fayan" (Speech at the expanded meeting of the central Politburo) (June 21, 1989). In *Peng Zhen wenxuan*, 659; *Lun xin Zhongguo de zhengfa gongzuo*, 436.

———. "Zhan zai geming he jianshe de zui qianxian" (Stand in the very front line of revolution and construction) (November 25, 1958). In *Peng Zhen wenxuan*, 313.

———. "Zhangwo zhengquan, fadong qunzhong" (Seize political power and mobilize the masses) (December 6, 1945). In *Peng Zhen wenxuan*, 111.

———. "Zhaokai qu renmin daibiao huiyi de chubu jingyan" (Preliminary experiences of the representative congresses in the open areas) (August 7, 1950). In *Peng Zhen wenxuan*, 202.

———. "Zheng-fa gongzuo de zhuyao renwu" (The main tasks of political–legal work) (September 16, 1953). In *Peng Zhen wenxuan*, 242.

———. "Zhonggong Jin Cha Ji bianqu zhi gezhong zhengce" (Various CPC policies for the Jin Cha Ji border region). N.p.: Unification press, 1942. Handwritten notes.

———. "Zhonggong zhongyang beifang fen ju guanyu Jin Cha Ji bianqu muqian shizheng gangling" (Outline of the Northern Bureau of the CCP Central Committee on the present conditions and policies in Jin Cha Ji) (1940). In Peng Zhen, *Guanyu Jin Cha Ji bianqu dang de gongzuo he juti zhengce baogao*, 210–14.

———. "Zhonghua renmin gongheguo quan guo renmin daibiao dahui changwu weiyuanhui de gongzuo baogao" (Report on the work of the NPC Standing Committee of the PRC) (passed July 5, 1955; delivered July 16, 1955). *Renmin shouce* (People's handbook) (1956): 110, 75–76, 240.

———. "Zhonghua renmin gongheguo quanguo renmin daibiao dahui changwu weiyuanhui de gongzuo baogao" (Report on the work of the NPC Standing Committee of the PRC) (June 14, 1956). *Renmin shouce* (People's handbook) (1957), 179.

———. "Zhonghua renmin gongheguo quan guo renmin daibiao dahui changwu weiyuanhui de gongzuo baogao" (Report on the work of the NPC Standing Committee of the PRC) (April 20, 1959). *Renmin shouce* (People's handbook) (1959), 110.

———. "Zijue di zou lishi biyou zhi lu" (Voluntarily tread the path mandated by history) (July 22, 1962). In *Peng Zhen wenxuan*, 331–39.

———. "Zuo hao sheng ji ren da changweihui de gongzuo" (Do a good job with the provincial level people's congresses) (June 24, 1983). In *Peng Zhen Lun xin shiqi de shehui zhuyi minzhu yu fazhi jianshe*, 196.

———. "Zuohao chengshi gongzuo yingjie geming de xin gaochao" (July 6, 1948). In *Peng Zhen wenxuan*, 143.

———. "Zuohao tongyi zhanxian gongzuo" (Do a good job in united front work) (January 6, 1949). In *Peng Zhen wenxuan*, 170–92.

———. *Zhonggong Jin Cha Ji bianqu zhi ge zhong zheng ce* (Various policies of the CPC in Jin Cha Ji border region) (1942). Hoover Institution. Folio.

"P'eng Chen on Contradictions Within the Ranks of the People." *Selections from China Mainland Press* (April 26, 1957): 5.

"P'eng Chen, Peking, and Peking University." *China News Analysis* 615 (June 10, 1966): 1–7.

"Peng Zhen Addresses Forum Marking CPC Founding." *Beijing Xinhua Domestic Service* June 28, 1990, in *FBIS Daily Report—China* (June 29, 1990): 20.

"Peng Zhen Attacks 'Leftist' Influence, Ideology." *Ching Pao* (The mirror, Hong Kong), September 5, 1992, in *FBIS Daily Report—China* (September 9, 1992): 27.

"Peng Zhen Calls for Political Reform." *Ching Pao* (The mirror, Hong Kong), March 5, 1993, in *FBIS Daily Report—China* (March 8, 1993): 26.

"Peng Zhen chanshu lixiang minzhu he fazhi" (Peng Zhen explains ideals of democracy and the legal system). *Renmin ribao* (People's daily), November 27, 1986: 4.

"Peng Zhen danxin zhong gong kuan yu tanwu, Deng gongzhu Jiang hua qili zhua jundui" (Peng Zhen worried that the CPC will collapse from corruption, Deng orders Jiang to energetically grasp the military). *Ching Pao* (The mirror, Hong Kong), July, 1993: 28.

"Peng Zhen de fandong heihua de zhaibian" (Collection of Peng Zhen's reactionary black utterances). *Cuijiu zhanbao* (Militant journal for smashing the old) (May 25, 1967): 1–3.

"Peng Zhen deng guizu laoye zai xiangshan" (Peng Zhen and the other aristocratic lords in the fragrant hills). In *Wenge dazibao jingxuan* (Selections from wall posters from the Cultural Revolution), edited by Tan Fang and Zhao Wumian, 488–91. Flushing, N.Y.: Mirror Books, 1996.

"Peng Zhen dies at age 95," *Xinhua* (New China News Agency), April 28, 1997.

"Peng Zhen Inscribes Name for Hebei Power Plant." Beijing *Xinhua* Domestic Service December 11, 1991, in *FBIS Daily Report—China* (December 12, 1991), 38.

"Peng Zhen Explains Mao 'Cult' to Cadre Children." *Ching Pao* (The mirror, Hong Kong), January 5, 1992, in *FBIS Daily Report—China* (January 17, 1992): 12.

"Peng Zhen: From Disgrace to Rehabilitation." *Issues and Studies* (September 1979): 93.

"Peng Zhen fuweiyuanzhang zuo ren da changweihui gongzuo baogao he guanyu jige falu cao'an de shuoming" (Vice chair Peng Zhen gives report on the work of the standing committee and an explanation of several draft laws). *Zhongguo fazhi bao* (Chinese legal system gazette) (September 5, 1980): 1, 3.

"Peng Zhen Meets Hong Kong Macao Reporters" (April 8, 1987). *FBIS Daily Report—China* (April 9, 1987): K1.

Peng Zhen nianpu (Chronology of the life of Peng Zhen). Beijing: Central Documents Press, 2002.

"Peng Zhen Reports on the Work of NPC Standing Committee." *Summary of World Broadcasts* FE / 6527 / C / 1 (September 19, 1980).

"Peng Zhen's Speech at Yanan Forum Viewed." *Renmin ribao* (People's daily), June 29, 1990, in *FBIS Daily Report—China* (July 5, 1990): 28.

"Peng Zhen Stresses Political Reform by Law." *Ching Pao* (The mirror, Hong Kong) September 5, 1991, in *FBIS Daily Report—China* (September 17, 1991): 20–21.

"Peng Zhen to Head New Legal Commission." *Summary of World Broadcasts* FE / 6053 / BH / s (February 27, 1979).

"Peng Zhen tongzhi de jianghua" (Peng Zhen's speech). *Zhongguo fazhi bao* (China legal system gazette) (November 25, 1985): 1.

"Peng Zhen tongzhi de shumian jianghua" (Written speech of comrade Peng Zhen). *Zhonggong dang shi tongxun* (CPC Party History Newsletter) 15 (March 25, 1991): 2.

"Peng Zhen tongzhi guancha Qinghuangdao laojiao suo" (Peng Zhen inspects the Qinghuangdao reform through labor post). *Zhongguo fazhi bao* (China legal system gazette) (September 4, 1981): 1.

"Peng Zhen tongzhi guanghui zhandou de yisheng" (The glorious militant life of Comrade Peng Zhen). In *Mianhuai Peng Zhen*, 1–12.

"Peng Zhen tongzhi tan jianchi hefeng xiyu de fangfa" (Comrade Peng Zhen discusses adhering to the methods of mild wind and gentle rain). *Renmin ribao* (People's daily), May 10, 1957: 1.

"Peng Zhen tongzhi xiang canjia quanguo gong, jian, fa youguan huiyi de tongzhi zuo zhongyao jianghua" (Comrade Peng Zhen gives an important speech to comrades participating in the national meetings on public security, procuracy, and the judiciary). *Xinhua yuebao* (New China monthly) 7 (1979): 28–29.

"Peng Zhen tongzhi zai Beijing shi renmin dai hui shang chanshu fanyou douzheng de weida yiyi" (Peng Zhen explains the huge significance of the anti-rightist struggle to a meeting of the Beijing Representative Congress) (speech, August 4, 1957). *Xin hua yue bao* (New China monthly) 17: 144.

"Peng Zhen tongzhi zai jiejian lifa gongzuo ganbu peixun xueyuan shi de jianghua yaodian" (Important points of a speech by Peng Zhen when receiving the Training Institute for Legislative Work Cadres) (notes from speech July 1, 1985, not reviewed by the speaker). *Gongzuo tongxun* (Work bulletin) (Hubei), August 9, 1985: 1.

"Peng Zhen weiyuanzhang zai ge sheng zizhiqu zhishashi renda changweihui fuzeren zuotanhui shang de jianghua yaodian" (Important points of Chairman Peng Zhen's speech to the conference of responsible persons from the people's congress standing committees of the provinces, autonomous regions and centrally administered cities). *Gongzuo tongxun* (Work bulletin) (Guizhou), January 30, 1986: 2.

Peng Zhen wenxuan (Collected works of Peng Zhen). Beijing: People's Press, 1991.

"Peng Zhen wenxuan jieshao" (Introducing Peng Zhen's collected works). *Renmin ribao* (People's daily), May 30, 1991: 5.

"Peng Zhen Writes Inscription for Middle School." *Shanxi ribao* (Shanxi daily), November 11, 1984, in *FBIS Daily Report—China* (November 30, 1984): K11.

"Peng Zhen Writes Preface to Book on Party Style." *Renmin ribao* (People's daily), May 6, 1988, in *FBIS Daily Report—China* (May 10, 1988): 23.

"Peng Zhen xiang wu jie renda si ci huiyi tichu guanyu jianyi tuichi xiugai xianfa wancheng qixian de shumian shuoming" (Peng Zhen delivers a written report to the Fourth Session of the Fifth NPC suggesting a postponement of the deadline for completing the revisions to the Constitution). *Xinhua yuebao* (New China monthly) 12 (1981): 34.

"Peng Zhen zai Beijing shi xuanchuan gongzuo huiyi shang de baogao" (Peng Zhen's report to the Beijing municipal propaganda work conference). *Renmin ribao* (People's daily), April 22, 1957: 1.

"Peng Zhen zai renda yubei huishang fabiao jianghua" (Peng Zhen delivers a speech at the NPC preparatory session). *Renmin ribao* (People's daily), March 27, 1985: 1.

"Peng Zhen zai wuchan jieji zhuanzheng fangmian de fan Mao Zedong sixiang yanlun" (Peng Zhen's opinions opposing the thought of Mao Zedong in the area of proletarian dictatorship). *Zheng-fa hongqi* (Politics and law red flag) (October 17, 1967): 1.

Pepper, Suzanne. *Civil War in China: The Political Struggle 1945–1949*. Berkeley: University of California Press, 1978.

Perry, Elizabeth, and Christine Wong, eds. *The Political Economy of Reform in Post-Mao China*. Cambridge, Mass.: Council on East Asian Studies, Harvard University, 1985.

Potter, Pitman B. *Chinese Foreign Business Law: Past Progress, Future Challenges*. San Francisco: The 1990 Institute, 1995.

———. "Peng Zhen: Evolving Views on Party Organization and Law." In *China's Establishment Intellectuals*, edited by Carol Lee Hamrin and Timothy Cheek, 21–50. Armonk, N.Y.: M. E. Sharpe, 1986.

———. "Riding the Tiger: Legitimacy and Legal Culture in Post-Mao China." *China Quarterly* 138 (June 1994): 327–58.

———. *The Chinese Legal System: Globalization and Local Legal Culture* (London: Routledge, 2001).

"PRC Regulations for the Punishment of Counterrevolutionaries." In *Zhongyang renmin zhengfu guanyu gongbu shixing Zhonghua renmin gongheguo zhengzhi fangeming tiaolie de mingling* (Orders of the Central People's Government Concerning Promulgation and Implementation of the PRC Law for Punishment of Counterrevolutionaries). Beijing, 1951.

"Propaganda Work Conference in Peking Discusses How to Handle Correctly the Contradiction Within the Ranks of the People." *Survey of China Mainland Press*, no. 1521 (May 2, 1957): 1.

Pu Yuhuo and Xu Shuangmi. *Dang de bai qu douzheng shihua* (Narrative of the party's struggle in the White Areas). Beijing: Central Part History Press, 1991.

"Qiao Shi's Words on Democracy in China." *China News Digest*. Available at: http://www.cnd.org (June 2, 1997).

Qiu Shi. *Gongheguo zhongda shijian he juece neimu* (Great events of the republic and the inside story of decisions). 2 vols. Beijing: Economic Daily Publishers, 1998.

———. *Gongheguo zhongda shijian juece shilu* (Record of important decisions of the republic). 2 vols. Beijing: Economic Daily Publishers, 1998.

Qiu Shi, ed. *Gongheguo zhongda juece chutai qian hou* (Before and after great decisions of the republic). 2 vols. Beijing: Economic Daily Publishers, 1998.

Qiu Zhizhuo and Lian Gangsheng, eds. *Liu Shaoqi de jiaoyin* (Footprints of Liu Shaoqi). Taiyuan: Shanxi People's Press, 1990.

"Quanguo zhengfa gongzuo hui zai jing juxing" (National political–legal work conference held in Beijing). *Zhongguo fazhi bao* (China legal system gazette) (July 30, 1982): 1.

"Quanguo zhengfa gongzuo huiyi zai Beijing juxing" (National political–legal work meeting convenes in Beijing). *Zhongguo fazhi bao* (China legal system gazette) (July 30, 1982): 1–2.

Reardon-Anderson, James. *Yenan and the Great Powers: The Origins of Chinese Communist Foreign Policy, 1944–1946*. New York: Columbia University Press, 1980.

Ren Dongyun, ed. *Gongheguo zhuxi de rong yu ru: Jian guo hou de Liu Shaoqi* (The honor and disgrace of the premier of the republic: Liu Shaoqi after the establishment of the country). Changchun: Changchun Publishing, 1993.

"Renda changweihui shisan ci huiyi tuanhui" (The thirteenth session of the NPC Standing Committee comes to a close). *Renmin ribao* (People's daily), November 23, 1985: 1, 4.

"Renmin wujing yao tigao suzhi shiying xin renwu" (The people's armed police should raise their quality to suit their new tasks). *Renmin ribao* (People's daily), January 11, 1985: 1.

"Renzhen xuexi he guanche zhixing xianfa" (Conscientiously study and thoroughly carry out the constitution). *Jingji ribao* (Economic daily), February 28, 1983: 1.

Resolution on CPC History (1949–1981). Beijing: Foreign Languages Press, 1981.

"Resolution on Law Interpretation" (National People's Congress Standing Committee, 1981). *Summary of World Broadcasts* FE / 67 48 / BII / 3 (June 1981): 3.

Rosen, Stanley. *Red Guard Factionalism and the Cultural Revolution in Guangzhou* (Canton). Boulder, Colo.: Westview Press, 1982.

Ruxue yu falu wenhua (Confucianism and legal culture). Shanghai: Fudan University Press, 1992.

Saich, Tony. "Introduction: The Chinese Communist Party and the Anti-Japanese War Base Areas." *China Quarterly* 140 (December 1994): 1000–6.

———. "Writing or Rewriting History? The Construction of the Maoist Resolution on Party History." In *New Perspectives on the Chinese Communist Revolution*, edited by Tony Saich and Hans van de Ven, 299–338. Armonk, N.Y.: M. E. Sharpe, 1995.

Saich, Tony, ed. *The Rise to Power of the Chinese Communist Party*. Armonk, N.Y.: M. E. Sharpe, 1996.

Saich, Tony, and Nancy Hearst, eds. "Li Rui: Lessons from the Lushan Plenum." *Chinese Law and Government* 29, no. 5 (September–October 1996).

"San shi san ge fangeming xiuzheng zhuyi fenzi" (Thirty-three counterrevolutionary revisionists) (1968). In *Wenge dazibao jingxuan* (Selections from wall posters from the Cultural Revolution), edited by Tan Fang and Zhao Wumian, 195–239. Flushing, N.Y.: Mirror Books, 1996.

Schoenhals, Michael. "Bo Yibo Has an Attitude Problem." In *China's Cultural Revolution, 1966–1969: Not a Dinner Party*, 122–35. Armonk, N.Y.: M. E. Sharpe, 1996.

———. "The Central Case Examination Group, 1966–1979." *China Quarterly* 145 (March 1966): 87–111.

Schoenhals, Michael, ed. *China's Cultural Revolution 1966–1969: Not a Dinner Party*. Armonk, N.Y.: M. E. Sharpe, 1996.

Schram, Stuart. *The Political Thought of Mao Tse-tung*. New York: Praeger, 1969, 1977.

Secretariat for the Party history materials collection meeting and the academic conference commemorating the CPC's sixtieth anniversary, ed. *Dang shi huiyi baogao ji* (Collection of reports from the Party history meetings). Beijing: Central Party School Press, 1982.

"Selected Edition on Liu Shao-ch'i's Counter-Revolutionary Revisionist Crimes." *Selections from China Mainland Magazines* 651 (April 22, 1969): 1, 39.

"Selected Edition on Liu Shao-ch'i's Counter-Revolutionary Revisionist Crimes." *Selections from China Mainland Magazines* 653 (May 5, 1969): 8.

"Selected Works of Peng Zhen Reviewed." *Beijing Xinhua Domestic Service*, May 28, 1991, in *FBIS Daily Report—China* (June 5, 1991): 27.

Sen Lin. "China's Decentralization and Provincial Economic Legislation." Ph.D. diss., University of Calgary, 1994.

Seymour, James. *China: The Politics of Revolutionary Reintegration*. New York: Thomas Crowell, 1976.

———. "Document No. 49, Peng Zhen" (from *Beijing Spring*). In *The Fifth Modernization: China's Human Rights Movement 1978–1979*, 194. Stanfordville, N.Y.: Human Rights Publishing Group, 1980.

———. Editor's introduction. In James D. Seymour, ed., *Chinese Law and Government* 21, no. 3 (fall 1988): 1–13 at 4.

———. *The Fifth Modernization: China's Human Rights Movement, 1978–1979*. Stanfordville, N.Y.: Human Rights Publishing Group, 1980.

Shabad, Theodore. *China's Changing Map: National and Regional Development, 1949–71*. New York: Praeger, 1972.

Shan Siyi. *Zai jiefang zhanzheng zhong fengfu fazhan* (Rich development during the war of liberation). Beijing: PLA Press, 1991.

Shanxi Party Committee History Research Office. *Peng Zhen sheng ping da shi nianbiao* (Chronology of major events in the life of Peng Zhen). Beijing: Central Party History Press, 1992.

Shanxi Provincial History Research Institute. "Renmin xinzhong de lishi fengbei" (An historical monument in the people's hearts). In *Mianhuai Peng Zhen*, 521–34.

Shao Chongzhu, ed. *Zhong gong fan tan da an zhong an* (Big cases and serious cases on the Chinese Communists' fight against corruption). Hong Kong: Xiafeier Publishers, 1998.

Shao Ding. "Ji He Long" (Remembering He Long). *Hong qi piao piao* (The red flag waving) 6 (February 1, 1958): 115.

Shi Dongbing. *Shanyu yulai* (The coming storm). Hong Kong: Fanrong chubanshe, 1992.

———. *Xuanze tupokou* (Choosing a breach). Hong Kong: Dragon Publishing, 1998.

———. *Zuichu de kangzheng: Peng Zhen zai "Wenhua da geming" qianxi* (The earliest resistance: Peng Zhen on the eve of the "Cultural Revolution"). Beijing: Central Party School, 1993.

"Shi yi renmin zhijie canjia guojia guanli de yi zhong zhongyao xingshi" (A form by which one billion people participate in the running of the country). *Renmin ribao* (People's daily), May 21, 1982.

Shi Zhongquan et al., eds. *Zhonggong ba da shi* (History of the Eighth CPC Congress). Beijing: People's Press, 1998.

Shirk, Susan. *The Political Logic of Economic Reform in China*. Berkeley: University of California Press, 1993.

"Shouci quanguo jingji fazhi gongzuo jingyan jiaoliu hui zai Beijing juxing" (The first national conference on exchanging experience in economic legal system work convenes in Beijing). *Renmin ribao* (People's daily), September 11, 1982: 4.

"Shouci quanguo jingji fazhi gongzuo jingyan jiaoliu hui zai jing juxing" (The first national conference on exchanging experiences in the economic law system is held in Beijing). *Zhongguo caimao bao* (China finance and trade gazette) (September 12, 1982).

Shoudu hong dai hui (Capital red congress) and Hebei Beijing shiyuan (Hebei Beijing normal college). "Peng Zei 'Huairuo diaocha' shi Liu Deng hei si ling bu yinmou bi ziben zhuyi de yanzhong buzhu" (Traitor Peng's "Huairou" investigation is a serious measure of the Liu Deng black headquarters plot to restore capitalism) (August 1, 1967). Fairbank Center for East Asian Research, Harvard University. Mimeographed.

Shu Si. "CCP Stresses Western Political System Does Not Conform to National Condition." *Chengming* (Hong Kong) 192 (October 1, 1993): 20–22. Reprint, *China Since Tiananmen: Political, Economic, and Social Conflicts*, edited by Lawrence R. Sullivan, 97–99. Armonk, N.Y.: M. E. Sharpe, 1995.

"Shui fandui Lin Biao tongzhi jiu zalan ta de goutou" (Whoever opposes comrade Lin Biao, we should smash his dog's head). *Zhandou bao* (Militant journal), no. 2 (January 1967): 4.

"Sixiang fangfa wenti" (Questions about methods of thinking). In *Yan'an zhongyang dangxiao de zhengfeng xuexi* (Studying the rectification of the Yan'an central Party school), 1:7–20. Beijing: Central Party School Press, 1987.

Solomon, Richard. *Mao's Revolution and the Chinese Political Culture*. Berkeley: University of California Press, 1971.

"Some Materials Regarding Certain Theoretical Issues." In "Party Documents on Anti-Bourgeois Liberalization and Hu Yaobang's Resignation, 1987," edited by James Tong, special issue of *Chinese Law and Government* 21, no. 1 (spring 1988): 63–102.

Song Rufen. "Mianhuai Peng Zhen tongzhi guangyu jingji lifa de jiaohui" (Recalling the teachings of comrade Peng Zhen concerning economic legislation). In *Mianhuai Peng Zhen*, 151–56.

Su Shuangbi and Wang Hongzhi. *Wen ge di yi yuan an: "San jia cun" wenzi yu shi mo* (The first unjust case of the Cultural Revolution: The literary inquisition of the "Three-family village" from beginning to end). Hong Kong: Cosmos Books, 2000.

Sullivan, Lawrence R., ed. "The Biography of An Ziwen and the History of the CCP Organization Department." *Chinese Law and Government* 21, no. 4 (winter 1988–1989).

Sun Sibai, ed. *Beijing daxue yi er jiu yundong huiyi lu* (Memoir of the December 9th Movement at Peking University). Beijing: Peking University Press, 1988.

Tai Huaiji. *Tiandi you zhengqi: Caolanzi jianyu douzheng yu liushi yi ren an* (Heaven and earth have upright spirit: The struggle in Caolanzi Prison and the 61-Man Case). Beijing: Beijing Publishers, 1982.

Talbot, Strobe, ed. *Khrushchev Remembers: The Last Testament*. Boston: Little Brown, 1974.

Tang, Peter S. H. *Communist China Today*. Vol. 1. Washington, D.C.: Research Institute on the Sino-Soviet Bloc, 1961.

Tang Tsou. "Back from the Brink of Revolutionary 'Feudal' Totalitarianism." In *State and Society in Contemporary China*, edited by Victor Nee and David Mozingo, 53–88 at 73 ff. Ithaca, N.Y.: Cornell University Press, 1983.

———. *The Cultural Revolution and Post-Mao Reforms: A Historical Perspective*. Chicago: University of Chicago Press, 1986.

———. "Party, Masses, and Citizens in Rebuilding the Chinese State." In *Foundations and Limits of State Power in China*, edited by Stuart R. Schram, 277. London: School of Oriental and African Studies; Hong Kong: Chinese University Press, 1987.

Tanner, Harold M. *Strike Hard!: Anti-Crime Campaigns and Chinese Criminal Justice, 1979–1985*. Ithaca, N.Y.: Cornell East Asia Program, 1999.

Tanner, Murray Scot. "Bureaucratic and Subcommittee Development in the National People's Congress." Paper presented at the annual meeting of the Association of Asian Studies, Los Angeles, Calif., 1993.

———. "How a Bill Becomes Law in China: Stages and Processes in Lawmaking." In special issue, "China's Legal Reforms." *China Quarterly* 141 (1995): 39–64.

———. "Organizations and Politics in China's Post-Mao Law-Making System." In *Domestic Law Reforms in Post-Mao China*, edited by Pitman B. Potter, 56–93. Armonk, N.Y.: M. E. Sharpe, 1994.

Tao Xijin. "Laoji wei ren jiaohui zuo hao gong an gongzuo" (Remember the education of criminals and do a good job in public security work). In *Mianhuai Peng Zhen*, 87–103.

Teiwes, Frederick C. "Establishment and Consolidation of the New Regime." In *The Cambridge History of China Vol. 14. The People's Republic of China Part 1—The Emergence of Revolutionary China 1949–1965*, edited by Denis Twitchett and John K. Fairbank, 51–143. Cambridge: Cambridge University Press, 1987.

———. "Leaders, Institutions, and the Origins of the Great Leap Forward." *Pacific Affairs* 66, no. 2 (summer 1993): 244–53.

———. *Politics and Purges in China: Rectification and the Decline of Party Norms, 1950–1965*. 1st ed. White Plains, N.Y.: M. E. Sharpe, 1979.

———. *Politics and Purges in China: Rectification and the Decline of Party Norms 1950–1965*. 2nd ed. Armonk, N.Y.: M. E. Sharpe, 1993.

———. *Politics at Mao's Court: Gao Gang and Party Factionalism in the Early 1950s*. Armonk, N.Y.: M. E. Sharpe, 1990.

Teiwes, Frederick C., and Warren Sun. "From a Leninist to a Charismatic Party: The CCP's Changing Leadership, 1937–1945." In *New Perspectives on the Chinese Communist Revolution*, edited by Tony Saich and Hans van de Ven, 339–87. Armonk, N.Y.: M. E. Sharpe, 1995.

———. "Mao, Deng Zihui, and the Politics of Agricultural Cooperativization." *Chinese Law and Government* 26, no. 3–4 (May–June / July–August 1993).

Thornton, Richard. *China: The Struggle for Power 1917–1972*. Bloomington: Indiana University Press, 1973.

"Thoroughly Disclosing the Inside Story of Chang Guan Lou Counterrevolutionary Incident." *Selections from the China Mainland Press*, no. 4001 (August 15, 1967): 1.

Tian Jiuru. "Peng Zheng tongzhi zai Yan'an" (Comrade Peng Zhen in Yan'an). In *Mianhuai Peng Zhen*, 322–28.

Tian Jiyun. "Xuyan" (Preface). In *Zhongguo gaige kaifang yu minzhu fazhi jianshe* (China's reform and opening up and construction of democracy and the legal system), edited by Tian Jiyun, 1–5. Beijing: China Democracy and Legal System Press, 2000.

Tian Jiyun, ed. *Zhongguo gaige kaifang yu minzhu fazhi jianshe* (China's reform and opening up and construction of democracy and the legal system). Beijing: China Democracy and Legal System Press, 2000.

Tianjin Dongfang daxue dongfang gongshe cui jiu congdui (Column for destroying the old of the East is Red commune at East is Red University in Tianjin). "Jiao si Wan Zhang fangeming xiuzheng zhuyi jituan de zhijie houtai Peng Zhen, Liu Ren" (Hang Peng Zhen and Liu Ren, the direct backstage backers of the Wan and Zhang counterrevolutionary revisionist clique). August 1967.

Tong, James. "Editor's Introduction." In "Party Documents on Anti-Bourgeois Liberalization and Hu Yaobang's Resignation, 1987," edited by James Tong, special issue of *Chinese Law and Government* 21, no. 1 (spring 1988): 3–17.

Unger, Jonathan. "The Struggle to Dictate China's Administration: The Conflict of Branches vs Areas vs Reform." *Australian Journal of Chinese Affairs* 18 (July 1987): 15–45.

Van Ness, Peter and Satish Raichur. "Dilemmas of Socialist Development: An Analysis of Strategic Lines in China, 1949–1981." In *China from Mao to Deng: The Politics and Economics of Socialist Development*, edited by Bulletin of Concerned Asian Scholars, 77–89. Armonk, N.Y.: M. E. Sharpe, 1983.

Van Slyke, Lyman P. *Enemies and Friends: The United Front in Chinese Communist History*. Stanford: Stanford University Press, 1967.

Vogel, Ezra F. *Canton Under Communism: Program and Politics in a Provincial Capital, 1949–1968*. Cambridge, Mass.: 1980.

Waller, Derek J. *The Government and Politics of the People's Republic of China*. London: Hutchinson, 1981.

Wang Chaobin. *San fan shi lu* (A record of the Three Anti Campaign). Beijing: Police Academy Press, 1992.

Wang Chongqing. "Dangxiao lishi shang guanche lilun lianxi shiji fangzhen de guanghui pianzhang" (Summary of brilliant writings fully integrating theory with practice in the history of the Party school). In *Yan'an zhongyang dangxiao de zhengfeng xuexi* (Studying the rectification of the Yan'an central Party school), 2:338–48. Beijing: Central Party School Press, 1989.

Wang Hanbin. "Peng Zhen tongzhi dui wo guo shehui zhuyi minzhu fazhi jianshe de zhuoyue gongxian" (The outstanding contributions of comrade Peng Zhen in the construction of our country's socialist democracy and legal system). In *Mianhuai Peng Zhen*, 28–55.

Wang Jianying. *Zhongguo gongchandang zuzhishi ziliao huibian* (Collection of materials on the organizational history of the CPC). Beijing: Red Flag Publishers, 1982.

Wang Li. "The First Year of the 'Cultural Revolution.'" *Chinese Law and Government* 32, no. 4 (July–August 1999).

Wang Lulin. "«Wu Qi zhishi»chutan" (Preliminary discussion of the "May 7 Circular"). In *Hui dao "Wen Ge"* (Revisiting the "Cultural Revolution"), edited by Zhang Hua et al., 161–72. Beijing: Party History Press, 2000.

Wang Ruoshui. "Mao Zedong yu [Wenhua da geming]" (Mao Zedong and the Cultural Revolution). *Tansuo zazhi* (Inquiry magazine). March 1993: 10; and April 1993: 60.

Weber, Max. *Economy and Society*. Edited by Guenther Roth and Claus Wittich. Berkeley: University of California Press, 1978.

Wei Li and Lucian W. Pye. "The Ubiquitous Role of the Mishu in Chinese Politics." *China Quarterly* 132 (December 1992): 913–36.

Wen Bi. *Zhonguo [zuo] huo* (The leftist plot in China). Beijing: Chaohua Press, 1993.

"Wenhua dageming" zhong de Zhou Enlai (Zhou Enlai during the "Cultural Revolution"). Beijing: Central Party School Press, 1997.

Whyte, Martin King. *Small Groups and Political Rituals in China*. Berkeley: University of California Press, 1975.

Wing-Tsit Chan. *A Source Book in Chinese Philosophy*. Princeton, N.J.: Princeton University Press, 1963.

Womack, Brantly. "Where Mao Went Wrong: Epistemology and Ideology in Mao's Leftist Politics." *Australian Journal of Chinese Affairs* 16 (July 1986): 24–38.

Wu Fumin. "Zou yifa zhiguo lu" (Walking the road of ruling the country by law). *Fazhi ribao* (Legal system daily) (April 19, 2000): 1–2.

Wu Jiemin, ed. *Yan'an Ma Lie xueyuan huijilu* (Memoirs of the Yan'an Marxism-Leninism Institute). Beijing: Academy of Social Sciences Press.

Wu Ningkun. *A Single Tear: A Family's Persecution, Love and Endurance in Communist China*. New York: Atlantic Monthly, 1993.

Xie Pengcheng. *Jiben falu jiazhi* (Basic legal values). Jinan: Shandong People's Press, 2000.

"«Xiuyang»he «Lun dang nei douzheng»shi zhenya geming pai de ruan daozi" (Self-cultivation and the theory of inner Party struggle are soft knives for suppressing the revolutionary school). [character indistinct] Beida ([character indistinct] Peking University). April 25, 1967.

"Xiuzheng zhuyi de dazahui «Beijing hauce»" (The revisionist miscellany

"Beijing Pictorial"). *Pi Peng zhan bao* (Militant journal for attacking Peng Zhen) (August 1967), 3:18–22.

Xu Taocheng. "'Yin mou'—1957" (The "Plot"). 1957. Folio, n.d.

Xue Qingzhao et al. *Di yi dai zhongyang lingdao jiti de xingcheng* (Shaping the first generation of the collective leadership of the centre). Beijing: Masses Press, 2001.

Yan Jiaqi and Gao Gao. *[Wenhua da geming] shi nian shi* (A ten-year history of the Cultural Revolution). Vol. 1. Hong Kong: Chaoliu Press, n.d.

Yan'an zhongyang dangxiao de zhengfeng xuexi (Studying the rectification of the Yan'an central Party school). Vol. 1. Beijing: Central Party School Press, 1987.

Yang, C. K. "The Cultural Revolution and Revisionism." In *China in Crisis 1: China's Heritage and the Communist Political System*, edited by Ping-ti Ho and Tang Tsou, 2:501–24. Chicago: University of Chicago Press, 1968.

Yang Chengwu. *Yang Chengwu huiyilu* (Memoirs of Yang Chengwu). Beijing: PLA Press, 1990.

Yang Shutang. "Peng Zhen tongzhi de geming jingshen jiang yongyuan jili women qianjin" (The revolutionary spirit of comrade Peng Zhen impels us forward). In *Mianhuai Peng Zhen*, 444–49.

Yang Xianzheng. "Tuzai zhong liang, zhongshen yinzei: Jielu Kang Sheng fangeming liang mina pai de zuilian" (A sinister plotter who butchered the loyal and innocent all his life: Exposing Keng Sheng's counterrevolutionary double-dealing features). *Hongqi* (Red flag) 1 (1981): 34–37.

Yao Yilin. "Yi er jiu yundong huiyi" (Memoir of the December 9th Movement). In *Yi er jiu yundong* (The December 9th Movement), edited by CPC Beijing Party Committee Party History Materials Compilation Committee, 321–31. Beijing: CPC Party History Materials Press, 1987.

Yao Yilin and Xu Jianguo. "Guangfan jinxing kang zhan de caizheng dongyuan" (Broadly promote finance activists who are carrying out the resistance war) (May 10, 1938). In *Jin Cha Ji kang Ri genju di* (The Jin Cha Ji base area for resistance to Japan), 1A:159. Beijing: CPC Party History Materials Publishers, 1988.

"Yi jiang sheng yong zhuijiu kou" (We must support the valiant and investigate bandits). *Beijing ribao* (Beijing daily), April 16, 1967: 1.

"Yi jiu si wu nian de renqu" (Tasks for 1945) (December 15, 1944). In *Zhonggong zhongyang wenjian xuanji* (Compilation of CPC central documents), edited by Central Archives, 14:414. Beijing: Central Party School, 1992.

Yi Ling and Wu Yuan. *Liu Shaoqi*. Chengdu: Sichuan People's Press, 1992.

"Yi shishi wei genju yi xianfa he falu wei junsheng lai tongyi sixiang" (Unify thought with facts as the basis and the constitution and law as the yardstick), and "Yong xianfa he falu tongyi sixiang" (Use the constitution and the law to unify thought). *Renmin ribao* (People's daily), May 30, 1989: 1.

"Yiding yao jianchi fazhi bu neng gao renzhi shei dou meiyou chaoyue xianfa he falu de tequan" (We must definitely uphold the rule of law and not pursue the rule of man, no one has the right to exceed the constitution and the law). *Zhongguo fazhi bao* (China legal system gazette) (May 30, 1989): 1.

Yifa zhiguo he yide zhiguo jiben fanglue xuexi duben (Basic general study text on ruling the country according to law and ruling the country according to morality). Beijing: Party Archives Press, 2001.

"Yonghu xuanju fa, kaizhan xuanju yundong" (Defend the electoral law, commence the election campaign). *Xin hua yue bao* (New China monthly) 3: 11.

You Lin. "Xuexi Makesi zhuyi de dianfan" (Study the paragon of Marxism). In *Mianhuai Peng Zhen*, 205–16.

You Lin and Yan Jianqi. "Important Documents for Building Socialist Democracy and the Legal System in the New Period." *Renmin ribao* (People's daily), August 20, 1990. In *FBIS Daily Report—China* (August 28, 1990): 19.

"You yi jian chumu jingxin de fangeming shijian" (A shocking counterrevolutionary incident). *Pi Peng zhan bao* (Militant journal for attacking Peng Zhen) 3 (August 1967): 14.

Young, Graham. "Mao Zedong and the Class Struggle in Socialist Society." *Australian Journal of Chinese Affairs* 16 (July 1986): 41–80.

Yu Wen et al. "Peng Zhen tongzhi shi renmin daibiao dahui zhidu jianshe de daitouren" (Comrade Peng Zhen is the exemplar of the people's representative Congress system). In *Mianhuai Peng Zhen*, 109–38.

Yu Xingzhong. "Legal Pragmatism in the People's Republic of China." *Journal of Chinese Law* 3, no. 29 (1989): 29–51.

Yuan Beijing shi wei jiguan hongqi bingtuan (Red flag corps of organs of the original Beijing CPC Committee) and Yuan Beijing shi wei jiguangeming zaofan dui (Revolutionary rebels of organs of the original Beijing CPC Committee). "Chedi qingsuan Liu Shaoqi he Peng Zhen fangeming xiuzheng zhuyi jituan zai renmin lai xin lai fang gongzuo zhong de taotian zuixing" (Thoroughly clear up the monstrous crimes of the Liu Shaoqi and Peng Zhen counterrevolutionary revisionist clique in people's letters and visits work). N.d. Mimeographed.

Yuan Beijing shiwei jiguan Mao Zedong sixiang hongqi bingduan (Mao Zedong thought red flag battalion of the original Beijing Municipal Committee organs), ed. *Da yexing jia, da yinmou jia: Peng Zhen zui 'e shi (1925–1966)* (Big careerist and plotter: The most odious history of Peng Zhen). Beijing: 1967.

"Zai gaodu minzhu de jichu shang gaodu jizhong lifa gongzuo jianchi lilun lianxi shiji" (On the basis of a high level of democracy the highly centralized drafting work must support the integration of theory with reality). *Renmin ribao* (People's daily), December 5, 1985: 1.

"Zai tan zhenli you meiyou jiejixing" (A further discussion on whether or not truth has class nature). *Qianxian* (Frontline) 17 (1965): 47–49.

Zhang Peng and Zhao Youfu. "Yi Peng Zhen tongzhi de Huairou xian nongcun diaocha" (Recalling comrade Peng Zhen's investigation of villages in Huairou county). In *Mianhuai Peng Zhen*, 230–48.

Zhang Qilin. "Peng Zhen tongzhi guanhuai Beijing kuang gong" (Comrade Peng Zhen looks after Beijing's mining industry workers). In *Mianhuai Peng Zhen*, 335–38.

Zhang Wenjian. "Xuexi Peng Zhen tongzhi qinfen gongzuo de jingshen"

(Studying the spirit of comrade Peng Zhen's industrious work). In *Mianhuai Peng Zhen*, 356–61.

Zhang Youyu, *Zhang Youyu xueshu lunzhu zixuan ji* (Self-selected compilation of Zhang Youyu's academic work). Beijing: Beijing Normal University Press, 1992.

Zhang Zhenglong. *Xue bai xue hong* (White snow red blood). Hong Kong: Great Earth Publishing, 1991.

Zhang Zhiming. *Cong minzhu xin lu dao yifa zhiguo* (From the new road of democracy to ruling the country according to law). Nanchang: Jiangxi Higher Education Press, 2000.

Zhang Zhiqing, Sun Li, and Bai Juntang. *Yan'an zhengfeng qianhou* (Before and after the Yan'an rectification). Jiangsu Arts Press, 1994.

Zhao Jin. "Peng Zhen tongzhi qi qi shibian qian zai Beijing" (Comrade Peng Zhen in Beiping prior to the July 7 incident). In *Mianhuai Peng Zhen*, 329–34.

Zheng Tianxiang, Liu Fuzhi, and Wang Hanbin. "Qieshi jiaqiang shehuizhuyi minzhu yu fazhi jianshe: Xuexi Peng Zhen wenxuan de tihui" (Really strengthen the construction of socialist democracy and the legal system: Learning from the study of Peng Zhen's collected works). *Renmin ribao* (People's daily), July 22, 1991: 5.

Zheng Xiaofeng and Shu Ling. *Tao Zhu zhuan* (Biography of Tao Zhu). Beijing: Youth Publishing, 1992.

Zheng Xuan. "Cuan dang cuan guo yinmou de da baolu: Ping Peng Zhen cehua de Changguanlou fangeming shijian" (Big Exposure of the Plot to Usurp the Party and State: A Commentary on the Changguanlou counterrevolutionary incident instigated by P'eng Chen). *Guangming ribao* (Bright daily), August 9, 1967.

"Zhengfa zhanxian tongzhi wei renmin li le gong yi nian duo lai shehui zhixu mingxian haozhuan" (Social order over the past year or more has taken a turn for the better due to meritorious service to the people by comrades on the political–legal front). *Renmin ribao* (People's daily), January 31, 1985: 1.

"'Zhenli mianqian ren ren pingdeng' de yao shan shi fou dingwan wuchan jieji zhuanzheng" (Is the target of "All are equal before the truth" not the finishing off of proletarian dictatorship?). *Tiyu zhanxian* (Athletics battle line) (May 20, 1967): 3.

"Zhishi fenzi qianjin de daolu: jinian «Zai Yan'an wenyi zuotanhui shang de jianghua»fabiao ershi zhou nian" (The road ahead for intellectuals: Issued to commemorate the twentieth anniversary of the "Yan'an forum on literature and art"). *Hongqi* (Red flag) 10 (1962): 1.

"Zhonggong Jin Cha Ji shengwei guanyu zai zhengquan jiguan zhong gongzuo de dangyuan bixu zunshou de tiaoli" (Regulations of the CPC Jin Cha Ji Provincial Committee that must be obeyed by Party members in the course of work in organs of political power) (May 14, 1938). In *Jin Cha Ji kang Ri genju di* (The Jin Cha Ji base area for resistance to Japan), 1A:164. Beijing: CPC Party History Materials Publishers, 1988.

"Zhonggong Shen-Gan-Ning bianqu zhengfu dang tuan guize (cao'an)" (Draft charter of the CPC party group in the Shen-Gan-Ning border region) (December 4, 1942). In *Shen Gan Ning bianqu kang Ri genju di* (The Shen Gan Ning base area for resistance to Japan), 2:531. Beijing: CPC Party History Materials Publishers, 1990.

"Zhonggong Shen Gan Ning bianqu zhongyangju dangxiao gongzuo baogao tigang" (Outline of the work report of the CPC central bureau of the Shen Gan Ning border area on the work of the party school) (February 5, 1941). In *Shen Gan Ning bianqu kang Ri genju di* (The Shen Gan Ning base area for resistance to Japan), 2:577. Beijing: CPC Party History Materials Publishers, 1990.

"Zhonggong zhongyang beifang fenju dui Jizhong gongzuo de zhishi xing" (Letter of instruction from the North China Subbureau of the CPC Centre on work in Central Hebei). In *Jin Cha Ji kang Ri genju di* (The Jin Cha Ji base area for resistance to Japan), 1A:269. Beijing: CPC Party History Materials Publishers, 1988.

"Zhonggong zhongyang beifang fenju guanyu er shi ge yue lai dang de gongzuo zongjie baogao tigang" (Outline of the CPC Central Committee North China Subbureau's comprehensive report on party work over the past twenty months) (August 1939). In *Jin Cha Ji kang Ri genju di* (The Jin Cha Ji base area for resistance to Japan), 1A:274. Beijing: CPC Party History Materials Publishers, 1988.

"Zhonggong zhongyang beifang fenju guanyu Ji Re Cha gongzuo de yijian" (Opinion of the CPC Centre North China Subbureau on work in Ji Re Cha). In *Jin Cha Ji kang Ri genju di* (The Jin Cha Ji base area for resistance to Japan), 1B:510. Beijing: CPC Party History Materials Publishers, 1989.

"Zhonggong zhongyang beifang fenju jiu yue kuangda ganbu huiyi de yiyi yu chenggong" (The significance and accomplishments of the September expanded cadres meeting of the CPC Centre's North China Subbureau). In *Jin Cha Ji kang Ri genju di* (The Jin Cha Ji base area for resistance to Japan), 1A:460. Beijing: CPC Party History Materials Publishers, 1988.

"Zhonggong zhongyang beifang ju jueding Hebei wenti de ba da gangling" (The Eight Point Program for problems in Hebei decided by the North China Bureau of the Party Centre). In *Jin Cha Ji kang Ri genju di* (The Jin Cha Ji base area for resistance to Japan), 1A:265. Beijing: CPC Party History Materials Publishers, 1988.

"Zhonggong zhongyang dui Jin Cha Ji gongzuo de zhishi" (Instruction from the CPC Centre on work in Jin Cha Ji) (September 27, 1939). In *Jin Cha Ji kang Ri genju di* (The Jin Cha Ji base area for resistance to Japan), 1A:289. Beijing: CPC Party History Materials Publishers, 1988. Also in *Zhonggong zhongyang wenjian xuanji* (Compilation of CPC central documents), edited by Central Archives, 12:178. Beijing: Central Party School. Periodical.

"Zhonggong zhongyang guanyu fandui quxiao Jin Cha Ji Bianqu he Jizhong guihuan Hebei deng qitu de zhishi" (Instruction from the CPC Centre concerning resisting the abolition of Jin Cha Ji Border Region, the return of Central Hebei to Hebei, and other schemes). In *Jin Cha Ji kang Ri genju di* (The Jin

Cha Ji base area for resistance to Japan), 1A:268. Beijing: CPC Party History Materials Publishers, 1988.

"Zhonggong zhongyang guanyu muqian shiju yu dang de renwu de jueding" (Decision of the CPC Centre on the present situation and the tasks of the party) (February 1, 1940). In *Zhonggong zhongyang wenjian xuanji* (Compilation of CPC central documents), edited by Central Archives, 12:261. Beijing: Central Party School. Periodical.

"Zhonggong zhongyang guanyu muqian xingshi yu dang de zhengce de jueding" (Decision of the CPC Centre on the present situation and Party policies) (July 7, 1940). In *Zhonggong zhongyang wenjian xuanji* (Compilation of CPC central documents), edited by Central Archives, 12:417–25. Beijing: Central Party School. Periodical.

"Zhonggong zhongyang guanyu shencha ganbu de jueding" (Decision of the CPC Centre concerning the investigation of cadres) (August 15, 1943). In *Zhonggong zhongyang wenjian xuanji* (Compilation of CPC central documents), edited by Central Archives, 14:89. Beijing: Central Party School, 1992.

"Zhonggong zhongyang guanyu Yan'an ganbu xuexiao de jueding" (Decision of the CPC Centre on the Yan'an cadres school) (December 17, 1941). In *Zhonggong zhongyang wenjian xuanji* (Compilation of CPC central documents), edited by Central Archives, 13:257. Beijing: Central Party School. Periodical.

"Zhonggong zhongyang guanyu zaizhi ganbu jiaoyu de jueding" (Decision of the CPC Centre on education of on-site cadres) (February 28, 1942). In *Zhonggong zhongyang wenjian xuanji* (Compilation of CPC central documents), edited by Central Archives, 13:347. Beijing: Central Party School. Periodical.

"Zhonggong zhongyang pijun zhongyang shi ren xiaozu guanyu fageming fenzi he qita huaifenzi de jieshi ji chuli de zhengce jiexian de zanxing guiding" (Provisional regulations of the Central Ten Person Small Group approved by the Party Centre concerning the limitations on policies toward defining and handling counterrevolutionaries and other bad elements) (March 10, 1956). In *Qingli jieji duiwu* (Purify class ranks), 89–96. Folio, c. 1969 (author's copy).

"Zhonggong zhongyang shi ren xiaozu 'Guanyu fageming fenzi he qita huaifenzi de jieshi ji chuli de zhengce jiexian de zanxing guiding' de buchong jieshi" (Supplemental interpretation of the provisional regulations of the Central Ten Person Small Group concerning the limitations on policies toward defining and handling counterrevolutionaries and other bad elements) (June 24, 1957). In *Qingli jieji duiwu* (Purify class ranks), 97–108. Folio, c. 1969 (author's copy).

"Zhonggong zhongyang shujichu guanyu Jizhong gongzuo de zhishi" (Instruction from the CPC Centre Secretariat on work in Central Hebei). In *Jin Cha Ji kang Ri genju di* (The Jin Cha Ji base area for resistance to Japan), 1A:291. Beijing: CPC Party History Materials Publishers, 1988.

"Zhongguo faxue hui chengli dahui longzhong kaimu" (Grand opening session of the China Law Society). *Zhongguo fazhi bao* (China legal system gazette) July 23, 1982): 1.

"Zhongguo faxue hui chengli dahui zai jing longzhong juxing" (Grand opening of the China Law Society held in Beijing). *Minzhu yu fazhi* (Democracy and the legal system) 8 (1982): 2.

Zhongguo geming shi gangyao (Outline of the history of the Chinese revolution). Lanzhou: Gansu People's Press, 1988.

Zhongguo gongchandang di ba ci quanguo daibiao dahui wenjian (Documents of the Eighth National CPC Representative Congress). Beijing: People's Press, 1956, 1980.

"Zhongguo gongchandang zhongyang dang xiao zhaoshou xinshen zige guiding" (Regulations on qualifications of newly admitted students to the CPC central Party school). In *Yan'an zhongyang dangxiao de zhengfeng xuexi* (Studying the rectification of the Yan'an central Party school), 1:326. Beijing: Central Party School Press, 1987.

"Zhongguo gongchandang zhongyang dangxiao di er qi zhaoshou xinsheng jianzhang" (Simple charter for new students recruited for the second term at the central CPC Party school of the PRC) (March 28, 1943). In *Yan'an zhongyang dangxiao de zhengfeng xuexi* (Studying the rectification of the Yan'an central party school), 2:332. Beijing: Central Party School Press, 1989.

Zhongguo renmin jiefangjun houqin xueyuan «xinghuo liaoyuan»geming zaofantuan (A single spark can start a prairie fire revolutionary resistance group of the Chinese People's Liberation Army Logistics Department). In "Chedi qingsuan Peng Zhen fandui Mao zhuxi de taotian zuixing" (Thoroughly clear up Peng Zhen's monstrous crimes of resisting Chairman Mao). June 14, 1967.

"Zhongguo Su-wei-ai zhongyang zhengfu, Zhongguo gongchandang zhongyang weiyuanhui wei kang ri qiu guo gao quanti tongbao shu" (Notice to all compatriots from the Chinese Soviet Central Government and the Central Committee of the Chinese Communist Party) (August 1, 1935). In *Yi er jiu yundong* (The December 9th Movement), edited by CPC Beijing Party Committee Party History Materials Compilation Committee, 21. Beijing: CPC Party History Materials Press, 1987.

"Zhongguo Yan'an jingshen yanjiu hui zai Beijing chengli" (The China Society for Research in the Yan'an Spirit is established in Beijing). *Dangshi tongxun* (Party history newsletter) 12, no. 36 (June 25, 1990): 1.

"Zhonghua renmin gongheguo di er jie quanguo renmin daibiao dahui di si ci hui guanyu di sanjie quanguo renmin daibiao dahui daibiao ming'e he xuanju wenti de jueyi" (Decision of the fourth session of the Second National People's Congress concerning questions about name lists and elections of the Third National People's Congress) (December 3, 1963). *Zhonghua renmin gongheguo di er jie quanguo renmin daibiao dahui changwu weiyuanhui gongbao* (PRC National People's Congress Standing Committee Reports) 73 (December 25, 1963): 12.

"Zhonghua renmin gongheguo di er jie quanguo renmin daibiao dahui fa an weiyuanhui guanyu di san jie quanguo renmin daibiao dahui daibiao ming'e he xuanju wenti de jueyi (cao'an) de shencha baogao" (Investigation report on the [draft] decision of the law drafting committee of the fourth session of the Second National People's Congress concerning questions about name lists and elections of the Third National People's Congress) (December 3, 1963). *Zhonghua renmin gongheguo di er jie quanguo renmin daibiao dahui changwu weiyuanhui gongbao* (PRC National People's Congress Standing Committee Reports) 73 (December 25, 1963): 13.

"Zhonghua renmin gongheguo quanguo renmin daibiao dahui daibiaotuan fangwen Sulian, Jie Ke Si Luo Fa Ke, Luo Man Ni Ya, Bao Jia Li Ya, A Er Ba Ni Ya, Nan Xi La Fa de baogao" (Report on the visit to the USSR, Czechoslovakia, Romania, Burgaria, Albania and Yugoslavia by the delegation from the National People's Congress of the PRC). *Renmin ribao* (People's daily), April 1, 1957: 1.

"Zhonghua renmin gongheguo chengzhi tanwu tiaoli" (PRC draft regulations for punishment of corruption) (April 21, 1952). *Renmin shouce* (People's handbook) (1952): 50–51.

"Zhongyang dangxiao jihua" (Plan for the central Party school). In *Yan'an zhongyang dangxiao de zhengfeng xuexi* (Studying the rectification of the Yan'an central Party school), 1:326. Beijing: Central Party School Press, 1987.

"Zhongyang dui Jinxibei caijing zhengce de zhishi" (Instructions from the Centre on finance and economic policies in northwest Shanxi) (May 18, 1940). In *Zhonggong zhongyang wenjian xuanji* (Compilation of CPC central documents), edited by Central Archives, 12:391. Beijing: Central Party School. Periodical.

"Zhongyang dui Jinxibei gongzuo de zhishi" (Instruction from the Centre on work in northwest Shanxi) (June 8, 1940). In *Zhonggong zhongyang wenjian xuanji* (Compilation of CPC central documents), edited by Central Archives, 12:403. Beijing: Central Party School. Periodical.

"Zhongyang gei beifang ju ji Hebei shengwei de zhishi xing" (Letter of instruction from the Centre to the North China Bureau and the Hebei CPC Committee) (August 5, 1936). In *Zhonggong zhongyang wenjian xuanji* (Compilation of CPC central documents), edited by Central Archives, 11:60. Beijing: Central Party School. Periodical.

"Zhongyang geming junshi weiyuanhui guanyu kang-Ri genjudi junshi jianshe de zhishi" (Instruction from the Central Revolutionary Military Commission on establishment of military affairs in the anti-Japanese base areas) (November 7, 1941). In *Zhonggong zhongyang wenjian xuanji* (Compilation of CPC central documents), edited by Central Archives, 13:212, 221, 226. Beijing: Central Party School. Periodical.

"Zhongyang guanyu banli dangxiao de zhishi" (Instruction from the Centre on the establishment of party schools) (February 5, 1940). In *Zhonggong zhongyang wenjian xuanji* (Compilation of CPC central documents), edited by Central Archives, 12:301. Beijing: Central Party School. Periodical.

"Zhongyang guanyu beifang ju lingdao renyuan fengong de jueding" (Decision of the Centre on the division of labor of leading personnel of the North China Bureau) (March 24, 1938). In *Zhonggong zhongyang wenjian xuanji* (Compilation of CPC central documents), edited by Central Archives, 11:477. Beijing: Central Party School. Periodical.

"Zhongyang guanyu cai jing gongzuo de zhishi" (Instruction from the Centre on finance and economic work) (February 1, 1940). In *Zhonggong zhongyang wenjian xuanji* (Compilation of CPC central documents), edited by Central Archives, 12:266. Beijing: Central Party School. Periodical.

"Zhongyang guanyu caizheng jingji zhengce de zhishi" (Instruction from the Centre on finance and economic policy) (April 15, 1940). In *Zhonggong zhongyang wenjian xuanji* (Compilation of CPC central documents), edited by Central Archives, 12:360. Beijing: Central Party School. Periodical.

"Zhongyang guanyu chengshi gongzuo de zhishi" (Instruction from the Centre on work in the cities) (June 5, 1944). In *Zhonggong zhongyang wenjian xuanji* (Compilation of CPC central documents), edited by Central Archives, 14:243. Beijing: Central Party School, 1992. Periodical.

"Zhongyang guanyu jianli chengshi gongzuo bumen de zhishi" (Instruction from the Centre on establishing urban work departments) (September 4, 1944). In *Zhonggong zhongyang wenjian xuanji* (Compilation of CPC central documents), edited by Central Archives, 14:319. Beijing: Central Party School, 1992. Periodical.

"Zhongyang guanyu jianli Dongbei changqi yongjiu genjudi gei Dongbei ju de zhishi" (Directive from the Centre to the Northeast Bureau concerning the establishment of long-term and permanent base areas in the Northeast) (December 21, 1945). In *Zhonggong zhongyang wenjian xuanji* (Compilation of CPC central documents), edited by Central Archives, 15:504. Beijing: Central Party School, 1992. Periodical.

"Zhongyang guanyu Jixi shibian jingguo ji jieshi fangzhen de zhishi" (Instruction from the Centre on passing of events in Western Hebei and the interpretation of policy). In *Zhonggong zhongyang wenjian xuanji* (Compilation of CPC central documents), edited by Central Archives, 12:249. Beijing: Central Party School. Periodical.

"Zhongyang guanyu Jizhong gongzuo de zhishi" (Instruction from the Party Centre on work in central Hebei) (October 28, 1939). In *Zhonggong zhongyang wenjian xuanji* (Compilation of CPC central documents), edited by Central Archives, 12:186. Beijing: Central Party School. Periodical.

"Zhongyang guanyu kaizhen manzhou gongzuo gei Jin Cha Ji fenju de zhishi" (Directive of the Centre to the Jin Cha Ji Subbureau concerning the work of developing Manchuria). In *Zhonggong zhongyang wenjian xuanji* (Compilation of CPC central documents), edited by Central Archives, 14:321. Beijing: Central Party School, 1992. Periodical.

"Zhongyang guanyu shencha ganbu wenti de zhishi" (Instruction from the Centre on the issue of cadre examination) (August 1, 1940). In *Zhonggong zhongyang wenjian xuanji* (Compilation of CPC central documents), edited by Central Archives, 12:444. Beijing: Central Party School. Periodical.

"Zhongyang guanyu Yan'an zaizhi ganbu xuexi de jueding" (Decision of the Centre on on-site cadre study in Yan'an) (December 1, 1941). In *Zhonggong zhongyang wenjian xuanji* (Compilation of CPC central documents), edited by Central Archives, 13:240. Beijing: Central Party School. Periodical.

"Zhongyang junwei guanyu Jixinan shijian ji women de fangzhen de zhishi" (Instruction from the Central Military Commission concerning the Southwest Hebei incident and our policies) (December 6, 1939). In *Zhonggong zhongyang wenjian xuanji* (Compilation of CPC central documents), edited by Central Archives, 12:215. Beijing: Central Party School. Periodical.

"Zhongyang junwei guanyu muqian xingshi he renwu de zhishi" (Directive from the Centre and the military committee concerning the present situation and tasks). In *Zhonggong zhongyang wenjian xuanji* (Compilation of documents of the Chinese Communist Party Centre), edited by Central Archives, 12:283–87. Beijing: Party History Press.

"Zhongyang junwei, zong zhengzhi bu dui yezhan zhengzhi bu zhaoji de zhengzhi gongzuo huiyi ji junqu bu ganbu huiyi de zhishi" (Instruction of the Central Military Commission and the Central Political Department on the political work meeting convened by the field operations political department and the military region cadres' meeting) (August 13, 1940). In *Zhonggong zhongyang wenjian xuanji* (Compilation of CPC central documents), edited by Central Archives, 12:448. Beijing: Central Party School. Periodical.

"Zhongyang shujichu bangongting guanyu zhengzhi ju dui dangxiao zuzhi ji jiaoyu fangzhen zhi xin jueding de tongzhi" (Notice of the Centre Secretariat General Office on the new decision of the Politburo concerning organization of the Party school and education policy) (March 2, 1942). In *Zhonggong zhongyang wenjian xuanji* (Compilation of CPC central documents), edited by Central Archives, 13:354. Beijing: Central Party School. Periodical.

"Zhongyang xuanchuan bu guanyu celue ganbu zhenglue jiaoyu de zhishi" (Instruction from the Central Propaganda Department on strengthening cadre education in policy) (August 13, 1940). In *Zhonggong zhongyang wenjian xuanji* (Compilation of CPC central documents), edited by Central Archives, 12:451. Beijing: Central Party School. Periodical.

"Zhongyang xuanchuan bu guanyu tigao Yan'an zai zhi ganbu jiaoyu zhiliang de jueding" (Decision of the Central Propaganda Department on raising the quality of education of Yan'an on-site cadres) (October 20, 1940). In *Zhonggong zhongyang wenjian xuanji* (Compilation of CPC central documents), edited by Central Archives, 12:524. Beijing: Central Party School. Periodical.

Zhou Weizhi. "Jin Cha Ji bianqu kang Ri genju di wen yi gongzuo huigu" (Recalling cultural work in the Jin Cha Ji Border Region resist Japan base area). In *Zhonggong dang shi ziliao* (Party history materials), edited by CPC Central Committee Party History Research Office, 33:52–110. Beijing: Party History Materials Publishers, 1990.

"Zhu De Peng Dehuai, Ren Bishi guanyu Jin Cha Ji junqu jiben renwu he gongzuo fangzhen de zhishi" (Instruction from Zhu De, Peng Dehuai, and

Ren Bishi concerning the basic tasks and work policies for Jin Cha Ji military region) (November 30, 1937). In *Jin Cha Ji kang Ri genjudi* (Jin Cha Ji Base Area for Resisting Japan), 1A:62–64. Beijing: CPC Party History Materials Press, 1988.

Zhu Liyu. *Peng Zhen minzhu fazhi sixiang yanjiu* (Research on Peng Zhen's thinking on democracy and the legal system). Beijing: People's University Press, 1999.

Zhuo Zeyuan. *Fa de jiazhi lun* (On the values of law). Beijing: Law Publishers, 1999.

Index